N. York. March 18th. 1787

for you the peccan Nuts have all been
when I recd. by the post about a dozen
by a French Gentleman in a Vessel bound
em himself to Paris, or consign them to
despair of being able to possess myself of
my endeavours have been equally un-
Maple, notwithstanding the different plans
begun a letter to you of some length which I
short notice I had of it, the tediousness of
unable interruptions make it doubtful

The Founding Fathers

Engraving after a painting by Gilbert Stuart

The Founding Fathers

JAMES MADISON

A Biography in His Own Words

Edited by
MERRILL D. PETERSON

With an Introduction by
ROBERT A. RUTLAND
Editor, *The Papers of James Madison*

JOAN PATERSON KERR
Picture Editor

Published by NEWSWEEK, New York
Distributed by HARPER & ROW, PUBLISHERS, INC.

We dedicate this series of books to the memory of
Frederick S. Beebe
friend, mentor, and "Founding Father" of Newsweek Books

James Madison, A Biography in His Own Words,
has been produced by the Newsweek Book Division:

Joseph L. Gardner, Editor

Janet Czarnetzki, Art Director

Judith Bentley, Copy Editor

Susan Storer, Picture Researcher

S. Arthur Dembner, Publisher

This book is based on *The Papers of James Madison*
edited by William T. Hutchinson and William M. E. Rachal (Vols. 1–7)
and by Robert A. Rutland and William M. E. Rachal (Vol. 8),
sponsored by The University of Virginia, published by
The University of Chicago Press, and copyright The University of Chicago.
The texts of all documents in this edition from the Madison Papers
have been supplied by Mr. Rutland.
Permission to reproduce excerpts has been granted through the courtesy
of The University of Chicago Press.
Other sources are acknowledged on page 408.

For information address Harper & Row, Publishers, Inc.
10 East 53rd Street, New York, N.Y. 10022
Published simultaneously in Canada by Fitzhenry & Whiteside Limited, Toronto.

ISBN: 06-013332-5
Library of Congress Catalog Card Number 72-92142
Copyright © 1974 by Newsweek, Inc.
All rights reserved. Printed and bound in the United States of America.
Endpapers: Madison to Thomas Jefferson, March 18, 1787;
SOL FEINSTONE COLLECTION, DAVID LIBRARY OF THE AMERICAN REVOLUTION, WASHINGTON CROSSING, PA.

Contents

Introduction   6

Chronology of Madison and His Times   10

1   A Revolutionary Vocation   13

2   Congressman at War   45

3   Radical Reformer   82

     A PICTURE PORTFOLIO: Man from Montpelier   111

4   Father of the Constitution   130

5   First Man in Congress   166

6   To the Revolution of 1800   209

7   Secretary of State   235

8   Gathering Storm Clouds   273

     A PICTURE PORTFOLIO: Mr. Madison's War   303

9   Second War for Independence   322

10   Last of the Fathers   365

     Selected Bibliography   408

     Acknowledgments   408

     Index   410

Introduction

by Robert A. Rutland
Editor, The Papers of James Madison

When John F. Kennedy accepted the first two volumes of *The Papers of James Madison* in 1962, he remarked with some earnestness that in his judgment Madison was probably "the most underrated of our Founding Fathers." President Kennedy was acknowledging the public's dim perception of Madison as Father of the Constitution, a view overlooking the rest of his long life and public career. Modern scholarship has sought to revive Madison as a total participant in the nation's birth and development, however; and the basis for a reevaluation lies in the papers he wrote or received, which he guarded at Montpelier until the end of his days and which now belong to the nation he usually alluded to as "our beloved Country."

In our age of instantaneous communications, an impersonalization of the written and spoken word has become so common that citizens are skimming and skipping, half listening or barely watching a great deal of the time. What a contrast with James Madison's world, where the pace of life was not dependent upon person-to-person telephone calls or vast electronic networks of programmed and stereotyped mass communications. Indeed, the scholar who delves into the papers of the Founding Fathers is invariably impressed by both the wisdom imparted and the sheer bulk of their writings. Surely Madison must have spent a good part of many days at Montpelier, Richmond, Philadelphia, Washington—wherever family or public duties took him—at the writing desk. The personal effort required, the thought processes involved, and the time consumed all make his correspondence, and that of all our early leaders, a monumental accomplishment.

The preservation of that achievement has become a public concern and a significant historical endeavor. Much of the record of history in Western society has been saved from the flames or insects only by chance. Public record keeping was still an infant art when the first Englishmen claimed their foothold on American soil, yet official records of that period abound. On the other hand, the survival of the colonists' diaries, personal letters, and family records was rather haphazard. By the time of the Revolution, however, American leaders often realized the importance of what they were doing and their unique position in history.

In the intellectual climate of the revolutionary era, Madison's generation brought together the elements for what has become an exemplary situation in world history. Never before was a nation created through joint efforts of pen and sword, with the chief participants fully conscious of the usefulness of both weapons. Burdened with such a sense of history, they carefully rewrote sentences, painstakingly called back letters written to departed colleagues, and guarded personal secrets by instructing surviving spouses to burn certain letters.

Fortunately for the nation they helped found, three Virginians—Washington, Jefferson, and Madison—were particularly aware of their role in history and anxious to preserve their niche by augmenting the memories of others with their own collections of personal papers. Their motives were not solely altruistic. Washington's vanity and a certain punctiliousness doubtless motivated him to collect and save the papers of a life that was to demand worldwide attention. Jefferson's epistolary activities were in part a protective shield to explain both his triumphs and his failures. Madison, probably in imitation of Jefferson's example, began to save papers as his public career developed and as he grew to recognize the magnitude of the revolutionary movement in which he was a participant.

Until Madison began to perceive his role in the American Revolution he was an indifferent collector of letters, although he was a young and eager spectator at the beginnings of the resistance. From his first writings in a commonplace book until his last letters were penned from Montpelier, Madison's seriousness is apparent. Many citizens—particularly Jefferson and Washington—were struck with the giant intellect of this small Virginian. His probity, logic, and tenacious pursuit of a national goal are discernible in so much of Madison's literary legacy that we are disappointed we know little of the other side of his personality. From such observers as Mrs. Samuel Harrison Smith and Harriet Martineau we learn that Madison could be jovial and even jocular on the right occasion, but the image most often projected in history books and fixed in the mind's eye is more to the turn of Washington Irving's unfortunate phrase, "Jemmy Madison—ah! poor Jemmy! He is but a withered little apple-John." The publication of Madison's papers, however, is bringing a more balanced view of a far different kind of person.

For most of his life Madison wrote with some reserve, but his letters to fellow Princetonian William Bradford between 1772 and 1775 reveal unguarded moments when the youthful Madison took solace in his collegiate attachments. "Friendship like all Truth delights in plainness and simplicity," Madison wrote "Dear Billey" from his "Obscure Corner" of the world. As young Whigs, they yearned to share in the excitement of the protest against British policies. Soon Madison moved from the role of a passive spectator to that of a drill-field marksman, and finally into more stirring action at Williamsburg.

After serving in the Virginia Convention of 1776 and participating in the Revolution as a privy councilor in Virginia, Madison entered the Continental Congress at Philadelphia in 1780 and began to save letters, memoranda, notes for speeches, and drafts of important documents made while the young nation struggled for its existence. His note-taking in Congress and later at the Federal Convention would in itself have assured Madison a special niche among the preservers of history; but Madison seems to have sensed the necessity for saving every scrap of paper related to his public career, either for its archival value or as an aid in writing a projected history of the Revolution (which he eventually abandoned).

Madison accumulated a great bulk of papers as he moved from the state legislature to Congress, advised President Washington, maintained his close ties with Jefferson, and became a leading figure in national politics. Except for a brief interval from 1797 to 1799, Madison remained active in the political life of his state and nation until his retirement from the Presidency on March 4, 1817. He lived another nineteen years, most of it spent at Montpelier, and during much of that time he was engaged in preparing his Federal Convention notes and other papers for eventual publication. His expenses were great and his income dwindled, but Madison believed that in his legacy of the primary sources of history he was securing a comfortable settlement for his devoted wife, Dolley.

Madison's plan to preserve history and secure needed income for his family was only partially successful. Interest in the Federal Convention of 1787 was great, as Madison realized, and the sparse information contained in the official journals released by the government in 1819 only whetted the public's expectations. Madison thought that the posthumous publication of his notes would bring his widow twelve thousand dollars and at the same time leave the nation with an accurate account of that historic conference. He hoped to set the record aright and provide future historians with a unique body of information. Not content to collect materials by recalling letters from the estates of important correspondents who had died, Madison began to revise his letters and documents in ways that have invariably obscured the record. In some instances, as with a coded letter to Jefferson concerning Lafayette, Madison attempted to alter and soften a contemporary judgment; but with other emendations, as in the Federal Convention notes, his tinkering caused doubts as to what was changed in 1787 for the sake of accuracy and what might have been altered much later as an outright distortion. Usually, the changes Madison made or caused his aides (Dolley Madison, her brother, and her son) to make can be easily discerned because of the ink or penmanship. But the fact that Madison, probably the most intellectual of the Founding Fathers, succumbed to the temptation to change the record tells us something about man's vanity. The full answer to why he did it is buried with Madison, of course, but his whole life was dedicated to making the American experiment in self-government succeed, and in his later years Madison was trying to erase old animosities and help secure the Union, which he perceived was in danger.

Madison died quietly on June 28, 1836. Dolley came into immediate possession of his papers, which she considered "Sacred, and no more to be infringed or altered than his last Will. He desired me to read them over and if any letter—line—or word struck me as being calculated to injure the feelings of any one or wrong in themselves that I would withdraw them or it." Thus the process of correcting and changing would continue "consonant to his wishes and directions, and made with my concurrence." Some of the personal letters between husband and wife were then destroyed or loaned out and later lost to history. Clerks made copies of the papers for a proposed edition of Madison's writings, but Mrs. Madison thought the publishers set too small a price on their worth. She figured the convention and congressional notes alone were worth one hundred thousand dollars—a stunning amount in that time—but finally accepted the thirty thousand Congress offered. These papers were published by Congress in three volumes in 1840, but meanwhile John C. Payne, Dolley's brother, had arranged additional papers and planned to offer a three or four-volume set from a commercial publisher. The original copies were deposited in a Washington bank while Mrs. Madison negotiated with the publishers, and during this period her impecunious son, John Payne Todd, had access to this treasure trove of early American history.

Todd drew on the papers to settle debts accumulated from his visits to the fleshpots in Washington. One of his chief creditors, James C. McGuire, ultimately came into the possession of hundreds of documents. Mrs. Madison herself displayed little evidence that she had much business acumen, and the sale of the rest of the papers became by 1848 a matter of some desperation. Four years of fruitless negotiations with a private firm had led to nothing, and in 1848 Congress offered Dolley Madison twenty-five thousand dollars for "all the unpublished papers" of her late husband still in her possession. The legislation was prudently conditioned on an immediate payment of five thousand dollars to Mrs. Madison's creditors and the establishment of a trust fund with the remaining money as an annuity for her.

As it developed, the Madison papers Dolley sold Congress were only a portion of those the aged Virginian had so carefully preserved. When Mrs. Madison died a year later, McGuire hauled trunkloads of papers from Montpelier to his Washington home as security for John Payne Todd's unpaid debts. Most of this material came to public attention when McGuire's collection was advertised for sale in 1892 and nearly three thousand letters to and from Madison were sold under the auctioneer's hammer. As late as 1903 some Madison documents, lent by Dolley Madison to a relative a short time before her death, were apparently burned by a descendant who wished to carry out a promise made by Anna C. Payne to the President's widow.

Despite the confusion and self-deception apparent in Dolley Madison's household, most of the Madison papers finally came to the Library of Congress in 1903. Important documents that had been plucked from the collection slowly returned to the main body through official channels, auction sales, and as gifts, while other valuable acquisitions were made by university and public libraries. Most of the twenty-two thousand Madison items are now found there, although some holdings remain in the Virginia State Library, Virginia Historical Society, the University of Virginia, the National Archives, and Princeton University. And although 125 years have elapsed since Dolley Madison thought she was turning the remnants of the President's papers over to a national custodian, a few major gaps remain. These important letters are in the hands of private manuscript collectors who guard their anonymity tenaciously, and their wishes are considered a sacred trust by some autograph dealers who regard an unpublished Madison letter as a tempting bit of merchandise. Perhaps several hundred Madison letters fall into this category. Eventually, they will reach the Library of Congress and rest in the manuscript depository of the James Madison Memorial annex to that storehouse of national scholarship.

The Library of Congress files are the basis of the ongoing *Papers of James Madison* project, which was jointly sponsored by the Universities of Chicago and Virginia from 1956 to 1970. Since 1971 the editorial offices have been at the University of Virginia and the publishing has continued at the University of Chicago. Following the scholarly guidelines laid down by Julian P. Boyd in *The Papers of Thomas Jefferson*, the editorial staff strives to produce accurate texts, duly annotated, of all the documents that affected the life of James Madison between 1759 and 1836. The previous editions of Madison's writings by Henry Gilpin (1840), William C. Rives and Philip R. Fendall (1865), and Gaillard Hunt (1900–10) all bore limitations that greatly restrict the modern scholar.

In this volume Merrill D. Peterson has brought together the panoramic view of Madison as a legislator, party leader, Cabinet officer, President, and senior statesman. From the files of his papers, Madison is presented in his own language as the dispassionate Founding Father whose chief interest in life was to prove that Americans had been chosen by Providence for an experiment to test man's capacity for self-government. The passion of James Madison's life was to make that experiment succeed.

Perhaps the reader of these excerpts will be able to make his own discovery as to the driving force in Madison's life. The consensus of biographers from Rives through Irving Brant, after they studied Madison's life with a sometimes microscopic eye, has been that Madison was primarily concerned with the survival of the American nation as a political unit. If the reader finds his own interpretation, then he will know the scholar's delight in uncovering new truths in the old repositories of knowledge.

EDITORIAL NOTE

Most of the Madison writings reprinted in this biography have been excerpted from the longer original documents being published in their entirety by the University of Chicago Press. Omissions at the beginning or ending of a document are indicated by ellipses only if the extract begins or ends in the middle of a sentence; omissions within a quoted passage are also indicated by ellipses. The original spellings have been retained; editorial insertions are set within square brackets.

Chronology of Madison and His Times

James Madison born in King George County, Virginia, March 16 (March 5, Old Style)	1751	
	1754	French and Indian War, 1754–63
	1760	Reign of George III of England, 1760–1820
Enrolled at Donald Robertson's school	1762	
	1765	Stamp Act
Studies with the Rev. Thomas Martin	1767	Parliament passes Townshend duties
Student at College of New Jersey in Princeton, 1769–72	1769	Nonimportation movement in Colonies
	1770	Townshend duties repealed; Boston Massacre; ministry of Lord North, 1770–82
Receives baccalaureate degree; continues study	1771	
Returns to Virginia; suffers from nervous disorder; letters to William Bradford	1772	
Legal studies begin	1773	Boston Tea Party
Visits Philadelphia; elected to Orange County Committee of Safety	1774	Coercive Acts; First Continental Congress; Louis XVI rules France, 1774–92
Colonel in Orange County militia	1775	Second Continental Congress; Battles of Lexington and Concord
Delegate to Virginia Convention and General Assembly	1776	Virginia Declaration of Rights; Declaration of Independence
Defeated in race for assembly, but chosen for Council of State, 1778–79	1777	Battle of Saratoga
Delegate to Continental Congress: investigates Lee's charges against Franklin, supports western lands motion, prepares instructions for Jay on Mississippi navigation	1780	Fall of Charleston; mutiny at Morristown
	1781	Virginia cedes Ohio lands; Articles of Confederation ratified; British campaign in Virginia; Battle of Yorktown
Urges impost unsuccessfully	1782	Preliminary peace treaty signed in Paris
Drafts new impost plan; end of engagement to Kitty Floyd; retires from Congress	1783	Congress ratifies peace treaty; British West Indies closed to American trade
Trip to Fort Stanwix with Lafayette; fight for religious liberty in Virginia assembly	1784	
"Memorial . . . against Religious Assessments"	1785	Congress moves to New York
Enactment of Virginia Statute for Religious Freedom; attends Annapolis Convention	1786	Shays' Rebellion
Returns to Continental Congress; supports a strong government at Federal Convention; contributes to *The Federalist*	1787	Adams's *A Defence of the Constitutions of Government of the United States . . .*
Fights for ratification at Virginia convention	1788	Constitution ratified
Elected to House of Representatives; sponsors Bill of Rights	1789	George Washington inaugurated as President; beginning of French Revolution
Compromise on funding and location of capital	1790	Hamilton's first *Report on the Public Credit*
Argues unconstitutionality of a national bank; tours the North with Jefferson; writes for Freneau's *National Gazette*	1791	*Report on Manufactures*; French Legislative Assembly, 1791–92; Thomas Paine's *The Rights of Man*
Leader of Republican opposition in Congress	1792	Hamilton and Jefferson feud in Philadelphia press; reelection of Washington
"Helvidius" essays; Citizen Genêt affair	1793	Execution of Louis XVI; France declares war on Britain; Proclamation of Neutrality

Seeks commercial restrictions against Britain; marries Dolley Payne Todd	1794	Jay mission to London; Whisky Rebellion
Opposes Jay's Treaty in House	1796	Washington's Farewell Address
Declines mission to France; voluntary retirement to Montpelier	1797	John Adams begins term as President; XYZ Affair
Virginia and Kentucky Resolutions; Address to the People	1798	Undeclared war with France; Alien and Sedition Acts
Elected to state legislature	1799	Adams sends new mission to Paris
Virginia Report on the Alien and Sedition Acts	1800	Federal capital moved to Washington; Spain cedes Louisiana to France
Secretary of State, 1801–9	1801	Electoral tie ends with selection of Jefferson as President; Tripolitan War, 1801–5
	1802	Peace of Amiens; Spain closes Mississippi
Louisiana Purchase	1803	Renewal of Napoleonic wars
	1804	William Pitt returns to power; Napoleon Bonaparte, Emperor of France, 1804–14
Investigates illegality of *Essex* decision	1805	Formation of the Third Coalition against France; Jefferson begins second term
Monroe-Pinkney Treaty	1806	Berlin Decree; Napoleon's Continental System
Chesapeake-Leopard affair; Embargo Act	1807	British orders in council
Inauguration as President with George Clinton as Vice President; Erskine agreement; nonintercourse with Britain	1809	Nonintercourse Act; repeal of embargo
Macon's Bill No. 2; resumption of French trade; annexation of West Florida	1810	Rambouillet Decree authorizes French seizure of American ships
Names Monroe Secretary of State	1811	Battle of Tippecanoe; Bank of the United States ends; War Hawks in Congress
War message to Congress	1812	Attempted invasion of Canada; capitulation of Detroit
Second inaugural with Elbridge Gerry as Vice President	1813	Britain blockades coast; Battles of Lake Erie and the Thames; Detroit retaken
Accepts British negotiations; Cabinet reorganization; end of embargo measures; flees Washington before British attack	1814	Napoleon abdicates; Congress of Vienna; Battle of Lake Champlain; Hartford Convention; Treaty of Ghent
Vetoes national bank; State of the Union message	1815	Battle of Waterloo; Battle of New Orleans; Congress ratifies peace treaty
	1816	Second Bank of the United States; peacetime tariff
Bonus bill veto; retires to Montpelier; president of Albemarle Agricultural Society; founder of American Colonization Society	1817	Presidency of James Monroe, 1817–25; Rush-Bagot Convention
	1820	Missouri Compromise
Refuses to publish Federal Convention notes	1821	
Lafayette visits Montpelier	1824	
Last visit with Jefferson	1825	University of Virginia opens; Presidency of John Quincy Adams, 1825–29
Succeeds Jefferson as rector of University of Virginia	1826	
Virginia constitutional convention	1829	Presidency of Andrew Jackson, 1829–37
Rebuts Hayne in *North American Review*	1830	Webster-Hayne debate; nullification controversy, 1830–33
	1831	Nat Turner insurrection
Resignation as rector; "Advice to My Country"	1834	
James Madison dies at Montpelier, June 28	1836	Establishment of Republic of Texas

For his unique contribution in drafting it, Madison was known as the Father of the Constitution.

Chapter 1

A Revolutionary Vocation

During the summer of 1769, James Madison, then a young gentleman of eighteen, left his home in the Virginia Piedmont to pursue his education at the College of New Jersey in Princeton. He traveled on horseback with two companions and a Negro servant, probably by the lowland route easterly from his native Orange County through Fredericksburg, Annapolis, and New Castle to the colonial metropolis of Philadelphia, thence across the Delaware to the sleepy village that was the seat of the college. The three-hundred-mile journey took perhaps a dozen days, and the Virginia uplander, who knew nothing of the bustle of towns and trade, must have marveled at the sights and sounds en route. All along the coast that summer, merchants were joining a nonimportation movement against Britain in retaliation for the hated Townshend Acts, which sought to raise revenue in America by imposing duties on certain goods imported by the Colonies. "No taxation without representation" was the cry, and in the provincial capitals through which the young Virginian passed—Annapolis, New Castle, Philadelphia—the agitation was especially warm. The education Madison was seeking lay at the end of the road in Princeton, but in the course of reaching it he was introduced to the spectacle of the American Revolution that would henceforth control his destiny.

The life of James Madison, more than the lives of his illustrious compatriots, was inseparable from the history of the revolutionary nation founded in 1776. There is virtually no accounting for him or of him apart from the great events of his time. Any chapter in the early life of the Republic is more important to his story than any chapter of merely personal history. And at the end, until his death in 1836, he stood as the lonely last sentinel of the Founding Fathers. Near the end, turning aside beseechers of autobiography, Madison said: "It has been remarked that the biography of an author must be a history of his writings. So must that of one whose whole life has in a manner been a public life, be gathered from

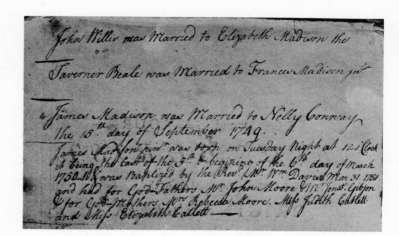

Part of a page from the Madison family Bible recording the birth of James Madison, Jr., on March 5, 1750 (March 16, 1751, New Style)

his official transactions, and his manuscript papers on public subjects...."
There was for him no life apart from his public career. He did, it is true,
finally dictate a hurried sketch of that career, "the merest skeleton" as he
observed; and predictably, this so-called "autobiography" draws a veil
over the person of James Madison. He devoted only two hundred words
to his life before the eighteenth year. (Until then the record of his papers
is a blank.) In retrospect, life began when he went to college, opened his
mind to the world of learning, and then, by measured steps, entered into
the actions and passions of his time.

He was born March 16, 1751, at his maternal grandparents' home in
King George County, but was at once taken inland to the Madison home,
Montpelier as he would later name it, in the deep-wooded, rolling hill country of Orange. His great-grandfather, James Taylor II, had explored this
wilderness and beyond to the Blue Ridge in 1716 as a member of Governor
Spotswood's land-surveying expedition, the "Knights of the Golden Horseshoe." Some years later he patented 13,500 acres on the Rapidan River in
what would become Orange County. A substantial portion of this land
descended to his eldest daughter, Frances Taylor, the wife of Ambrose
Madison. The Madisons traced their Virginia ancestry back two generations
to John Maddison, a ship's carpenter who came from England about the
middle of the seventeenth century. They, like the Taylors, had prospered
and, like many of the Tidewater gentry in the early part of the eighteenth
century, cast their gaze and their fortunes westward to the virgin red lands
of the Virginia Piedmont. Not long after the death of James Taylor II in
1729, Ambrose Madison settled his family in Orange. His eldest son, James
Madison, was then only a child, but he grew up with the country, became
one of its first citizens, and managed an estate of some four thousand acres.
In 1749 he married Nelly Conway, the seventeen-year-old daughter of a
planter in the low country. James Madison, Jr., was the first of twelve children born to them; only seven survived infancy.

Looking back two centuries from the lovely hills of Orange today, one imagines an idyllic rural boyhood for young Madison. He never lacked companionship. Not only were there brothers and sisters to play with and look after, but the country rapidly filled with families as large and often as comfortable as his own, and the network of cousinship extended well beyond the boundaries of Orange. Doubtless, with other Virginia boys, he liked to ride and to shoot, though in these favored pastimes he was neither physically nor temperamentally to the manner born. He was baptized and raised in the Anglican faith, the established religion of the colony. The nearest church, Brick Church, of which his father was a vestryman, lay six miles east of Orange Court House. These two places, church and court, were prominent landmarks in the youth's meagerly provisioned world.

Orange was no longer on the frontier, and Indians were about as rare as buffalo; yet the unusual interest that the upland planters felt in the land beyond the mountains was enough to raise apprehensions during the French and Indian War. Neighbors went off to fight and rumors of Indian attack spilled over the Blue Ridge. The West thus early became a fixture of Madison's consciousness. The war ended gloriously in British conquest to the Mississippi; nearer home and recurrent were the plagues of drought and disease, especially smallpox which reached epidemic proportions when Madison was about ten. His family must have suffered, along with most Virginia planters, from the frequently short crops and the depression of tobacco prices in the 1760s. This reversal of fortunes put a heavy strain on the province's relationship with the mother country. Yet with all these

Page of an autobiographical sketch written by Madison in later life, describing his schoolmaster Donald Robertson as having a "warm temper"

difficulties over several years, Madison's father built a spacious new mansion at Montpelier. The rectangular brick dwelling, simple but graceful in design, beautifully situated and offering the vista of the Blue Ridge, would become Madison's home for the rest of his life.

At about this time, in 1762, the lad was sent to a celebrated school kept by Donald Robertson in King and Queen County some seventy miles from home. Robertson had been educated in Scotland. His most famous pupil remembered him fondly as "a man of extensive learning, and a distinguished Teacher." To the small stock of rudimentary education acquired at Montpelier, Madison now added Latin and Greek, French, algebra and geometry, geography, and "miscellaneous literature." In 1767, after five years at the Robertson school, he returned home for further study under the tutelage of the Reverend Thomas Martin, newly appointed rector of Brick Church, who lived with the family and taught Madison's younger brothers and sisters as well. A recent graduate of the College of New Jersey, Martin seems to have steered Madison in that direction. Most college-bound Virginians went to William and Mary in the capital at Williamsburg. But the Madisons, father and son, feared the miasmal climate of the Tidewater, and they had doubtless heard stories about the rowdyism of students and the debauchery of Anglican professors at William and Mary. In contrast to the sinking reputation of William and Mary, they received glowing

accounts from Martin, himself an exemplary model of piety and learning, of the young College of New Jersey.

Founded in 1746 under Scottish Presbyterian auspices, the college had just come under the dynamic leadership of Dr. John Witherspoon, the learned divine who had risen to eminence in the Church of Scotland before accepting the call from the academic citadel of Presbyterianism in the New World. Without in any way diverting the institution from its religious mission, Witherspoon gave to the college an equally vital civil character. As the American Revolution came on, Princeton was imbued with the patriot cause in which many of its graduates, together with its president, would distinguish themselves. Under Witherspoon, aided by such earnest alumni as Thomas Martin, the reputation of the college spread far beyond the reaches of the Delaware. Still, in 1769 Madison was among the first southern youths to attend Princeton—part of the vanguard of a virtual army to come —and being both Virginian and Anglican he must have felt somewhat out of place. It was a venturesome step, and it paid off not simply in the standard currency of education but in the education of a man whose personal identifications were neither Virginian nor Anglican, but American.

One massive building, Nassau Hall, its long, cold gray walls crowned by a sky-piercing tower, contained the entire college. Here, spread over four floors, were student rooms, classrooms, dining hall, library, and chapel

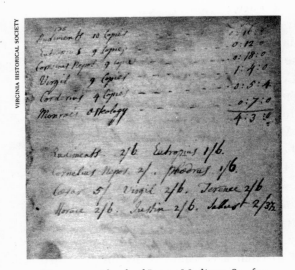

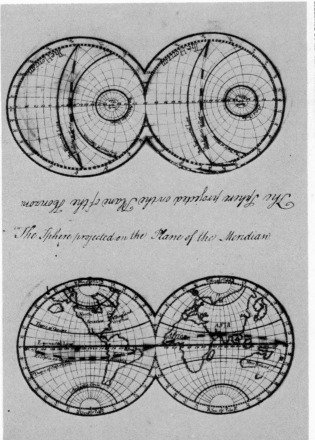

The Sphere projected on the Plane of the Meridian

The account book of James Madison, Sr., for December 11, 1755 (left) listed expenses "To building a house . . . ," probably referring to his mansion (far left, as sketched at a later date). In Donald Robertson's school young "Jamie" began his study of Latin and bought a number of the books listed above in Robertson's ledger. He also made the astronomical drawings seen at right.

—all the essentials for the care and instruction of some one hundred young men. Classes were in session when Madison arrived in midsummer. Discovering that he was a year or two older and also better prepared than most entering students, he commenced his studies at once in hopes of catching up with the freshman class, though final examinations were only a few weeks away. "The near approach of examination occasions a surprising application to study on all sides, and I think it very fortunate that I entered College immediately after my arrival," Madison wrote to Martin in August—the earliest letter from his pen that has survived. He passed the freshman examinations in English, Latin and Greek, mathematics, and the New Testament and was to finish the ordinary college course in two years. Following the commencement in September, the youth wrote to his father.

Nassau-Hall, September 30th. 69.

Hond. Sir,

I received your letter by Mr. Rosekrans, and wrote an Answer; but as it is probable this will arrive sooner which I now write by Doctor Witherspoon, I shall repeat some circumstances to avoid obscurity.

On Wednesday last we had the annual commencement. Eighteen young gentlemen took their Batchelors' degrees, and a considerable number their Masters Degrees; the Degree of Doctor of Law was bestowed on Mr. Dickenson the Farmer [author of *Letters From a Farmer in Pennsylvania*] and Mr. Galloway, the Speaker of the Pennsylvania Assembly, a distinguishing mark of Honour, as there never was any of that kind done before in America. The Commencement began at 10 O'Clock, when the President walked first into the Church, a board of Trustees following, and behind them those that were to take their Master's degrees, and last of all, those that were to take their first Degrees; After a short Prayer by the President, the Head Oration, which is always given to the greatest Scholar by the President & Tutors, was pronounced in Latin by Mr. Samuel [Stanhope] Smith son of a Presbyterean Minister in Pennsylvania. Then followed the other Orations, Disputes and Dialogues, distributed to each according to his merit, and last of all was pronounced the Valedictory Oration by Mr. John Henry son of a Gentleman in Maryland. This is given to the greatest *Orator*. We had a very great Assembly of People, a considerable number of whom came from N. York. Those at Philidelphia were most of them detained by Racis [horse races] which were to follow on the next day.

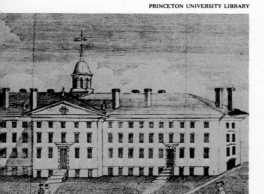

Amos Doolittle's engraving of Nassau Hall at Princeton, New Jersey

Earliest surviving letter from Madison's pen was to Thomas Martin.

David Rittenhouse's orrery

Since Commencement the Trustees have been sitting about Business relative to the College, and have chose for Tutors the ensuing year, for the junior class Mr. Houston from N. Carolina in the room of Mr. Periam, for the Freshman class Mr. Reeves (a gentleman who has for several years kept a School at Elizabeth Town) in the room of Mr. Pemberton: the Sophomore Tutor Mr. Thomsom still retains his place, remarkable for his skill in the sophomore Studies having taken care of that class for several years past. Mr. Halsey was chosen Junior Tutor but refused. The Trustees have likewise appointed Mr. Caldwel, a Minister at Elizabeth Town, to take a journey through the Southern Provinces as far as Georgia to make collections by which the College Fund may be inabled to increase the Library, provide an apparatus of mathematical and Philosophical Instruments & likewise to support Professors which would be a great addition to the advantages of this College. Doctr. Witherspoon's business to Virginia is nearly the same as I conjecture and perhaps to form some acquaintance to induce Gentlemen to send their sons to this College.

I am very sorry to hear of the great drought that has prevailed with you, but am in some hopes the latter part of the year may have been more seasonable for you[r] crops. Your caution of frugality on consideration of the dry weather shall be carefully observed; but I am under a necesity of spending much more than I was apprehensive, for the purchasing of every small trifle which I have occasion for consumes a much greater sum than one wou[ld] suppose from a calculation of the necessary expences....

I recollect nothing more at present worth relating, but as often as opportunity and any thing worthy your attention shall occur, be assured you shall hear from your

Affectionate Son
JAMES MADISON

The letter is full of information, some of it faintly familiar. The poor collegian, then as now, pleads with his father for money. The poor college president, then as now, goes off on a fund-raising tour. (Witherspoon's southern tour was remarkably successful; part of the proceeds purchased David Rittenhouse's ingenious orrery, from which Madison learned the Newtonian wonders of the solar system.) Honorary degrees are conferred on the great men of the day, in this case on the Whig patriots John Dickinson and Joseph Galloway, the first honorary doctorates of laws conferred in America. (John Hancock, the Massachusetts hero, received an honorary A.M., though Madison does not mention him.) And the scholar of the class discourses in Latin. Samuel Stanhope Smith, whom Madison would come to know as a tutor and friend, later founded Hampden-Sydney College in Virginia, distinguished himself in natural history, and eventually became president of Princeton.

Madison was a diligent scholar. Witherspoon later remarked that he never knew him to do anything wrong. In the Presbyterian confines of Nassau Hall, shielded from the vices and follies of the world, young men found little opportunity to do wrong. Discipline, if not severe, was rigorous. Beginning with the five o'clock bell, followed by chapel at six, the daily schedule was carefully prescribed. The curriculum was classical and also Christian, as was customary, but Princeton had gone further than most academies in introducing newer liberal studies, such as natural science, modern philosophy, and modern literature, including French. If Princeton aimed to discipline the mind and strengthen character, it also aimed to cultivate reason and critical inquiry. "In the instruction of youth," said one account of the college, "care is taken to cherish a spirit of liberty, and free enquiry; and not only to permit, but even to encourage their right of private judgment, without presuming to dictate with an air of infallibility...." Learning this, Madison learned the best that Princeton had to teach. The ascendant intellectual spirit was that of the Scottish Enlightenment. In the culminating course of the senior year, moral philosophy, as taught by President Witherspoon himself, Madison read the Scottish luminaries—Francis Hutcheson, Adam Ferguson, Lord Kames, and others—who affirmed the natural reasonableness and benevolence of mankind. The persistent Scottish strain in Madison's education, curiously mixing Calvinistic Presbyterianism with Enlightenment liberalism, shaped a mental outlook in which the recognition of man's potentiality for virtuous freedom never lost sight of his potentiality for evil.

Madison's education as a political thinker came later, though he formed an early acquaintance with the tradition of political theory from Plato and Aristotle to the moderns, especially Locke and the English Whigs of the late-seventeenth and eighteenth centuries. Equally significant in this respect were the lively extracurricular debates on public issues. Studious, painfully shy, and averse to the platform, Madison nevertheless entered into the round of collegiate activities, both the frivolous and the serious. As a member of the Whig Society, a literary fellowship, he penned many sheets of harsh sophomoric doggerel for the "paper war" on the rival Cliosophic Society. Judging by the theses Princeton graduates expounded at commencement exercises, the libertarian issues in the Anglo-American controversy stirred the minds of the students. Resistance to tyranny, religious toleration, promotion of American manufactures, and nonimportation were among the theses defended in 1770. The despised Townshend Acts were repealed in the spring, but apparently the young Princetonians favored continued agitation. Writing to his father in July, mainly of trivial matters but also of his journey home during the coming fall vacation, Madison expressed his political feelings.

One of Madison's poems for Whig Society was "Clio's Proclamation."

Nassau Hall. July 23d. 1770

Inclosed are the measures of my Neck & rists. I believe my Mother need not hurry herself much about my shirts before I come for I shall not want more than three or four at most. I should chuse she would not have them ruffled 'till I am present myself. I have not yet procured a horse for my Journey, but think you had better not send me one as I cant wait long enough to know whether or not you'll have an opportunity without losing my chance, most of the horses being commonly engaged by the Students sometime before vacation begins. If I should set off from this place as soon as I expect you may look for me in October perhaps a little before the middle if the weather should be good. We have no publick news but the base conduct of the Merchants in N. York in breaking through their spirited resolutions not to import, a distinct account of which I suppose will be in the Virginia Gazete before this arrives. their Letter to the Merchants in Philadelphia requesting their concurrence was lately burnt by the Students of this place in the college Yard, all of them appearing in their black Gowns & the bell Tolling. The number of Students has increased very much of late; there are about an hundred & fifteen in College & the Grammar School, twenty two commence this Fall, all of them in American Cloth.

At the time of Madison's graduation a year later, in September, 1771, nonimportation had collapsed everywhere and the political waters were calm again. He refrained from any public part in the commencement exercises. The audience heard a rousing patriotic poem, "The Rising Glory of America," by two of his classmates, Philip Freneau and Hugh Henry Brackenridge.

And here fair freedom shall forever reign.
I see a train, a glorious train appear,
Of Patriots plac'd in equal fame with those
Who nobly fell for Athens or for Rome.
The sons of Boston, resolute and brave,

The firm supporters of our injur'd rights,
Shall lose their splendours in the brighter beams
Of patriots fam'd and heroes yet unborn.

The long poem was a hymn to the New World, a testament to the "spirit of liberty" abroad at Princeton, and a leitmotiv to the young men who would make their careers as poets, ministers, soldiers, and statesmen of the new nation. Brackenridge would become one of the first American novelists; Freneau the first patriot poet as well as a partisan journalist closely associated with Madison. Several of his classmates later served valiantly in the Revolutionary War, and one of them, Gunning Bedford, Jr., of Delaware, would reappear in the Federal Convention of 1787. The paths of other college friends, though not of the Class of '71—Henry Lee ("Light-horse Harry" of Revolutionary War fame) and Aaron Burr—would cross and re-cross Madison's own.

Not knowing what to do when he graduated and reluctant to exchange the exuberant intellectual life of Nassau Hall for the doldrums of Virginia, Madison stayed on at Princeton for six months to study Hebrew and theology under Dr. Witherspoon's direction. In poor health at this time, he grew worse after returning home in April, 1772. Madison and his friends traced the illness to the "doubled labour" of taking the bachelor's degree in two years. Whatever may have been the cause of the disease, he suffered from a severe nervous disorder that threw a pall over his future. In this distressed state of mind, he continued his course of study mainly along theological lines; then, as the melancholy cloud of eternity lifted, he shifted to the study of law without, however, any determination to become a lawyer. Indeed Madison's illness only complicated further the youthful ordeal of finding a proper vocation in life. The choices were few in eighteenth-century Virginia. In view of his education under Witherspoon's guiding hand, he must have considered the ministry for a time. Its charms soon passed, however. The law appealed to his reason, but he found the reading "coarse and dry" and dropped any thought of a career at the bar.

During this personal "time of troubles" Madison entered into correspondence with his former college friend William Bradford of Philadelphia. Bradford, whose father published the widely read *Pennsylvania Journal,* initiated this remarkable exchange of letters in October, 1772, on a soul-sick note that was more than reciprocated by Madison's despondency. "The value of a college-life like most other blessing[s] is seldom known but by its loss," the Pennsylvanian began. After Nassau Hall, he expected no happiness, only "trouble & anxiety," and he knew not what business to pursue in life. Madison replied in kind.

Orange Virginia Novr. 9th. 1772

My dear Billey,

You moralize so prettily that if I were to judge from some parts of your letter of October 13 I should take you

Few books from Madison's extensive library are known to have survived; this 1676 volume is among them.

William Bradford by St. Mémin

for an old Philosopher that had experienced the emptiness of Earthly Happiness. And I am very glad that you have so early seen through the romantic paintings with which the World is sometimes set off by the sprightly imaginations of the Ingenious. You have happily supplied by reading and observation the want of experiment and therefore I hope you are sufficiently guarded against the allurements and vanities that beset us on our first entrance on the Theatre of Life. Yet however nice and cautious we may be in detecting the follies of mankind and framing our Oeconomy according to the precepts of Wisdom and Religion I fancy there will commonly remain with us some latent expectation of obtaining more than ordinary Happiness and prosperity till we feel the convincing argument of actual disappointment. Tho I will not determine whether we shall be much the worse for it if we do not allow it to intercept our views towards a future State, because strong desires and great Hopes instigate us to arduous enterprizes fortitude and perseverance. Nevertheless a watchful eye must be kept on ourselves lest while we are building ideal monuments of Renown and Bliss here we neglect to have our names enrolled in the Annals of Heaven. These thoughts come into my mind because I am writing to you and thinking of you. As to myself I am too dull and infirm now to look out for any extraordinary things in this world for I think my sensations for many months past have intimated to me not to expect a long or healthy life, yet it may be better with me after some time tho I hardly dare expect it and therefore have little spirit and alacrity to set about any thing that is difficult in acquiring and useless in possessing after one has exchanged Time for Eternity. But you have Health Youth Fire and Genius to bear you along through the high tract of public Life and so may be more interested and delighted in improving on hints that respect the temporal though momentous concerns of man. . . .

As you seem to require that I should be open and unreserved (which is indeed the only proof of true friendship) I will venture to give you a word of advice though it be more to convince you of my affection for you than from any apprehension of your needing it. Pray do not suffer those impertinent fops that abound in every City to divert you from your business and philosophical amusements. You may please them more by admitting them to the enjoyment of your company but you will make them respect and admire you more by shewing your indignation at their follies and by keeping them at a becoming distance. I am luckily out of the way of such troubles, but I know you are cirrounded with them for they breed in Towns and populous places, as naturally as flies do in the Shambles, because there they get food enough for their Vanity and impertinence.

I have undertaken to instruct my brothers and Sisters in some of the first rudiments of literature, but it does not take up so much of my time but I shall always have leisure to receive and answer your letters which are very grateful to me I assure you, and for reading any performances you may be kind enough to send me whether of Mr. Freneau or any body else. I think myself happy in your correspondence and desire you will continue to write as often as you can as you see I intend to do by the early and long answer I send you. You are the only valuable friend I have settled in so public a place and must rely on you for an account of all literary transactions in your part of the world. . . .

And now my friend I must take my leave of you, but with such hopes that it will not be long before I receive another epistle from you as make me more cheerfully conclude and Subscribe myself Yr. Sincere and Affecte. friend

JAMES MADISON JUNR.

Your Direction [address] was right however the addition of Junr. to my name would not be improper.

Madison's opening correspondence with his friend William Bradford

Another letter to Bradford, written nearly a year later, reveals Madison's growing inclination toward the study of law.

[Orange, Virginia,] Septr. 25th 1773

Since you first hinted to me your suspense as to the settled business of your life, I have partook of your anxiety & [though it] has been often in my thoughts I feel a backwardness to offer my opinion in so critical a matter and the more so for the weight you are pleased to give it. I have too much esteem and affection for you and am too conscious of my want of capacity and experience to direct in so important an Affair. I must therefore premise that it is my earnest request that you would act the candid open friend as well as in rejecting as in asking advice; for I consult nothing but your real interest, and am sensible of my insufficiency to be a counsellor much more a preceptor. You forbid any recommendation of Divinity by suggesting that you have insuperable objections therefore I can only condole with the Church on the loss of a fine Genius and persuasive Orator. I cannot however suppress thus much of my advice on that head that you would always keep the Ministry obliquely in View whatever your profession be. This will lead you to cultivate an acquaintance occasionally with the most sublime of all Sciences and will qualify you for a change of public character if you should hereafter desire it. I have sometimes thought there could not be a stronger testimony in favor of Religion or against temporal Enjoyments even the most rational and manly than for men who occupy the most honorable and gainful departments and are rising in reputation and wealth, publicly to declare their unsatisfatoriness by becoming fervent Advocates in the cause of Christ, & I wish you may give in your Evidence in this way. Such Instances have seldom occurred, therefore they would be more striking and would be instead of a "Cloud of Witnesses.["] If I am to speak my Sentiments of Merchandize, Physic and Law I must say they are all honorable and usefull professions and think you ought to have more regard to their Suitableness to your Genius than to their comparative Excellence. As far as I know your endowments I should pronounce Law the most eligeble. It alone can bring into use many parts of knowledge you have acquired and will still have a taste for, & pay you for cultivating the Arts of Eloquence. It is a sort of General Lover that wooes all the Muses and Graces. This cannot be said so truly of commerce and Physic & therefore less Learning & smaller understanding will do for them. The objection founded on the number of Lawyers should stimulate to Assiduity rather than discourage the Attempt. I greatly commend your determined adherence to probity and Truth in the Character of a Lawyer but fear it would be impracticable. Misrepresentation from a client or intricacy in a cause must often occasion doubt and ignorance till the matter has been considerably debated at the bar; Though it must be allowed there are a thousand cases in which your rule would be safe and highly commend-

BOTH: HISTORICAL SOCIETY OF PENNSYLVANIA

The London Coffee House, where Madison had stopped en route to Princeton, and the bookstore next door were both operated by the family of William Bradford.

able. I must add after all that if you should enter on a mercantile State (to which peculiar reasons for ought I know may advise) I should be loth to disapprove.

Madison closed this letter with mention of the hardships caused by "a very great scarcity of circulating cash" in Virginia, then abruptly broke off, "I do not meddle with Politicks." In truth he had not and would not for several months yet. However, the course of legal study soon led him into the great questions of freedom and self-government thrown up by the onrushing tide of the American Revolution; and as his mind took hold of these questions and as his health slowly mended as well, Madison's spirits revived and the youthful melancholy disappeared to be replaced by vigorous and life-fulfilling purpose.

Madison's political feelings were most aroused, oddly enough, not by the imperial issues of trade and taxation, but by the repressions and abuses of the Anglican Church in Virginia. Schooled at Princeton in the dissenting tradition and straitlaced Presbyterian morality, he was shocked by the corruptions of the Anglican clergy and the persecuting intolerance of the established church toward nonconforming sectarians in his own neighborhood. Although by 1774 he could denounce the Tea Act and cheer the Boston mob, it was the union of Church and State that set him on fire. The cause of religious freedom became Madison's passport to revolution, as is evident in his letters to Bradford.

[Orange, Virginia,] Dec. 1. 1773.
I am glad you have rescued yourself from your anxiety and suspence and have come to a determination to engage in the study of the Law, which I hope you had better reasons for chusing than I could suggest. I intend myself to read Law occasionally and have procured books for that purpose so that you need not fear offending me by Allusions to that Science. Indeed any of your remarks as you go along would afford me entertainment and instruction. The principles & Modes of Government are too important to be disregarded by an Inquisitive mind and I think are well worthy [of] a critical examination by all students that have health & Leisure. I should be well pleased with a scetch of the plan you have fixed upon for your studies, the books & the order you intend to read them in; and when you have obtained sufficient insight into the Constitution of your Country and can make it an amusement to yourself send me a draught of its Origin & fundamental principals of Legislation; particularly the extent of your religious Toleration. Here

*As a young man, Madison was often
referred to as pale and sickly.*

allow me to propose the following Queries. Is an Ecclesiastical Establishment absolutely necessary to support
civil society in a supream Government? & how far it is
hurtful to a dependant State? I do not ask for an immediate answer but mention them as worth attending to in
the course of your reading and consulting experienced
Lawyers & Politicians upon. When you have satisfied
yourself in these points I should listen with pleasure to
the Result of your reserches.

You recommend sending for the Reviews as the best
way to know the present State of Literature and the
Choicest Books published. This I have done and shall
continue to do: but I find them loose in their principals
[and] encourage[r]s of free enquiry even such as destroys
the most essential Truths, Enemies to serious religion &
extreamly partial in their Citations, seeking them rather
to Justify their censures and Commendations than to
give the reader a just specimen of the Authors genius. I
can rely with greater confidence on you[r] judgment after
you have read the Authors or have known their Character
from you[r] judicious friends. I am meditating a Journey
to Philada which I hope to accomplish early in the spring
if no unforeseen hindrances stop me. I shall bring a
brother with me to put to school somewhere there, perhaps at Mr. Smith's. I need not say how far the desire of
seeing you and others is a powerful Inducement and that
my imagination daily anticipates the pleasure of this
Tour. Who were the authors of the Sermons you sent me?
What is the exchange with you now & what is it likely to
be in the spring? Write speedily & forgive my troublesome questions.

Writing to Bradford in January and April, Madison
relayed developments in Virginia and commented on events in Philadelphia:
citizens there had forced a ship laden with East India Company tea to return to sea, threatening otherwise to tar and feather the captain.

[Orange, Virginia,] Jan 24. 1774
I congratulate you on your heroic proceedings in Philada.
with regard to the Tea. I wish Boston may conduct matters with as much discretion as they seem to do with boldness: They seem to have great Tryals and difficulties
by reason of the obduracy ... of their Governour. However Political Contests are necessary sometimes as well

as military to afford exercise and practise and to instruct in the Art of defending Liberty and property. I verily believe the frequent Assaults that have been made on America Boston especially will in the end prove of real advantage. If the Church of England had been the established and general Religion in all the Northern Colonies as it has been among us here and uninterrupted tranquility had prevailed throughout the Continent, It is clear to me that slavery and Subjection might and would have been gradually insinuated among us. Union of Religious Sentiments begets a surprizing confidence and Ecclesiastical Establishments tend to great ignorance and Corruption all of which facilitate the Execution of mischievous Projects. But away with Politicks! Let me address you as a Student and Philosopher & not as a Patriot now. I am pleased that you are going to converse with the Edwards and Henry's & Charles &c&c who have swayed the British Sceptre though I believe you will find some of them dirty and unprofitable Companions unless you will glean Instruction from their follies and fall more in love with Liberty by beholding such detestable pictures of Tyranny and Cruelty. I was afraid you would not easily have loosened your Affections from the Belles Lettres. A Delicate Taste and warm imagination like yours must find it hard to give up such refined & exquisite enjoyments for the coarse and dry study of the Law: It is like leaving a pleasant flourishing field for a barren desert; perhaps I should not say barren either because the Law does bear fruit but it is sour fruit that must be gathered and pressed and distilled before it can bring pleasure or profit. I perceive I have made a very awkward Comparison but I got the thought by the end and had gone to far to quit it before I perceived that it was too much entangled in my brain to run it through. And so you must forgive it. I myself use to have too great a hankering after those amusing Studies. Poetry wit and Criticism Romances Plays &c captivated me much: but I begin [to] discover that they deserve but a moderate portion of a *mortal's* Time. and that something more substantial more durable more profitable befits a riper Age. It would be exceeding improper for a labouring man to have nothing but flowers in his Garden or to determine to eat nothing but sweet-meats and Confections. Equally absurd would it be for a Scholar and man

As Madison's correspondence with Bradford continued, he wrote in January, 1774, that it was "too far advanced to req[uire a]pologies for bad writing & [b]lots."

of Business to make up his whole Library with Books of Fancy and feed his Mind with nothing but such Luscious performances.

When you have an Opportunity and write to Mr. Brackinridge pray tell him I often think of him and long to see him and am resolved to do so in the Spring. George Luckey was with me at Christmas and we talked so much about old Affairs & Old Friends that I have a most insatiable desire to see you all. Luckey will accompany me and we are to set off on the 10th. of April if no disaster befalls either of us. I want again to breathe your free Air. I expect it will mend my Constitution & confirm my principles. I have indeed as good an Atmosphere at home as the Climate will allow: but have nothing to brag of as to the State and Liberty of my Country. Poverty and Luxury prevail among all sorts: Pride ignorance and Knavery among the Priesthood and Vice and Wickedness among the Laity. This is bad enough But It is not the worst I have to tell you. That diabolical Hell conceived principle of persecution rages among some and to their eternal Infamy the Clergy can furnish their Quota of Imps for such business. This vexes me the most of any thing whatever. There are at this [time?] in the adjacent County not less than 5 or 6 well meaning men in close Goal [gaol] for publishing their religious Sentiments which in the main are very orthodox. I have neither patience to hear talk or think of any thing relative to this matter, for I have squabbled and scolded abused and ridiculed so long about it, [to so lit]tle purpose that I am without common patience. So I [leave you] to pity me and pray for Liberty of Conscience [to revive among us.]

I expect to hear from you once more before I see you if time will admit: and want to know when the Synod meets & where: What the Exchange is at and as much about my friends and other Matters as you can and think worth notice. Till I see you Adieu.

JM

NB Our Correspondence is too far advanced to req[uire a]pologies for bad writing & [b]lots.

April 1st. 1774. Virginia Orange Cy. Our Assembly is to meet the first of May When It is expected something will be done in behalf of the Dissenters: Petitions I hear are already forming among the

The closing of the port of Boston was pictured in a British cartoon showing the caged Bostonians being fed codfish by their sympathizers.

Persecuted Baptists and I fancy it is in the thoughts of the Presbyterians also to intercede for greater liberty in matters of Religion. For my part I can not help being very doubtful of their succeeding in the Attempt. The Affair was on the Carpet during the last Session; but such incredible and extravagant stories were told in the House [of Burgesses, the lower house of the assembly] of the monstrous effect of the Enthusiasm prevalent among the Sectaries and so greedily swallowed by their Enemies that I believe they lost footing by it and the bad name they still have with those who pretend too much contempt to examine into their principles and Conduct and are too much devoted to the ecclesiastical establishment to hear of the Toleration of Dissentients, I am apprehensive, will be again made a pretext for rejecting their requests. The Sentiments of our people of Fortune & fashion on this subject are vastly different from what you have been used to. That liberal catholic and equitable way of thinking as to the rights of Conscience, which is one of the Characteristics of a free people and so strongly marks the People of your province is but little known among the Zealous adherents to our Hierarchy. We have it is true some persons in the Legislature of generous Principles both in Religion & Politicks but number not merit you know is necessary to carry points there. Besides the Clergy are a numerous and powerful body have great influence at home by reason of their connection with & dependence on the Bishops and Crown and will naturally employ all their art & Interest to depress their rising Adversaries; for such they must consider dissenters who rob them of the good will of the people and may in time endanger their livings & security.

You are happy in dwelling in a Land where those inestimable privileges are fully enjoyed and public has long felt the good effects of their religious as well as Civil Liberty. Foreigners have been encouraged to settle amg. you. Industry and Virtue have been promoted by mutual emulation and mutual Inspection, Commerce and the Arts have flourished and I can not help attributing those continual exertions of Gen[i]us which appear among you to the inspiration of Liberty and that love of Fame and Knowledge which always accompany it. Religious bondage shackles and debilitates the mind and unfits it for every noble enterprize every expanded prospect. How far this is the Case with Virginia will more clearly appear when the ensuing Trial is made.

I am making all haste in preparing for my Journey.

The journey took Madison to Philadelphia, where he was visiting with college friends when news arrived of the act closing the port of Boston. The first of Parliament's Coercive Acts in retaliation upon Massachusetts for the Boston Tea Party of December 16, 1773, the act inflamed the continent and led to demands from one colonial capital to another for a continental congress and for the revival of economic coercion against the mother country. Madison returned from the ferment in Philadelphia full of eagerness for the movement that had suddenly acquired a national dimension. In Virginia the House of Burgesses, having been dissolved by Governor Dunmore, had gone into business for itself and, among other forward actions, called for the election of delegates to a revolutionary convention to meet in Williamsburg in August. Madison was now obsessed by politics. He devoured the pamphlets Bradford sent him from Philadelphia and rejected counsels of caution such as he detected in the proceedings of the Pennsylvania assembly. A few months earlier he could exclaim, with charming insouciance, "But away with Politicks!" and break into discourse on the pleasures of belles lettres. No longer. His only regret now was that he had not put off his northern journey until September, when the leading patriots of all the colonies were to assemble in Philadelphia. Excerpts from additional letters to Bradford chart his course.

[Orange, Virginia,] July 1. 1774.

I am once more got into my native land and into the possession of my customary enjoyments Solitude and Contemplation, though I must confess not a little disturbed by the sound of War blood and plunder on the one Hand and the Threats of Slavery and Oppression on the Other. From the best accounts I can obtain from our Frontiers The Savages are determined in the extirpation of the Inhabitants, and no longer leave them the alternative of Death or Captivity....

As to the Sentiments of the people of this Colony with respect to the Bostonians I can assure [you] I find them generally very warm in their favour. The Natives are very unanimous and resolute, are making resolves in almost every County and I believe are willing to fall in with the Other Colonies in any expedient measure, even if that should be the universal prohibition of Trade. It must not be denied though that the Europeans especially the Scotch and some interested Merchants among the

Another British cartoon showed Virginia Loyalists being forced to sign resolutions drawn up by the 1774 convention in Williamsburg.

natives discountenance such proceedings as far as they dare alledging the Injustice and perfidy of refusing to pay our debts to our Generous Creditors at Home. This Consideration induces some honest moderate folks to prefer a partial prohibition extending only to the *Importation* of Goods.

[Orange,] Virginia August 23. 1774
I have seen the instructions of your committee to your representatives & greately admire the wisdom of the advice & the elegance and cogency of the diction. In the latter especially they are vastly superior to what has been done by our convention. But do you not presume too much on the generosity & Justice of the crown, when you propose deffering all endeavours on our part till such important concessions & novel regulations are obtained; Would it not be advisable as soon as possible to begin our defence & to let its continuance or cessation depend on the success of a petition presented to his majesty. Delay on our part emboldens our adversaries and improves their schemes; whilst it abates the ardor of the Americans inspired with recent Injuries and affords opportunity to our secret enemies to disseminate discord & disunion. But I am mounting into the sphere of the general Congress to whose wisdom and Judgment all private opinions must give place. This Colony has appointed seven delegates to represent it on this grand occasion, most of them glowing patriots & men of Learning & penetration. It is however the opinion of some good Judges that one or two might be exchanged for the better. The Conduct of your Assembly in chusing [a conservative, Joseph] galloway & Humphries [Charles Humphreys, a Quaker] seems to forbode difficulties and divisions which may be strengthened by the deputees from N.Y. It also seems to indicate a prevalency of selfish Quakers in your House which frustrate the generous designs & manly efforts of the real friends to American Freedom. I assure you I heartily repent of undertaking my Journey to the North when I did. If I had it to perform now, the opportunity of attending the Congress would be an infinite addition to the pleasures of it. I cannot help congratulating you on your happy situation in that respect. I comfort myself however under the privation of such an happiness with the hope that you will befriend

Madison wrote to Bradford that the naming of Joseph Galloway to the Pennsylvania assembly "seems to forebode difficulties."

Carpenters' Hall in Philadelphia

me in sending a brief account of whatever is singular and important in their proceedings that can not be gathered from the public papers. Indeed I could wish their Debates were to be published which might greatly illuminate the minds of the thinking people among us and I would hope there would be sufficient abilities displayed in them to render us more respectable at Home.

Madison had found his vocation in the American Revolution. Bradford reported from Philadelphia that the city had "become another Cairo; with this difference that the one is a city swarming with Merchants, the other with politicians & Statesmen." Congress sat behind the closed doors of Carpenters' Hall, one room of which housed the city library supposed to be much used by the delegates, "by which we may conjecture that their measures will be wisely plan'd since they debate on them like philosophers; for by what I was told Vattel, Barlemaqui Locke & Montesquie seem to be the standar[d]s to which they refer either when settling the rights of the Colonies or when a dispute arises on the Justice or propriety of a measure." Madison, if he had not already read these philosophers, and others of lesser fame, would soon do so. The demiphilosophers in Philadelphia repudiated the authority of Parliament, called upon the people to arm, and adopted the system of nonintercourse. Madison heartily approved these bold measures. In December, 1774, he was elected to the Orange County Committee of Safety, which was charged to enforce the economic boycott—the Continental Association—and which quickly became the revolutionary local government. Of the eleven members, his father being chairman, Madison was much the youngest. Some months later the provincial committee of safety in Williamsburg commissioned him a colonel in the Orange County militia. But for his uncertain health, he might have taken to the field in 1775. As it was, although the honorific "Colonel" clung to him for many years, his only military service was on the parade ground, and that briefly. Of Orange and Virginia events, of his hopes and his fears, Madison wrote in letters to Bradford.

[Orange,] Virginia Nov: 26. 1774.
The pamphlets & letters you sent me were safely delivered about ten days after the date of them. . . .

The proceedings of the Congress are universally approved of in this Province & I am persuaded will be faithfully adheared to. A spirit of Liberty & Patriotism animates all degrees and denominations of men. Many publickly declare themselves ready to join the Bostonians as soon as violence is offered them or resistance thought expedient. In many counties independent companies are forming and voluntaraly subjecting themselves to military discipline that they may be expert & prepared against a time of Need. I hope it will be a general thing thro'ought this province. Such firm and provident steps will either intimidate our enemies or enable us to defy them. By an epistle from the yearly meeting of the Quakers in your City to their bretheren & friends in our Colonies I observe they are determined to be passive on this Critical occasion from a regard to their religious principles mixed I presume with the Leaven of civil policy.

If america & Britain should come to an hostile rupture I am afraid an Insurrection among the slaves may & will be promoted. In one of our Counties lately a few of those unhappy wretches met together & chose a leader who was to conduct them when the English Troops should arrive—which they foolishly thought would be very soon & that by revolting to them they should be rewarded with their freedom. Their Intentions were soon discovered & proper precautions taken to prevent the Infection. It is prudent such attempts should be concealed as well as suppressed.

Virginia Orange County Jany 20. 1775
We are very busy at present in raising men and procuring the necessaries for defending ourselves and our friends in case of a sudden Invasion. The extensiveness of the Demands of the Congress and the pride of the British Nation together with the Wickedness of the present Ministry, seem, in the Judgment of our Politicians to require a preparation for extreme events. There will by the Spring, I expect, be some thousands of well trained High Spirited men ready to meet danger whenever it appears, who are influenced by no mercenary Principles, bearing their own expences and having the prospect of no recompence but the honour and safety of their Country. I suppose the Inhabitants of your Province are more reserved in their behaviour if not more easy in their Apprehensions, from the prevalence of Quaker principles and politics. The Quakers are the only people with us who refuse to accede to the Continental Association.... When I say they refuse to accede to the Association my meaning is that they refuse to Sign it, that being the method used among us to distinguish friends from foes and to oblige the Common people to a more strict observance

Madison's commission as a colonel in the Orange County militia

A 1775 cartoon showing George III in his carriage being driven to destruction by his advisers while America burns in the background

The logo of Rivington's Gazetteer

of it: I have never heard whether the like method has been adopted in the other governments.

[Orange, Virginia, *c.* March 10, 1775]
We had a report here a few days [ago] that the New Yorkers had again given way & that the assembly had voted the proceedings of the Congress illegal. It raised a surprizing spirit of indignation & resentment which however Subsided on the report's being contradicted. The intimation you gave me of the state of affairs there prepared me to hear it without Surprize.

I lately saw in one of our Gazettes a pamphlet in answer to the friendly address [a tract by an Anglican clergyman] &c: by what you informed me I conjecture it to have been written by Genl. [Charles] Lee. It has much Spirit and Vivacity & contains some very sensible remarks. Some of our old bigots did not altogether approve the Strictures on the Clergy & King Charles; but it was generally, nay with this exception, universally, applauded. I wish most heartily we had [James] Rivington [a Tory newspaper editor] & his ministerial Gazetteers for 24. hours in this place. Execrable as their designs are, they would meet with adequate punishment. How different is the Spirit of Virginia from that of N York? A fellow was lately tarred & feathered for treating one [of] our county committees with disre[s]pect;

in N Y. they insult the whole Colony and Continent with impunity!

[Orange,] Virginia May 9th. 1775

We have lately had a great alarm here about the Governor's removing a large quantity of powder from our magazine and conveying it on board a ship of war: Not less [than] 600 men well armed and mounted assembled at Fredg. on this occasion, with a view to proceed to Wmsburg. [to] recover the powder & revenge the insult: The propriety of such a step was warmly agitated and weighty arguments aduced both for & against it: At length the advice of Peyton Randolph, Edm. Pendleton, Richd. H. Lee, and George Washington Esqrs. delegates for the Congress, to return home was complied with. The reasons however that induced these Gentlement to give this advice did not appear satisfactory to Patrick Henry Esqr. another of our delegates whose sentiments were not known at Fredg. This Gentleman after the dispersion of the troops at the above named place under the authority of the committee of his County and at the head of an Independant Company undertook to procure redress, which he resolutely accomplished by taking of the King's Quit-rents as much money as would replace the powder which had been removed so far that it could not be come at. This affair has prevented his appearing at the [Second Continental] Congress as early as his Colleagues, and has afforded me this opportunity of sending you a few lines [via Henry]. I expect his conduct as contrary to the opinion of the other delegats will be disapproved of by them, but it [has] gained him great honor in the most spirited parts of the Country and addresses of thanks are already presenting to him from different Quarters: The Gentlemen below [planters along the lower reaches of the York and James rivers] whose property will be exposed in case of a civil war in this Colony were extremely alarmed lest Government should be provoked to make reprisals. Indeed some of them discovered a pusilanimity little comporting with their professions or the name of Virginian.

I sent last fall to England for a few books, among which was priestly's treatise on Government. The present state of our affairs seems to threaten that it may be a long time before our commercial intercourse will be renewed: If

The Old Magazine in Williamsburg from which Lord Dunmore, the royal governor, had powder removed

this sd. appear to you to be the Case (& the session of the Congress will enable you to form a good guess) and it should be convenient in other respects, I should be glad you would send me the above treatise by the return of Mr. S. Smith.

On April 19, 1775, the first skirmishes of the American Revolution took place at Lexington and Concord. A few weeks later, American militiamen led by Ethan Allen captured Fort Ticonderoga and Crown Point in upper New York. Rumors of further encounters flew through the Colonies. Two days after the defeat of American forces at Bunker Hill, a report had reached Virginia of a great American victory in Boston. The rumor later proved unfounded, as Madison suspected it would.

[Orange, Virginia,] June 19th. 1775

A rumour is on the wing that the provincials have stormed Boston & with the Loss of 7,000 have cutt off or taken Gage & all his men. It is but little credited. Indeed the fact is extremely improbable: but the times are so remarkable for strange events; that improbability is almost become an argument for their truth.

Our friend Mr Wallace I hear is well & has entered into the Connubial state with one Miss McDowell, daughter of one of the representatives of Bottatourt County. Since I wrote last a Dysentry hath made an Irruption in my father's family. It has carried off a little sister about seven & a brother about four years of age. It is still among us but principally among the blacks. I have escaped hitherto, & as it is now out of the house I live in, I hope the danger is over. It is a disorder pretty incident to this Country & from some symptoms I am afraid will range more generally this year than common. Our Burgesses from the County are not yet returned from Willmsbg. where they hold their Assembly. So I cannot give you any particulars of their proceedings. The news papers will do that I expect: I understand Lord Dunmore by deserting his Palace & taking Sanctuary on board the Ship of War, under pretence of the fear of an Attack on his person, has surprized & incensed them much, As they thought it incredible he should be actuated on that occasion by the Motive he alledges. It is judged more likly to have proceeded from some intelligence or Instructions he has received from his friends or superiors to the North. It is said the Governor of N Carolina has treated

While minutemen in Massachusetts participated in battles such as Lexington, Colonel Madison was becoming a marksman in Orange.

his Assembly nearly in the same manner. Some will have it that Lord Dunmore removed from Wmsbg. & pretended danger that he might with more force & consistency misrepresent us to the ministry. His unparralled malice to the people of this Colony since the detection of his false & wicked letters, sent home at the time he was professing an ardent friendship for us must lead us to suppose he will do us all the Injury in his power. But we defy his power as much as we detest his Villany. We have as great unanimity & as much of the Military Ardor as you can possibly have in your government; & the progress we make in discipline & hostile preparations is as great as the Zeal with which these things were undertaken. The strength of this Colony will lie chiefly in the rifle-men of the Upland Counties, of whom we shall have great numbers. You would be astonished at the perfection this art is brought to. The most inexpert hands recon on it an indifferent shot to miss the bigness of a man's face at the distance of 100 Yards. I am far from being among the best & should not often miss it on a fair trial at that distance. If we come into an engagement, I make no doubt but the officers of the enemy will fall at the distance before they get withing 150 or 200 Yards. Indeed I believe we have men that would very often hit such a mark 250 Yds. Our greatest apprehensions proceed from the scarcity of powder but a little will go a great way with such as use rifles. It is imagined our Governor has been tampering with the Slaves & that he has it in contemplation to make great Use of them in case of a civil war in this province. To say the truth, that is the only part in which this Colony is vulnerable; & if we should be subdued, we shall fall like Achilles by the hand of one that knows that secret. But we have a good cause & great Courage which are a great support. I shall just add that among other incouragement we have a prospect of immense crops of Grain.

Virginia Orange: July 28—1775
Our convention is now sitting, and I believe intends to strike a considerable sum of money & to raise 3 or 4,000 men as an Army to be in immediate pay. The independants [minutemen], who I suppose will be three times that number will also have their pay commence as soon as they are called to action. The Preparations for War are

Lord Dunmore

every where going on in a most vigorous manner. But the Scarcity of Ammunition is truly alarming. Can you tell how they are supplied in N England and what steps are taking to procure a sufficiency for the time to come. I was a little induced from the confident assertion of the Congress that foreign Assistance if necessary was ["] *undoubtedly* attainable," to think & hope that some secret Overtures had been made to them. If so I imagine they are wrapped up in impenetrable secresy as yet. . . .

A Letter to Mr Smith is in company with this. It is directed to him at Princeton to the care of Plum. If he should be in Philada. at the time you get this I should be glad you would give him notice of it. Or if by going to Princeton you think it will miss of him in that case you would oblige me by taking it out of the office and conveying it to him. I have requested him to bring me two pamphlets "An apology for the Church of England as by Law Established" &c by Josiah Tucker—and An Essay on Toleration with a particular view to the late Application of the Dissenting Ministers to Parliament &c. by Phil. Furneaux. If he should not be in Town after he recieves this & you could procure them and send them to him with Priestly before he sets off for Virginia you would lay me under another Obligation.

A Scotch Parson in an adjoining County refused to observe the fast or preach on that day [a day designated for "public humiliation, Fasting and prayer" by the Continental Congress]. When called on he pleaded Conscience, alledging that it was his duty to pay no regard to any such appointments made by unconstitutional authority. The Committee it seems have their Consciences too: they have ordered his Church doors to be shut and his salary to be stopped, and have sent to the convention for their advice. If the Convention should connive at their proceedings I question, should his insolence not abate if he does not get ducked in a coat of Tar & surplice of feathers and then he may go in his new Canonicals and act under the lawful Authority of Gen. Gage if he pleased. We have one of the same Kidney in the parish I live in. He was sometime ago published in the Gazette for his insolence and had like to have met with sore treatment; but finding his protection to be not so much in the law as the favor of the people he is grown very supple & obsequious.

Virginia, HOWE

Nineteenth-century engraving of the site of Lord Dunmore's Palace

The war was a year old; Lord Dunmore and his Loyalist band had been driven to sea; and the movement for independence had made great strides when, on April 25, 1776, the twenty-five-year-old colonel of militia was elected by the freeholders of Orange to the Virginia Convention in Williamsburg. Early in the next month, he set out on his first journey to the capital village a hundred miles away. A stranger to the town, he found familiar faces in the convention, which was the revolutionary successor to the House of Burgesses. Among the delegates were kinsmen and friends of the family who helped smooth the way for Madison. Several of the celebrated Virginia patriots—George Washington, Richard Henry Lee, Thomas Jefferson—were on other errands; but Patrick Henry—the most celebrated of them all—and Edmund Pendleton, the presiding officer, were not only among Madison's relations, but among the great men of Virginia in the convention. On May 15, the delegates instructed the Virginians in Congress to propose a united declaration of independence. Without waiting for the formalities to be completed in Philadelphia, the convention at once set to work to form a new government for Virginia.

Pendleton named Madison to the committee that was to prepare a constitution and a declaration of rights. George Mason, a wealthy planter from Fairfax who was well versed in Whig theory, was the dominant force in the committee. The new constitution, adopted in convention on June 28, bore no traces of Madison's hand, and he would later join with Jefferson in efforts to reform it in democratic directions. But toward the proposed declaration of rights the freshman delegate overcame his reserve and offered an important amendment to Mason's article on religion. Madison recalled

the episode in an account written years later, in which he referred to himself in the third person.

Certificate of election (above) of James Madison, Jr., and William Moore to the convention that met at Williamsburg in the second capitol (left, below), built in 1751

"Autobiographical Notes," 1832

Being young & in the midst of distinguished and experienced members of the Convention he [Madison] did not enter into its debates; tho' he occasionally suggested amendments; the most material of which was a change of the terms in which the freedom of Conscience was expressed in the proposed Declaration of Rights. This important and meritorious instrument was drawn by Geo. Mason, who had inadvertently adopted the word *"toleration"* in the article on that subject. The change suggested and accepted, substituted a phraseology which —declared the freedom of conscience to be a *natural* and absolute right.

This account merits some elaboration. Mason had proposed "the fullest Toleration in the Exercise of Religion." The concept of toleration, as in the English Toleration Act previously in force in the colony and in Locke's celebrated *Letter Concerning Toleration*, assumed an official and preferred religion along with the right of the State to grant or to withhold favor from "dissenting" religions. Perhaps one-half the inhabitants of Virginia were dissenters from the Anglican Church in 1776. Some sectarians, especially the Baptists, had been persecuted; all had been regulated, and they demanded not merely toleration but equality. Having earlier championed their cause at home, Madison now attempted to push it to conclusion in Williamsburg. For Mason's words he proposed to substitute a clause stating that "all men are equally entitled to the full and free exercise of [religion] according to the dictates of Conscience." This was not all. It followed from the first principle "therefore that no man or class of men ought, on account of religion to be invested with peculiar emoluments or privileges." The second principle looked to the separation of Church and State and, of course, threatened to dethrone the Anglican clergy. Madison prevailed upon Patrick Henry to introduce the amendment on the floor. It failed mainly because it struck at the established Church. Seeing that he might win one point without permanently jeopardizing the other, Madison took the road to compromise—a road he would travel often during his long career. He revised the amendment, dropping the directive toward separation but maintaining the latitude of the principle of religious freedom. In this form it was adopted. The Virginia Declaration of Rights became a model for the new American states, and indeed for revolutionary peoples everywhere. The right of religious freedom enunciated by James Madison acquired the force of authority it had never had before. In Virginia the victory was the first in a long campaign—Madison always at the fore—climaxed in 1786 with the passage under his leadership of Thomas Jefferson's Statute for Religious Freedom.

Madison returned to Williamsburg for the October, 1776, session of the general assembly, the legislative body established by the new Virginia Constitution. But he was defeated—his first and last defeat at the polls—in the ensuing April election. There was a special reason for his defeat, as he explained many years later.

MANUSCRIPT DIVISION, LIBRARY OF CONGRESS

Madison's handwritten amendment on his copy of the printed broadside of Virginia Declaration of Rights

"Autobiographical Notes," 1832

Previous to the Revolution the election of County Representatives, was as in England, septennial, and it was as there the usage for the candidates to recommend themselves to the voters, not only by personal solicitation, but by the corrupting influence of spirituous liquors, and other treats, having a like tendency. Regarding these as equally inconsistent with the purity of moral and of republican principles; and anxious to promote, by his example, the proper reform, he [Madison] trusted to the new views of the subject which he hoped would prevail with the people; whilst his competitors adhered to the old practice. The consequence was that the election went against him; his abstinence being represented as the effect of pride or parsimony.

Fortunately for Madison, the assembly valued his services and promptly elected him to the Council of State. Headed by the governor, who also received his office from the all-powerful legislature, the eight-man council was the executive power under the new constitution. Since it met daily the year around, except during the "sickly season" in the Tidewater, Madison took up residence with his second cousin, the Reverend James Madison, president of William and Mary, who occupied a charming Georgian house in the college yard. Before long the young councilor wrote to his father.

Williamsburg Jany. 23rd. 1778

Hond Sir

I got safe to this place on Tuesday following the day I left home, and at the earnest invitation of my Kinsman Mr. Madison have taken my lodgings in a Room of the Presidents house, which is a much better accomodation than I could have promised myself. It would be very agreeable to me if I were enabled by such rarities as our part of the County furnishes, particularly dried fruit &tc which Mr. Madison is very fond of to make some

Virginia, HOWE

The College of William and Mary

The Reverend James Madison

little returns for the Culinary favours I receive. Should any opportunity for this purpose offer I hope they will be sent. You will see by the inclosed Acct. of Sales what money you have in Mr. Lee's hands [William Lee, his business agent], and if you chuse to draw for it, you can transmit me your Bills for Sale. You will be informed in due time by Advertisement from the Governor what is proper to be done with the Shoes &tc. collected for the Army. You will be able to obtain so circumstantial an Acct. of public affairs from Majr. Moore that I may spare myself the trouble of anticipating it. Majr. Moore also has for my Mother 4 Oz. of Bark [quinine]. The other Articles wanted by the family are not at present to be had. Whenever I meet with them I shall provide and transmit them. I hope you will not forget my parting request that I might hear frequently from home and whenever my brother returns from the Army I desire he may be informed I shall expect he will make up by letter the loss of intelligence I sustain by my removal out of his way. With the sincerest affection for yourself & all others whom I ought particularly to remember on this occasion,

I am Dear Sir Your Affecte. son

JAMES MADISON JNR.

What Madison himself contributed to the council's work cannot be determined, but it must have given him a liberal education in the hardships and frustrations of wartime government. Problems of taxation and finance, of recruitment, trade, Indian affairs, public works, the navy, supply and logistics, and so on, were constantly on the council's agenda, and they grew more difficult with the passage of time. Patrick Henry was governor, as he had been since 1776. Madison worked hand-in-glove with Henry; only in later years would they become political enemies. Thomas Jefferson succeeded Henry in June, 1779, just after the first of several British invasions by way of Hampton Roads. Government became a task of Sisyphus as the enemy converged on the defenseless state from the Carolinas and the Chesapeake. Madison was not around for the finish in 1780–81. Having been elected a Virginia delegate to the Continental Congress in December, 1779, he had moved on to a larger theater. But the invasion devastated Jefferson, who was left to cope almost single-handedly with the war.

The fifty-year friendship between these two Virginians, Jefferson and Madison, is the most remarkable in the annals of statesmanship. Madison first knew Jefferson as a member of the assembly, where he was equally ardent in his support of the war and in his advocacy of liberal reforms for Virginia. Not until they labored together as governor and councilor, however, did they become political intimates. In some respects they were much alike. They came from the same part of the country—Monticello was only thirty miles from Madison's home—belonged to the same class, responded to the same intellectual currents, and shared the same republican principles. Yet they were men of fundamentally different personal styles and temperaments, and from this, rather than from their similarities, stemmed the creative genius of their partnership. Jefferson, the older man by eight years, was tall, angular, and robust; Madison, slight of build—five feet six inches tall—frail, with soft features and a bleached skin that resembled parchment. Jefferson was the bolder thinker, easily caught up in philosophical speculation, looking less to the *is* than to the *ought to be*. Madison's was the tougher, more probing, persistent, and sagacious mind: he helped keep his friend's feet on the ground: Jefferson had the gift of brilliant rhetoric, which Madison lacked, though it was John Marshall who said that if eloquence included the unadorned power of reasoned persuasion, Madison was "the most eloquent man I ever heard." Both men were reticent in social intercourse; some observers thought them cold, stiff, and aloof. Jefferson, nevertheless, radiated political magnetism, and Madison, without this aura, shone in caucuses and committees. He genuinely liked politics and thought it a worthy vocation. Jefferson soon came to consider politics a curse and would have gladly thrown it off for the pleasures of the arts and sciences if he could have.

In 1780, while Jefferson struggled with the discouraging problems of the Virginia magistracy, Madison entered the continental stage where the problems were different but no less intractable. Each in his own station would be the eyes and ears and helping hand to the other, and this great collaboration would endure, with scarcely a ripple between them, as long as they lived.

Royal arms of colonial Virginia

COLONIAL WILLIAMSBURG

44

Chapter 2

Congressman at War

Madison was delighted to exchange Williamsburg for Philadelphia. The city on the Delaware was not only the political but also the cultural and intellectual capital of the new nation. The Quaker imprint remained strong. Philadelphia was enlightened, wealthy, moral, and staid. The neatly patterned and treelined streets with their rows of sedate, red brick and white-trimmed houses expressed the city's sober charm. Benjamin Franklin once said that if there existed an atheist in the universe he would be converted on seeing Philadelphia—everything was so well arranged. In this aspect, certainly, the city appealed to the earnest young Virginian. Arriving in March after unusually heavy snows had melted in Virginia, he took up residence in Mrs. House's boardinghouse at Fifth and Market streets, only a block from the State House where Congress met. Madison served in Congress continuously, almost never away from his seat, for three and a half years. And Philadelphia, not Montpelier, not Virginia, would be the principal seat of his life for the next twenty years.

The early months of 1780 were the gloomiest of the war. No one could remember a harsher winter. For the soldiers of the Continental Army encamped at Morristown, New Jersey, conditions were worse than at Valley Forge the year before; supplies ran low, rations were cut, and money, so far as the soldiers saw any, was as worthless as oak leaves. Mutiny broke out in May and was quickly crushed. Between the opposing armies in the North, things were at a stalemate. Unable to destroy General Washington's army, the British commander in chief, Sir Henry Clinton, pursued a more promising strategy: "to unravel the thread of rebellion from the southward." Georgia had already fallen to the British, and Charleston was under siege when Madison entered Congress. It would fall on May 12, the darkest day of the war. Weak, broke, and bitterly divided, Congress was unable to rally the country. Although twelve states had at last, after two years, ratified the Articles of Confederation, Maryland still balked on the ground that the western lands claimed by several of the states should become the property of the Union. Much of the discord in Congress flowed from the French alliance. The acrimonious dispute between Silas Deane and Arthur Lee, commissioners with Franklin in negotiating the alliance, had been dumped into the lap of Congress in 1778, and the political forces that formed around these rivals led to pro-French and anti-French factions which kept Congress in turmoil until peace came. France had drawn her ally Spain into the war in 1779, and she would soon deliver on the promise of an army to fight alongside the Americans. Without France the war could not be won; her power, accordingly, was bound to be felt for good or ill in the peace. Peace was a dim prospect, yet Congress had, some months before Madison's arrival, hammered out preliminary terms and sent John Adams to Europe to negotiate whenever the time grew ripe.

Money was the fundamental problem facing Congress. From the beginning the war had been floated on a sea of paper money. Depreciation set in early and it ran rampant in 1780. As the Continental presses printed more and more money, the more and more worthless it became. The state currencies were caught in the same dizzy spiral. Government could not pay its bills, credit was undermined, and disaffection spread among soldiers and civilians alike. Alert to the problem, Madison, while snowbound at Montpelier, had made a study of public finance and recorded his views in a little essay called "Money." Attacking the quantity theory of money as

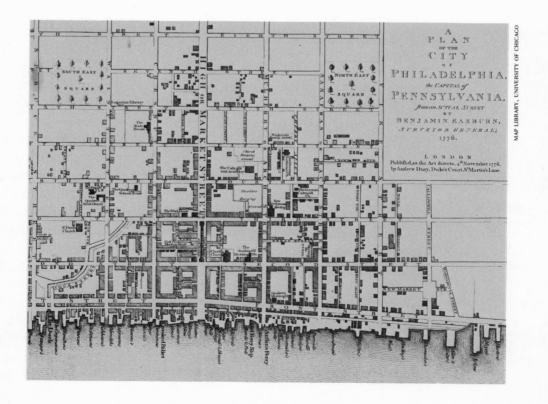

expounded by David Hume, he argued that the value of money depended not on its quantity but on public confidence in the issuing authority, in this case the government. To create that confidence he recommended a loan of specie from abroad, increased taxes, rigorous economy, and the kind of leadership that would raise the public's faith in the ability of the government to meet its obligations.

Congress was ready to act, though not exactly along the lines of Madison's thought. On the day he arrived in Philadelphia it adopted a bold "new plan of finance." Congress printed no more money; the dollar was devalued to two and a half cents; as the states retired the old currency through tax collections, they would issue new paper which Congress pledged to redeem in coin after five years. Another part of the plan substituted supplies in kind from the states for requisitions of money. It was a hazardous experiment. Congress surrendered the one real power it had over its own affairs—the power of issuing money—and threw the responsibility of supporting the continent, including the Continental Army, upon the states. Madison was apprehensive for the plan's success. He expressed his views in two letters to Governor Jefferson.

A plan of the city of Philadelphia published in 1776 (left), and James Madison's credentials as a delegate to the Continental Congress which was meeting there in 1780

Philadelphia March 27th. 1780

Among the various conjunctures of alarm and distress which have arisen in the course of the revolution, it is with pain I affirm to you Sir, that no one can be singled out more truly critical than the present. Our army threatened with an immediate alternative of disbanding or living on free quarter; the public treasury empty; public credit exhausted, nay the private credit of purchasing Agents employed, I am told, as far as it will bear, Congress complaining of the extortion of the people; the people of the improvidence of Congress, and the army of both; our affairs requiring the most mature & systematic measures, and the urgency of occasions admitting only of temporizing expedients, and those expedients generating new difficulties. Congress from a defect of adequate Statesmen more likely to fall into wrong measures and of less weight to enforce right ones, recommending plans to the several states for execution and the states separately rejudging the expediency of such plans, whereby the same distrust of concurrent exertions that has damped the ardor of patriotic individuals, must produce the same effect among the States themselves. An old system of finance discarded as incompetent to our necessities, an untried & precarious one substituted, and a total stagnation in prospect between the end of the former & the operation of the latter: These are the outlines of the true picture of our public situation. I leave it to your own imagination to fill them up. Believe me Sir as things now stand, if the States do not vigorously proceed in collecting the old money and establishing funds for the credit of the new, that we are undone; and let them be ever so expeditious in doing this still the intermediate distress to our army and hindrance to public affairs are a subject of melancholy reflection. Gen Washington writes that a failure of bread has already commenced in the army, and that for any thing he sees, it must unavoidably increase. Meat they have only for a short season and as the whole dependance is on provisions now to be procured, without a shilling for the purpose and without credit for a shilling. I look forward with the most pungent apprehensions.

Philada. May 6th. 1780

I am sorry I can give you no other account of our public situation than that it continues equally perplexed & alarming as when I lately gave you a sketch of it. Our army has as yet been kept from starving, and public measures from a total stagnation, by draughts on the States for the unpaid requisitions. The great amount of these you may judge of, from the share that has fallen to Virginia. The discharge of debts due from the purchasing departments has absorbed a great proportion of them, and very large demand still remain.... A punctual compliance on the part of the States with the specific supplies will indeed render much less money necessary than would otherwise be wanted, but experience by no means affords satisfactory encouragement that due and unanimous exertions will be made for that purpose not to mention that our distress is so pressing that it is uncertain whether any exertions of that kind can give relief in time. It occurs besides, that as the ability of the people to comply with the pecuniary requisitions is derived from the sale of their commodities, a requisition of the latter must make the former proportionally more difficult and defective: Congress have the satisfaction however to be informed that the legislature of Connecticut have taken the most vigorous steps for supplying their quota both of money & commodities; and that a body of their principal merchants have

For the NATIONAL GAZETTE.

MONEY.

[OBSERVATIONS *written posterior to the circular* ADDRESS *of* CONGRESS *in Sept.* 1779, *and prior to their Act of March,* 1780.]

IT has been taken for an axiom in all our reasonings on the subject of finance, that supposing the quantity and demand of things vendible in a country to remain the same, their price will vary according to the variation in the quantity of the circulating medium; in other words, that the value of money will be regulated by its quantity. I shall submit to the judgment of the public some considerations which determine mine to reject the proposition as founded in error. Should they be deemed not absolutely conclusive, they seem at least to shew that it is liable to too many exceptions and restrictions to be taken for granted as a fundamental truth.

If the circulating medium be of universal value as specie, a local increase or decrease of its quantity, will not, whilst a communication subsists with other countries, produce a correspondent rise or fall in its value. The reason is obvious. When a redundancy of universal money prevails in any one country, the holders of it know their interest too well to waste it in extravagant prices, when it would be worth so much more to them elsewhere. When a deficiency happens, those who hold commodities, rather than part with them at an undervalue in one country, would carry them to another. The variation of prices, in these cases, cannot therefore exceed the expence and insurance of transportation.

Suppose a country totally unconnected with Europe, or with any other country, to possess specie in the same proportion to circulating property that Europe does; prices there would correspond with those in Europe. Suppose that so much specie were thrown into circulation as to make the quantity exceed the proportion of Europe tenfold, without any change in commodities, or in the demand for them: as soon as such an augmentation had produced its effect, prices would rise tenfold; or which is the same thing, money would be depreciated tenfold. In this state of things, suppose again, that a free and ready communication were opened between this country and Europe, and that the inhabitants of the former, were made sensible of the value of their money in the latter; would not its value among themselves immediately cease to be regulated by its quantity, and assimilate itself to the foreign value?

Madison's essay "Money," written in 1780, was published in the National Gazette *in 1791.*

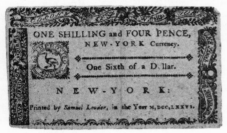

Examples of the paper money issued by the state of New York during the Revolutionary War

associated for supporting the credit of the new paper, for which purpose they have in a public address pledged their faith to the Assembly to sell their merchandise on the same terms for it as if they were to be paid in specie. A Similar vigor throughout the Union may perhaps produce effects as far exceeding our present hopes as they have heretofore fallen short of our wishes.

It is to be observed that the situation of Congress has undergone a total change from what it originally was. Whilst they exercised the indefinite power of emitting money on the credit of their constituents they had the whole wealth & resources of the continent within their command, and could go on with their affairs independently and as they pleased. Since the resolution passed for shutting the press, this power has been entirely given up and they are now as dependent on the States as the King of England is on the parliament. They can neither enlist pay nor feed a single soldier, nor execute any other pu[r]pose but as the means are first put into their hands. Unless the legislatures are sufficiently attentive to this change of circumstances and act in conformity to it, every thing must necessarily go wrong or rather must come to a total stop. All that Congress can do in future will be to administer public affairs with prudence vigor and oeconomy. In order to do which they have sent a Committee to Head Quarters with ample powers in concert with the Commander in chief and the Heads of the departments to reform the various abuses which prevail and to make such arrangements, as will best guard against a relapse into them....

With great regard, I am Dr Sir Yr Obt Servt

JAMES MADISON JNR.

Madison's fears proved justified. The new currency was cheapened before it could be launched in the states, and the system of specific supplies encountered massive logistical problems. In October, Madison penned a grim analysis for his good friend in Virginia, Joseph Jones, and urged harsh measures by the state's legislature, of which Jones was a member. If the people would not voluntarily support the cause of liberty and union, Madison would force them to it.

Philada. Octr. [24,] 1780

We continue to receive periodical alarms from the Commissary's & Quarter Master's departments. The season

Madison's good friend, Joseph Jones

The southeast corner of Third and Market streets in Philadelphia, two blocks from Madison's lodgings

is now arrived when provision ought to be made for a season that will not admit of transportation, and when the monthly supplies must be subject to infinite disappointments even if the States were to do their duty. But instead of Magazines being laid in our army is living from hand to mouth, with a prospect of being soon in a condition still worse. How a total dissolution of it can be prevented in the course of the winter is for any resources now in prospect utterly inexplicable, unless the States unanimously make a vigorous & speedy effort to form Magazines for the purpose. But unless the States take other methods to procure their specific supplies than have prevailed in most of them, their utmost efforts to comply with the requisitions of Congress can be only a temporary relief....

As you are at present a *legislator* I will take the liberty of hinting to you an idea that has occurred on this subject. I take it for granted that taxation alone is inadequate to our situation. You know as well as I do how far we ought to rely on loans to supply the defect of it. Specific taxes as far as they go are a valuable fund but from local and other difficulties will never be universally and sufficiently adopted. Purchase with State money or certificates will be substituted. In order to prevent this evil and to insure the supplies therefore I would propose, that they be diffused and proportioned among the people as accurately as circumstances will admit, that they be *impress*[ed] with vigor and impartiality, and paid for in certificates not transferrible & be redeemable at some period subsequent to the war at specie value and bearing an intermediate interest. The advantage of such a scheme is this, that it would anticipate during the war the future revenues of peace, as our Enemies and all other modern nations do. It would be compelling the people to lend the public their commodities, as people elsewhere lend their money to purchase commodities. It would be a permanent resourse by which the war might be supported as long as the earth should yield its increase. This plan differs from specific taxes only in this that as an equivalent is given for what is received much less nicely would be requisite in apportioning the supplies among the people, and they might be taken in places where they are most wanted. It differs from the plan of paying for supplies in state emissions or common certificates in this, that the latter produce all the evils of a redundant medium, whereas the former not being transferrible can not have that effect, and moreover do not require the same degree of taxes during the war.

The financial crisis continued for months, even years, but disaster was eventually averted by the vigorous efforts of Robert Morris, the Philadelphia merchant-capitalist who was appointed Superintendent of Finance by Congress in 1781. Charges of "dictator" and "profiteer" were thrown at Morris, but Madison supported him. Meanwhile, in all matters, Madison won a place of leadership in Congress. The eminence which distinguished that body in its birth was no longer present, and Madison, though at age twenty-nine the youngest member, put his head for legislative business and his nationalist ardor to good use. Amidst the turbulence of congressional politics, which sickened and disgusted so many, Madison seemed to flourish. In the fall of 1780 the Lee-Deane affair surfaced again, this time with malicious intent to destroy the chief American architect of the French alliance in Paris, Benjamin Franklin. Madison was named chairman of a committee to investigate Lee's charges. The committee rebuffed Lee, and in the ensuing turmoil Madison did what he could to sustain Franklin and the alliance. He thus allied himself with the pro-French faction, which included Morris and other leading Middle State men as well as most Virginians, against the anti-Gallicans led by the Massachusetts brace of Adamses, John and Samuel, the Virginia Lees, and prominent South Carolinians. The commitment colored Madison's position on all the great issues before Congress during the next three years.

One of these issues concerned western lands. Of the seven states boasting western lands, Virginia's claim above the Ohio River and to the Mississippi was by far the largest. The Articles of Confederation left these virgin lands with the states. The so-called "landless states" were unhappy with this arrangement and one of them, Maryland, held out against ratification. They argued that the lands should be ceded to Congress for the "common benefit." Behind this mask of high-mindedness was the speculative greed of private land companies, especially powerful in Maryland and Pennsylvania, which sought to validate old titles allegedly obtained from the Crown or from Indian tribes. In the final analysis, of course, the future of the Transappalachian West hung on the outcome of the war. To win this stake the Confederation must be completed, Congress strengthened, and the jealousies of the states sunk in the common cause. Among Virginians in 1780 these political realities overcame the niceties of the state's legal title; on the strength of that claim, however, Virginia set conditions to the western cession that would annihilate the pretensions of the speculators. In September, Congress called upon Virginia to cede without conditions.

Joseph Jones, then a Virginia delegate to Congress, countered with a motion seconded by Madison stipulating the conditions. The Ohio lands would be carved into separate and independent states; Virginia would be secured in her remaining territory, which included Kentucky; she would be reimbursed for the costs of defending her "back lands"; and all the company claims would be denied. Later, when Jones was called home, Madison became the Virginia spokesman on this question. Writing in September to Edmund Pendleton, a prominent figure in Virginia politics, Madison advocated, with unwarranted optimism, Virginia's cession of its western land claims.

Phila. Sepr. 12th. 1780

Congress have also at length entered seriously on a plan for finally ratifying the confederation. Convinced of the necessity of such a measure, to repress the hopes with which the probable issue of the campaign will inspire our Enemy, as well as to give greater authority & vigor to our public councils, they have recommended in the most pressing terms to the States claiming unappropriated back lands, to cede a liberal portion of them to the general benefit. As these exclusive claims formed the only obstacle with Maryland there is no doubt that a compliance with this recommendation will bring her into the confederation. How far the States holding the back lands may be disposed to give them up cannot be so easily determined. From the sentiments of the most intelligent persons which have come to my knowledge, I own I am pretty sanguine they will see the necessity of closing the union in too strong a light to oppose the only expedient that can accomplish it.

A month later Madison reported to Jones the outcome of their motion. Congress adopted the Virginia principle of erecting new republican states in the West and agreed to assume the defense expenses incurred by the ceding states; but Congress refused to guarantee their remaining territory or to slam the door on the speculators.

Philada. Oct. 17th. 1780

Congress have at length been brought to a final consideration of the clause relating to Indian purchases. It was debated very fully and particularly, and was in the result lost by a division of the house. Under the first impression of the chagrin I had determined to propose to my colleagues to state the whole matter to the [Virginia General] Assembly with all the circumstances and reasonings of the opponents to the measure. But on cooler

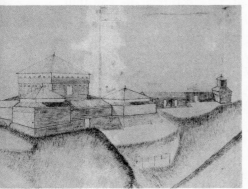

*Fort Franklin, below Lake Erie, was
typical of the frontier outposts
in the western part of America.*

reflection I think it best to leave the fact in your hands
to be made use of as your prudence may suggest. I am
the rather led to decline the first determination because
I am pretty confident that whatever the views of particular members might be it was neither the wish nor
intention of many who voted with them to favor the
purchasing companies. Some thought such an assurance
from Congress unnecessary because their receiving the
lands from the States as vacant & unappropriated excluded all individual claims, and because they had given
a general assurance that the cession should be applied
to the common benefit. Others supposed that such an
assurance might imply that without it Congress would
have a right to dispose of the lands in any manner they
pleased, and that it might give umbrage to the states
claiming an exclusive jurisdiction over them. All that now
remains for the Ceding States to do is to annex to their
cessions the express condition that no private claims be
complied with by Congress. Perhaps it would not be
going too far, by Virginia who is so deeply concerned to
make it a condition of her grant that no such claims be
admitted even within the grants of others, because when
they are given up to Congress she is interested in them
as much as others, and it might so happen, that the benefit of all other grants except her own might be transferred
from the public, to a few land mongers. I can not help
adding however that I hope this incident in Congress will
not discourage any measures of the Assembly which
would otherwise have been taken for ratifying the Confederation. Under the cautions I have suggested, they
may still be taken with perfect security.

At the beginning of the new year, the Virginia assembly
voted to cede the unappropriated Ohio lands with the original conditions.
It was enough to complete the Confederation: Maryland ratified in March,
1781. But rather than acknowledge the Virginia claim Congress spurned
her gift. Madison vented his irritation to Jefferson.

Philada: Jany. 15th. 1782
The machinations which have long been practised by
interested individuals agst. this claim are well known to
you. The late proceedings within the walls of Congress
in consequence of the territorial cessions produced by
their recommendations to the States claiming the West-

ern Country were many weeks ago transmitted for the Legislature by a Capt. Irish. By the same conveyance I wrote to you on the subject. We have the mortification to find by our latest letters from Richmond that this Gentleman had not at the date of them appeared there. As it is uncertain whether that information may not have totally miscarried it will be proper to repeat to you that the States besides Virga. from which the cessions came were Connecticut & N York. The cession of the former consisted of all her claim west of N. York as far as the Missippi. That of the latter of all her claims beyond a certain western limit drawn on the occasion. The cession of Con[necticu]t extended to the soil only expressly reserving the jurisdiction. That of N.Y. made no reservation. These cessions with that of Virga. & sundry memorials from the Ind[ian]a & other land Companies were referred to a Committee composed of a Member from N.H. R.I. N.J. Pa. & Maryld. The ingredients of this composition prepared us for the complexion of their proceedings. ... The upshot of the whole was a report to Congress rejecting the Cessions of Virga. & Cont. and accepting that of N.Y.; disallowing also, the claims of the Companies N.W. of the Ohio but justifying that of the Inda. Compy. The report seems to distrust the doctrine hitherto maintained, of territorial rights being incident to the U.S. Collectively which are not comprehended within any individual State; substituting the expedient of recognizing the title of N.Y. stretching it over the whole country claimed by the other ceding States, & then accepting a transfer of it to the U.S. In this state the business now rests, the report having never been taken into consideration, nor do we wish it should, till it shall have undergone the consideration of Virga.

In whatever light the policy of this proceeding may be viewed it affords an additional proof of the industry & perseverance with which the territorial rights of Virga. are persecuted, & of the necessity of fortifying them with every precaution which their importance demands. As a very obvious & necessary one we long since recommended to the State an accurate & full collection of the documents which relate to the subject.... we have no hope at present of being enabled from any other sources than the voluntary aids of individuals to contradict even verbally the misrepresentations & calumnies which are

Thomas Paine opposed Virginia's western land claims in this 1780 pamphlet entitled Public Good.

daily levelled agst. the claims of Va. & which can not fail to prepossess the public with errors injurious at present to her reputation & which may affect a future decision on her rights. Col. Masons industry & kindness have supplied us with some valuable papers & remarks. Mr. Jones has also recd. from Mr. Pendleton some judicious remarks on the subject. We are still notwithstandg. far from possessing a complete view of it. Will you permit me to ask of you such information as your researches have yielded, with the observations which you have made in the course of them. I would not obtrude such a request on you if the subject were not of public importance & if it could have been addressed with equal prospect of advantage elsewhere. Indeed if you cd. prevail on yourself to spare as much time as would Survey the whole subject, beginning with the original charter, pursuing it thro' the subsequent charters & other public acts of the crown thro' the Govs. of Virga., & referring to all the transactions with the Indians which have been drawn into the question, the public utility I am persuaded wd. sufficiently reward you for the labor.

Jefferson declined this task. Unable to muster either the troops or the finances needed to fight off the British invasion of Virginia, he had finally resigned as governor and, wanting nothing more to do with public life, had retired to Monticello. As the western land affair dragged on in Congress, it became associated with other sensitive issues, among them that of Vermont. The Vermonters demanded statehood against the competing claims made on their territory by Massachusetts, New Hampshire, and New York. New England congressmen purposely delayed resolution of the western land problem in hopes of logrolling Maryland and Pennsylvania votes on Vermont. Virginia opposed independence for Vermont because it would set a precedent for dismembering large states and, of course, add to northeastern political power in the Union. For his own edification Madison wrote an analysis of the intricate political issue.

May 1st. 1782.

The two great objects which predominate in the policies of Congress at this juncture are I. Vermont. II. Western territory.

I The independence of Vermont and its admission into the Confederacy are patronised by the Eastern States (N. Hampshire excepted) 1. from ancient prejudice agst. N York: 2. the interest which Citizens of those

*The first American map of the
United States was made by Abel
Buell in 1784. He extended the
southern states to the Mississippi.*

States have in lands granted by Vermont. 3. but principally from the accession of weight they will derive from it in Congress. N. Hampshire having gained its main object by the exclusion of its territory East of Connecticut River from the claims of Vermont, is already indifferent to its independence, and will probably soon combine with other Eastern States in its favor.

The same patronage is yielded to the pretensions of Vermont by Pennsylvania & Maryland with the sole view of reinforcing the opposition to claims of Western territory particularly those of Virginia and by N. Jersey & Delaware with the additional view of strengthening the interest of the little States. Both of these considerations operate also on Rhode Island in addition to those above mentioned.

The independence of Vermont and its admission into the Union are opposed by N. York for reasons obvious & well known.

The like opposition is made by Virginia N. Carolina

S. Carolina, and Georgia. The grounds of this opposition are. 1. an habitual jealosy of a predominance of Eastern Interests. 2. the opposition expected from Vermont to Western claims. 3. the inexpediency of admitting so unimportant a State, to an equal vote in deciding on peace & all the other grand interests of the Union now depending. 4. the influence of the example on a premature dismemberment of other States. These considerations influence the four States last mentioned in different degrees. The 2. & 3. to say nothing of the 4. ought to be decisive with Virginia.

II The territorial claims, particularly those of Virginia are opposed by Rhode Island, N. Jersey, Pennsylvania Delaware & Maryland. Rhode Island is influenced in her opposition by 1. a lucrative desire of sharing in the vacant territory as a fund of revenue. 2. by the envy & jealousy naturally excited by superior resources & importance. N.J. Penna: Delaware, Maryland, are influenced partly by the same considerations; but principally by the intrigues of their Citizens who are interested in the claims of land Companies. The decisive influence of this last consideration is manifest from the peculiar, and persivering opposition made agst. Virginia within whose limits those claims lye.

The Western claims, or rather a final settlement of them, are also thwarted by Massachusetts and Connecticut. This object with them is chiefly subservient to that of Vermont, as the latter is with Pennsylvania & Maryland to the former. The general policy and interests of these two States are opposed to the admission of Vermont into the Union, and if the case of the Western territory were once removed, they would instantly divide from the Eastern States in the case of Vermont. Of this Massachusetts & Connecticut are not insensible, and therefore find their advantage in keeping the territorial Controversy pending. Connecticut may likewise conceive some analogy between her claim to the Western Country & that of Virginia, and that the acceptance of the cession of the latter, would influence her sentiments in the controversy between the former & Pennsylvania.

The Western claims are espoused by Virga. N & S. Carolinas, Georgia & N. York, all of these States being interested therein S. Carolina is the least so. The claim of N. York is very extensive, but her title very flimsy. She

Vermont did not become a state until 1791, almost ten years after Madison wrote his analysis.

urges it more with the hope of obtaining some advantage, or credit, by its cession, than of ever maintaining it. If this Cession should be accepted, and the affair of Vermont terminated, as these are the only ties which unite her with the Southern States, she will immediately connect her policy with that of the Eastern States; as far at least, as the remains of former prejudices will permit.

The vexing question of western lands would be settled at last in 1784, more or less on Virginia's terms. The Virginia empire became the foundation of American empire. Coveting the West, the Virginians also coveted the navigation of the Mississippi, without which the Transappalachian lands would be next to worthless. Spain ruled west of the Mississippi and sought the return of the Floridas from Britain. Aiming at this conquest, Spain had no intention of spoiling it by inviting the imperious Americans to navigate the Mississippi through New Orleans to the Gulf. France sided with Spain. It was a clear case of conflicting ambitions between the new nation and its allies. The United States needed Spanish help in the war, but must the Mississippi be sacrificed to obtain it? In August, 1779, when Congress drew up preliminary peace terms, the answer had been no. The United States demanded free navigation of the Mississippi, and John Jay, the American Minister to Spain, was so instructed. Jay quickly ran into trouble at Madrid. Spain would not throw herself into the war unless the Americans receded on the Mississippi. In August, 1780, Jay wrote to Congress asking for clarification of his instructions. Madison came into the affair at this point. He steered through Congress a report that had been written by his colleague Jones reaffirming the American ultimatum. Then, in October, Madison drafted new instructions to Jay. The first of many important diplomatic papers from his pen, it was also a landmark statement of American policy on the Mississippi. He took up the matter of navigation and commerce after making a defense of the American territorial claim to the 31st parallel, the northern boundary of the Floridas.

[October 17, 1780]

The next object of the instructions is the free navigation of the Mississippi for the citizens of the United States in common with the subjects of his C M [Catholic Majesty].

On this subject the same inference may be made from Art: 7 of the Treaty of Paris [1763] which stipulates this right in the amplest manner to the King of G. Britain, and the devolution of it to the United States as was applied to the territorial claims of the latter. Nor can Congress hesitate to believe that even if no such right could be inferred from that treaty that the generosity of his C. M.

would suffer the inhabitants of these States to be put into a worse condition in this respect by their alliance with him in the character of a sovereign people, than they were in when subjects of a power who was always ready to turn their force against the Majesty; especially as one of the great objects of the proposed alliance is to give greater effect to the common exertions for disarming that power of the faculty of disturbing others.

Besides, as the United States have an indisputable right to the possession of the East bank of the Mississippi for a very great distance, and the navigation of that river will essentially tend to the prosperity and advantage of the Citizens of the United States that may reside on the Mississippi or the waters running into it, it is conceived that the circumstance of Spain's being in possession of the banks on both sides near its mouth, cannot be deemed a natural or equitable bar to the free use of the river. Such a principle would authorize a nation disposed to take advantage of circumstances to contravene the clear indications of nature and providence, and the general good of mankind.

The Usage of nations accordingly seems in such cases to have given to those holding the mouth or lower parts of a river no right against those above them, except the right of imposing a moderate toll, and that on the equitable supposition that such toll is due for the expence and trouble the former may have been put to.

"An *innocent passage* (says Vattel) [a Swiss jurist] is due to all nations with whom a State is at peace; and this duty comprehends troops equally with individuals." If a right to a passage by land through other countries may be claimed for troops which are employed in the destruction of Mankind; how much more may a passage by water be claimed for commerce which is beneficial to all nations.

Here again it ought not to be concealed that the inconveniences which must be felt by the inhabitants on the waters running westwardly under an exclusion from the free use of the Mississippi would be a constant and increasing source of disquietude on their part, of more rigorous precautions on the part of Spain, and of an irritation on both parts, which it is equally the interest and duty of both to guard against.

But notwithstanding the equitable claim of the United

Early view on the upper Mississippi

States to the *free* navigation of the Mississippi and its great importance to them, Congress have so strong a disposition to conform to the desires of his C. M that they have agreed that such equitable regulations may be entered into as may be a Requisite security against contraband; provided the point of right be not relinquished and *a free port or ports below the 31st: degree of N. L. and accessible to Merchant ships be stipulated to them.*

The reason why a port or ports as thus described was required must be obvious. Without such a stipulation the free use of the Mississippi would in fact amount to no more that a free intercourse with New Orleans and the other ports of Louisiana. From the rapid current of this river it is well known that it must be navigated by vessels of a peculiar construction and which will be unfit to go to sea. Unless therefore some place be assigned to the U.S. where the produce carried down the river and the merchandis [a]rriving from abroad may be reposited till they can be respectively taken away by the proper vessels there can be no such thing as a foreign trade.

There is a remaining consideration respecting the navigation of the Mississippi, which deeply concerns the maritime powers in general but more particularly their most Christian and Catholic Majesties. The Country watered by the Ohio with its large branches having their sources near the lakes on one side, and those running N. Westward and falling into it on the other sides will appear from a single glance on a map to be of vast extent. The circumstance of its being so finely watered, added to the singular fertility of its soil and other advantages presented by a new country, will occasion a rapidity of population not easy to be conceived. The spirit of emigration has already shewn itself in a very strong degree, notwithstanding the many impediments which discourage it. The principal of these impediments is the war with Britain which can not spare a force sufficient to protect the emigrants against the incursions of the Savages. In a very few years after peace shall take place this Country will certainly be overspread with inhabitants. In like manner as in all other new settlements, agriculture, not manufactures will be their employment. They will raise wheat corn Beef Pork tobacco hemp flax and in the southern parts perhaps, rice and indigo in great quantities. On the other hand their consumption of foreign man-

First page of the new instructions Madison drafted for Jay in Madrid on navigation of the Mississippi

ufactures will be in proportion, if they can be exchanged for the produce of their soil. There are but two channels through which such commerce can be carried on—the first is down the river Mississippi—the other is up the rivers having their sources near the lakes, thence by short portages to the lakes or the rivers falling into them, and thence through the lakes and down the St. Lawrence. The first of these channels is manifestly the most natural and by far the most advantageous. Should it however be obstructed, the second will be found far from an impracticable. If no obstructions should be thrown in its course down the Mississippi, the exports from this immense tract of Country will not only supply an abundance of all necessaries for the W. Indies Islands, but serve for a valuable basis of general trade, of which the rising spirit of commerce in France & Spain will no doubt particularly avail itself. The imports will be proportionally extensive and from the climate as well as other causes will consist in a great degree of the manufactures of the same countries. On the other hand should obstructions in the Mississippi force this trade into a contrary direction through Canada, France and Spain and the other maritime powers will not only lose the immediate benefit of it to themselves, but they will also suffer by the advantage it will give to G. Britain. So fair a prospect would not escape the commercial sagacity of this nation. She would embrace it with avidity; she would cherish it with the most studious care; and should she succeed in fixing it in that channel, the loss of her exclusive possession of the trade of the United States might prove a much less decisive blow to her maritime preeminence and tyranny than has been calculated.

Theodorick Bland

These were brave words. But in the fall of 1780, when Cornwallis was marching through the Carolinas and Virginia lay defenseless before the enemy, the United States could not place the future interests of the West ahead of survival. Theodorick Bland, the only other Virginian then in Congress, broke with Madison on the Mississippi question. The two men were frequently at odds; they belonged to different factions. In this case Bland was responding to fears that peace would be negotiated by the Russian-led League of Armed Neutrality on the basis of *uti possidetis*, that is, a peace in which the belligerents would retain the territories they held at the time the agreement was signed. Accordingly, Georgia and South

Carolina would remain British colonies. Bland urged the Virginia legislature to drop the Mississippi demand in exchange for military assistance from Spain, which was urgently needed. Of this discouraging development Madison wrote to Jones.

Philada. Novr. 25th. 1780

I informed you some time ago that the instructions to Mr. Jay had passed Congress in a form which was entirely to my mind. I since informed you that a Committee was preparing a letter to him explanatory of the principles & objects of the instructions. This letter also passed in a form equally satisfactory. I did not suppose that any thing further would be done on the subject, at least till further intelligence should arrive from Mr. Jay. It now appears that I was mistaken. The Delegates from Georgia & South Carolina, apprehensive that a *Uti possidetis* may be obtruded on the belligerent powers by the armed neutrality in Europe and hoping that the accession of Spain to the Alliance will give greater concert & success to the military operations that may be pursued for the recovery of these States, and likewise add weight to the means that may be used for obviating a *Uti possidetis*, have moved for a reconsideration of the Instructions in order to empower Mr. Jay in case of necessity to yield to the claims of Spain on condition of her guarantieng our independence and affording us a handsome subsidy. The expediency of such a motion is further urged from the dangerous negociations now on foot by British Emissaries for detaching Spain from the war. Wednesday last was assigned for the consideration of this motion and it has continued the order of the day ever since without being taken up. What the fate of it will be I do not predict; but whatever its own fate may [be] it must do mischief in its operation. It will not probably be concealed that such a motion has been made & supported, and the weight which our demands would derive from unanimity & decision must be lost. I flatter myself however that Congress will see the impropriety of sacrificing the acknowledged limits and claims of any State without the express concurrence of such State. Obsticles enough will be thrown in the way of peace, if [it] is to be bid for at the expence of particular members of the Union. The Eastern States must on the first suggestion take the alarm for their fisheries. If they will not support other States in their rights, they cannot expect to be supported themselves when theirs come into question.

In this important business, which so deeply affects the claims & interests of Virginia & which I know she has so much at heart, I have not the satisfaction to harmonise in Sentiment with my Colleague [Bland]. He has embraced an opinion that we have no just claim to the subject in controversy between us & Spain, and that it is the interest of Virginia not to adhere to it. Under this impression he drew up a letter to the Executive to be communicated to the Legislature, stating in general the difficulty Congress might be under, & calling their attention ,to a revision of their instructions to their Delegates on the subject. I was obliged to object to such a step, and in order to prevent it observed that the instructions were given by the Legislation of Virga. on mature consideration of the case, & on a supposition that Spain would make the demands she has done . . . that Mr. Jay's last despatches encouraged us to expect that Spain would not be inflexible if we wer[e] so, that [we] might every day expect to have more satisfactory information from him. that finally if it should be thought expedient to listen to the pretensions of Spain, it would be best before we took any decisive step in the matter to take the Counsel of those who best know the interests & have the greatest influence on the opinions of our Constituents, that as you were both a member of Congress & of the Legislature & were not with the latter, you would be an unexceptionable medium for effecting this, and that I would write to you for the purpose, by the first safe conveyance.

These objections had not the weight with my Colleague which they had with me. He adhered to his first determination & has I believe sent the letter above mentioned by Mr. Walker who will I suppose soon forward it to the Governour. You will readily conceive the embarrassments this affair must have cost me. All I have to ask of you is that if my refusing to concur with my Colleague in recommending to the legislature a revision of their instructions should be misconstrued by any, you will be so good as to place it in its true light, and if you agree with me as to the danger of giving express power to concede, or the inexpediency of conceding at all, that you will consult with gentlemen of the above description and acquaint me with the result.

John Jay at the time of his mission to Spain, in a portrait by Caleb Boyle

For several weeks Madison held out against any change of policy. Early in the new year, however, amidst the devastation left by the traitor Arnold's invasion of the state, the Virginia assembly reversed itself, and Madison grudgingly shelved the Mississippi demand for the duration of the war. He did not yield the principle or the interest behind that demand. The right of navigation of the Mississippi was essential to the Union, in his opinion, and he would pursue that right until it was finally wrested from Spain in 1795. Cornwallis followed Arnold into Virginia. The state was terrorized from the Chesapeake to the Blue Ridge. Outraged by the enemy's "atrocities," Madison formed a consuming hatred of Great Britain. His report to Philip Mazzei, an Italian who had lived in Virginia, suggests the inflamed state of his feelings.

Philada. July 7th. 1781

No description can give you an adequate idea of the barbarity with which the Enemy have conducted the war in the Southern States. Every outrage which humanity could suffer has been committed by them. Desolation rather than conquest seems to have been their object. They have acted more like desperate bands of Robbers or Buccaneers than like a nation making war for dominion. Negroes, Horses, Tobacco &c not the standards and arms of their antagonists are the trophies which display their success. Rapes, murders & the whole catalogue of individual cruelties, not protection & the distribution of justice are the acts which characterize the sp[h]ere of their usurped Jurisdiction. The advantage we derive from such proceedings would, if they were purchased in other terms than the distresses of our Citizens, fully compensate for the injury occurring to the public. They are a daily lesson to the people of the U. States of the necessity of perseverance in the contest, and where ever the pressure of their local tyranny is removed the subjects of it rise up as one man to avenge their wrongs and prevent a repetition of them. Those who have possessed a latent partiality for them as their resentments are embittered by their disappointments generally feel most sensibly their injuries & insults and are the foremost in retaliating them. It is much to be regretted that these things are so little known in Europe. Were they published to the World in their true colours, the British nation would be hated by all nations as much as they have heretofore been feared by any, and all nations would be sensible of the policy of abridging a power which nothing else can prevent the abuse of.

Gallant action in Amelia County, Virginia, by Peter Francisco (above) who fought his way clear of British dragoons; French troops marching toward Yorktown (opposite)

CHÂTEAU DE VERSAILLES

Three months later, Madison asked Congress to issue a manifesto directing field commanders to retaliate for the firing of American towns and villages by executing enemy officers held as prisoners of war. Congress tabled the proposal, nor would Congress support his opposition to treaty provision for the restitution of property belonging to British subjects. The prospects of a "glorious peace" — a peace laid in victory — brightened in October, 1781, upon the surrender of Cornwallis at Yorktown. "With what hope or with what view can they [the British] try the fortunes of another campaign?" Madison asked, adding "it seems scarcely possible for them much longer to shut their ears against the voice of peace." In his posture toward the negotiation of peace, Madison adhered to the French alliance. In June, 1781, when victory was still a dream, Congress had instructed its peace commission to seek little more than the recognition of American independence and to be governed in all matters by French advice. A year later, as negotiations actually began in Paris, Congress not only raised its sights but spurned the indignity of subservience to France. The Lee-Adams faction led this anti-Gallic revolt. Arthur Lee himself, now a Virginia delegate, offered a resolution to revoke the clause placing the American commissioners on cue from Versailles. Opposed to revocation, Madison spoke against a milder substitute for Lee's motion. His remarks were recorded in Secretary Charles Thomson's notes of the debate.

"Debates in the Congress" [August 8, 1782]
Mr. Madison grants that the instructions given are a sacrifice of national dignity. But it was a sacrifice of dignity to policy. The situation of affairs and circumstances at the time rendered this sacrifice necessary. Nothing essential is given up, nor did it render our situation less precarious than it was before; nay he was per-

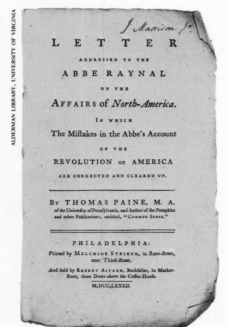

In October, 1781, Madison drafted a "Manifesto" (above) seeking retaliation against the British; below, a pamphlet on the Revolution that survives from his library

suaded that this mark of confidence gave an additional security to our interests as the Court of France must be sensible that the odium of unequal or hard conditions will now rest wholly on her. At least he was sure that the instructions given did not weaken that security. Our interests are as safe in her hands now as they were before or as if the ministers were left wholly to their discretion. Our ministers may still, notwithstanding the instructions given, state & assert our claims and contend with the utmost earnestness for our rights, and it is only in the last extremity when all their pleas, all their reasoning and all their most earnest endeavours prove ineffectual that they are ultimately to govern themselves by the advice and opinion of the Court of France; and must not this have been the case if the instructions had never been given? France has voluntarily bound herself by the treaties she has entered into with us to secure and guarantee our independence & sovereignty absolute and unlimited as well in matters of government as commerce. What indication has she given of any alteration of sentiment or conduct towards us? It is her interest as well as policy to secure the affections of the people of these States and forever separate us from G. Britain. She can never think us formidable to her while we continue absolutely independent, nor will she ever object to our enlarging our boundaries or increasing our commerce & naval power unless we give her reason to suspect a want of confidence in her and a disposition to reunite ourselves with her ancient enemy. In that case interest and policy will both unite and induce her to keep us as weak as possible. Whether withdrawing our confidence at this critical moment will not give just grounds of suspicion and jealousy he leaves gentlemen to determine. There was a passage in Mr Jay's letter lately read which made a strong impression on him; he did not know whether it made the same on others. He meant that passage which mentioned the fears and suspicions occasioned by the late change in the British administration, lest the men now in office who had always professed themselves friends to America and had in such severe terms condemned the war might influence the councils and conduct of the Americans. The withdrawing the instructions given on the 15th June, 1781 ... will increase that jealousy.

Let us consider how it will operate on Great Britain. Tired with the war and disappointed in all her attempts to separate us from France, there is reason to think there are serious thoughts of peace, but flushed with her late success [a defeat of the French Fleet in the West Indies] and flattered with the hopes of rising dissentions & jealousies between us & the other belligerent, will she not be encouraged to prosecute the war with new vigour & try by redoubled efforts to reduce us to her power?

But it is said our dignity is stained, and that we must revoke the instructions in order to wipe off that stain and restore its lustre. But will this do? Will it repair our loss of dignity in the eyes of the nations of Europe to convince them we are a people unstable in our councils & measures, governed wholly by circumstances, *abject & profuse* of promises when in distress and difficulties, but who veer about on a change of circumstances & on whose promises and professions no reliance can be placed? In a word, continued he, I am persuaded that a change in the instructions will not add to our security. I am persuaded that it will give umbrage to our ally, and by a seeming act of ingratitude or of diffidence awaken her suspicions and jealousies, and abate her zeal in our favour. I am persuaded that the umbrage and jealousy which this measure will excite will be prejudicial to us and will give encouragement to our enemy to prosecute

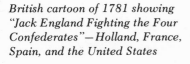

British cartoon of 1781 showing "Jack England Fighting the Four Confederates"—Holland, France, Spain, and the United States

the war. I am persuaded it is now too late to alter, and that withdrawing our confidence will not cure the wound given to our national dignity. For all these reasons I shall be against touching the instructions given. But if any member thinks that anything farther can be done to secure to the United States the several objects claimed, by them, I shall have no objections to that, it being well understood that no encroachment is to be made on the instructions given, but they are to remain in their full force. I shall therefore move that the motion before the house be postponed.

Madison prevailed. The motion was postponed, only to be renewed in December with the same result. Dispatches from two of the commissioners, Jay and Adams, had refueled the hostility to France in Congress. Like the third commissioner, Franklin, Madison was well aware of Versailles's concern to hold the Americans in check and to deny their claim to the Newfoundland fisheries and their ambitions in the West; but, again like Franklin, he felt that the country had placed its trust to France at a desperate time, that any withdrawal of confidence would risk the loss of French aid and support and draw down upon the new nation "the reproach of ingratitude," and, finally, that the United States was "more in danger of being seduced by Britain than sacrificed by France." If American and French interests did not perfectly coincide, as on the Mississippi, they

Instructions drafted by Madison to peace commissioners in 1782 (right); and the Department of Foreign Affairs where the Proclamation of Peace was drafted in 1783 (above)

British cartoon of 1783 entitled
"Blessed are the Peace Makers"

were not "diametrically opposed." In peace as in war Britain remained the enemy in Madison's eyes. For that reason alone it was necessary to maintain the French alliance.

News of the preliminary peace treaty with Great Britain reached Philadelphia in March, 1783. Madison thought the terms "extremely liberal." Britain recognized the independence of the United States, gave the Americans liberty to fish in Newfoundland waters, agreed to the Mississippi as the western boundary, and, so far as it was Britain's to grant, consented to the right of navigation of that great river. Madison was nevertheless disturbed. The American commissioners had been decoyed by their British counterparts into negotiating independently of the French ministry. "In this business," he wrote cryptically to a friend, "Jay has taken the lead & proceeded to a length of what you can form little idea. Adams has followed with cordiality. Franklin has been dragged into it." Moreover, the treaty contained a secret article on the Florida boundary that put the new nation in the dishonorable position of betraying its allies. (If in the treaty to come between Britain and Spain the former retained the Floridas, the boundary would be one hundred miles north of where it would be if the Floridas passed to Spain, as they did.) Madison and his friends cried "betrayal," but the treaty stood.

The nation had won its independence, but could it survive? Could it hold the West and secure its frontiers against the British to the north and the Spanish to the south? Could it recover old markets within the British commercial system or, excluded from that, find new markets for its products? Above all, could it create a government strong enough to bind the quarreling states and attend the national interest? Since his entrance into Congress, Madison had been a dedicated nationalist. He advocated financial independence of the Confederation from the member states; he advocated the reform of Congress and the creation of executive departments; he advocated vesting Congress with all the means necessary to carry out its powers.

Scarcely had the Articles of Confederation gone into effect than he proposed an amendment—which was never adopted—authorizing Congress to *enforce* obedience upon the states. Of this he wrote candidly to Jefferson.

Philada. April 16th. 1781

The necessity of arming Congress with coercive powers arises from the shameful deficiency of some of the States which are most capable of yielding their apportioned supplies, and the military exactions to which others already exhausted by the enemy and our own troops are in consequence exposed. Without such powers too in the general government, the whole confederacy may be insulted and the most salutary measures frustrated by the most inconsiderable State in the Union. At a time when all the other States were submitting to the loss and inconveniency of an embargo on their exports, Delaware absolutely declined coming into the measure, and not only defeated the general object of it, but enriched herself at the expense of those who did their duty.

The expediency however of making the proposed application to the States will depend on the probability of their complying with it. If they should refuse, Congress will be in a worse situation than at present: for as the confederation now stands, and according to the nature even of alliances much less intimate, there is an implied right of coer[c]io[n] against the delinquent party, and the exercise of it by Congress whenever a palpable necessity occurs will probably be acquiesced in.

It may be asked perhaps by what means Congress could exercise such a power if the States were to invest them with it? As long as there is a regular army on foot a small detachment from it, acting under Civil authority, would at any time render a voluntary contribution of supplies due from a State, an eligible alternative. But there is a still more easy and efficacious mode. The situation of most of the States is such, that two or three vessels of force employed against their trade will make it their interest to yield prompt obidience to all just requisitions on them. With respect to those States that have little or no foreign trade of their own it is provided that all inland trade with such states as supply them with foreign merchandize may be interdicted and the concurrence of the latter may be enforced in case of refusal by operations on their foreign trade.

There is a collateral reason which interests the States

Madison's committee report of June 19, 1782, which recommended suppressing "illicit and infamous" trade with the enemy

*Portion of Madison's expense
account as a delegate in Congress*

who are feeble in maritime resources, in such a plan. If a naval armament was considered as the proper instrument of general Government, it would be both preserved in a respectable State in time of peace, and it would be an object to mann it with Citizens taken in due proportio[ns] from every State. A Navy so formed and under the orders of the general Council of the States, would not only be a guard against aggression & insults from abroad; but without it what is to protect the Southern States for many years to come against the insults & aggressions of their N. Brethern.

Money became even more of a problem as the pressures of war lifted. The state legislatures, with problems enough of their own and no longer under compulsion to unite against a common enemy, repeatedly failed to meet the requisitions of Congress. This seeming indifference extended to the states' delegates in Philadelphia. Madison went months without pay, living on the funds advanced by the generous patriot Haym Salomon, as he explained in a letter to Edmund Randolph, Virginia's Attorney General.

> September 30. 1782
> The remittance to Col: Bland is a source of hope to his brethren. I am almost ashamed to reiterate my wants so incessantly to you, but they begin to be so urgent that it is impossible to suppress them. The kindness of our little friend in Front Street near the Coffee House is a fund which will preserve me from extremities, but I never resort to it without great mortification, as he obstinately rejects all recompense. The price of money is so usurious that he thinks it ought to be extorted from none but those who aim at profitiable speculations. To a necessitous Delegate he gratuitously spares a supply out of his private stock.

Madison was a leading member of the small cadre of nationalists that formed in Congress in 1781. Centered around Robert Morris, it was composed mainly of young men—men who had made their careers in Congress or the Continental Army—and it overlapped the "French party," just as the opposition to centralization overlapped the Lee-Adams faction. The paramount plank in the nationalists' platform was an independent revenue to be obtained by a uniform tax on imports. This "impost," as it was called, would enable Congress to pay the army, service the huge debt, and meet the other needs of the Confederation. Behind this fiscal necessity was a shrewd political calculation. By attaching the interests of creditors and soldiers to Congress, the central government would be strengthened at the expense of the states. The first attempt at an impost failed in November, 1782. Congress had asked the states to ratify an amendment to the Articles of Confederation empowering Congress to levy a duty of 5 percent ad valorem on imports. Twelve legislatures ratified; Rhode Island stubbornly refused. And the Articles could be changed only with unanimous consent. More decisive in the defeat, however, was Virginia's repeal in December, 1782, of what it had earlier approved. Bewildered and mortified, Madison expressed himself in letters to Randolph who, having just retired from Congress, took up the nationalist cause in Richmond.

Madison's notes on the debates in Congress for November 4, 1782

Philada. Novr. 26th. 1782

The obstinacy of Rhode Island in rejecting the Impost, is a subject of very general and pointed crimination not only among the public creditors and their friends who deem it equivalent to a denial of justice but among the most enlightened patrons of the foederal interests who pronounce it a blow to our credit abroad as well as our future credit at home And in truth who can combine this consideration with the paltry payments on the last requisition of Congress and not shudder at the prospect. This obstinacy on the part of R. I. is supposed, on good grounds, to be much cherished by the limited manner in which other states have acceded to the impost from which she infers a latent repugnance to the measure. Would it not then be prudent in Virginia to revise and enlarge her act of compliance? If her example should prove less efficatious than might be wished it would at least have a conciliating effect on other states and gain her general credit. I see no possible objection; unless indeed, she wishes the plan to be frustrated; in which case I can only give it as my firm opinion that a thorough knowledge of public affairs would speedily reconcile her to it. If your own ideas correspond with those here expressed, and the temper of the Legislature be not unfavorable, you will give such suggestions as may be best adapted to the object, and make them the subject of a future paragraph.

Philadelphia, January 22, 1783

The repeal of the impost act of Virginia is still considered as covered with some degree of mystery....Many have surmised that the enmity of Doctor Lee against Morris is at the bottom of it. But had that been the case, it can scarcely be supposed that the repeal would have passed so quietly. By this time, I presume, you will be able to furnish me with its true history, and I ask the favor of you to do it. Virginia could never have cut off this source of public relief at a more unlucky crisis than when she is protesting her inability to comply with the continental requisitions. She will, I hope, be yet made sensible of the impropriety of the step she has taken, and make amends by a more liberal grant. Congress cannot abandon the plan as long as there is a spark of hope. Nay, other plans on a like principle must be added. Justice, gratitude, our reputation abroad, and our tranquility at home, require provision for a debt of not less than fifty millions of dollars, and I pronounce that this provision will not be adequately met by separate acts of the States. If there are not revenue laws which operate at the same time through all the States, and are exempt from the control of each—the mutual jealousies which begin already to appear among them all will assuredly defraud both our foreign and domestic creditors of their just claims.

The deputies of the army are still here, urging the objects of their mission. Congress are thoroughly impressed with the justice of time, and are disposed to do every thing which depends on them. But what can a Virginia Delegate say to them, whose constituents declare that they are unable to make the necessary contributions, and unwilling to establish funds for obtaining them elsewere?

Silhouette of James Madison, by Joseph Sansom, made in Philadelphia while he was a member of Congress

The nationalists at once renewed their campaign for a permanent revenue. The deputation from the army proved a powerful incentive, while Morris's threatened resignation evoked images of impending chaos. Creditors were turning to the state governments to receive their due, and, of course, if the states took over the debt, there would be no rock upon which to build a national government. Madison and his friends spoke of Congress becoming a mere "rope of sand," to which Arthur Lee replied, "he had rather see Congress a rope of sand than a rod of Iron." The debate raged for two months. Madison kept Randolph posted on its progress.

Philada. Feby. 25th. 1783.

Congress are still engaged on the subject of providing adequate revenues for the public debts, particularly that due to the army. The recommendation of the Impost will be renewed with perhaps some little variation, to which will be superadded probably a duty on a few enumerated articles. Master [John Francis] Mercer [another Virginia delegate] altho' he continues to be adverse to the measure declares now that he will not carry his opposition out of Congress. Whether any other general revenues will be recommended is very uncertain. A poll tax seems to be the only one sufficiently simple & equal for the purpose, and besides other objections to which even that is liable, the Constitution of Maryland which interdicts such a tax is an insuperable bar. The plan talked of by some for supplying the deficiency is to call on the States to provide each its proportion of a permanent revenue within itself, and, to appropriate it to the continental debt. The objections against this plan are that as the execution of it will depend on a unanimous & continued punctuality in the 13 States; it is a precarious basis for public credit—that the precariousness will be increased by mutual jealousies among the States that others may be sparing themselves exertions which they are submitting to; and that these jealousies will be still more increased by the mutual opinion which prevails that they are comparatively in advance to the U. States; an opinion which cannot be corrected without closing the accounts between all of them & the U. States; prerequisites to which are a valuation of the land, and a final discrimination of such parts of the separate expenditures of the States as ought to be transferred to the common mass, from such parts as ought in justice to fall on the particular States themselves. Some States also will contend and it would seem neither agst. the principles of justice nor the spirit of the Confederation, for a retrospective abatement of their share of the past debt according to their respective disabilities from year to year throughout the war. What will be the end of this complication of embarrassments time only can disclose. But a greater embarrassment than any is s[t]ill behind. The discontents and designs of the army are every day takeing a more solemn form. It is now whispered that they have not only resolved not to lay down their arms til justice shall be done them [but] that to prev[en]t surprize a public declaration will be made to that effect. It is added and I fear with too much certainty, that the influence of General [Washington] is rapidly decreaseing in the army insomuch that it is even in contemplation to substitute some less scrupulous guard-

Robert Morris

ian of their interests. . . .

You will suffer me to renew my exhortations to an exchange of your office [Attorney General] under the State for a seat in the Legislature. It depends much in my opinion on the measures which may be pursued by Congress & the several States within the ensuing period of 6 months whether prosperity & tranquility, or confusion and disunion are to be the fruits of the Revolution. The seeds of the latter are so thickly sown that nothing but the most enlightened and liberal policy will be able to stifle them. The easetern states particularly Massachusetts conceiv that compared with the Southern they are greatly in advance in the general account.

A respectable delegate from Massachusetts a few days ago being a little chafed by some expressions of Masters Lee and Mercer unfavorable to loan office creditors said that if notice was not to be obtained thro the general confederacy, the sooner it was known the better that some states might be forming other confederacys adequate to the purpose adding that some had suffered immensely from the want of a proportional compliance with deman[ds] for men & mon[ey] by others. However erroneous these ideas may be, do they not merit serious attention? Unless some amicable & adequate arrangements be speedily taken for adjusting all the subsisting accounts and discharging the public engagements, a dissolution of the union will be inevitable. Will not in that event the S[outhern] S[tates] which at sea will be opulent and weak, be an easey prey to the easetern which will be powerful and rapacious? and particularly if supposed c[l]aims of justice are on the side of the latter will they not be a ready prete[x]t for reprisals? The consequence of such a situation would probably be that alliances would be sougt first by the weaker and then by the stronger party and this country be made subservi-[ent] to the wars and politics of Europe.

John Francis Mercer

Reluctantly, Madison was no longer insisting on the "whole loaf." In March he drafted a new impost plan more consistent with the character of the Confederation as a league of states. The tax would be limited to a period of twenty-five years and the revenue applied only to the principal and interest of the debt. Collectors would be appointed by the respective states which would retain the revenue until requisitioned by Congress. Madison's colleague from New York, Alexander Hamilton, scorned the compromise. It passed, however, as part of·a package containing a number of provisions in addition to the impost, and all this had now to run the gauntlet of the legislatures. In an artful address to the states, Madison explained the proposition in detail and concluded with an elevated appeal.

"Address to the States," April 26. 1783

The plan thus communicated and explained by Congress must now receive its fate from their Constituents. All the objects comprized in it are conceived to be of great importance to the happiness of this confederated republic, are necessary to render the fruits of the Revolution, a full reward for the blood, the toils, the cares and the calamities which have purchased it. But the object of which the necessity will be peculiarly felt, and which it is peculiarly the duty of Congress to inculcate, is the provision recommended for the national debt. Altho' this debt is greater than could have been wished, it is still less on the whole than could have been expected, and when referred to the cause in which it has been incurred, and compared with the burdens which wars of ambition and of vain glory have entailed on other nations, ought to be borne not only with cheerfulness but with pride. But the magnitude of the debt makes no part of the question. It is sufficient that the debt has been fairly contracted and that justice & good faith demand that it should be fully discharged. Congress had no option but between different modes of discharging it. The same option is the only one that can exist with the States. The mode which has after long & elaborate discussion been preferred, is, we are persuaded, the least objectionable of any that would have been equal to the purpose. Under this persuasion, we call upon the justice & plighted faith of the several States to give it its proper effect, to reflect on the consequences of rejecting it, and to remember that Congress will not be answerable for them.

If other motives than that of justice could be requisite on this occasion, no nation could ever feel stronger. For to whom are the debts to be paid?

To an Ally, in the first place, who to the exertion of his arms in support of our cause, has added the succours of his Treasurer; who to his important loans has added liberal donations; and whose loans themselves carry the impression of his magninimity and friendship. . . .

To individuals in a foreign country in the next place

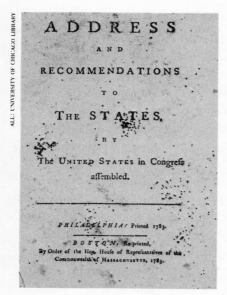

ADDRESS

AND

RECOMMENDATIONS

TO

THE STATES,

BY

The UNITED STATES in Congress
assembled.

PHILADELPHIA: Printed 1783.

BOSTON: Reprinted,
By Order of the Hon. House of Representatives of the
Commonwealth of Massachusetts, 1783.

*Madison's "Address to the States,"
printed in Philadelphia in 1783*

who were the first to give so precious a token of their confidence in our justice, and of their friendship for our cause; and who are members of a republic which was second in espousing our rank among nations. . . .

Another class of Creditors is that illustrious & patriotic band of fellow Citizens, whose blood and bravery have defended the liberties of their Country, who have patiently borne, among other distresses the privation of their stipends, whilst the distresses of their Country disabled it from bestowing them; and who even now ask for no more than such a portion of their dues as will enable them to retire from the field of victory & glory into the bosom of peace & private citizenship, and for such effectual security for the residue of their claims as their Country is now unquestionably able to provide. . . .

The remaining class of Creditors is composed partly of such of our fellow Citizens as originally lent to the public the use of their funds or have since manifested most confidence in their Country by receiving transfers from the lenders; and partly of those whose property has been either advanced or assumed for the public service. To discriminate the merits of these several descriptions of creditors would be a task equally unnecessary & invidious. If the voice of humanity plead more loudly in favor of some than of others; the voice of policy, no less than of justice pleads in favor of all. A wise nation will never permit those who relieve the wants of their Country, or who rely most on its faith, its firmness and its resources, when either of them is distrusted, to suffer by the event.

Let it be remembered finally that it has ever been the pride and boast of America, that the rights for which she contended were the rights of human nature. By the blessing of the Author of these rights on the means exerted for their defence, they have prevailed against all opposition and form the basis of thirteen independant States. No instance has heretofore occurred, nor can any instance be expected hereafter to occur, in which the unadulterated forms of Republican Government can pretend to so fair an opportunity of justifying themselves by their fruits. In this view the Citizens of the U.S. are responsible for the greatest trust ever confided to a Political Society. If justice, good faith, honor, gratitude & all the other Qualities which enable the character of a nation, and fulfil

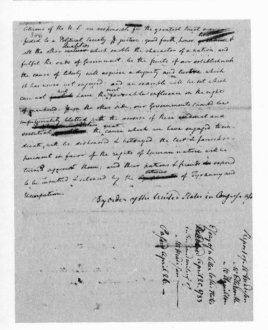

Two pages in Madison's handwriting of draft for "Address to the States"

Elias Boudinot, president of the Continental Congress

the ends of Government, be the fruits of our establishments, the cause of liberty will acquire a dignity and lustre, which it has never yet enjoyed; and an example will be set which can not but have the most favorable influence on the rights of mankind. If on the other side, our Governments should be unfortunately blotted with the reverse of these cardinal and essential Virtues, the great cause which we have engaged to vindicate, will be dishonored & betrayed: the last & fairest experiment in favor of the rights of human nature will be turned against them; and their patrons & friends exposed to be insulted & silenced by the votaries of Tyranny and Usurpation.

Alas, the new plan—"the budget of Congress," as Madison called it—would have no more success than the old. As peace came to the United States, all incentive to tighten the continental belt seemed to disappear. The Confederation became a work of futility, Congress a joke. The ultimate disgrace struck on June 20 when a mutiny of soldiers drove Congress from Philadelphia. Suddenly Madison found himself back in Princeton where the fleeing statesmen reconvened. His third annual term would expire in November, and he had already planned to leave Congress. He had not been home since March, 1780. He was tired. He was discouraged. The nationalist cadre was breaking up. Hamilton was about to leave; Morris's departure could be expected at any time. But Madison had an additional reason: he had fallen in love. The young lady, only sixteen years old in April, was Kitty (Catherine) Floyd, daughter of a New York delegate who stayed under the same boardinghouse roof with Madison. Although there was a rival for Kitty's affections in the person of a young medical student, she and Madison quietly became engaged in the spring and expected to wed at the end of the year, when Madison's term in Congress expired.

Jefferson, who encouraged this match, was also in Philadelphia, under the same roof, during the early months of 1783. He had lost his wife the previous September and, heeding the pleas of Madison and other friends to return to service, had accepted congressional appointment as a peace commissioner. Peace came before he could embark for France, however. Stranded in Philadelphia, he drew closer to Madison. The two men exchanged views on many subjects, joined forces to reform the Virginia Constitution, and concerted the first of several ciphers to be employed in their political correspondence. Jefferson was then preparing a catalogue of his personal library. From it and from other sources, Madison compiled a list of some three hundred titles which he embodied in a report to Congress recommending the establishment of a congressional library. He recorded the reasons for this proposal and for its defeat in his notes of the congressional debate.

By His EXCELLENCY

Elias Boudinot, Esquire,

Prefident of the United States in Congrefs Affembled.

A PROCLAMATION.

WHEREAS a body of armed Soldiers in the fervice of the United States, and quartered in the Barracks of this City, having mutinoufly renounced their obedience to their Officers, did, on Saturday the Twenty-firft Day of this inftant, proceed, under the direction of their Serjeants, in a hoftile and threatning manner, to the Place in which Congrefs were affembled, and did furround the fame with Guards: And whereas Congrefs in confequence thereof, did on the fame Day, refolve, " That the Prefident and Supreme Executive Council of this State " fhould be informed, that the authority of the United States having been, that Day, groffly infulted by the " diforderly and menacing appearance of a body of armed Soldiers, about the Place within which Congrefs were affem- " bled; and that the Peace of this City being endangered by the mutinous Difpofition of the faid Troops then in the " Barracks; it was, in the Opinion of Congrefs, neceffary, that effectual Meafures fhould be immediately taken for " fupporting the public Authority." And alfo whereas Congrefs did at the fame Time appoint a Committee to con- fer with the faid Prefident and Supreme Executive Council on the practicability of carrying the faid Refolution into due effect: And alfo whereas the faid Committee have reported to me, that they have not received fatisfactory Affurances for expecting adequate and prompt exertions of this State for fupporting the Dignity of the federal Government: And alfo whereas the faid Soldiers ftill continue in a ftate of open Mutiny and Revolt, fo that the Dignity and Authority of the United States would be conftantly expofed to a repetition of Infult, while Congrefs fhall continue to fit in this City, I do therefore, by and with the Advice of the faid Committee, and according to the Powers and Authorities in me vefted for this Purpofe, hereby fummon the honourable the Delegates compofing the Congrefs of the United States, and every of them, to meet in Congrefs on Thurfday the Twenty Sixth Day of June inftant, at Princeton, in the ftate of New-Jerfey, in order that further and more effectual Meafures may be taken for fuppreffing the prefent Revolt, and maintaining the Dignity and Authority of the United States, of which all Officers of the United States, civil and military, and all others whom it may concern, are defired to take Notice and govern themfelves accordingly.

GIVEN under my Hand and Seal at Philadelphia, in the ftate of Pennfylvania, this Twenty-Fourth Day of June, in the Year of Our Lord One Thoufand Seven Hundred and Eighty-Three, and of our Sovereignty and Inde- pendence the feventh.

ELIAS BOUDINOT.

Atteft,

SAMUEL STERETT, *Private Secretary*.

Philadelphia, Printed by DAVID C. CLAYPOOLE.

Boudinot issued this proclamation summoning congressmen to meet in Princeton after the mutiny of soldiers at Philadelphia.

"Notes on Debates," Thursday Jany. 23 [1783] In favr. of the Rept. it was urged as indispensable that Congress sd. have at all times at command such authors on the law of Nations, treaties Negociations &c as wd. render their proceedings in such cases conformable to propriety; and it was observed that the want of this in- formation was manifest in several important acts of Con- gress. It was further observed that no time ought to be lost in collecting every book & tract which related to American Antiquities & the affairs of the U.S. since many of the most valuable of these were every day becoming extinct, & they were necessary not only as materials for a Hist: of the U.S. but might be rendered still more so by future pretensions agst. their rights from Spain or other powers which had shared in the discoveries & possessions of the New World. Agst. the Report were urged 1st. the inconveniency of advancing even a few hundred pounds at this crisis; 2dly. the difference of expence between procuring the books during the war & after a peace. These objections prevailed, by a considerable majority. A mo- tion was then made by Mr. Wilson 2ded. by Mr. Madison to confine the purchase for the present to the most es- sential part of the books. This also was negatived.

After Jefferson's return to Virginia, Madison informed him, bluntly, of the discouraging state of public affairs and, delicately, of the miscarriage of his personal affair with Miss Floyd, who had apparently had a change of heart in favor of the medical student.

Philada. Aug: 11th. 1783.
At the date of my letter in April I expected to have had the pleasure by this time of being with you in Virginia. My disappointment has proceeded from several dilatory circumstances on which I had not calculated. One of them was the uncertain state into which the object I was then pursuing had been brought by one of those incidents to which such affairs are liable. The result has rendered the time [of] my return to Virga. less material, as the neces- sity of my visiting the State of N.Jy: no longer exists. It would be improper by this communication to send par- ticular explanations, and perhaps needless to [trou]ble you with them at any time.... My journey to Virga. tho' still somewhat contingent in point of time cannot now be very long postponed. I need not I trust renew my assur-

Motion, in Madison's handwriting, to appoint Jefferson a peace commissioner in November, 1782

ances that it will not finally stop on this side of Monticello.

The reserve of our foreign Ministers still leaves us the sport of misinformations concerning the def[initive]: Treaty. . . . Congs. remain at Princeton utterly undecided both as to their ultimate seat and their intermediate residence. Very little business of moment has been yet done at the new Metropolis, except a ratification of the Treaty with Sweeden. In particular nothing has been [d]one as to a foreign establishment. With regard to an internal peace [es]tablishment, though it has been treated with less inattention, it has undergone little discussion. The Commander cheif has been invited to Princeton with a view to obtain his advice and sanction to the military branches of it, and is every day expected [t]here. The Budget of Congs. is likely to have the fate of many of their other

Madison wrote to Jefferson (above) in April, 1783, in cipher (crossed-out passages in letter at left) to tell him of the progress of his romance with Catherine Floyd.

propositions to the States. Delaware is the only one among those which have bestowed a consideration on it that has acceded in toto. Several Legislatures have adjourned without giving even that mark of their [co]ndescension. In the Southern States a jealousy of Congressional usur[p]ations is likely to be the bane of the system: in the Eastern an aversion to the half-pay [pensions for veterans] provided for by it. New Jersey & Maryland have adopted the impost, the other funds recommended being passed for one year only by one of these States, and postponed by the other.... Massts. has in the election of delegates for the ensuing year stigmatized the concurrence of those now in place in the provision for half-pay, by substituting a new representation; and has sent a Memorial to Congs. which I am told is pregnant with the most penurious ideas not only on that subject but on several others which concern the national honor & dignity. This picture of our affairs is not a flattering one; but we have been witnesses of so many cases in which evils & errors have been the parents of their own remedy, that we can not but view it with the consolations of hope.

Jefferson was back in Philadelphia in October, this time to take a Virginia seat in Congress. That vagabond crew, it turned out, would next meet in Annapolis. Madison wound up his affairs in Philadelphia and, on his way home, accompanied Jefferson as far as the Maryland capital. Before leaving he presumably sold, in some form, his slave Billy who had been his personal servant for many years. Explaining his dilemma to his father, Madison revealed both his abhorrence of slavery and his complicity in the wretched system.

Philada. Sepr. 8. 1783.
On a view of all circumstances I have judged it most prudent not to force Billey back to Va. even if could be done; and have accordingly taken measures for his final separation from me. I am persuaded his mind is too thoroughly tainted to be a fit companion for fellow slaves in Virga. The laws here do not admit of his being sold for more than 7 years [of servitude]. I do not expect to get near the worth of him; but cannot think of punishing him by transportation merely for coveting that liberty for which we have paid the price of so much blood, and have proclaimed so often to be the right, & worthy the pursuit, of every human being.

Chapter **3**

Radical Reformer

At home with his family, Madison seemed uncertain of what to do with himself. His father, hale and hearty, and his younger brother Ambrose looked after Montpelier; the long absent son was not needed in this work, and such was his distaste for slavery that he occasionally fancied removing himself altogether from Virginia. He resumed the study of law, thinking perhaps to attain independence through this profession; but, as before, his efforts were halfhearted. *Coke upon Littleton*, part of the great seventeenth-century work on English law, occupied the morning hours, he later recalled; in the afternoon, he "indulged in miscellaneous reading, which embraced among other works of philosophical cast, those of Buffon whose views of nature, however fanciful and even absurd in some instances were highly attractive in others, and especially by the fascinating eloquence which distinguishes them." Jefferson had put him on to Buffon and then engaged Madison in his campaign to demolish the great naturalist's theory of biological degeneracy in the New World. With Jefferson's help, too, Madison was building his own library, giving first place to political titles, though not omitting the scientific and the literary. The older man sympathized with Madison's isolation in Orange and, knowing well his own need for companionship, proposed that he come to live in the neighborhood of Monticello as two other young friends, James Monroe and William Short, had already planned to do. "With such a society," wrote Jefferson, "I could once more venture home and lay myself up for the residue of life, quitting all its contentions which grow daily more and more insupportable." Jefferson knew of a farm only two miles from Monticello, but Madison declined the invitation, while drawing upon Jefferson for books and other scarce items.

Orange [Virginia,] March 16. 1784

The winter has been so severe that I have never renewed my call on the library of Monticello, and the time is now drawing so near when I may pass for a while into a different scene, that I shall await at least the return to my studies. . . . I lately got home the Trunk which contained my Buffon, but have barely entered upon him. My time begins already to be much less my own than during the winter blockade. I must leave to your discretion the occasional purchase of rare and valuable books, disregarding the risk of duplicates. You know tolerably well the objects of my curiosity. I will only particularize my wish of whatever may throw light on the general Constitution and droit public of the several confederacies which have existed. I observe in Boinauds Catalogue [a listing from a Philadelphia bookstore] several pieces on the Du[t]ch, the German and the Helvetic. The operations of our own must render all such lights of consequence. Books on the Law of N. and N. [Nature and Nations] fall within a similar remark. The tracts of Bynkershoek which you mention I must trouble you to get for me and in french if to be had rather than latin. Should the body of his works come nearly as cheap, as these select publications perhaps it may [be] worth considering whether the whole would not be preferable. Is not Wolfius also worth having. I recollect to have seen at Pritchards a copy of Hawkin's Abridgt. of Co: Litt: I would willingly take it if it be still there and you have an opportunity. A copy of Deane's letters which were printed in New York and which I failed to get before I left Philada. I should also be glad of. I use this freedom in confidence that you will be equally free in consulting your own conveniency whenever I encroach upon it; I hope you will be so particularly in the request I have to add. One of my parents would be considerably gratified with a pair of good spectacles which can not be got here. The particular readiness of Dudley to serve you inclines me to think that an order from you would be well executed. Will You therefore be so good as to get from him one of his best pebble and double jointed pair, for the age of fifty five or thereabouts with a good case; and forward them by the first safe conveyance to me at Orange or at Richmond as the case may be.

PRES'T. MADISON'S LIBRARY, AT AUCTION.

AT Orange Court House, Virginia, on Tuesday the 37th day of June, prox., being the day after the County Court of Orange in that montßc I shall sell at public auction, to the highest bidder, that part of the Library of the late James Madison, which, in a recent division of his books with the University of Virginia, fell to the share of my testator; and at the same time I will sell other books, the property of my said testator. In all there are some

SEVEN OR EIGHT HUNDRED VOLUMES,

among which are many very rare and desirable works, some in Greek, some in Latin, numerous others in French, and yet more in English, in almost all the departments of Literature; not a few of them being in this manner exposed to sale only because the University possessed already copies of the same editions. The sale beginning on the day above mentioned, will be continued from day to day till all the books shall have been sold, on the following terms:

Cash will be required of each purchaser whose aggregate purchases shall amount to no more than Five dollars; those whose purchases shall exceed that amount, will have the privilege either to pay the cash or to give bond with approved security, bearing interest from the date, and payable six months thereafter.

ELHANON ROW, Administrator, with the will annexed of John P. Todd, dec'd.

May 30, 1854.

Madison's library, collected over the years, was bequeathed in part to the University of Virginia. The remainder was sold to pay gambling debts of his stepson, John Todd.

Madison's retirement was mercifully short. In the spring of 1784 the freeholders of Orange elected him to the House of Delegates, the lower house of the general assembly. He was in Richmond for the May session, returned home briefly, and then embarked on a northerly tour. Falling in with the Marquis de Lafayette, the gallant Frenchman who was himself on tour, Madison journeyed all the way to old Fort Stanwix deep in the Mohawk Valley west of Albany, New York. He would never travel so far again. The Mississippi question weighed on Madison's mind—he had written to Jefferson at length on the subject—and he did not hesitate to press his views on Lafayette, as he reported to Jefferson, then a commissioner in France and soon to succeed Franklin as American minister.

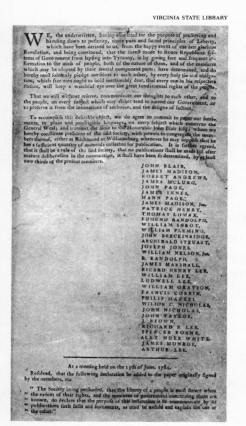

While a delegate in Richmond, Madison signed this declaration by the short-lived Constitutional Society of Virginia, whose alleged purpose was to revise the state constitution.

Philada. Sepr. 7th. 1784.

Some business, the need of exercise after a very sedentary period, and the view of extending my ramble into the Eastern States which I have long had a curiosity to see have brought me to this place.... At Baltimore I fell in with the Marquis de la Fayette returning from a visit to Mount Vernon. Wherever he passes he receives the most flattering tokens of sincere affection from all ranks. He did not propose to have left Virginia so soon but Genl. Washington was about setting out on a trip to the Ohio, and could not then accompany him on some visits as he wished to do. The present plan of the Marquis is to proceed immediately to New York, thence by Rhode Island to Boston, thence through Albany to Fort Stanwix where a treaty with the Indians is to be held the latter end of this month, thence to Virginia so as to meet the Legislature at Richmond. I have some thoughts of making this tour with him, but suspend my final resolution till I get to N.Y. whither I shall follow him in a day or two.

The relation in which the Marquis stands to France and America has induced me to enter into a free conversation with him on the subject of the Mississippi. I have endeavored emphatically to impress on him that the ideas of America and of Spain irreconcilably clash, that unless the mediation of France be effectually exerted an actual rupture is near at hand, that in such an event the connection between France and Spain will give the enemies of the former in America the fairest opportunity of involving her in our resentments against the latter and of introducing Great Brit. as a party with us against both, that America can not possibly be diverted from her object and therefore France is bound to set every engine at work to divert Spain from hers and that France has besides a great interest in a trade with the western country thro the Missisipi. I thought it not unwise also to suggest to him some of the considerations which seem to appeal to the prudence of Spain. He admitted the force of every thing I said, told me he would write in the most [approving?] terms to the Count de Vergennes [the French Minister of Foreign Affairs] by the packet which will probably carry this and let me see his letter at N. York before he sends it. He thinks that Spain is bent on excluding us from the Missisipi and mentioned several anecdotes which happened while he was at Madrid in proof of it.

The business at Fort Stanwix was a boundary settlement with the Iroquois. Congress had sent commissioners, including General Oliver Wolcott and Arthur Lee, to negotiate, but as it happened the Marquis upstaged the Americans and confounded the British, the old allies of the Six Nations. Lafayette reaped new glory and doubtless contributed to the eventual treaty. Upon his return to Philadelphia, Madison gave Jefferson an amusing as well as insightful account of the proceedings.

Philada. Octr. 17. 1784

It seems that most of the Indian tribes particularly those of the Iroquois retain a strong predilection for the French and most of the latter an enthusiastic idea of the marquis. This idea has resulted from his being a Frenchman, the figure he has made during the war and the arrival of several important events which he foretold to them soon after he came to this country. Before he went to Fort Schuyler [another name for Stanwix] it had been suggested, either in compliment or sincerity that his presence and influence might be of material service to the treaty. At Albany the same thing had been said to him by General Wolcot. On his arrival at Fort S. Mr. [Samuel] Kirkland [a missionary] recommended an exertion of his influence as of essential consequence to the treaty, painting in the strongest colours the attachment of the Indians to his person, which seemed indeed to be verified by their caresses and the artifices employed by the British partizans to frustrate the objects of the treaty, among which was a pretext that the alliance between the United States and France was insincere and transitory and consequently the respect of the Indians for the later ought to be no motive for their respecting the former. Upon these circumstances the M. grounded a written message to the Commissioners before they got up intimating his disposition to render the United States any service his small influence over the Indians might put in his power and

Bust of Lafayette by Houdon
VIRGINIA STATE CAPITOL BUILDING

Atotarho, a founder of the Iroquois League, appears at right as a Medusa-headed figure; the Indian at center wears a British redcoat.

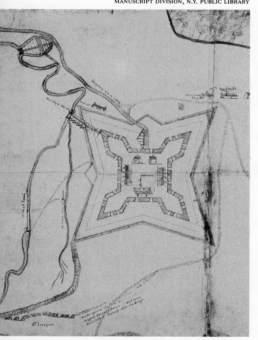

Plan of Fort Stanwix

desiring to know what the Commissioners would chuse him to say. The answer in Mr. Lee's hand consisted of polite acknowledgments and information that the Commissioners would be happy in affording him an opportunity of saying what ever he might wish forbearing to advise or suggest what it would be best for him to say. The M. perceived the caution but imputed it to Lee alone. As his stay however was to be very short it was necessary for him to take provisional measures before the arrival of the commissioners and particularly for calling in the Oneida Cheifs who were at their town. It fell to my lot to be consulted in his dilemma. My advice was that he should invite the chiefs in such a way as would give him an opportunity of addressing them publicly, if on a personal interview with the Commissioners it should be judged expedient; or of satisfying their expectations with a friendly entertainment in return for the civilities his visit to their town had met with. This advice was approved; but the Indians brought with them such ideas of his importance as no private reception would probably have been equal to. When the Commissioners arrived the M. consulted them in person. They were reserved, he was embarrassed. Finally they changed their plan and concurred explicitly in his making a Speech in form. He accordingly prepared one, communicated it to the Commissioners and publicly pronounced it, the Commissioners premising such an one as was thought proper to introduce his. The answer of the sachems, as well as the circumstances of the audience denoted the highest reverence for the orator. The cheif of the Oneidas said that the words which he had spoken to them early in the war had prevented them from being misled to the wrong side of it. During this scene and even during the whole stay of the M. he was the only conspicuous figure. The Commissioners were eclipsed. All of them probably felt it. Lee complained to me of the immoderate stress laid on the influence of the M., and evidently promoted his departure. The M. was not insensible of it, but consoled himself with the service which he thought the Indian speech would witness that he had rendered to the United States. I am persuaded that the transaction is also pleasing to him in another view as it will form a bright column in the gazettes of Europe, and that he will be impatient for its appearance there without seeing any mode in which it can happen of course. As it is blended with the proceedings of the Commissioners, it will probably not be published in America very soon, if at all. The time I have lately passed with the M. has given me a pretty thorough insight into his character. With great natural frankness of temper he unites much address; with very considerable talents, a strong thirst of praise and popularity. In his politics he says his three hobbyhorses are the alliance between France and the United States, the Union of the latter and the manumission of the slaves. The two former are the dearer to him as they are connected with his personal glory. The last does him real honor, as it is a proof of his humanity. In a word, I take him to be as amiable a man as his vanity will admit, and as sincere an American as any Frenchman can be; one whose past services gratitude obliges us to acknowledge and whose future friendship prudence requires us to cultivate.

*First page of the treaty concluded
at Fort Stanwix in October, 1784*

During the period Jefferson lived in France Madison was his tireless informant, not only of the great events in Richmond and Philadelphia but of the little events at home; and in the two-way exchange of knowledge between the continents Madison was both recipient and contributor. Jefferson supplied him with the fascinating curiosities of the French capital—phosphorous matches, a pedometer, the new Argand cylinder lamp—and news of recent balloon ascensions. But mostly he supplied him with books. Although the choices were often Jefferson's, he endeavored to meet his friend's requests, as Madison gratefully acknowledged.

Orange [Virginia,] April 27. 1785.

I have received your two favors of Novr. 11 and Decr. 8.

Along with the former I received the two pamphlets on animal magnetism and the last aeronautic expedition, together with the phosphoretic matches. These articles were a great treat to my curiosity.... I thank you much for your attention to my literary wants. All the purchases you have made for me, are such as I should have made for myself with the same opportunities. You will oblige me by adding to them the Dictionary [of Law] in 13 vol. 4°. by Felice and others, also de Thou in French. If the utility of [the historical dictionary by] Moreri be not superseded by some better work I should be glad to have him too. I am afraid if I were to attempt a catalogue of my wants I should not only trouble you beyond measure, but exceed the limits which other considerations ought to prescribe to me. I cannot however abridge the commission you were so kind as to take on yourself in a former letter, of procuring me from time to time such books as may be "either old and curious or new and useful." Under this description will fall those particularised in my former letters, to wit treatises on the ancient or modern foederal republics, on the law of Nations, and the history natural and political of the New World; to which I will add such of the Greek and Roman authors where they can be got very cheap, as are worth having and are not on the common list of School classics. Other books which particularly occur, are the translation [French] of the Historians of the Roman Empire during its decline by _____, Paschals provincial letters—Don Ulloa in the Original—Lynnaeus best edition—Ordinances Marines—Collection of Tracts in french on the Œconomies of different nations. I forget the full title. It is much referred to by Smith on the wealth of nations. I am told a Monsr. Amelot has lately published his travels into China, which if they have any merit must be very entertaining. Of Buffon I have his original work of 31 vol., 10 vol. of Supplemt. and 16 vol. on birds. I shall be glad of the continuation as it may from time to time be published. I am so pleased with the new invented lamp that I shall not grudge two guineas for one of them. I have seen a pocket compass of somewhat larger diameter than a watch and which may be carried in the same way. It has a spring for stopping the vibration of the needle when not in use. One of these would be very convenient in case of a ramble into the Western Country. In my walks for exercise or

A list of books that Jefferson bought in Paris for James Madison

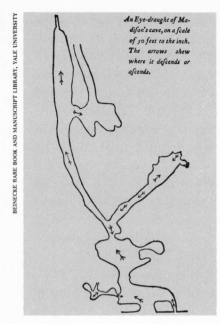

An Eye-draught of Madison's cave, on a scale of 50 feet to the inch. The arrows shew where it descends or ascends.

Jefferson's line drawing of a cave he described in Notes on Virginia

amusements, objects frequently present themselves, which it might be matter of curiosity to inspect, but which it is difficult or impossible to approach. A portable glass would consequently be a source of many little gratifications. I have fancied that such an one might be fitted into a Cane without making it too heavy. On the outside of the tube might be engraved a scale of inches &c. If such a project could be executed for a few Guineas I should be willing to submit to the price; if not, the best substitute I suppose will be a pocket-telescope, composed of several tubes so constructed as to slide the lesser into the greater. I should feel great remorse at troubling you with so many requests, if your kind and repeated offers did not stifle it in some measure. Your proposal for my replacing here advances for me without regard to the exchange is liable to no objection except that it will probably be too unequal in my favour. I beg that you will enable me as much as you can to keep those little matters balanced.

The balance was struck, imperfectly, by Madison's caring for Jefferson's nephews, the Carrs, and by dispatching American plants, seeds, specimens of animals, and other curiosities Jefferson wished to introduce to the Old World. To this enterprise, which was part of the vindication of American nature launched by Jefferson's *Notes on the State of Virginia*, Madison was a zealous friend. The two Virginians had often discussed the deficiencies and errors of the state constitution, and Madison upon entering the general assembly sought a convention for its reform. The people had had no vote in making the constitution; all power was concentrated in the legislative branch, which implied despotism on the theory of "separation of powers" derived from Montesquieu; representation was unequal, the court system inadequate, and fundamental personal liberties poorly protected. Unfortunately, as he had feared, Patrick Henry stood in "violent opposition," and reform was defeated. Henry held sway in the assembly. Because of his demagogic and parochial leadership, taxes were suspended, planters were secured from paying their prewar British debts, commerce languished, and Virginia retreated from her national responsibilities. Madison would emerge victorious in the end, but in the frustrating years 1785–87 he must have often felt, as Jefferson did, that the only thing to do was devoutly to pray for Henry's death.

Constitutional reform failing, Madison turned to statutory reform. He secured the printing of the *Report of the Committee of Revisors*, which Jefferson, George Wythe, and Edmund Pendleton had submitted to the legislature in 1779. Some of the revisors' reforms of colonial and English law had been enacted, but the original aim of a revised code had miscarried. Madison hoped to reverse this outcome or at least to see that the landmark bills of the revisal, "this mine of legislative wealth," became law. Among these were Jefferson's plan for establishing a public school system, his Bill for Proportioning Crimes and Punishments, and his Bill for Establishing Religious Freedom. With the last Madison scored a stunning legislative triumph. By 1780, the Anglican establishment was doomed in Virginia. Its friends, however, aided by religionists of other sects, had come up with a new principle in Church-State relations: government support of Christianity as the religion of the commonwealth. Under this principle all citizens would be taxed for the support of all Christian ministers regardless of sect. Earlier diverted, this "general assessment" plan was revived under Henry's auspices in 1784. Madison briefed Jefferson on the issue after the fall session.

A petition that was submitted to the Virginia General Assembly during Madison's 1785 term by Virginians west of the Alleghenies

Richmond Jany. 9th. 1785.

A resolution for a legal provision for the "teachers of Christian Religion" had early in the Session been proposed by Mr. Henry, and in spite of all the opposition that could be mustered, carried by 47 against 32 votes. Many Petitions from below the blue ridge had prayed for such a law; and though several from the presbyterian laity beyond it were in a contrary Stile, the Clergy of that Sect favoured it. The other sects seemed to be passive. The Resolution lay some weeks before a bill was brought in, and the bill some weeks before it was called for; after the passage of the incorporating act it was taken up, and on the third reading, ordered by a small majority to be printed for consideration. The bill in its present dress proposes a tax of blank per Ct. on all taxable property for support of Teachers of the Christian Religion. Each person when he pays his tax is to name the society to which he dedicates it, and in case of refusal to do so, the tax is to be applied to the maintenance of a school in the county. As the bill stood for some time, the application in such cases was to be made by the Legislature to pious uses. In a committee of the whole it was determined by a majority of 7 or 8 that the word "Christian" should be exchanged for the word "Religious." On the report to the House the pathetic zeal of the late Governor Harrison gained a like majority for reinstating discrimination. Should the bill ever pass into a law in its present form it may and will be easily eluded. It is chiefly obnoxious on account of its dishonorable principle and dangerous tendency.

To the Honorable the GENERAL ASSEMBLY of the COMMON-
WEALTH of VIRGINIA.

A MEMORIAL and REMONSTRANCE.

The broadside George Mason had printed of Madison's "Memorial and Remonstrance against Religious Assessments" in June, 1785

To gain time, Madison supported an incorporation act for the Protestant Episcopal Church in exchange for postponement of decision on the general assessment bill. Baptists, Presbyterians, and Methodists rallied against it; the people voiced their opposition to this "alarming usurpation" in the spring elections of 1785; and in June Madison wrote his "Memorial and Remonstrance against Religious Assessments." Printed and circulated as a petition throughout the state, the argument was one of the strongest ever made for the twin principles of religious freedom and separation of Church and State.

[June, 1785]

We the subscribers.... remonstrate against the said Bill.

1.⁰ Because we hold it for a fundamental and undeniable truth "that Religion or the duty which we owe to our Creator and the manner of discharging it, can be directed only by reason and conviction, not by force or violence" [Virginia Declaration of Rights, Article 16]. The Religion then of every man must be left to the conviction and conscience of every man; and it is the right of every man to exercise it as these may dictate. This right is in its nature an unalienable right. It is unalienable, because the opinions of men, depending only on the evidence contemplated by their own minds cannot follow the dictates of other men: It is unalienable also, because what is here a right towards men, is a duty towards the Creator. It is the duty of every man to render to the Creator such homage and such only as he beleives to be acceptable to him. This duty is precedent, both in order of time and in degree of obligation, to the claims

The old capitol where the general assembly met from 1780 to 1788

Ancient Church, near Smithfield.

A Religious Encampment in a Forest.

The engravings above and opposite, from two nineteenth-century books, give a sampling of the churches in Virginia; Madison felt that some churches "instead of maintaining the purity and efficacy of Religion, have had a contrary operation."

of Civil Society. . . . We maintain therefore that in matters of Religion, no mans right is abridged by the institution of Civil Society and that Religion is wholly exempt from its cognizance. True it is, that no other rule exists, by which any question which may divide a Society, can be ultimately determined, but the will of the majority; but it is also true that the majority may trespass on the rights of the minority.

2.⁰ Because if Religion be exempt from the authority of the Society at large, still less can it be subject to that of the Legislative Body. The latter are but the creatures and vicegerents of the former. Their jurisdiction is both derivative and limited: it is limited with regard to the co-ordinate departments, more necessarily is it limited with regard to the constituents. The preservation of a free Government requires, not merely, that the metes and bounds which separate each department of power be invariably maintained: but more especially that neither of them be suffered to overleap the greater Barrier which defends the rights of the people. The Rulers who are guilty of such an encroachment, exceed the commission from which they derive their authority, and are Tyrants. The people who submit to it are governed by laws made neither by themselves nor by an authority derived from them, and are slaves.

3.⁰ Because it is proper to take alarm at the first experiment on our liberties. We hold this prudent jealousy to be the first duty of citizens, and one of the noblest characteristics of the late Revolution. . . . Who does not see that the same authority which can establish Christianity, in exclusion of all other Religions, may establish with the same ease any particular sect of Christians, in exclusion of all other Sects? that the same authority which can force a citizen to contribute three pence only of his property for the support of any one establishment, may force him to conform to any other establishment in all cases whatsoever?

4.⁰ Because the Bill violates that equality which ought to be the basis of every law, and which is more indispensable, in proportion as the validity or expediency of any law is more liable to be impeached. If "all men are by nature equally free and independent" [Virginia Declaration, Article 1], all men are to be considered as entering into Society on equal conditions; as relinquishing no more, and therefore retaining no less, one than another, of their natural rights. Above all are they to be considered as retaining an "equal title to the free exercise of Religion according to the dictates of Conscience" [Article 16]. Whilst we assert for ourselves a freedom to embrace, to profess and to observe the Religion which we believe to be of divine origin, we cannot deny an equal freedom to those whose minds have not yet yielded to the evidence which has convinced us. If this freedom be abused, it is an offence against God, not against man: To God, therefore, not to man, must an account of it be rendered....

5.⁰ Because the Bill implies either that the Civil Magistrate is a competent Judge of Religious Truth; or that he may employ Religion as an engine of Civil policy. The first is an arrogant pretension falsified by the contradictory opinions of Rulers in all ages, and throughout the world; the second an unhallowed perversion of the means of salvation.

6.⁰ Because the establishment proposed by the Bill is not requisite for the support of the Christion Religion. To say that it is, is a contradiction to the Christian Religion itself, for every page of it disavows a dependence on the powers of this world: it is a contradiction to fact; for it is known that this Religion both existed and flourished, not only without the support of human laws, but in spite of every opposition from them; and not only during the period of miraculous aid, but long after it had been left to its own evidence and the ordinary care of Providence; nay, it is a contradiction in terms, for a Religion not invented by human policy, must have pre existed and been supported, before it was established by human policy....

7.⁰ Because experience witnesseth that ecclesiastical establishments, instead of maintaining the purity and efficacy of Religion, have had a contrary operation. During almost fifteen centuries has the legal establishment of Christianity been on trial. What have been its fruits? more or less in all places, pride and indolence in the Clergy, ignorance and servility in the laity; in both, superstition, bigotry and persecution. Enquire of the Teachers of Christianity for the ages in which it appeared in its greatest lustre; those of every sect, point to the ages prior to its incorporation with Civil policy. Propose a restoration of this primitive state, in which its Teachers depended on the voluntary rewards of their flocks, many

BOTH: *Old Churches and Families of Virginia*
BY WILLIAM MEADE, 1857

ST. PAUL'S CHURCH, NORFOLK, VA.

ST. JOHN'S CHURCH, RICHMOND, VA.

of them predict its downfall. On which side ought their testimony to have greatest weight, when for or when against their interest?

8.⁰ Because the establishment in question is not necessary for the support of Civil Government.... If Religion be not within the cognizance of Civil Government, how can its legal establishment be necessary to Civil Government? What influence in fact have ecclesiastical establishments had on Civil Society? In some instances they have been seen to erect a spiritual tyranny on the ruins of the Civil authority: in many instances they have been seen upholding the thrones of political tyranny: in no instance have they been seen the guardians of the liberties of the people. Rulers who wished to subvert the public liberty, may have found an established Clergy convenient auxiliaries. A just Government instituted to secure & perpetuate it needs them not. Such a government will be best supported by protecting every Citizen in the enjoyment of his Religion with the same equal hand which protects his person and his property; by neither invading the equal rights of any Sect, nor suffering any Sect to invade those of another.

9.⁰ Because the proposed establishment is a departure from that generous policy, which, offering an asylum to the persecuted and oppressed of every Nation and Religion, promised a lustre to our country, and an accession to the number of its citizens. What a melancholy mark is the Bill of sudden degeneracy! Instead of holding forth an asylum to the persecuted, it is itself a signal of persecution. It degrades from the equal rank of Citizens, all those whose opinions in Religion do not bend to those of the Legislative authority. Distant as it may be in its present form from the Inquisition, it differs from it only in degree. The one is the first step, the other the last in the career of intolerance.

An ACT *for establishing* RELIGIOUS FREEDOM; *passed in the assembly of Virginia in the beginning of the year* 1786.

WELL aware that Almighty God hath created the mind free ; that all attempts to influence it by temporal punishments or burthens , or by civil incapacitations , tend only to beget habits of hypocrisy and meanness , and are a departure from the plan of the Holy Author of our religion , who , being Lord both of body and mind , yet chose not to propagate it by coercions on either , as was in his Almighty power to do ; that the impious presumption of legislators and rulers civil , as well as ecclesiastical who , being themselves but fallible and uninspired men , have assumed dominion over the faith of others , setting up their own opinions and modes of thinking as the only true and infallible , and as such endeavouring to impose them on others , hath established and maintained false religions over the greatest part of the world , and through all time : That to compel a man to furnish contributions of money for the propagation of opinions which he disbelieves , is sinful and tyrannical ; that even the forcing him to support this or that teacher of his own religious persuasion , is depriving him of the comfortable liberty of giving his contributions to the particular pastor whose

Printed text of Jefferson's Act for Establishing Religious Freedom

Six additional points, fifteen in all, completed Madison's argument. Meanwhile, Patrick Henry had been elected governor, thus depriving proponents of the assessment bill of their chief spokesman in the legislature. When the assembly convened in the fall, the bill died quietly. Madison capped the victory with passage of Jefferson's bill written in 1779 legalizing religious freedom. Thus was "extinguished forever the ambitious hope of making laws for the human mind," he wrote with justifiable pride to his friend in Paris. Decades later it still seemed to him, as it always did to Jefferson, one of his best achievements. "It was the Universal opinion of the Century preceding the last," he wrote in 1819, "that Civil Government could not stand without the prop of a Religious establishment, and that the Christion religion itself, would perish if not supported by a legal provision for its Clergy. The experience of Virginia conspicuously corroborates the disproof of both opinions." Jefferson was indebted to Madison for taking up the unfinished work of the revisal and, of course, shared his disappointment that more was not accomplished. After leaving the assembly in 1786, Madison reported the final outcome.

One of Madison's own horses had been stolen at Williamsburg in 1779; he put this ad in the Virginia Gazette.

New York Feby. 15th. 1787

My last was from Richmond on the 4th. of December, and contained a sketch of our legislative proceedings prior to that date. The principal proceedings of subsequent date relate as nearly as I can recollect 1st. to a rejection of the Bill on crimes and punishments, which after being altered so as to remove most of the objections as was thought, was lost by a single vote. The rage against Horse stealers had a great influence on the fate of the Bill. Our old bloody code is by this event fully restored, the prerogative of conditional pardon having been taken from the Executive by a Judgment of the Court of Appeals, and the temporary law granting it to them having expired and been left unrevived. I am not without hope that the rejected bill will find a more favorable disposition in the next Assembly. 2dly. to the bill for diffusing knowledge. It went through two readings by a small majority and was not pushed to a third one. The necessity of a systematic provision on the subject was admitted on all hands. The objections against that particular provision were   1. the expence, which was alleged to exceed the ability of the people.   2. the difficulty of executing it in the present sparse settlement of the Country.   3. the inequality of the districts as contended by the Western members. The latter objection is of little weight and might have been easily removed if it has been urged in an early stage of the discussion. The bill now rests on the same footing with the other unpassed bills in the Revisal. 3dly. to the Revisal at large. It was found impossible to get thro' the system at the late session for several reasons.   1. the changes which have taken place since its compilement, in our affairs and our laws, particularly those relating to our Courts, called for changes in some of the bills which could not be made with safety

In New York Congress held its sessions at the old City Hall, which later became Federal Hall.

by the Legislature. 2. the pressure of other business which tho' of less importance in itself, yet was more interesting for the moment. 3. the alarm excited by an approach toward the Execution Bill which subjects land to the payment of debts. This bill could not have been carried, was too important to be lost, and even too difficult to be amended without destroying its texture. 4. the danger of passing the Repealing Bill at the end of the Code before the operation of the various amendments &c. made by the Assembly could be leisurely examined by competent Judges. Under these circumstances it was thought best to hand over the residue of the work to our successors, and in order to have it made compleat, Mr. Pendleton, Mr. Wythe and Blair were appointed a Committee to amend the unpassed bills and also to prepare a supplemental revision of the laws which have been passed since the original work was executed.

Madison had meanwhile returned to Congress, then meeting in New York. Even when the laboring oar was in Virginia, his mind was on the deepening crisis of the Confederation. Nationalists like himself, anxious to stiffen the arm of Congress, had shifted their aim from the tax power to the power to regulate commerce, though the latter might encompass the former. Britain had lost an empire but she seemed determined to hold her former colonies in commercial bondage. Old markets in the West Indies were closed to the Americans; British ships took the lion's share of the carrying trade; and merchants and planters found no escape from the web of British credit. The signs of economic depression—money scarcity, falling prices, stagnation of trade—became evident in 1784. Commercial discontents produced a wave of legislation, especially in the eastern states, in retaliation against British and in favor of American trade. But thirteen separate states, each pursuing its own commercial interest, could not secure the national interest. Congress in 1784 had asked the legislatures for power to enact a uniform navigation law. It floundered, and Congress backed away from a proposed amendment vesting full power to regulate commerce in the Confederation. Madison thought such power essential. It was not only subservience to Britain that he feared but jealousies and dissensions among the states with their discordant economic interests—commercial, agricultural, manufacturing—which England would surely exploit. He expressed himself to James Monroe, then a Virginia delegate in Congress.

Orange [Virginia,] Aug: 7. 1785

Viewing in the abstract the question whether the power of regulating trade, to a certain degree at least, ought to be vested in Congress, it appears to me not to admit of a doubt, but that it should be decided in the affirmative. If it be necessary to regulate trade at all, it surely is necessary to lodge the power, where trade can be regulated with effect, and experience has confirmed what reason foresaw, that it can never be so regulated by the States acting in their separate capacities. They can no more exercise this power separately, than they could separately carry on war, or separately form treaties of alliance or Commerce. The nature of the thing therefore proves the former power, no less than the latter, to be within the reason of the fœderal Constitution. Much indeed is it to be wished, as I conceive, that no regulation of trade, that is to say, no restrictions or imposts whatever, were necessary. A perfect freedom is the System which would be my choice. But before such a system will be eligible perhaps for the U.S. they must be out of debt; before it will be attainable, all other nations must concur in it. Whilst any one of these imposes on our Vessels seamen &c in their ports, clogs from which they exempt their own, we must either retort the distinction, or renounce not merely a just profit, but our only defense against the danger which may most easily beset us. Are we not at this moment under this very alternative? The policy of G.B. (to say nothing of other nations) has shut against us the channels without which our trade with her must be a losing one; and she has consequently the triumph, as we have the chagrin, of seeing accomplished her prophetic threats, that our independence, should forfeit commercial advantages for which it would not recompence us with any new channels of trade. What is to be done? Must we remain passive victims to foreign politics; or shall we exert the lawful means which our independence has put into our hands, extorting redress? The very question would be an affront to every Citizen who loves his Country. What then are those means? Retaliating regulations of trade only. How are these to be effectuated? Only by harmony in the measures of the States. How is this harmony to be obtained? Only by an acquiescence of all the States in the opinion of a reasonable majority. If Congress as they are now constituted, can not be trusted with the power of digesting and enforcing this opinion, let them be otherwise constituted: let their numbers be encreased, let them be chosen

Madison's notes for the speech on federal regulation of commerce that he made in Congress in 1785

Lower New York from the harbor

oftener, and let their period of service be shortned; or if any better medium than Congress can be proposed, by which the wills of the States may be concentered, let it be substituted; or lastly let no regulation of trade adopted by Congress be in force untill it shall have been ratified by a certain proportion of the States. But let us not sacrifice the end to the means: let us not rush on certain ruin in order to avoid a possible danger. I conceive it to be of great importance that the defects of the foederal system should be amended, not only because such amendments will make it better answer the purpose for which it was instituted, but because I apprehend danger to its very existence from a continuance of defects which expose a part if not the whole of the empire to severe distress. The suffering part, even when the minor part, can not long respect a Government which is too feeble to protect their interest; But when the suffering part come to be the major part, and they despair of seeing a protecting energy given to the General Government, from what motives is their allegiance to be any longer expected. Should G.B. persist in the machinations which distress us, and seven or eight of the States be hindered by the others from obtaining relief by foederal means, I own, I tremble at the anti-foederal expedients into which the former may be tempted.

Considerations such as these led to the movement for full-scale constitutional reform. That the initiative should have come from Virginia, a staple-producing state, was surprising. But on the invitation of the Virginia assembly in 1786, nine states agreed to send delegates to a commercial convention. Madison, who would be a delegate, explained the plan to Jefferson with more than a trace of despair for its success.

Orange [Virginia,] March 18th. 1786
A Quorum of the deputies appointed by the Assembly for a Commercial Convention had a meeting at Richmond shortly after I left it, and the Attorney [General, Edmund Randolph] tells me, it has been agreed to propose Annapolis for the place, and the first Monday in Sepr. for the time of holding the Convention. It was thought prudent to avoid the neighbourhood of Congress, and the large Commercial towns in order to disarm the adversaries to the object of insinuations of influence from either of these quarters. I have not heard what opinion is enter-

tained of this project at New York, nor what reception it has found in any of the States. It if should come to nothing, it will I fear confirm G.B. and all the world in the belief that we are not to be respected, nor apprehended as a nation in matters of Commerce. The States are every day giving proofs that separate regulations are more likely to set them by the ears, than to attain the common object. When Massts. set on foot a retaliation of the policy of G. B. Connecticut declared her ports free. N. Jersey served N. York in the same way. And Delaware I am told has lately followed the example in opposition to the commercial plans of Penna. A miscarriage of this attempt to unite the States in some effectual plan will have another effect of a serious nature. It will dissipate every prospect of drawing a steady revenue from our imports either directly into the federal treasury, or indirectly thro' the treasuries of the commercial States, and of consequence the former must depend for supplies solely on annual requisitions, and the latter on direct taxes from the property of the Country. That these dependencies are in an alarming degree fallacious is put by experience out of all question. The payments from the States under the calls of Congress have in no year borne any proportion to the public wants. . . . Another unhappy effect of a continuance of the present anarchy of our commerce will be a continuance of the unfavorable balance on it, which by draining us of our metals furnishes pretexts for the pernicious substitution of paper money, for indulgences to debtors, for postponements of taxes. In fact most of our political evils may be traced up to our commercial ones, as most of our moral may to our political. The lessons which the mercantile interests of Europe have received from late experience will probably check their propensity to credit us beyond our resources, and so far the evil of an unfavorable balance will correct itself. But the Merchants of G.B. if no others will continue to credit us at least as far as our remittances can be obtained, and that is far enough to perpetuate our difficulties unless the luxurious propensity of our own people can be otherwise checked.

This view of our situation presents the proposed Convention as a remedial experiment which ought to command every assent; but if it be a just view it is one which assuredly will not be taken by all even of those

Pictorial Field Book of the Revolution BY BENSON J. LOSSING, 1852

The State House at Annapolis

Diego de Gardoqui

whose intentions are good. I consider the event therefore as extremely uncertain, or rather, considering that the States must first agree to the proposition for sending deputies, that these must agree in a plan to be sent back to the States, and that these again must agree unanimously in a ratification of it. I almost despair of success. It is necessary however that something should be tried and if this be not the best possible expedient, it is the best that could possibly be carried thro' the Legislature here. And if the present crisis cannot effect unanimity, from what future concurrence of circumstances is it to be expected?

When the convention met in September, only five states were actually represented. The delegates threw away the script and addressed Congress to call a new convention at Philadelphia in May, 1787, for the purpose of discussing all matters requisite "to render the constitution of the Federal Government adequate to the exigencies of the Union." Congress complied, and although the convention was called "for the sole and express purpose of revising the Articles of Confederation," politicians of Madison's persuasion had converted the specter of commercial disaster into a glorious opportunity to create a truly national government.

Fears outran hopes in the later months of 1786, however. Almost at the time of the Annapolis Convention, Congress authorized Secretary of Foreign Affairs John Jay, then negotiating with the Spanish minister, Don Diego de Gardoqui, to suspend the American demand for navigation of the Mississippi in exchange for a treaty of commerce with Spain. Madison was outraged. For years he had viewed the navigation of the Mississippi as essential to the future of the West and of the Union. What faith could westerners place in a government that bargained away their most vital interest? Indeed what confidence could any state or section have in a government that so cavalierly sacrificed one part to gratify another? Madison communicated his indignation over the Jay-Gardoqui proposal to Monroe.

Orange [Virginia,] June 21st. 1786.
Your favor of the 31st. ult. did not come to hand till two days ago. As I expected to see you in a short time, I will suspend the full communication of my ideas on the subject of it till I have that pleasure. I cannot however forbear in the mean time expressing my amazement that a thought should be entertained of surrendering the Mississippi and of guarantying the possessions of Spain [in] America. In the first place has not Virga., have not Congress themselves, and the Ministers of Congs. by their

orders, asserted the right of those who live on the waters of the Missisipi to use it as the high road given by nature to the sea. This being the case, have Congress any more authority to say that the western citizens of Virga. shall not pass thro the capes of Missisipi than to say that her eastern citizens shall pass thro the capes Henry and Charles. It should be remembered that the United States are not now extricating themselves from war, a crisis which often knows no law but that of necessity. The measure in question would be a voluntary barter in time of profound peace of the rights of one part of the empire to the interests of another part. What would Massachusets say to a proposition for ceding to Britain her right of fishery as the price of some stipulations in fa[vor] of to[ba]cco.

Again can there be a more shortsighted or dishonorable policy than to concur with Spain in frustrating the benev- olent views of nature to sell the affections of our ultra- montane brethr[en], to depreciate the richest fund we possess, to distrust an ally [France] whom we know to be able to befriend us and to have an interest in doing it against the only na[tion] whose enmity we can dread, and at the same time to court by the most precious sacri- fices the alliance of a nation whose impotency is notorious, who has given no proof of regard for us and the genius of whose government religion & manners unfit them, of all the nations in Christendom for a coalition with this country. Can any thing too, as you well observe, be more unequal than a stipulation which is to open all our ports to her and some only and those the least valuable of hers to us; and which places the commercial freedom of our ports against the fettered regulations of those in Spain. I always thought the stipulation with France and Holland of the privileges of the most favoured nation as unequal, and only to be justified by the influence which the treaties could not fail to have on the event of the war. A stipulation putting Spanish subjects on the same foot- ing with our own citizens is carrying the evil still farther without the same pretext for it; and is the more to be dreaded, as by making her the most favoured nation it would let in the other nations with whom we are now connected to the same privileges, whenever they may find it their interest to make the same compensation for them whilst we have not a reciprocal right to force them

Madison is listed as one of three delegates from Virginia to the Annapolis Convention of 1786.

James Monroe circa 1786

into such an arrangement in case our interest should dictate it. A guaranty is if possible still more objectionable. If it be insidious we plunge ourselves into infamy. If sincere, into obligations the extent of which cannot easily be determined. In either case we get farther into the labyrinth of European politics from which we ought religiously to keep ourselves as free as possible. And what is to be gained by such a rash step? Will any man in his senses pretend that our territory needs such a safeguard, or that if it were in danger, it is the arm of Spain that is to save it. Viewing the matter in this light I cannot but flatter myself, that if the attempt you apprehend should be made, it will be rejected with becoming indignation.

Because of the Jay-Gardoqui affair, Madison hastened to return to Congress in 1787. So vehement was the sectional opposition, however, that Jay himself quietly shelved the project. Congress was in a pitiable state, much worse than when Madison had left it three years before. To his fears of congressional collapse and disunion were added dreads of social disorder. The news of Shays' Rebellion met him in New York where Congress convened. He could not pass off this insurgency in Massachusetts with the philosophical aplomb of his friend Jefferson who remarked: "I like a little rebellion now and then. It is like a storm in the atmosphere." No, Shays' Rebellion, along with the rage for paper money in states such as Rhode Island, underscored the need to recast the balance between liberty and authority. For the present, Congress could do nothing but wait the turn of events in Philadelphia. Madison summed up the uncertain prospect for Edmund Pendleton.

New York Feby. 24. 1787.
What the issue of it [the Federal Convention] will be is among the other arcana of futurity and nearly as inscrutable as any of them. In general I find men of reflection much less sanguine as to a new than despondent as to the present System. Indeed the present System neither has nor deserves advocates; and if some very strong props are not applied will quickly tumble to the ground. No money is paid into the public Treasury; no respect is paid to the federal authority. Not a single State complies with the requisitions, several pass them over in silence, and some positively reject them. The payments ever since the peace have been decreasing, and of late fall short even of the pittance necessary for the Civil list of the

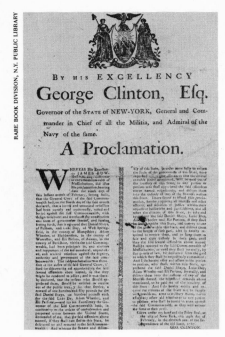

New York Governor George Clinton urged the capture of Daniel Shays.

Confederacy. It is not possible that a Government can last long under these circumstances. If the approaching Convention should not agree on some remedy, I am persuaded that some very different arrangement will ensue. The late turbulent scenes in Massts. & infamous ones in Rhode Island, have done inexpressible injury to the republican character in that part of the U. States; and a propensity towards Monarchy is said to have been produced by it in some leading minds. The bulk of the people will probably prefer the lesser evil of a partition of the Union into three more practicable and energetic governments. The latter idea I find after long confinement to individual speculations & private circles, is beginning to shew itself in the Newspapers. But tho' it is a lesser evil, it is so great a one that I hope the danger of it will rouse all the real friends to the Revolution to exert themselves in favor of such an organization of the Confederacy, as will perpetuate the Union, and redeem the honor of the Republican name.

Madison had prepared himself well for the work that lay before him in Philadelphia. Quite aside from his practical experience, he had over the last three years read widely in the history and theory of government both ancient and modern. This was not an academic exercise; it was reading with a clear political purpose in view. With knowledge and insight drawn from the whole range of human experience, he believed that government might be made a science and that man might control his political destiny. Among his contemporaries none fretted as much as he over the theoretical basis of federal government. The failures of the Confederation doubtless caused him to toss and turn when everybody else at Montpelier was sleeping soundly. Poring over the books Jefferson sent him from Paris, Madison searched the history of confederations in order to discover the solution for America. The lesson of the past was always the same: weakness at the center led to jealousies, dissensions, and disorders in and among the members. Sometime before the Federal Convention he digested what he had learned in a series of "Notes on Ancient and Modern Confederacies." Drawing on this rich fund of analogy, he then wrote a paper commonly entitled "Vices of the Political System of the United States."

[April, 1787]

1. Failure of the States to comply with the Constitutional requisitions.... This evil has been so fully experienced both during the war and since the peace, results so naturally from the number and independent authority

of the States and has been so uniformly exemplified in every similar Confederacy, that it may be considered as not less radically and permanently inherent in, than it is fatal to the object of, the present System.

2. Encroachments by the States on the federal authority.... Examples of this are numerous and repetitions may be foreseen in almost every case where any favorite object of a State shall present a temptation. Among these examples are the wars and Treaties of Georgia with the Indians, ... the troops raised and to be kept up by Massts.

3. Violations of the law of nations and of treaties.... From the number of Legislatures, the sphere of life from which most of their members are taken, and the circumstances under which their legislative business is carried on, irregularities of this kind most frequently happen. Accordingly not a year has passed without instances of them in some one or other of the States. The Treaty of peace, the treaty with France, the treaty with Holland have each been violated....

As yet foreign powers have not been rigorous in animadverting on us. This moderation however cannot be mistaken for a permanent partiality to our faults, or a permanent security agst. those disputes with other nations, which being among the greatest of public calamitees, it ought to be least in the power of any part of the Community to bring on the whole

4. Trespasses of the States on the rights of each other.... These are alarming symptoms, and may be daily apprehended as we are admonished by daily experience. See the law of Virginia restricting foreign vessels to certain ports, of Maryland in favor of vessels belonging to her own citizens....

Paper money, instalments of debts, occlusion of Courts, making property a legal tender, may likewise be deemed aggressions on the rights of other States....

The practice of many States in restricting the commercial intercourse with other States, and putting their productions and manufactures on the same footing with those of foreign nations, though not contrary to the federal articles, is certainly adverse to the spirit of the Union, and tends to beget retaliating regulations, not less expensive & vexatious in themselves than they are destructive of the general harmony.

5. Want of concert in matters where common in-

terest requires it. . . . This defect is strongly illustrated in the state of our commercial affairs. How much has the national dignity, interest, and revenue suffered from this cause? Instances of inferior moment are the want of uniformity in the laws concerning naturalezation & literary property; of provision for national seminaries, for grants of incorporation for national purposes, for canals and other works of general utility, wch. may at present be defeated by the perverseness of particular states whose concurrence is necessary.

6. Want of general Guaranty to the States of their Constitutions & laws against internal violence. . . . The confederation is silent on this point and therefore by the second article the hands of the federal authority are tied according to Republican Theory. . . .

7. Want of sanction to the laws, and of coercion in the government of the Confederacy. . . . A sanction is essential to the idea of law, as coercion is to that of Government. The federal system being destitute of both, wants the great vital principles of a Political Cons[ti]tution. Under the form of such a constitution, it is in fact nothing more than a treaty of amity and of commerce and of alliance, between so many independent and sovereign states. . . .

8. Want of ratification by the people of the articles of Confederation. . . . In some of the States the Confederation is recognized by, and forms a part of the constitution. In others however it has received no other sanction than that of the Legislative authority. From this defect two evils result: 1. Whenever a law of a state happens to be repugnant to an act of Congress . . . it will be at least questionable whether the former must not prevail, and as the question must be decided by the Tribunals of the State, they will be most likely to lean on the side of the State.

2. As far as the Union of the States is to be regarded as a league of sovereign powers, and not as a political Constitution by virtue of which they are become one sovereign power, so far it seems to follow from the doctrine of compacts that a breach of any of the articles of the confederation by any of the parties to it, absolves the other parties from their respective obligations, and gives them a right if they chuse to exert it, of dissolving the union altogether.

[Madison went on to describe still other evils: multiplicity of laws in the states, mutability of laws, injustice of laws. The fatal cause of injustice lay in the selfishness of different interests and factions in the community. Neither morality nor religion offered an adequate check. In "little republics" there was all the more danger that "a common passion or interest" would unite a majority against the rest of the people. The solution was to be found, said Madison with a flash of insight, in an "enlargement of the sphere" of government.]

If an enlargement of the sphere is found to lessen the insecurity of private rights, it is not because the impulse of a common interest or passion is less predominant in this case with the majority; but because a common interest or passion is less apt to be felt and the requisite combinations less easy to be formed by a great than by a small number. The Society becomes broken into a greater variety of interests, of pursuits, and of passions, which check each other, whilst those who may feel a common sentiment have less opportunity of communication and concert. It may be inferred that the inconveniences of popular States contrary to the prevailing Theory, are in proportion not to the extent, but to the narrowness of their limits.

The great desideratum in Government is such a modification of the Sovereignty as will render it sufficiently neutral between the different interests and factions, to controul one part of the Society from invading the rights of another, and at the same time sufficiently controuled itself, from setting up an interest adverse to that of the whole Society. . . .

An auxiliary desideratum for the melioration of the Republican form is such a process of elections as will most certainly extract from the mass of the Society the purest and noblest characters which it contains; such as will at once feel most strongly the proper motives to pursue the end of their appointment, and be most capable to devise the proper means of attaining it.

So formidable had the vices become in Madison's eyes that he made a quantum leap from the confederate pattern of government, in which the states were the sovereign members, to a government of "national supremacy" founded on the authority of the people and armed with great powers. He sketched his ideas—a sketch of what would become the Virginia Plan—in a letter to General Washington a month before the convention met in Philadelphia. It was, as he confessed, a "radical" program. Indeed, it amounted to a repudiation of the centrifugal republicanism of the revolutionary era.

New York April 16th. 1787.

I have been honored with your letter of the 31. March, and find with much pleasure that your views of the reform which ought to be pursued by the Convention, give a sanction to those I entertained. Temporising applications will dishonor the Councils which propose them, and may foment the internal malignity of the disease, at the same time that they produce an ostensible paliation of it. Radical attempts, although unsuccessful, will at least justify the authors of them.

Having been lately led to revolve the subject which is to undergo the discussion of the Convention, and formed in my mind *some* outlines of a new system, I take the liberty of submitting them without apology, to your eye.

Conceiving that an individual independence of the States is utterly irreconcileable with their aggregate sovereignty; and that a consolidation of the whole into one simple republic would be as inexpedient as it is unattainable, I have sought for some middle ground, which may at once support a due supremacy of the national authority, and not exclude the local authorities wherever they can be subordinately useful.

I would propose as the ground-work that a change be made in the principle of representation. According to the present form of the Union in which the intervention of the States is in all great cases necessary to effectuate the measures of Congress, an equality of suffrage, does not destroy the inequality of importance, in the several members. No one will deny that Virginia and Massachusetts have more weight and influence both within and without Congress than Delaware or Rhode Island. Under a system which would operate in many essential points without the intervention of the State Legislatures, the case would be materially altered. A vote in the national Councils from Delaware, would then have the same effect and value as one from the largest State in the Union. I am ready to believe that such a change would not be attended with much difficulty. A majority of the States, and those

Mezzotint of George Washington by Charles Willson Peale, dated 1787

107

Cd. Fes. for Vol.1.
Dear Sir.

New York April 16th 1787.

I have been honored with your letter of the 31. March, and find with much pleasure that your views of the reform which ought to be pursued by the Convention, give a sanction to those I entertained. Temporising applications will dishonor the Councils which proposed them, and may foment the internal malignity of the disease, at the same time that they produce an ostensible palliation of it. Radical attempts, although unsuccessful, will at least justify the authors of them.

Having been lately led to revolve the subject which is to undergo the discussion of the Convention, and formed in my mind some outlines of a new system, I take the liberty of submitting them without apology, to your eye.

Conceiving that an individual independence of the States is utterly irreconcilable with their aggregate sovereignty; and that a consolidation of the whole into one simple republic would be as inexpedient as it is unattainable, I have sought for some middle ground, which may at once support a due supremacy of the national authority, and not exclude the local authorities wherever they can be subordinately useful.

I would propose as the ground-work that a change be made in the principle of representation. According to the present form of the Union in which the intervention of the States is in all great cases necessary to effectuate the measures of Congress, an equality of suffrage, does not destroy the inequality

Genl. Washington

Madison's letter to Washington sketching his ideas for a "radical" program to present at the coming Constitutional Convention

of greatest influence, will regard it as favorable to them. To the northern States it will be recommended by their present populousness; to the Southern by their expected advantage in this respect. The lesser States must in every event yield to the predominant will. But the consideration which particularly urges a change in the representation is that it will obviate the principal objections of the larger States to the necessary concessions of power.

I would propose next that in addition to the present federal powers, the national Government should be armed with positive and compleat authority in all cases which require uniformity; such as the regulation of trade, including the right of taxing both exports and imports, the fixing the terms and forms of naturalization &c. &c.

Over and above this positive power, a negative *in all cases whatsoever* on the legislative acts of the States, as heretofore exercised by the Kingly prerogative, appears to me to be absolutely necessary, and to be the least possible encroachment on the State jurisdictions. Without this defensive power every positive power that can be given on paper will be evaded or defeated. The States will continue to invade the national jurisdiction, to violate treaties and the law of Nations and to harass each other with rival and spiteful measures dictated by mistaken views of interest. Another happy effect of this prerogative would be its controul on the internal vicissitudes of State policy, and the aggressions of interested majorities on the rights of minorities and of individuals. The great desideratum which has not yet been found for Republican Governments, seems to be some disinterested and dispassionate umpire in disputes between different passions and interests in the State. The majority who alone have the right of decision, have frequently an interest real or supposed in abusing it. . . . Might not the national prerogative here suggested be found sufficiently disinterested for the decision of local questions of policy, whilst it would itself be sufficiently restrained from the pursuit of interests adverse to those of the whole Society? There has not been any moment since the peace at which the representatives of the Union would have given an assent to paper money or any other measure of a kindred nature.

The national supremacy ought also to be extended as I conceive to the Judiciary departments. If those who are to expound and apply the laws, are connected by their interests and their oaths with the particular States wholly, and not with the Union, the participation of the Union in the making of the laws may be possibly rendered unavailing. It seems at least necessary that the oaths of the Judges should include a fidelity to the general as well as local Constitution, and that an appeal should be to some national tribunals in all cases to which foreigners or inhabitants of other States may be parties. The admiralty jurisdiction seems to fall entirely within the purview of the national Government.

The national supremacy in the Executive departments is liable to some difficulty, unless the officers administering them could be made appointable by the supreme Government. The Militia ought certainly to be placed in some form or other under the authority which is entrusted with the general protection and defence.

A Government composed of such extensive powers should be well organized and balanced. The Legislative department might be divided into two branches; one of them chosen every   years by the people at large, or by the Legislatures; the other to consist of fewer members, and to go out in such a rotation as always to leave in office a large majority of old members. Perhaps the negative on the laws might be most conveniently exercised by this branch. As a further check, a council of revision including the great ministerial officers might be superadded.

A national Executive must also be provided. I have scarcely ventured as yet to form my own opinion either of the manner in which it ought to be constituted or of the authorities with which it ought to be cloathed.

An article should be inserted expressly guarantying the tranquility of the States against internal as well as external dangers.

In like manner the right of coercion should be expressly declared. With the resources of commerce in hand, the national administration might always find means of exerting it either by sea or land; But the difficulty & awkwardness of operating by force on the collective will of a State, render it particularly desirable that the necessity of it might be precluded. Perhaps the negative on the laws might create such a mutuality of dependence between the general and particular authorities, as to answer this purpose. Or perhaps some defined objects of taxation might be submitted along with commerce, to the general authority.

To give a new system its proper validity and energy, a ratification must be obtained from the people, and not merely from the ordinary authority of the Legislatures. This will be the more essential as inroads on the *existing Constitutions* of the States will be unavoidable.

In sum, this man so often portrayed as mild, timid, and the soul of prudence struck out for Independence Hall with boldness in his eyes and a prescription for radical reform in his pocket.

A Picture Portfolio

Man from Montpelier

A New and Accurate
MAP OF
VIRGINIA
Wherein most of the
COUNTIES
are laid down from
ACTUAL SURVEYS.
With
A Concise Account of the
Number of
Inhabitants, the Trade, Soil, and Produce
of that
PROVINCE.
By JOHN HENRY.
Engraved by Thomas Jefferys Geographer to the KING.

HOME OF A LIFETIME

For most of his eighty-five full and productive years, James Madison called home a plantation in the beautiful hill country of Orange County, Virginia. Over the years his father had built it into a splendid estate, which Madison, as the eldest son, inherited in 1801. In the detail of the 1770 map at left, drawn by John Henry—the father of another of Virginia's most famous sons, Patrick Henry—Orange County can be seen just to the southeast of the magnificent Blue Ridge Mountains which cut diagonally across the top left corner. The Madison house, perched on the side of a mountain of its own, had a fine view of the Blue Ridge some thirty miles away across broad meadows and sweeping forests. When Madison was about ten, the family moved from a simple wooden house to the handsome brick mansion below that they were building nearby. Madison made many improvements to the house over the years and first called it Montpelier in the late 1790s. When the Baroness Hyde de Neuville, wife of the French Minister to the United States, painted this charming watercolor in 1818, the classic portico designed by Thomas Jefferson, Madison's closest friend and Virginia neighbor, had long since been added and the two flanking wings completed.

EARLY INFLUENCES

Madison's mother, Nelly Conway Madison, and his father, James Madison, Sr., both came from families who had decided early to leave Virginia's Tidewater region and settle in the sparsely inhabited area to the west known as the Piedmont. The two families prospered there and James Madison, Sr., became as prominent locally as his son was to become nationally. Of the Madisons' twelve children, eleven are indicated on the bottom line of the family tree James Madison, Jr., drew sometime between 1813 and 1819 (right); another son lived for only one day. Young "Jemmy" was exceptionally fortunate in his schooling. In 1762, and for five years thereafter, he was sent away to a school run by Donald Robertson, of whom Madison has been quoted as saying: "All that I have been in my life I owe largely to that man." Surviving among Madison's papers is a copybook kept during those school years. Two of its 102 pages are reproduced at far right, showing Madison's youthful doodle of a human face in the center of Copernicus's solar system and a page of sophisms copied in a careful hand. For two more years he was tutored at home, along with his brothers and sisters, by the Reverend Thomas Martin, the new rector of the local church and a graduate of the College of New Jersey.

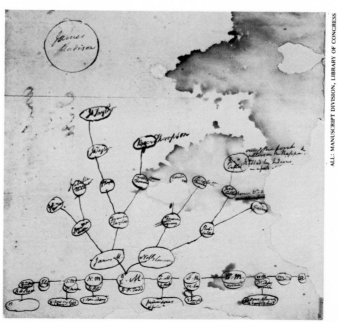

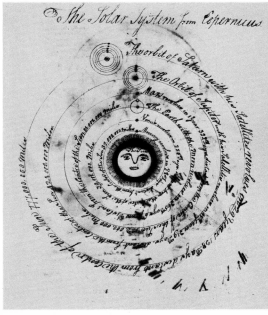

The Solar System from Copernicus

116

NORTH TO COLLEGE

Unlike many young Virginians of his day, Madison did not go to the College of William and Mary in Williamsburg but instead headed north to the College of New Jersey in Princeton, where the moral and religious tone was more to the liking of his father and his recent tutor. There he found an imposing building, Nassau Hall (below), where more than a hundred students slept, dined, studied, and went to church under one roof. The president, whose house is at right in this old print, was an impressive Scottish Presbyterian minister, Dr. John Witherspoon (left). His advice to his students for conduct in public life was succinct: "Lads, ne'er do ye speak unless ye ha' something to say, and when ye are done, be sure and leave off." Madison worked extremely hard, to the great detriment of his health, and completed the four-year course in two. He received his diploma (far left) in the fall of 1771 but stayed another six months for further study with Dr. Witherspoon.

of the President's House in New Jersey

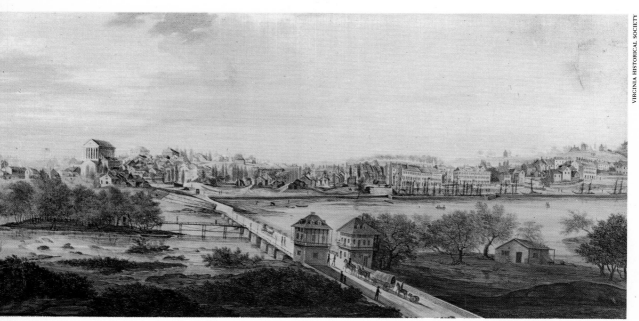

VIRGINIA LEGISLATOR

For several years following his graduation from Princeton, Madison remained at Montpelier regaining his health and reading voraciously. Politics soon became his main interest, fanned by the events leading to the Revolution. In 1776 when he was first elected to the Virginia Convention, he visited Williamsburg, the small but elegant capital seen at right in a French map of the period. Madison lived with his second cousin, the Reverend James Madison, president of William and Mary, in the charming house to the right of the college buildings in the view at top. In 1780 the capital was moved to Richmond. When Madison served there as an Orange County delegate to the Virginia General Assembly for four sessions beginning in 1784, Mayo Bridge, shown in the 1822 watercolor above, had not yet been built and the James River was crossed by ferryboat.

39.ᵉ Camp à Williams'burg le 26. Septembre, 7. miles de Arche's hupe
le 27. Sejour.

Queens - Creek

chemin d'habitations

chemin de York

chemin Burwell

chemin d'habitations Rochambeau

Williams'burg

Capitole

casernement

Maisons des Colleges

Collége

Collége Landing

Collége Creek

Raich mill's

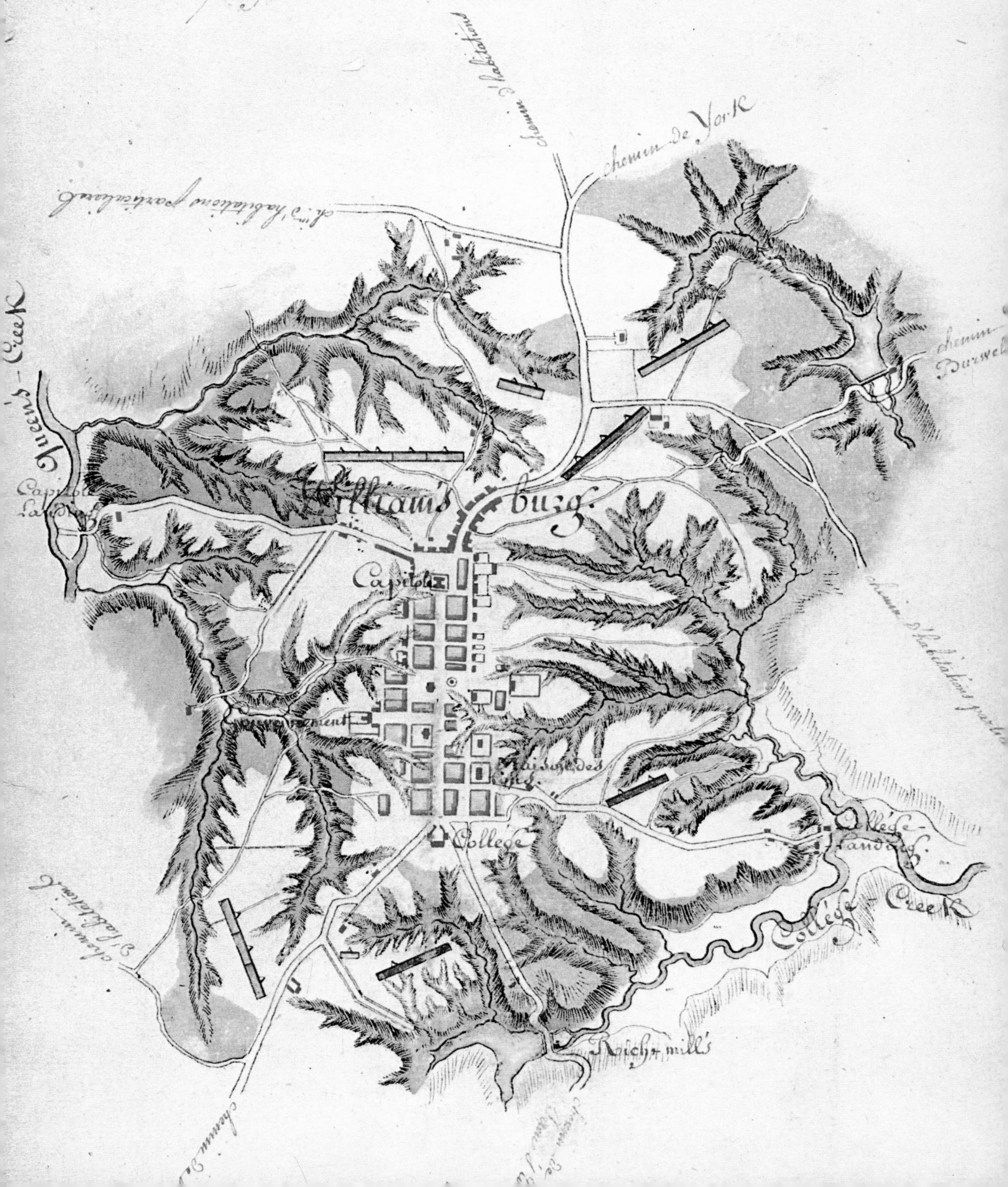

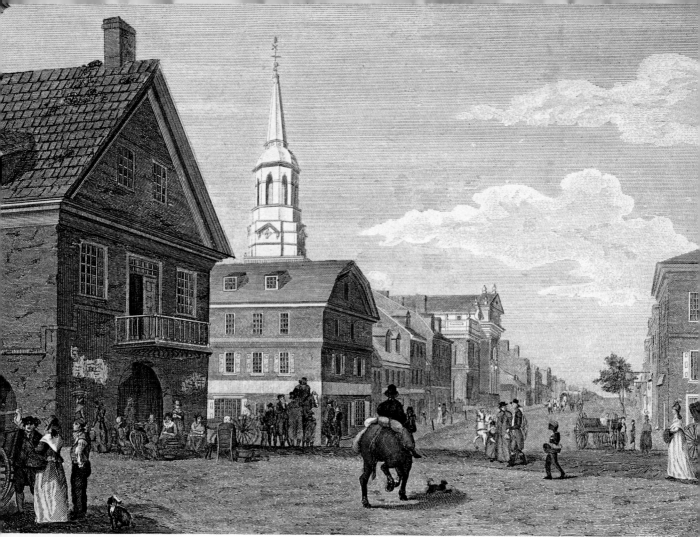

YOUNGEST DELEGATE

When Madison was appointed to the Continental Congress at Philadelphia in 1779, he was, at age twenty-nine, the youngest delegate. As the miniature below shows, however, he looked considerably younger, "no bigger than half a piece of soap," and was described by a delegate's wife as "a gloomy stiff creature...nothing engaging or even bearable in his manners." He took lodgings with Mrs. Mary House at Fifth and Market streets, three blocks west of the junction of Market and Second pictured in the Birch engraving at left and only a block from the Pennsylvania State House (left, below) where Congress held its sessions. The year after Madison arrived, the steeple on the State House decayed so badly that it had to be dismantled and replaced by the low roof seen here. As was characteristic of him, Madison kept at his post for nearly four years with only two short breaks—a remarkable and unmatched record. But his life was briefly brightened by a charming young lady (below right), not yet sixteen, who also lived at Mrs. House's with her father William Floyd, a delegate from New York. When Charles Willson Peale painted these miniatures in 1783, Madison and Kitty Floyd planned to be married. But Miss Floyd changed her mind, and Madison wrote sorrowfully to Jefferson of her "profession of indifference at what has happened."

FATHER OF THE CONSTITUTION

In 1787 Madison returned to Philadelphia to take part in the Federal Convention that would draft the Constitution of the United States. No man was better prepared for the task. In addition to his practical legislative experience, he had pored over countless volumes on the history and theory of government, and he took his seat in the handsome east chamber of the State House (depicted in the nineteenth-century painting above during the signing ceremony) with a well-thought-out program. He chose a seat in the front row where he could hear everything and take copious notes; his first page is at left. For the major role he played in the Convention, he has been called the Father of the Constitution. A fellow delegate wrote that "he always comes forward the best informed man of any point in debate. The affairs of the United States, he perhaps has the most correct knowledge of, of any man in the union."

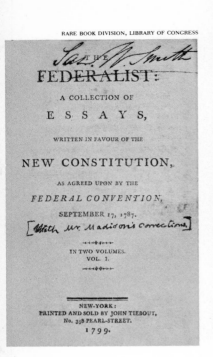

POLITICAL STRATEGISTS

Drafting the Constitution was one thing; getting the states to ratify it was quite another. Brilliant, thirty-year-old Alexander Hamilton of New York (right) chose to fight for adoption with a series of newspaper articles designed to convince the doubters. As his collaborators he picked John Jay, an experienced diplomat (above), and James Madison. Under the collective pen name of Publius, these three young men produced seventy-seven essays in six months. With eight more they were published in book form as *The Federalist* (above, left), which is generally considered to be the outstanding work on the basic theory of American government. When the states debated ratification, some pressed for amendments, including a bill of rights. In order to assure widespread support after ratification, Madison condensed their demands and shepherded twelve of them (above, far right) through the new Congress as it met in New York's Federal Hall (above, right). The first two were never ratified, but the ten that remained became those amendments to the Constitution known as the Bill of Rights.

"THE GREAT LITTLE MADISON"

"Thou must come to me," Dolley Payne Todd wrote her best friend in May, 1794. "Aaron Burr says that the great little Madison has asked to be brought to see me this evening." Dolley, an effervescent and attractive young woman (right, in Gilbert Stuart's portrait now on loan to the White House), had lost her husband and one of her two sons in the yellow fever epidemic of the previous year and was one of Philadelphia's most eligible widows. Madison, now forty-three, had been back in that city ever since Congress returned there in 1790 and inevitably became aware of the twenty-six-year-old charmer whose home was only a block from the State House. Few letters exist between them; they were seldom separated after their marriage that September, only four months after being introduced. The fragment below is of a letter Madison wrote in August after receiving Dolley's acceptance of his proposal. When Jefferson became President in 1801, he appointed his old and close friend Secretary of State. A description of him made at this time closely parallels the Madison seen in the fine portrait by Thomas Sully at left: "I never knew him to wear any other color than black . . . his breeches short, with buckles at the knees, black silk stockings, and shoes with strings. . . ."

BY GILBERT STUART, 1804; PENNSYLVANIA ACADEMY OF THE FINE ARTS, COURTESY WHITE HOUSE HISTORICAL ASSOCIATION

UNDER ☆ MY ☆ ☆WINGS☆ ☆ EVERY☆ ☆THING☆ ☆ ☆ PROSPERS

SECRETARY OF STATE

When the Madisons moved to Washington in May, 1801, they lived for a short time in the President's House (above), and Dolley was able to exercise her talents as a hostess for the widower Jefferson (above, left). Her husband, in his office a few blocks away, was demonstrating his own skills as the President's indispensable first minister. For eight years Jefferson had many occasions to appreciate fully "the rich and ready resources" of the "luminous and discriminating mind" of his Secretary of State. One of the high points of their administration was the skillful negotiation with France leading to the Louisiana Purchase in 1803. Not only did this include the strategic port of New Orleans (painted at left in the year of the transfer), which both Jefferson and Madison considered crucial, but also 828,000 square miles of land that doubled the size of the United States overnight. When his term was ended, Jefferson wrote in tribute: "Mr. Madison is justly entitled to his full share of the measures of my administration. Our principles were the same, and we never differed sensibly in our application of them."

129

Chapter 4

Father of the Constitution

In his own lifetime James Madison would be venerated as the Father of the Constitution. He thought this more praise than belonged to him. The Constitution was not "like the fabled Goddess of Wisdom, the offspring of a single brain," but rather "the work of many heads and many hands." Fifty-five heads to be exact. They came from twelve states (Rhode Island was not represented); they were lawyers, merchants, planters, and physicians and ranged in age from twenty-six to eighty-one; thirty-nine of them had served in Congress, hence were schooled in the frustrations of the Confederation. At thirty-six years of age, one of seven elected Virginia delegates, Madison was in his prime. He had studied politics as a science and practiced it as his profession. One delegate, William Pierce of Georgia, wrote of him: "Every person seems to acknowledge his greatness. He blends together the profound politician, with the scholar.... The affairs of the United States, he perhaps has the most correct knowledge of, of any man in the Union."

Arriving on May 3, one of the first delegates on the scene, Madison took his usual lodgings at Mrs. House's boardinghouse. The convention was scheduled to open on May 14, but it was not until the twenty-fifth that a quorum of seven states could be mustered. Meanwhile, Madison enjoyed the pleasures of Philadelphia. He met and dined with the celebrated Franklin, himself a delegate; he joined with Washington and others in an outing along the Schuylkill. For the most part, however, he laid his plans for the convention and pressed his views on the delegates tumbling into Philadelphia. When the Virginia corps was completed on May 17, Madison brought them together to hammer out the Virginia Plan. It was Madison's plan, essentially, and it became the basis for the deliberations of the convention. Most of what is known about the debates in the convention derives from Madison. The delegates met behind closed doors; although a secretary was appointed, he kept only a journal of proceedings. But Madison, realizing the importance of the event for the nation's history and for the science of government, kept extensive notes on the debates. They would not be published until Congress bought them and authorized their publication in 1840, four years after his death. In a preface written in the 1830s, Madison explained his role as unofficial chronicler of the convention.

Debates in the Federal Convention
[*c.* 1830–36]

The curiosity I had felt during my researches into the History of the most distinguished Confederacies, particularly those of antiquity, and the deficiency I found in the means of satisfying it more especially in what related to the process, the principles, the reasons, & the anticipations, which prevailed in the formation of them, determined me to preserve as far as I could an exact account of what might pass in the Convention whilst executing its trust, with the magnitude of which I was duly impressed, as I was with the gratification promised to future curiosity by an authentic exhibition of the objects, the opinions, & the reasonings from which the new System of Govt was to receive its peculiar structure & organization. Nor was I unaware of the value of such a contribution to the fund of materials for the History of a Constitution on which would be staked the happiness of a people great even in its infancy, and possibly the cause of Liberty throughout the world.

In pursuance of the task I had assumed I chose a seat in front of the presiding member, with the other members on my right & left hands. In this favorable position for hearing all that passed, I noted in terms legible & in abbreviations & marks intelligible to myself what was read from the Chair or spoken by the members; and losing not a moment unnecessarily between the adjournment & reassembling of the Convention I was enabled to write out my daily notes during the session or within a few finishing days after its close in the extent and form preserved in my own hand on my files.

In the labour & correctness of doing this, I was not a little aided by practice & by a familiarity with the style and the train of conversation & reasoning which characterized the principal speakers. It happened, also that I was not absent a single day, nor more than a casual fraction of an hour in any day, so that I could not have lost a single speech, unless a very short one.

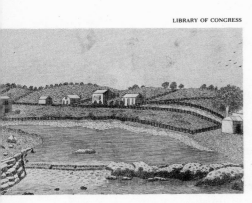

A view of the Falls of Schuylkill, five miles above Philadelphia

The convention met daily, six days a week, from late morning to early evening for almost four months. When not in his seat at the State House (Independence Hall), Madison spent countless hours over his notes in his quarters at Mrs. House's. He wrote few letters and, under the injunction of secrecy, had virtually nothing to communicate. After the business began, he wrote to Jefferson about the delegates, explained the restraint on his pen, and passed typically unflattering comments on Patrick Henry, who had disdained the convention because he "smelt a rat," and on John Adams, whose *A Defence of the Constitutions of Government of the United States of America* had just appeared.

Philada. June 6th. 1787.

In furnishing you with this list of names, I have exhausted all the means which I can make use of for gratifying your curiosity. It was thought expedient in order to secure unbiased discussion within doors, and to prevent misconceptions and misconstructions without, to establish some rules of caution which will for no short time restrain even a confidential communication of our proceedings. The names of the members will satisfy you that the States have been serious in this business. The attendance of Genl. Washington is a proof of the light in which he regards it. The whole Community is big with expectation. And there can be no doubt but that the result will in some way or other have a powerful effect on our destiny.

Mr. Adams' Book which has been in your hands of course, has excited a good deal of attention. An edition has come out here and another is on the press at N. York. It will probably be much read, particularly in the Eastern States, and contribute with other circumstances to revive the predilections of this Country for the British Constitution. Men of learning find nothing new in it, Men of taste many things to criticize. And men without either, not a few things, which they will not understand. It will nevertheless be read, and praised, and become a powerful engine in forming the public opinion. The name and character of the Author, with the critical situation of our affairs, naturally account for such an effect. The book also has merit, and I wish many of the remarks in it, which are unfriendly to republicanism, may not receive fresh weight from the operations of our Government.

I learn from Virginia that the appetite for paper money grows stronger every day. Mr. H-n-y is an avowed

John Adams by Mather Brown

The city and port of Philadelphia
as it was in the eighteenth century

patron of the scheme, and will not fail I think to carry it through unless the County which he is to represent shall bind him hand and foot by instructions. I am told that this is in contemplation. He is also said to be unfriendly to an acceleration of Justice. There is good reason to believe too that he is hostile to the object of the convention and that he wishes either a partition or total dissolution of the confederacy.

The Virginia Plan, presented by Governor Edmund Randolph and adopted as the working model on May 29, called for a vigorous national government founded in the authority of the people and acting directly on them. A national legislature in two branches, the first elected by the people, the second by the first branch; a body empowered "to legislate in all cases to which the separate states are incompetent," to negate all state laws contravening the articles of the Union, and to coerce the states where necessary; a separate national executive and national judiciary—these were the principal features of the "supreme national government" proposed by Virginia. A big step toward its realization was taken on June 6 when the committee of the whole voted for popular election of the lower house. On this matter Madison spoke as follows.

Edmund Randolph's notes of May 29 on discussion of the Virginia Plan

Debates in the Federal Convention
June 6, 1787

Mr. Madison considered an election of one branch at least of the Legislature by the people immediately, as a clear principle of free Govt. and that this mode under proper regulations had the additional advantage of securing better representatives, as well as of avoiding too great an agency of the State Governments in the General one.—He differed from the member from Connecticut [Mr. Sharman] in thinking the objects mentioned to be all the principal ones that required a National Govt. Those were certainly important and necessary objects; but he combined with them the necessity of providing more effectually for the security of private rights, and the steady dispensation of Justice. Interferences with these were evils which had more perhaps than any thing else, produced this convention. Was it to be supposed that republican liberty could long exist under the abuse of it practised in some of the States. The gentleman [Mr. Sharman] had admitted that in a very small State, faction & oppression wd. prevail. It was to be inferred then that wherever these prevailed the State was too small. Had they not prevailed in the largest as well as the smallest tho' less than in the smallest; and were we not thence admonished to enlarge the sphere as far as the nature of the Govt. would admit. This was the only defence agst. the inconveniences of democracy consistent with the democratic form of Govt. All civilized Societies would be divided into different Sects, Factions, & interests, as they happened to consist of rich & poor, debtors & creditors, the landed, the manufacturing, the commercial interests, the inhabitants of this district or that district, the followers of this political leader or that political leader, the disciples of this religious Sect or that religious Sect. In all cases where a majority are united by a common interest or passion, the rights of the minority are in danger. What motives are to restrain them? A prudent regard to the maxim that honesty is the best policy is found by experience to be as little regarded by bodies of men as by individuals. Respect for character is always diminished in proportion to the number among whom the blame or praise is to be divided. Conscience, the only remaining tie, is known to be inadequate in individuals: In large numbers, little is to be expected from

Delegates passing through the State House garden (above) were besieged by prisoners begging through the windows of Walnut Street Prison (below) and forced to endure their "foul and horrid imprecations."

it. Besides, Religion itself may become a motive to persecution & oppression.—These observations are verified by the Histories of every Country antient & modern. In Greece & Rome the rich & poor, the creditors & debtors, as well as the patricians & plebians alternately oppressed each other with equal unmercifulness. What a source of oppression was the relation between the parent cities of Rome, Athens & Carthage, & their respective provinces: the former possessing the power, & the latter being sufficiently distinguished to be separate objects of it? Why was America so justly apprehensive of Parliamentary injustice? Because G. Britain had a separate interest real or supposed, & if her authority had been admitted, could have pursued that interest at our expence. We have seen the mere distinction of colour made in the most enlightened period of time, a ground of the most oppressive dominion ever exercised by man over man. What has been the source of those unjust laws complained of among ourselves? Has it not been the real or supposed interest of the major numbers? Debtors have defrauded their creditors. The landed interest has borne hard on the mercantile interest. The Holders of one species of property have thrown a disproportion of taxes on the holders of another species. The lesson we are to draw from the whole is that where a majority are united by common sentiment, and have an opportunity, the rights of the minor party become insecure. In a Republican Govt. the Majority if united have always an opportunity. The only remedy is to enlarge the sphere, & thereby divide the community into so great a number of interests & parties, that in the 1st. place a majority will not be likely at the same moment to have a common interest separate from that of the whole or of the minority; and in the 2d. place, that in case they shd. have such an interest, they may not be apt to unite in the pursuit of it. It was incumbent on us then to try this remedy, and with that view to frame a republican system on such a scale & in such a form as will controul all the evils wch. have been experienced.

This speech, of course, had its basis in Madison's studies prior to the convention and also anticipated the fully developed "theory of factions" in the most famous of *The Federalist* papers. In reaction against the abuses of majoritarian democracy as practiced by the lower houses of the state legislatures, Madison had come to believe that the salvation of the Republic lay in enlarging the sphere of government so as to embrace a greater number of interests and factions. The theory turned the conventional wisdom from Aristotle to Montesquieu on its head. The idea that a republican government could not exist in a large territory, such as the United States, was wrong; in truth, said Madison, it could exist in no other. He had come to see this clearly after reading David Hume's "Idea of a Perfect Commonwealth," an explicit rebuttal of the equation of republicanism with smallness; but experience, too, had been his guide. Interests founded on property were the moving forces of government, he had learned. And because these interests cut across state lines, the great conflict that had broken out in the convention between large and small states was, in fact, a figment of the imagination, as he pointed out to his colleagues.

George Washington presiding over the Constitutional Convention

Debates in the Federal Convention
June 30, 1787

He [Mr. Madison] admitted that every peculiar interest whether in any case of citizens, or any description of States, ought to be secured as far as possible. Wherever there is danger of attack there ought be given a constitutional power of defence. But he contended that the States were divided into different interests not by their difference of size, but by other circumstances; the most material of which results partly from climate, but principally from the effects of their having or not having slaves. These two causes concurred in forming the great division of interests in the U. States. It did not lie between the large & small States: It lay between the Northern & Southern.

M adison's experience in the struggle for religious freedom in Virginia had also been important, for he had discovered that the principle could be best secured in a pluralistic environment of competing sects, no one of which could tyrannize over the others. The theory of factions applied to the political sphere a truth drawn from the religious sphere.

For six weeks the small-state bloc, fearing their powerlessness in the proposed government, fought to secure the representation of the states in the legislative branch. On June 7 it was agreed that the members of the upper house should be appointed by the state legislatures. Only the most strident nationalists, like Madison and James Wilson of Pennsylvania, opposed this concession to federalism. By itself it offered no protection to the small states, for the Virginia Plan still called for proportional representation in both branches. The committee of the whole went on record in favor of this rule on June 11. At this point the small-state leaders brought forth the so-called New Jersey Plan as a substitute for the Virginia Plan. Presented by William Paterson of New Jersey, the plan looked to amendment rather than overturn of the Articles of Confederation. A national executive and national judiciary would be created, but Congress would receive, sparingly, only additional enumerated powers, and equal representation of the states would remain the rule. "You see the consequence of pushing things too far," John Dickinson of Delaware said to Madison. "Some of the members from the small States wish for two branches in the General Legislature and are friends to a good National Government; but we would sooner submit to a foreign power than submit to be deprived of an equality of suffrage in both branches of the Legislature, and thereby be thrown under the domination of the large States." But on this issue Madison was immovable.

The New Jersey Plan was soon set aside, and the convention, unable to resolve the great question of representation, went on to less contentious matters. One of these was the duration of the term of members of the upper house. Already some men were conceiving of this body (the Senate) as the representation of the states with the lower house the representation of the people in the government. This was not Madison's conception. He viewed the Senate as a necessary check on the democracy—"the fickleness and passion"—of the lower house.

Debates in the Federal Convention
June 26, 1787

John Dickinson of Delaware

Mr. Madison. In order to judge of the form to be given to this institution, it will be proper to take a view of the ends to be served by it. These were first to protect the people agst. their rulers: secondly to protect the people agst. the transient impressions into which they themselves might be led. A people deliberating in a temperate moment, and with the experience of other nations before them, on the plan of Govt. most likely to secure their happiness, would first be aware, that those chargd. with the public happiness, might betray their trust. An obvious precaution agst. this danger wd. be to divide the trust between different bodies of men, who might watch & check each other.... It wd. next occur to such a people, that they themselves were liable to temporary errors, thro' want of information as to their true interest, and that men chosen for a short term, & employed but a small portion of that in public affairs, might err from the same cause. This reflection wd. naturally suggest that the Govt. be so constituted, as that one of its branches might have an oppy. of acquiring a competent knowledge of the public interests. Another reflection equally becoming a people on such an occasion, wd. be that they themselves, as well as a numerous body of Representatives, were liable to err also, from fickleness and passion. A necessary fence agst. this danger would be to select a portion of enlightened citizens, whose limited number, and firmness might seasonably interpose agst. impetuous councils. It ought finally to occur to a people deliberating on a Govt. for themselves, that as different interests necessarily result from the liberty meant to be secured, the major interest might under sudden impulses be tempted to commit injustice on the minority. In all civilized Countries the people fall into different classes havg a real or supposed difference of interests. There will be creditors & debtors, farmer, merchts. & manufacturers. There will be particularly the distinction of rich & poor. It was true as had been observd. [by Mr. Pinkney] we had not among us those hereditary distinctions, of rank which were a great source of the contests in the ancient Govts. as well as the modern States of Europe, nor those extremes of wealth or poverty which characterize the latter. We cannot however be regarded even at this time, as one homogeneous mass, in which every thing that affects a part will affect in the same manner the whole. In framing a system which we wish to last for ages, we shd. not lose sight of the changes which ages will produce. An increase of population will of necessity increase the proportion of those who will labour under all the hardships of life, & secretly sigh for a more equal distribution of its blessings. These may in time outnumber those who are placed above the feelings of indigence. According to the equal laws of suffrage, the power will slide into the hands of the former. No agrarian attempts have yet been made in this Country, but symtoms, of a leveling spirit, as we have understood, have sufficiently appeared in a certain quarters to give notice of the future danger. How is this danger to be guarded agst. on republican principles? How is the danger in all cases of interested coalitions to oppress the minority to be guarded agst? Among other means by the establishment of a body in the Govt. sufficiently respectable for its wisdom & virtue to aid on such emergencies, the preponderance of justice by throwing its weight into that scale. Such being the objects of the second branch in the proposed Govt. he [Mr. Madison] thought a considerable duration ought to be given to it.

On July 17 a group of delegates, including Madison, rode out to visit William Bartram's gardens.

James Wilson of Pennsylvania

He did not conceive that the term of nine years could threaten any real danger; but in pursuing his particular ideas on the subject, he should require that the long term allowed to the 2d. branch should not commence till such a period of life, as would render a perpetual disqualification to be re-elected little inconvenient either in a public or private view. He observed that as it was more than probable we were now digesting a plan which in its operation wd. decide for ever the fate of Republican Govt. we ought not only to provide every guard to liberty that its preservation cd. require, but be equally careful to supply the defects which our own experience had particularly pointed out.

Whatever the theoretical merits of Madison's position on representation, more and more delegates were becoming convinced it was impractical. The country, after all, was composed of corporate political units—states—and they could not be left out of the general government. On July 2 Connecticut moved for state equality in the upper house. A tie vote resulted; stalemate was complete. When a motion was made to send the issue to a committee for decision, Madison smelled a compromise and opposed it. But the committee was appointed, and the next day it reported the "great compromise": equal representation of the states in the upper house, proportional representation in the lower, provided that all money bills originate in the latter. Madison and the hardcore nationalists fought the compromise until July 16, when it was narrowly adopted. The ultranationalists had lost control of the convention. From this point the strongly "consolidated" union envisioned by the Virginia Plan was replaced by the moderate conception of a government with a "mixed constitution," partly national, partly federal, of which, ironically, James Madison himself would become the great expounder in *The Federalist.*

Without compromise there would have been no new government, but the price of compromise was a garbled and mutilated constitution. Certainly this was Madison's belief as he watched other parts of the Virginia Plan cut away and discarded. Instead of a congressional negative over state laws, the convention relied upon the expedient of the New Jersey Plan declaring the constitution and the laws made under it "the supreme law of the land" in the several states. Instead of a plenary grant of legislative power, the convention chose to enumerate specific powers granted to Congress. Madison fought for the negative without success. He tried to expand the list of enumerated powers—powers to establish a national university, to promote useful knowledge, to grant corporate charters, to tax exports—again without success. When it came to the executive, Madison himself took leave of the Virginia Plan. Wishing a strong and independent executive, one that would express the will of the nation and not be answerable to partial interests or congressional cabals, he saw the importance of founding the appointment directly on the popular suffrage. His speech arguing this position is spiced with his pessimistic opinion of human nature when arrayed in the garments of power.

Debates in the Federal Convention
July 25, 1787

Mr. Madison. There are objections agst. every mode that has been, or perhaps can be proposed. The election must be made either by some existing authority under the Natl. or State Constitutions—or by some special authority derived from the people—or by the people themselves.—The two Existing authorities under the Natl. Constitution wd. be the Legislative & Judiciary. The latter he presumed was out of the question. The former was in his Judgment liable to insuperable objections. Besides the general influence of that mode on the independence of the Executive, 1. the election of the Chief Magistrate would agitate & divide the legislature so much that the public interest would materially suffer by it. Public bodies are always apt to be thrown into contentions, but into more violent ones by such occasions than by any others. 2. the candidate would intrigue with the Legislature, would derive his appointment from the predominant faction, and be apt to render his administration subservient to its views. 3. The Ministers of foreign powers would have and make use of, the opportunity to mix their intrigues & influence with the Election. Limited as the powers of the Executive are, it will be an object of great moment with the great rival powers of Europe who have American possessions, to have at the head of our Governmt. a man attached to their respective politics & interests. No pains, nor perhaps expence, will be spared, to gain from the Legislature an appointmt. favorable to their wishes....The existing authorities in the States are the Legislative, Executive & Judiciary. The appointment of the Natl. Executive by the first, was objectionable in many points of view, some of which had been already mentioned. He would mention one which of itself would decide his opinion. The Legislatures of the States had betrayed a strong propensity to a variety of pernicious measures. One object

Washington was a guest in Robert Morris's home during the summer of 1787. As President, he and Martha lived in the same house.

Robert Morris of Pennsylvania

of the Natl. Legislr. was to controul this propensity. One object of the Natl. Executive, so far as it would have a negative on the laws, was to controul the Natl. Legislature, so far as it might be infected with a similar propensity. Refer the appointmt. of the Natl. Executive to the State Legislatures, and this controuling purpose may be defeated. The Legislatures can & will act with some kind of regular plan, and will promote the appointmt. of a man who will not oppose himself to a favorite client. Should a majority of the Legislatures at the time of election have the same object, or different objects of the same kind, The Natl. Executive would be rendered subservient to them.... The option before us then lay between an appointment by Electors chosen by the people—and an immediate appointment by the people. He thought the former mode free from many of the objections which had been urged agst. it, and greatly preferable to an appointment by the Natl. Legislature. As the electors would be chosen for the occasion, would meet at once, & proceed immediately to an appointment, there would be very little opportunity for cabal, or corruption.... The remaining mode was an election by the people or rather by the qualified part of them, at large. With all its imperfections he liked this best. He would not repeat either the general argumts. for or the objections agst. this mode. He would only take notice of two difficulties which he admitted to have weight. The first arose from the disposition in the people to prefer a Citizen of their own State, and the disadvantages this wd. throw on the smaller States. Great as this objection might be he did not think it equal to such as lay agst. every other mode which had been proposed. He thought too that some expedient might be hit upon that would obviate it. The second difficulty arose from the disproportion of qualified voters in the N. & S. States and the disadvantages which this mode would throw on the latter. The answer to this objection was 1. that this disproportion would be continually decreasing under the influence of the Republican laws introduced in the S. States, and the more rapid increase of their population. 2. That local considerations must give way to the general interest. As an individual from the S. States he was willing to make the sacrifice.

Indirect election of the President through the medium of an electoral college was, of course, the mode finally chosen. It was quite acceptable to Madison. The convention finished its work on September 17. Only thirty-eight of the original fifty-five delegates were still in attendance. The summer's heat had taken its toll; some delegates had been called home, others had walked out in protest. After the final reading of the engrossed Constitution, the aged Franklin rose to plead for unanimous approval. "I consent, Sir, to this Constitution, because I expect no better, and because I am not sure, that it is not the best." Madison could subscribe to this philosophy. More ardent centralists than he—Alexander Hamilton, James Wilson, Gouverneur Morris—signed the document. The three who did not, Elbridge Gerry of Massachusetts and the Virginians George Mason and Edmund Randolph, feared the strength, not the weakness, of the new government.

The delegates had provided for ratification of the Constitution by popularly elected conventions in the several states, the approval of nine states only being sufficient to establish the government. Some men had balked at this "new set of ideas," strangely democratic and unknown to the Articles of Confederation, but the majority had readily assented to Madison's argument that the legitimacy of the government must be founded in the sovereignty of the people.

Debates in the Federal Convention
July 23, 1787

Mr. Madison thought it clear that the Legislatures were incompetent to the proposed changes. These changes would make essential inroads on the State Constitutions,

Resolution (left) submitting the Constitution to Congress with the signature of George Washington, president; aged Benjamin Franklin (above) pleaded for its approval.

and it would be a novel & dangerous doctrine that a Legislature could change the constitution under which it held its existence. There might indeed be some Constitutions within the Union, which had given a power to the Legislature to concur in alterations of the federal Compact. But there were certainly some which had not; and in the case of these, a ratification must of necessity be obtained from the people. He considered the difference between a system founded on the Legislatures only, and one founded on the people, to be the true difference between a *league* or *treaty*, and a *Constitution*. The former in point of *moral obligation* might be as inviolable as the latter. In point of *political operation*, there were two important distinctions in favor of the latter. 1. A law violating a treaty ratified by a preexisting law, might be respected by the Judges as a law, though an unwise or perfidious one. A law violating a constitution established by the people themselves, would be considered by the Judges as null & void. 2. The doctrine laid down by the law of Nations in the case of treaties is that a breach of any one article by any of the parties, frees the other parties from their engagements. In the case of a union of people under one Constitution, the nature of the pact has always been understood to exclude such an interpretation. Comparing the two modes in point of expediency he thought all the considerations which recommended this Convention in preference to Congress for proposing the reform were in favor of State Conventions in preference to the Legislatures for examining and adopting it.

Madison returned to Congress to plan the strategy of the ratification campaign. The Constitution was well below his expectations, but he embraced it in the confidence it was the strongest medicine the public would swallow. In the wider controversy now beginning he would bury his doubts and scruples, though he did not disguise them in a lengthy report sent to Jefferson in France on the convention and its work.

New York Octr. 24. 1787

You will herewith receive the result of the Convention, which continued its session till the 17th of September. I take the liberty of making some observations on the subject which will help to make up a letter, if they should answer no other purpose.

Gouverneur Morris of Pennsylvania was known as "an eternal speaker."

It appeared to be the sincere and unanimous wish of the Convention to cherish and preserve the Union of the States. No proposition was made, no suggestion was thrown out in favor of a partition of the Empire into two or more Confederacies.

It was generally agreed that the objects of the Union could not be secured by any system founded on the principle of a confederation of sovereign States. A voluntary observance of the federal law by all the members could never be hoped for. A compulsive one could evidently never be reduced to practice, and if it could, involved equal calamities to the innocent and the guilty, the necessity of a military force both obnoxious and dangerous, and in general, a scene resembling much more a civil war, than the administration of a regular Government.

Hence was embraced the alternative of a government which instead of operating, on the States, should operate without their intervention on the individuals composing them: and hence the change in the principle and proportion of representation.

This ground-work being laid, the great objects which presented themselves were 1. to unite a proper energy in the Executive and a proper stability in the Legislative departments, with the essential characters of Republican Government. 2. To draw a line of demarkation which would give to the Central Government every power requisite for general purposes, and leave to the States every power which might be most beneficially administered by them. 3. To provide for the different interests of different parts of the Union. 4. To adjust the clashing pretensions of the large and small States. Each of these objects was pregnant with difficulties. The whole of them together formed a task more difficult than can be well conceived by those who were not concerned in the execution of it. Adding to these considerations the natural diversity of human opinions on all new and complicated subjects, it is impossible to consider the degree of concord which ultimately prevailed as less than a miracle.

The first of these objects as it respects the Executive, was peculiarly embarrassing. On the question whether it should consist of a single person, or a plurality of coordinate members, on the mode of appointment, on the duration in office, on the degree of power, on the re-eligibility, tedious and reiterated discussions took place. The plurality of co-ordinate members had finally but few advocates. Governour Randolph was at the head of them. The modes of appointment proposed were various, as by the people at large—by electors chosen by the people—by the Executives of the States—by the Congress, some preferring a joint ballot of the two Houses—some a separate concurrent ballot allowing to each a negative on the other house—some a nomination of several candidates by one House, out of whom a choice should be made by the other.... The expedient at length adopted seemed to give pretty general satisfaction to the members. As to the duration in office, a few would have preferred a tenure during good behaviour—a considerable number would have done so in case an easy and effectual removal by impeachment could be settled. It was much agitated whether a long term, seven years for example, with a subsequent and perpetual ineligibility, or a short term with a capacity to be re-elected, should be fixed.... The questions concerning the degree of power turned chiefly on the appointment to offices and the controul on the Legislature. An absolute appointment to all offices—to some offices—to no offices, formed the scale of opinions of the first point. On the second, some contended for an absolute negative, as the only possible mean of reducing to practice, the theory of a free government which forbids a mixture of the Legislative and Executive powers. Others would be content with a revisionary power to be overruled by three fourths of both Houses. It was warmly urged that the judiciary department should be associated in the revision. The idea of some was that a separate revision should be given to the two departments—that if either objected two thirds; if both three fourths, should be necessary to overrule.

In forming the Senate, the great anchor of the Government, the questions as they came within the first object turned mostly on the mode of appointment, and the duration of it. The different modes proposed were, 1. by the House of Representatives, 2. by the Executive, 3. by electors chosen by the people for the purpose, 4. by the State Legislatures. On the point of duration, the propositions descended from good behavior to four years, through the intermediate terms of nine, seven, six and five years. The election of the other branch was first determined to

Jared Ingersoll of Pennsylvania did not speak during the entire summer.

be triennial, and afterwards reduced to biennial.

The second object, the due partition of power, between the General and local Governments, was perhaps of all, the most nice and difficult. A few contended for an entire abolition of the States: Some for indefinite power of Legislation in the Congress, with a negative on the laws of the States: some for such a power without a negative: some for a limited power of legislation, with such a negative: the majority finally for a limited power without the negative. The question with regard to the Negative underwent repeated discussions, and was finally rejected by a bare majority. As I formerly intimated to you my opinion in favor of this ingredient, I will take this occasion of explaining myself on the subject. . . .

1. Without such a check in the whole over the parts, our system involves the evil of imperia in imperio [a government within a government]. If a compleat supremacy some where is not necessary in every Society, a controuling power at least is so, by which the general authority may be defended against encroachments of the subordinate authorities, and by which the latter may be restrained from encroachments on each other. If the supremacy of the British Parliament is not necessary as has been contended, for the harmony of that Empire, it is evident I think that without the royal negative or some equivalent controul the unity of the system would be destroyed. The want of some such provision seems to have been mortal to the antient Confederacies and to be the disease of the modern. . . . Still more to the purpose is our own experience both during the war and since the peace. Encroachments of the States on the general authority, sacrifices of national to local interests, interferences of the measures of different States, form a great part of the history of our political system. It may be said that the new Constitution is founded on different principles, and will have a different operation. I admit the difference to be material. It presents the aspect rather of a feudal system of republics, if such a phrase may be used, than of a Confederacy of independent States. And what has been the progress and event of the feudal Constitutions? In all of them a continual struggle between the head and the inferior members, until a final victory has been gained in some instances by one, in others, by the other of them. . . . It may be said that the Judicial

Three delegates refused to sign the Constitution: George Mason (top left) and Edmund Randolph (bottom left), Virginia; Elbridge Gerry, Massachusetts (top). Luther Martin, Maryland (above), had left early.

authority under our new system will keep the States within their proper limits, and supply the place of a negative on their laws. The answer is that it is more convenient to prevent the passage of a law, than to declare it void after it is passed; that this will be particularly the case where the law aggrieves individuals, who may be unable to support an appeal against a State to the supreme Judiciary, that a State which would violate the Legislative rights of the Union, would not be very ready to obey a Judicial decree in support of them, and that a recurrence to force, which in the event of disobedience would be necessary, is an evil which the new Constitution meant to exclude as far as possible.

2. A Constitutional negative on the laws of the States seems equally necessary to secure individuals against encroachments on their rights. The mutability of the laws of the States is found to be a serious evil. The injustice of them has been so frequent and so flagrant as to alarm the most stedfast friends of Republicanism. I am persuaded I do not err in saying that the evils issuing from these sources contributed more to that uneasiness which produced the Convention, and prepared the public mind for a general reform, than those which accrued to our national character and interest from the inadequacy of the Confederation to its immediate objects. A reform therefore which does not make provision for private rights, must be materially defective. . . . It may be asked how private rights will be more secure under the Guardianship of the General Government than under the State Governments, since they are both founded on the republican principle which refers the ultimate decision to the will of the majority, and are distinguished rather by the extent within which they will operate, than by any material difference in their structure. . . . I will state some of the ideas which have occurred to me on this subject. Those who contend for a simple Democracy, or a pure republic, actuated by the sense of the majority, and operating within narrow limits, assume or suppose a case which is altogether fictitious. They found their reasoning on the idea, that the people composing the Society enjoy not only an equality of political rights; but that they have all precisely the same interests and the same feelings in every respect. Were this in reality the case, their reasoning would be conclusive. The interest

147

of the majority would be that of the minority also; the decisions could only turn on mere opinion concerning the good of the whole of which the major voice would be the safest criterion; and within a small sphere, this voice could be most easily collected and the public affairs most accurately managed. We know however that no Society ever did or can consist of so homogeneous a mass of Citizens. In the savage State indeed, an approach is made towards it; but in that state little or no Government is necessary. In all civilized Societies, distinctions are various and unavoidable. A distinction of property results from that very protection which a free Government gives to unequal faculties of acquiring it. There will be rich and poor; creditors and debtors; a landed interest, a monied interest, a mercantile interest, a manufacturing interest. . . . If then there must be different interests and parties in Society; and a majority when united by a common interest or passion can not be restrained from oppressing the minority, what remedy can be found in a republican Government, where the majority must ultimately decide, but that of giving such an extent to its sphere, that no common interest or passion will be likely to unite a majority of the whole number in an unjust pursuit. In a large Society, the people are broken into so many interests and parties, that a common sentiment is less likely to be felt, and the requisite concert less likely to be formed, by a majority of the whole. The same security seems requisite for the civil as for the religious rights of individuals. If the same sect form a majority and have the power, other sects will be sure to be depressed. Divide et impera [divide and rule], the reprobated axiom of tyranny, is under certain qualifications, the only policy, by which a republic can be administered on just principles. It must by observed however that this doctrine can only hold within a sphere of a mean extent. As in too small a sphere oppressive combinations may be too easily formed against the weaker party; so in too extensive a one a defensive concert may be rendered too difficult against the oppression of those entrusted with the administration. The great desideratum in Government is, so to modify the sovereignty as that it may be sufficiently neutral between different parts of the Society to controul one part from invading the rights of another, and at the same time sufficiently controuled itself, from

setting up an interest adverse to that of the entire Society.... In the extended Republic of the United States, the General Government would hold a pretty even balance between the parties of particular States, and be at the same time sufficiently restrained by its dependence on the community, from betraying its general interests.

Begging pardon for this immoderate digression, I return to the third object abovementioned, the adjustment of the different interests of different parts of the Continent. Some contended for an unlimited power over trade including exports as well as imports, and over slaves as well as other imports; some for such a power, provided the concurrence of two thirds of both Houses were required; some for such a qualification of the power, with an exemption of exports and slaves, others for an exemption of exports only. The result is seen in the Constitution. [The importation of slaves could not be prohibited prior to 1808; trade could be regulated by vote of a simple majority.] S. Carolina and Georgia were inflexible on the point of the slaves.

The remaining object, created more embarrassment, and a greater alarm for the issue of the Convention than all the rest put together. The little States insisted on retaining their equality in both branches, unless a compleat abolition of the State Governments should take place; and made an equality in the Senate a sine qua non. The

Scenes familiar to convention delegates included Chestnut Street, where Congress Hall was being built that summer (opposite), and the markets along High Street.

large States on the other hand urged that as the new Government was to be drawn principally from the people immediately and was to operate directly on them, not on the States; and consequently as the States would lose that importance which is now proportioned to the importance of their voluntary compliances with the requisitions of Congress, it was necessary that the representation in both Houses should be in proportion to their size. It ended in the compromise which you will see, but very much to the dissatisfaction of several members from the large States.

The advocates of the new system took the name of Federalists. Those in opposition were perforce Antifederalists, though they professed to be the true friends of both federalism and republicanism. "Since the world began," a Pennsylvanian remarked, "I believe no question has ever been more repeatedly and strictly scrutinized or more fairly and freely argued, than the proposed Constitution." The most distinguished product of this debate was the series of seventy-seven letters of "Publius" contributed to the New York press and later published collectively with eight more as *The Federalist*. Publius was the composite creation of two New Yorkers, John Jay and Alexander Hamilton, and Madison. Hastily written in the heat of campaign, *The Federalist* nevertheless became the classic commentary on the Constitution. Twenty-nine of the papers may be credited to Madison. Most important at the time were those in which Madison, with statesmanlike ingenuity, gave theoretical form and coherence to the disjointed work of the convention. Suppressing his own disappointments, allaying the fears of his opponents, Madison fabricated a working model of the new system such as had scarcely been imagined before, and so compelling was it that it could never be escaped thereafter. In Number 39, for example, he set forth the idea of a "compound republic," partly national and partly federal, which overcame the polarity of these terms and laid the basis for political accommodation.

[January 16, 1788]

In order to ascertain the real character of the government it may be considered in relation to the foundation on which it is to be established; to the sources from which its ordinary powers are to be drawn; to the operation of those powers; to the extent of them; and to the authority by which future changes in the government are to be introduced.

On examining the first relation, it appears on one hand that the Constitution is to be founded on the assent and ratification of the people of America, given by deputies elected for the special purpose; but on the other, that this assent and ratification is to be given by the people, not as individuals composing one entire nation; but as composing the distinct and independent States to which they respectively belong. It is to be the assent and ratification of the several States, derived from the supreme authority in each State, the authority of the people themselves. The act therefore establishing the Constitution, will not be a *national* but a *federal* act.

That it will be a federal and not a national act, as these terms are understood by the objectors, the act of the people as forming so many independent States, not as forming one aggregate nation, is obvious from this single consideration that it is to result neither from the decision of a *majority* of the people of the Union, nor from that of a *majority* of the States. It must result from the *unanimous* assent of the several States that are parties to it, differing no other wise from their ordinary assent than in its being expressed, not by the legislative authority, but by that of the people themselves. Were the people regarded in this transaction as forming one nation, the will of the majority of the whole people of the United States, would bind the minority; in the same manner as the majority in each State must bind the minority; and the will of the majority must be determined either by a comparison of the individual votes; or by considering the will of a majority of the States, as evidence of the will of a majority of the people of the United States. Neither of these rules has been adopted. Each State in ratifying the Constitution, is considered as a sovereign body independent of all others, and only to be bound by its own voluntary act. In this relation then the new Constitution will, if established, be a *federal* and not a *national* Constitution.

The next relation is to the sources from which the ordinary powers of government are to be derived. The house of representatives will derive its powers from the people of America, and the people will be represented in the same proportion, and on the same principle, as they are in the Legislature of a particular State. So far the Government is *national* not *federal*. The Senate on the other hand will derive its powers from the States, as political and co-equal societies; and these will be represented on the principle of equality in the Senate, as

John Jay (above, by John Trumbull) and Alexander Hamilton (below, by James Sharples) collaborated with Madison on The Federalist.

52   THE FEDERALIST.

long as it exifts by a conftitutional neceffity for local purpofes, though it fhould be in perfect fubordination to the general authority of the union, it would ftill be, in fact and in theory, an affociation of ftates, or a confederacy. The propofed conftitution, fo far from implying an abolition of the ftate governments, makes them conftituent parts of the national fovereignty by allowing them a direct reprefentation in the fenate, and leaves in their poffeffion certain exclufive and very important portions of fovereign power.—This fully correfponds, in every rational import of the terms, with the idea of a federal government.

In the Lycian confederacy, which confifted of twenty-three CITIES, or republics, the largeft were intitled to *three* votes in the COMMON COUNCIL, thofe of the middle clafs to *two*, and the fmalleft to *one*. The COMMON COUNCIL had the appointment of all the judges and magiftrates of the refpective CITIES. This was certainly the moft delicate fpecies of interference in their internal adminiftration; for if there be any thing that feems exclufively appropriated to the local jurifdictions, it is the appointment of their own officers. Yet Montefquieu, fpeaking of this affociation, fays, " Were I to give a model of an excellent " confederate republic, it would be that of Lycia." Thus we perceive that the diftinctions infifted upon were not within the contemplation of this enlightened civilian, and we fhall be led to conclude, that they are the novel refinements of an erroneous theory.

PUBLIUS.

NUMBER X.
The fame Subject continued.

AMONG the numerous advantages promifed by a well conftructed union, none deferves to be more accurately developed than its tendency to break and control the violence of faction. The friend of popular governments,

Number 10 of The Federalist *was the most celebrated of the twenty-nine essays credited to Madison.*

they now are in the existing Congress. So far the government is federal, not national. The executive power will be derived from a very compound source. The immediate election of the President is to be made by the States in their political characters. The votes alloted to them, are in a compound ratio, which considers them partly as distinct and co-equal societies; partly as unequal members of the same society. The eventual election, again is to be made by that branch of the Legislature which consists of the national representatives; but in this particular act, they are to be thrown into the form of individual delegations from so many distinct and co-equal bodies politic. From this aspect of the Government, it appears to be of a mixed character presenting at least as many *federal* as *national* features.

The difference between a federal and national Government as it relates to the *operation of the Government* is supposed to consist in this, that in the former, the powers operate on the political bodies composing the confederacy, in their political capacities: In the latter, on the individual citizens, composing the nation, in their individual capacities. On trying the Constitution by this criterion, it falls under the *national*, not the *federal* character; though perhaps not so compleatly, as has been understood. . . .

But if the Government be national with regard to the *operation* of its powers, it changes its aspect again when we contemplate it in relation to the *extent* of its powers. The idea of a national Government involves in it, not only an authority over the individual citizens; but an indefinite supremacy over all persons and things, so far as they are objects of lawful Government. Among a people consolidated into one nation, this supremacy is compleatly vested in the national Legislature. Among communities united for particular purposes, it is vested partly in the general, and partly in the municipal Legislatures. In the former cases, all local authorities are subordinate to the supreme; and may be controuled, directed or abolished by it at pleasure. In the latter the local or municipal authorities form distinct and independent portions of the supremacy, no more subject within their respective spheres to the general authority, than the general authority is subject to them, within its own sphere. In this relation then the proposed Government cannot be deemed a *national* one; since its jurisdiction extends to certain enumerated objects only, and leaves to the several States a residuary and inviolable sovereignty over all other objects. It is true that in controversies relating to the boundary between the two jurisdictions, the tribunal which is ultimately to decide, is to be established under the general Government. But this does not change the principle of the case. The decision is to be impartially made, according to the rules of the Constitution; and all the usual and most effectual precautions are taken to secure this impartiality. Some such tribunal is clearly essential to prevent an appeal to the sword, and a dissolution of the compact; and that it ought to be established under the general, rather than under the local Governments; or to speak more properly, that it could be safely established under the first alone, is a position not likely to be combated.

If we try the Constitution by its last relation, to the authority by which amendments are to be made, we find it neither wholly *national*, nor wholly *federal*. Were it wholly national, the supreme and ultimate authority would reside in the *majority* of the people of the Union; and this authority would be competent at all times, like that of a majority of every national society, to alter or abolish its established Government. Were it wholly federal on the other hand, the concurrence of each State in the Union would be essential to every alteration that would be binding on all. The mode provided by the plan of the Convention is not founded on either of these principles. In requiring more than a majority, and particularly, in computing the proportion by *States*, not by *citizens*, it departs from the *national*, and advances towards the *federal* character: In rendering the concurrence of less than the whole number of States sufficient, it loses again the *federal*, and partakes of the *national* character.

The proposed Constitution therefore is in strictness neither a national nor a federal constitution; but a composition of both. In its foundation, it is federal, not national; in the sources from which the ordinary powers of the Government are drawn, it is partly federal, and partly national: in the operation of these powers, it is national, not federal: In the extent of them again, it is federal, not national: And finally, in the authoritative

By the United States in Congress assembled,

SEPTEMBER 13, 1788.

WHEREAS the Convention assembled in Philadelphia, pursuant to the Resolution of Congress of the 21st February, 1787, did, on the 17th of September in the same year, report to the United States in Congress assembled, a Constitution for the People of the United States; whereupon Congress, on the 28th of the same September, did resolve unanimously, " That the said report, with the Resolutions and Letter accompanying the same, be transmitted to the several Legislatures, in order to be submitted to a Convention of Delegates chosen in each State by the people thereof, in conformity to the Resolves of the Convention made and provided in that case:" And whereas the Constitution so reported by the Convention, and by Congress transmitted to the several Legislatures, has been ratified in the manner therein declared to be sufficient for the establishment of the same, and such Ratifications duly authenticated have been received by Congress, and are filed in the Office of the Secretary--- therefore,

RESOLVED, That the first Wednesday in January next, be the day for appointing Electors in the several States, which before the said day shall have ratified the said Constitution; that the first Wednesday in February next, be the day for the Electors to assemble in their respective States, and vote for a President; and that the first Wednesday in March next, be the time, and the present Seat of Congress the place for commencing Proceedings under the said Constitution.

Chas Thomson sy

Madison's essay Number 39 stated: "The immediate election of the President is to be made by the States...." A broadside issued a year later announced the date for the electors to vote for President.

mode of introducing amendments, it is neither wholly federal, nor wholly national.

In December, as the first state conventions assembled, Madison sent another report to Jefferson.

New York. Decr. 9th. 1787

The Constitution proposed by the late Convention engrosses almost the whole political attention of America. All the Legislatures except that of R. Island, which have been assembled, have agreed in submitting it to State Conventions. Virginia has set the example of opening a door for amendments, if the Convention there should chuse to propose them. Maryland has copied it. The States which preceded, referred the Constitution as recommended by the General Convention, to be ratified or rejected as it stands. The Convention of Pennsylvania, is now sitting. There are about 44 or 45, on the affirmative and about half that number on the opposite side. ... The returns of deputies for the Convention of Connecticut are known, and prove, as is said by those who know the men that a very great majority will adopt it in that State. The event in Massachusetts lies in greater uncertainty. The friends of the New Government continue to be sanguine. N. Hampshire from every account, as well as from some general inducements felt there, will pretty certainly be on the affirmative side. So will New Jersey and Delaware. N. York is much divided. She will hardly dissent from N. England, particularly if the conduct of the latter should coincide with that of N. Jersey and Pennsylva. A more formidable opposition is likely to be made in Maryland than was at first conjectured. ... The body of the people in Virgina. particularly in the upper and lower Country, and in the Northern Neck, are as far as I can gather, much disposed to adopt the new Constitution. The middle Country, and the South side of James River are principally in the opposition to it. As yet a large majority of the people are under the first description. As yet also are a majority of the Assembly. What change may be produced by the united influence of exertions of Mr. Henry, Mr. [George] Mason, and the Governor with some pretty able auxiliaries, is uncertain. My information leads me to suppose there must be three parties in Virginia. The first for adopting without

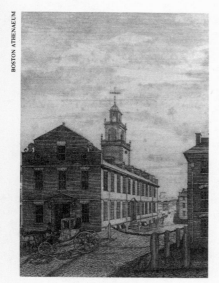

BOSTON ATHENAEUM

The State House in Boston where the Massachusetts convention for ratification of the Constitution met

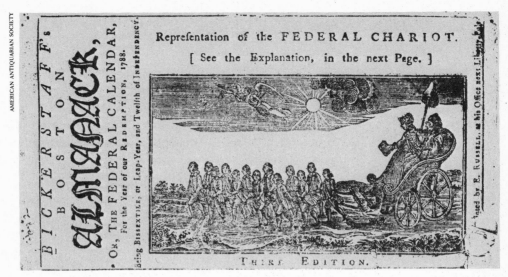

Representation of the FEDERAL CHARIOT.

[See the Explanation, in the next Page.]

THIRD EDITION.

The cover of this 1788 Almanac crudely depicts George Washington and Benjamin Franklin escorting the new Constitution to its ratification by the states.

attempting amendments. This includes Genl. W and the other deputies who signed the Constitution, Mr. Pendleton (Mr. Marshal I believe), Mr. Nicholas, Mr. Corbin, Mr. Zachy. Johnson, Col. Innis, (Mr. B. Randolph as I understand) Mr. Harvey, Mr. Gabl. Jones, Docr. Jones, &c. &c. At the head of the 2d. party which urges amendments are the Govr. & Mr. Mason. These do not object to the substance of the Governt. but contend for a few additional guards in favor of the Rights of the States and of the people. I am not able to enumerate the characters which fall in with their ideas, as distinguished from those of a third Class, at the head of which is Mr. Henry. This class concurs at present with the patrons of amendments, but will probably contend for such as strike at the essence of the System, and must lead to an adherence to the principle of the existing Confederation, which most thinking men are convinced is a visionary one, or to a partition of the Union into several Confederacies.... Mr. Henry is the great adversary who will render the event precarious. He is I find with his usual address, working up every possible interest, into a spirit of opposition. It is worthy of remark that whilst in Virga. and some of the other States in the middle & Southern Districts of the Union, the men of intelligence, patriotism, property, and independent circumstances, are thus divided: all of this description, with a few exceptions, in the Eastern States, and most of the middle States, are zealously attached to the proposed Constitution. In N. England, the men of letters, the principal officers of Government, the Judges and Lawyers, the Clergy, and men of property, furnish only here and there an adversary. It is not less worthy of remark that in Virginia where the mass of the people have been so much accustomed to be guided by their rulers on all new and intricate questions, they should on the present which certainly surpasses the judgment of the greater part of them, not only go before, but contrary to their most popular leaders. And the phenomenon is the more wonderful as a popular ground is taken by all the adversaries to the new Constitution. Perhaps the solution in both these cases, would not be very difficult; but it would lead to observations too diffusive; and to you unnecessary. I will barely observe that the case in Virga. seems to prove that the body of sober and steady people, even of the lower order, are tired of the vicisitudes, injustice and follies which have so much characterised public measures, and are impatient for some change which promises stability and repose.

Madison was rightly apprehensive about Virginia. Six states were under the new roof when he left New York for home in March, 1788, to seek election to the Virginia convention. He was successful, and it was generally thought the Federalists had won a slight edge in the delegate count. Eight states had ratified (Rhode Island had rejected the Constitution and the New Hampshire convention had adjourned without decision) when the delegates assembled in Richmond on June 2. All eyes were on Virginia, not simply because she would make the ninth state but because without Virginia the Union would be impoverished, cut in two, deprived of Washington's leadership, probably rebuffed by New York, and left to waste away. Madison did not underestimate his opposition. Patrick Henry, bespectacled, bewigged, slightly stooped now, still flashed the oratorical brilliance that had electrified the colonists in 1765. Ably assisted though he was, Henry was the colossus of the Antifederalists. Conjuring up the specter of "one great consolidated empire," he mocked and scorned the Constitution. Federal tax gatherers would suck the blood of the people; a standing army would oppress them; the states would be annihilated; and a northern sectional majority in Congress would ride roughshod over the farmers of the South, abandon the Mississippi, and even strike at slavery.

"What can avail your specious, imaginary balances, your rope-dancing, chain-rattling ridiculous ideal checks and contrivances?" The Constitution had "an awful squinting," said Henry, touching on the executive; "it squints at monarchy, and does not this raise indignation in the breast of every true American?"

To Henry's frightful rhetoric, Madison opposed dispassionate reason. He had no other eloquence: frail in body, frail in voice, he was not a commanding figure; but he spoke to the point with calmness and composure, and he addressed the intelligence, not the fears, of the delegates. "In fine," it was later said, "the good genius of the country was in him personified." The following is taken from Madison's first reply to Henry.

Debates of the Convention of Virginia
June 6, 1788

Patrick Henry

We ought sir, to examine the Constitution on its own merits solely: we are to inquire whether it will promote the public happiness: its aptitude to produce this desirable object ought to be the exclusive subject of our present researches. In this pursuit, we ought not to address our arguments to the feelings and passions, but to those understandings and judgments which were selected by the people of this country, to decide this great question by a calm and rational investigation. I hope that gentlemen, in displaying their abilities on this occasion, instead of giving opinions and making assertions, will condescend to prove and demonstrate, by a fair and regular discussion. It gives me pain to hear gentlemen continually distorting the natural construction of language, for it is sufficient if any human production can stand a fair discussion.... I must take the liberty to make some observations on what was said by another gentleman, (Mr. Henry.) He told us that this Constitution ought to be rejected because it endangered the public liberty, in his opinion, in many instances. Give me leave to make one answer to that observation: Let the dangers which this system is supposed to be replete with be clearly pointed out: if any dangerous and unnecessary powers be given to the general legislature, let them be plainly demonstrated, and let us not rest satisfied with general assertions of danger, without examination. If powers be necessary, apparent danger is not a sufficient reason against conceding them. He has suggested that licentiousness has seldom produced the loss of liberty; but that the tyranny of rulers has almost always effected it. Since the general civilization of mankind, I believe there are more instances of the abridgment of the freedom of the people by gradual and silent encroachments of those in power, than by violent and sudden usurpations; but, on a candid examination of history, we shall find that turbulence, violence, and abuse of power, by the majority trampling on the rights of the minority, have produced factions and commotions, which, in republics, have, more frequently than any other cause, produced despotism. If we go over the whole history of ancient and modern republics, we shall find their destruction to have generally resulted from those causes. If we consider the peculiar situation of the United States, and what are the sources of that diversity of sentiment which pervades its inhabitants, we shall find great danger to fear that the same causes may terminate here in the same fatal effects which they produced in those republics. This danger ought to be wisely guarded against. . . .

I must confess I have not been able to find his usual consistency in the gentleman's argument on this occasion. He informs us that the people of the country are at perfect repose,—that is, every man enjoys the fruits of his labor peaceably and securely, and that every thing is in perfect tranquility and safety. I wish sincerely, sir, this were true. If this be their happy situation, why has every state acknowledged the contrary? Why were deputies from all the states sent to the general Convention? Why have complaints of national and individual distresses been echoed and re-echoed throughout the continent? Why has our general government been so shamefully disgraced, and our Constitution violated? Wherefore have laws been made to authorize a change, and wherefore are we now assembled here? A federal government is formed for the protection of its individual members. Ours has attacked itself with impunity. Its authority has been disobeyed and despised. I think I perceive a glaring inconsistency in another of his arguments. He complains of this Constitution, because it requires the consent of at least three fourths of the states to introduce amendments which shall be necessary for the happiness of the people. The assent of so many he urges as too great an obstacle to the admission of salutary amendments, which, he strongly insists, ought to be at the will of a bare majority. We hear this argument, at the very moment we are called

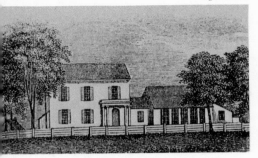

Virginia, HOWE

*Red Hill in Charlotte County,
Virginia, Patrick Henry's home*

upon to assign reasons for proposing a constitution which puts it in the power of nine states to abolish the present inadequate, unsafe, and pernicious Confederation! In the first case, he asserts that a majority ought to have the power of altering the government, when found to be inadequate to the security of public happiness. In the last case, he affirms that even three fourths of the community have not a right to alter a government which experience has proved to be subversive of national felicity! nay, that the most necessary and urgent alterations cannot be made without the absolute unanimity of all the states! Does not the thirteenth article of the Confederation expressly require that no alteration shall be made without the unanimous consent of all the states? Could any thing in theory be more perniciously improvident and injudicious than this submission of the will of the majority to the most trifling minority? Have not experience and practice actually manifested this theoretical inconvenience to be extremely impolitic? Let me mention one fact, which I conceive must carry conviction to the mind of any one: the smallest state in the Union has obstructed every attempt to reform the government; that little member has repeatedly disobeyed and counteracted the general authority; nay, has even supplied the enemies of its country with provisions. Twelve states had agreed to certain improvements which were proposed, being thought absolutely necessary to preserve the existence of the general government; but as these improvements, though really indispensable, could not, by the Confederation, be introduced into it without the consent of every state, the refractory dissent of that little state prevented their adoption. The inconveniences resulting from this requisition, of unanimous concurrence in alterations in the Confederation, must be known to every member in this Convention; it is therefore needless to remind them of them. Is it not self-evident that a trifling minority ought not to bind the majority? Would not foreign influence be exerted with facility over a small minority? Would the honorable gentlemen agree to continue the most radical defects in the old system, because the petty state of Rhode Island would not agree to remove them? . . .

But the honorable member has satirized, with peculiar acrimony, the powers given to the general government by this Constitution. I conceive that the first question on

A November, 1788, resolution from
the Virginia assembly calling for
a second constitutional convention

this subject is, whether these powers be necessary; if they be, we are reduced to the dilemma of either submitting to the inconvenience or losing the Union. Let us consider the most important of these reprobated powers; that of direct taxation is most generally objected to. With respect to the exigencies of government, there is no question but the most easy mode of providing for them will be adopted. When, therefore, direct taxes are not necessary, they will not be recurred to. It can be of little advantage of those in power to raise money in a manner oppressive to the people. To consult the conveniences of the people will cost them nothing, and in many respects, will be advantageous to them. Direct taxes will only be recurred to for great purposes. What has brought on other nations those immense debts, under the pressure of which many of them labor? Not the expenses of their governments, but war. If this country should be engaged in war, — and I conceive we ought to provide for the possibility of such a case, — how would it be carried on? By the usual means provided from year to year. As our imports will be necessary for the expenses of government and other common exigencies, how are we to carry on the means of defence? How is it possible a war could be supported without money or credit? And would it be possible for a government to have credit without having the power of raising money? No; it would be impossible for any government, in such a case, to defend itself. Then I say, sir, that it is necessary to establish funds for extraordinary exigencies, and to give this power to the general government; for the utter inutility of previous requisitions on the states is too well known....

But it is urged that its consolidated nature, joined to the power of direct taxation, will give it a tendency to destroy all subordinate authority; that its increasing influence will speedily enable it to absorb the state governments. I cannot think this will be the case. If the general government were wholly independent of the governments of the particular states, then, indeed, usurpation might be expected to the fullest extent. But, sir, on whom does this general government depend? It derives its authority from these governments, and from the same sources from which their authority is derived. The members of the federal government are taken from the same men from whom those of the state legislatures are taken.

If we consider the mode in which the federal representatives will be chosen, we shall be convinced that the general will never destroy the individual governments; and this conviction must be strengthened by an attention to the construction of the Senate. The representatives will be chosen probably under the influence of the members of the state legislatures; but there is not the least probability that the election of the latter will be influenced by the former. One hundred and sixty members represent this commonwealth in one branch of the legislature, are drawn from the people at large, and must ever possess more influence than the few men who will be elected to the general legislature.

In the end the Virginia debate came down to the question of whether amendments should be sought before or after the ratification of the Constitution. Some of the amendments proposed by the Antifederalists were plainly designed to cripple the new government; others, however, were intended to meet the widespread demand for a bill of rights. Madison and his associates firmly opposed amendments of the first class, and Federalists everywhere had taken high ground against a bill of rights. But in a bid to reconcile moderate Antifederalists to the Constitution, the Virginia advocates pledged to seek subsequent amendments that would secure the fundamental liberties of the citizens without crippling the government. Henry spurned the pledge. "Do you enter into a compact first, and afterwards settle the terms of the government?" he asked scornfully. But Henry was defeated on the resolution for prior amendments, and on June 25 the convention approved the Constitution, 89 for, 79 against. Unknown to the delegates, New Hampshire already had become the ninth state to ratify; nevertheless, it was the Virginia verdict that set the wheels of the new system in motion and exerted a powerful influence on the outcome in the main Antifederalist stronghold, New York.

Madison at once set out for New York. The changeover to the new government must go smoothly under the ministrations of the old; New York must ratify; Antifederalist demands for a "second convention" must be put down. A visiting Frenchman in New York described Madison as tired, worn out by the labors of the past year, and still burdened with cares. "His expression was that of a stern censor; his conversation disclosed a man of learning; and his countenance was that of a person conscious of his talents and of his duties." From all sides, pressures mounted for a federal declaration or bill of rights. Without conceding the merits of the case, Madison came to see the political prudence of the measure. It would be a gesture of conciliation. Quieting apprehensions of the new system, it would at one and the same time steal the Antifederalists' thunder and allow them to save face while yielding to the Constitution. Even so, the project had no charms for him, as he explained in a letter to Jefferson.

New York Ocr. 17. 1788

The little pamphlet herewith inclosed will give you a collective view of the alterations which have been proposed for the new Constitution. Various and numerous as they appear they certainly omit many of the true grounds of opposition. The articles relating to Treaties, to paper money, and to contracts, created more enemies than all the errors in the System positive and negative put together. It is true nevertheless that not a few, particularly in Virginia have contended for the proposed alterations from the most honorable and patriotic motives; and that among the advocates for the Constitution there are some who wish for further guards to public liberty and individual rights. As far as these may consist of a constitutional declaration of the most essential rights, it is probable they will be added; though there are many who think such addition unnecessary, and not a few who think it misplaced in such a Constitution. There is scarce any point on which the party in opposition is so much divided as to its importance and its propriety. My own opinion has always been in favor of a bill of rights; provided it be so framed as not to imply powers not meant to be included in the enumeration. At the same time I

In October, 1788, Madison wrote these observations on the "Draught of a Constitution for Virginia."

*Notes made of a speech Hamilton
gave in defense of the Constitution*

have never thought the omission a material defect, nor been anxious to supply it even by subsequent amendment, for any other reason than that it is anxiously desired by others. I have favored it because I supposed it might be of use, and if properly executed could not be of disservice. I have not viewed it in an important light 1. because I conceive that in a certain degree, though not in the extent argued by Mr. Wilson, the rights in question are reserved by the manner in which the federal powers are granted. 2 because there is great reason to fear that positive declaration of some of the most essential rights could not be obtained in the requisite latitude. I am sure that the rights of conscience in particular, if submitted to public definition would be narrowed much more than they are likely ever to be by an assumed power. One of the objections in New England was that the Constitution by prohibiting religious tests opened a door for Jews Turks and infidels. 3. because the limited powers of the federal Government and the jealousy of the subordinate Governments, afford a security which has not existed in the case of the State Governments, and exists in no other. 4. because experience proves the inefficacy of a bill of rights on those occasions when its controul is most needed. Repeated violations of these parchment barriers have been commited by overbearing majorities in every State. In Virginia I have seen the bill of rights violated in every instance where it has been opposed to a popular current. Notwithstanding the explicit provision contained in that instrument for the rights of Conscience it is well known that a religious establishment would have taken place in that State, if the legislative majority had found as they expected, a majority of the people in favor of the measure; and I am persuaded that if a majority of the people were now of one sect, the measure would still take place and on narrower ground than was then proposed, notwithstanding the additional obstacle which the law has since created. Wherever the real power in a Government lies, there is the danger of oppression. In our Governments the real power lies in the majority of the Community, and the invasion of private rights is chiefly to be apprehended, not from acts of Government contrary to the sense of its constituents, but from acts in which the Government is the mere instrument of the major number of the constituents. This is a truth of great importance, but not yet sufficiently attended to: and is probably more strongly impressed on my mind by facts, and reflections suggested by them, than on yours which has contemplated abuses of power issuing from a very different quarter [that is, from the despotism of European princes]. Wherever there is an interest and power to do wrong, wrong will generally be done, and not less readily by a powerful and interested party than by a powerful and interested prince. . . . What use then it may be asked can a bill of rights serve in popular Governments? I answer the two following which though less essential than in other Governments, sufficiently recommend the precaution. 1. The political truths declared in that solemn manner acquire by degrees the character of fundamental maxims of free Government, and as they become incorporated with the national sentiment, counteract the impulses of interest and passion. 2. Altho' it be generally true as above stated that the danger of oppression lies in the interested majorities of the people rather than in usurped acts of the Government, yet there may be occasions on which the evil may spring from the latter sources; and on such, a bill of rights will be a good ground for an appeal to the sense of the community. Perhaps too there may be a certain degree of danger, that a succession of artful and ambitious rulers, may by gradual & well-timed advances, finally erect an independent Government on the subversion of liberty. Should this danger exist at all, it is prudent to guard against it, especially when the precaution can do no injury. At the same time I must own that I see no tendency in our governments to danger on that side. It has been remarked that there is a tendency in all Governments to an augmentation of power at the expense of liberty. But the remark as usually understood does not appear to me well founded. Power when it has attained a certain degree of energy and independence goes on generally to further degrees. But when below that degree, the direct tendency is to further degrees of relaxation, until the abuses of liberty beget a sudden transition to an undue degree of power. With this explanation the remark may be true; and in the latter sense only is it in my opinion applicable to the Governments in America. It is a melancholy reflection that liberty should be equally exposed to danger whether the Government have too much or too little power; and that

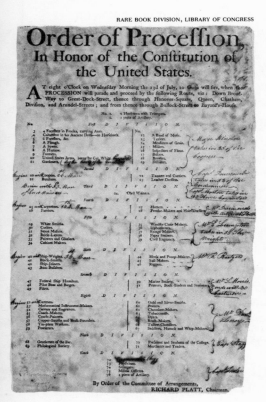

Triumphal "Order of Procession" for a parade held in New York City in honor of the Constitution

the line which divides these extremes should be so inaccurately defined by experience.

Supposing a bill of rights to be proper the articles which ought to compose it, admit of much discussion. I am inclined to think that absolute restrictions in cases that are doubtful, or where emergencies may overrule them, ought to be avoided. The restrictions however strongly marked on paper will never be regarded when opposed to the decided sense of the public; and after repeated violations in extraordinary cases, they will lose even their ordinary efficacy. Should a Rebellion or insurrection alarm the people as well as the Government, and a suspension of the Hab. Corp. [habeas corpus] be dictated by the alarm, no written prohibitions on earth would prevent the measure. Should an army in time of peace be gradually established in our neighbourhood by Britn: or Spain, declarations on paper would have as little effect in preventing a standing force for the public safety. The best security agst these evils is to remove the pretext for them.

If Madison saw the problem in America as the creation of a government strong enough to preserve liberty, Jefferson, on the scene of Europe at the dawn of the French Revolution, naturally saw the problem in a different light. The people were always entitled to the most sovereign guarantees of their personal liberties. Whatever the deficiency of "parchment barriers," they were better than no barriers. "The inconveniences of the Declaration [of Rights] are that it may cramp government in its useful exertions. But the evil of this is shortlived, moderate, and reparable. The inconveniences of the want of a Declaration are permanent, afflicting and irreparable: they are in constant progression from bad to worse." Jefferson's cool but shattering argument did not convert Madison to the cause; political necessity had accomplished that in Richmond, in his own congressional district, and in his calculus of the national interest. But Jefferson's letter, aided by his own reflection, led Madison to champion the cause of a bill of rights with the ardor of a true believer. In the face of formidable apathy, even of those who had paraded in this cause, Madison almost singlehandedly framed and pushed through the First Congress those amendments to the Constitution that compose the Bill of Rights. Ironically, the Bill of Rights, like the Constitution of which he would become the legendary father, was in some sense a political afterthought of Madison's original conception. If this is a sobering reflection, it does not reduce one whit—indeed it magnifies—the creative genius that infused the work.

Chapter 5

First Man in Congress

In what capacity Madison would be permitted to serve the new government was quite uncertain as the year 1788 came to a close. The Antifederalist complexion of Virginia politics embarrassed his prospects in that
quarter. His name was put in candidacy for the United States Senate, but
Henry and company elected two of their own and then, in carving out the
congressional districts, joined Madison's Orange constituency with neighboring counties disposed to Antifederalism. To counteract these "machinations," Madison's friends begged him to return home and declare for
Congress. His own preference, clearly, was for a seat in the House of Representatives, but he was not eager to take to the hustings. An executive appointment was in reach; Washington, whose political confidant Madison had
become, would surely use him in some high office. After pondering his
course for several weeks and observing the strength of Federalism in the
elections of members to the First Congress from other states, Madison
decided to go home and make the race. He explained himself to Jefferson.

Philadelphia Decr. 8. 1788.

Notwithstanding the formidable opposition made to the
new federal Government, first in order to prevent its
adoption, and since in order to place its administration
in the hands of disaffected men, there is now both a certainty of its peaceable commencement in March next,
and a flattering prospect that it will be administred by
men who will give it a fair trial. General Washington will
certainly be called to the Executive department. Mr.
Adams who is *pledged to support him* will probably be
the vice president. The enemies to the Government, at
the head the most inveterate of whom, is Mr. Henry are
laying a train for the election of Governour [George]
Clinton [of New York], but it cannot succeed unless the

federal votes be more dispersed than can well happen. Of the seven States which have appointed their Senators, Virginia alone will have antifederal members in that branch....In the House of Representatives the proportion of antifederal members will of course be greater, but can not, if present appearances are to be trusted, amount to a majority, or even a very formidable minority. The election for this branch has taken place as yet no where except in Penna. and here the returns are not yet come in from all the Counties. It is certain however that seven out of the eight, and probable that the whole eight representatives will bear the federal stamp. Even in Virginia where the enemies to the Government form 2/3 of the *legislature* it is computed that more than half the number of Representatives, who will be elected by the *people,* formed into districts for the purpose, will be of the same stamp. By some it is computed that 7 out of the 10, allotted to that State, will be opposed to the politics of the present Legislature....

...I shall leave this place in a day or two for Virga. where my friends who wish me to cooperate in putting our political machine into activity as a member of the House of Representatives, press me to attend. They made me a candidate for the Senate, for which I had not allotted my pretensions. The attempt was defeated by Mr. Henry who is omnipotent in the present legislature and who added to the expedients common on such occasions, a public philippic agst. my federal principles. He has taken equal pains in forming the Counties into districts for the election of Reps. to associate with Orange such as are most devoted to his politics, and most likely to be swayed by the prejudices excited agst. me. From the best information I have of the prevailing temper of the district, I conclude that my going to Virga. will answer no other purpose than to satisfy the Opinions and intreaties of my friends. The trip is in itself very disagreeable both on account of its electioneering appearance, and the sacrifice of the winter for which I had assigned a task with the intermission of Congressional business would have made convenient at New York.

James Monroe, Madison's friendly rival in first congressional race

Madison's low-keyed electioneering proved successful. Against a friendly opponent, James Monroe, he won with ease. In the process, however, he discovered firsthand the popularity of Antifederalism and trimmed his political sails accordingly. He went to Congress not only pledged to a bill of rights but also convinced that only under a course of moderation could the perils of Antifederalism be avoided and the Constitution make its way into the affections of the people. En route to New York he stopped at Mount Vernon, as had become his habit, and wrote the draft of the brief inaugural address that Washington would deliver from the portico of Federal Hall (formerly the City Hall of New York) on April 30, 1789. In the new Congress Madison at once resumed the leadership he had had in the old. Everyone saw him as "our first man." The First Congress, though covered with confusion and perplexity, must have an extraordinary influence on the future of the government. Rising to this responsibility, Madison coped with measures creating the executive departments, forming the judiciary, establishing the revenue system, framing the Bill of Rights, and so on. In the third month of the session he reported to Jefferson.

New York June 30. 1789.

The federal business has proceeded with a mortifying tardiness, chargeable in part on the incorrect draughts of Committees, and the prolixity of discussion incident to a public body, every member of which almost takes a positive agency, but principally resulting from the novelty and complexity of the subjects of Legislation. We are in a wilderness without a single footstep to guide us. Our successors will have an easier task, and by degrees the way will become smooth short and certain.

My last informed you of some of the difficulties attending a regulation of the duties. The bill on that subject has at length received the fiat of both Houses and will be forthwith made a law by the concurrence of the President. The rates are not precisely on the scale first settled by the House of Reps. . . .

The Senate has prevailed on another point in the bill which had undergone more discussion and produced more difficulty. It had been proposed by the H. of Reps. that, besides a discrimination in the tonnage, a small reduction should be made in the duty on distilled spirits imported from countries in treaty with the U. States. The Senate were opposed to any discrimination whatsoever, contending that even G. Britain should stand on the same footing with the most favored nations. The arguments on that side of the question were that the U.S. were not bound by treaty to give any commercial preferences to particular nations—that they were not bound by gratitude, since our allies had been actuated by their own interest and had obtained their compensation in the dismemberment of a rival empire—that in national and particularly in commercial measures, gratitude was moreover, no proper motive, interest alone being the Statesman's guide—that G.B. made no discrimination against the U.S. compared with other nations; but on the contrary distinguished them by a number of advantages—that if G.B. possessed almost the whole of our trade it proceeded from causes which proved that she could carry it on for us on better terms than the other nations of Europe—that we were too dependent on her trade to risk her displeasure by irritating measures which might induce her to put us on a worse footing than at present—that a small discrimination could only irritate without operating on her interests or fears—that if any thing were done it would be best to make a bolder stroke at once, and that in fact the Senate had appointed a committee to consider the subject in that point of view.—On the other side it was contended that it would be absurd to *give* away every thing that could *purchase* the stipulations wanted by us, that the motives in which the new Government originated, the known sentiments of the people at large, and the laws of most of the States subsequent to the peace shewed clearly that a distinction between nations in Treaty and nations not in Treaty would coincide with the public opinion, and that it would be offensive to a great number of citizens to see G.B. in particular put on the footing of the most favored nations, by the first act of a Government instituted for the purpose of uniting the States in the vindication of their commercial interests against her monopolizing regulations—that this respect to the sentiments of the people was the more necessary in the present critical state of the Government—that our trade at present entirely contradicted the advantages expected from the Revolution, no new channels being opened with other European nations, and the British channels being narrowed by a refusal of the most natural and valuable one to the U.S.—that this evil proceeded from the deep hold the British monopoly had taken of our Country, and the difficulty experienced by France Holland, &c. in entering into competition with her—that in order to break this monopoly, those nations ought to be aided till they could contend on equal terms—that the market of France was particu-

Madison often stopped at Mount Vernon en route from Montpelier to meetings of Congress.

Madison went to Washington's house on Cherry Street to escort him to Federal Hall for the inauguration.

larly desirable to us—that her disposition to open it would depend on the disposition manifested on our part &c. &c. . . . —that it would be sufficient to begin with a moderate discrimination, exhibiting a readiness to invigorate our measures as circumstances might require—that we had no reason to apprehend a disposition in G.B. to resort to a commercial contest, or the consequences of such an experiment, her dependence on us being greater than ours on her. The supplies of the United States are necessary to the existence, and their markets to the value, of her islands. The returns are either superfluities or poisons. In time of famine, the cry of which is heard every three or four years, the bread of the United States is essential. In time of war, which is generally decided in the West Indies, friendly offices, not violating the duties of neutrality, might effectually turn the scale in favor of an adversary. In the direct trade with Great Britain, the consequences ought to be equally dreaded by her. The raw and bulky exports of the United States employ her shipping, contribute to her revenue, enter into her manufactures, and enrich her merchants who stand between the United States and the consuming nations of Europe. A suspension of the intercourse would suspend all these advantages, force the trade into rival channels from which it might not return, and besides a temporary loss of a market for 1/4 of her exports, hasten the establishment of manufactures here, which would so far cut off the market forever. On the other side, the United States would suffer but little. The manufactures of Great Britain, as far as desirable, would find their way through other channels, and if the price were a little augmented it would only diminish an excessive consumption. They could do almost wholly without such supplies, and better without than with many of them. . . . The event of the tonnage bill, in which the discrimination was meant to be most insisted on by the House of Representatives, is not yet finally decided. But here, also, the Senate will prevail. It was determined yesterday in that House to *adhere* to their amendment for striking out the clause, and there is no reason to suppose that the other House will let the Bill be lost. . . .

The other bills depending relate to the collection of the Impost, and the establishment of a war, foreign, and Treasury Department. The bills on the two first of these departments have passed the House of Representatives, and are before the Senate. They gave birth to a very interesting constitutional question—by what authority removals from office were to be made. The Constitution being silent on the point, it was left to construction. Four opinions were advanced: 1. That no removal could be made but by way of impeachment. To this it was objected that it gave to every officer, down to tide waiters and tax gatherers, the tenure of good behavior.   2. That it devolved on the Legislature, to be disposed of as might be proper. To this it was objected that the Legislature might then dispose of it to be exercised by themselves, or even by the House of Representatives.   3. That it was incident to the power of appointment, and therefore belonged to the President and Senate. To this it was said that the Senate, being a *Legislative* body, could not be considered in an *Executive* light farther than was expressly declared; that such a construction would transfer the trust of seeing the laws duly executed from the President, the most responsible, to the Senate, the least responsible branch of the Government; that officers would intrench themselves behind a party in the Senate, bid defiance to the President, and introduce anarchy and discord into the Executive Department; that the Senate were to be Judges in case of impeachment, and ought not, therefore, to be previously called on for a summary opinion on questions of removal; that in their Legislative character they ought to be kept as cool and unbiased as possible, as the constitutional check on the passions and parties of the other House, and should, for that reason also, be as little concerned as possible in those *personal* matters, which are the great source of factious animosities.   4. That the Executive power being generally vested in the President, and the Executive function of removal not expressly taken away, it remained with the President. To this was objected the rule of construction on which the third opinion rested, and the danger of creating too much weight in the Executive scale. After very long debates the 4th opinion prevailed, as most consonant to the text of the Constitution, to the policy of mixing the Legislative and Executive Departments as little as possible, and to the requisite responsibility and harmony in the Executive Department. What the decision of the Senate will be cannot yet be even conjectured.

As one might surmise from this letter, it was Madison's opinion that prevailed on the question of executive removal power—a constitutional decision of great import for the office of the Presidency—while his opinion was defeated on the question of commercial discrimination. It proved a costly defeat, one that he and Jefferson would try repeatedly to reverse but without success. The commercial aspirations that had brought the Constitution into being could not be fulfilled, Madison thought, if Congress began by discarding the weapon of commercial discrimination. To combat British monopoly and British influence, to encourage American shipping and navigation, to open new markets in a widening system of free trade pivoted on the French alliance—these were Madison's objectives, and he argued that the national government was morally committed to their realization. But interests as different as those of southern planters and eastern merchants, each in its own way tied into the British system, combined to defeat Madison's project. The division on this issue presaged the great conflict still to come.

Early in 1790, Alexander Hamilton, who had been appointed Secretary of the Treasury, gave Congress his *Report on the Public Credit.* Hamilton had been Madison's choice for the Treasury post; they were political allies and expected to remain so. With much of Hamilton's plan for paying the debt and establishing the public credit Madison was in complete accord. Under this plan the national debt of some fifty-two million dollars, of which twelve million was owed abroad, would be funded by the government, interest paid, and provision made for discharge. But justice was revolted, Madison said, by the Secretary's proposition to put original and present holders of the domestic debt on the same footing and to fund the whole at face value in specie. In the course of depreciation over the years, the debt had become an article of speculation. The needs of the original creditors—soldiers, farmers, tradesmen—had led them to sell their securities at a fraction of their nominal value. Probably not more than one-fifth of the debt remained in the hands of the wartime creditors. Hamilton's plan rewarded the speculative greed of the few to the exclusion of justice for the many. Madison, although he had earlier rejected the idea, proposed a discrimination between the two classes of creditors. Original holders would be paid in full; holders by transfer would be paid at the market value, with the difference between the face value and the market value going to the primary creditors. Whatever the justice of the arrangement, it was full of difficulties and met defeat in the House.

Madison was more successful in opposing Hamilton's plan for the assumption of the state debts, estimated at about twenty-five million dollars. The issue for Madison was not "state rights" or excessive taxation or fear of the power to be erected on this mass of debt. Again, the issue was justice. Since the war the states had moved to pay their debts at a very uneven pace. For the general government simply to assume these debts as they stood in

1790 would be to penalize the fiscally responsible states to the benefit of the delinquents. So Madison argued that the debts should be assumed as they stood in 1783 and, in addition, that more generous provision be made for allocating "common charges" among the states. Obviously, this plan would have increased the national debt substantially above the level set by Hamilton. Others opposed assumption on other grounds, though equity was always a consideration. Madison discussed both discrimination and assumption in a letter to Edmund Pendleton, a district judge in Virginia.

N. York March 4. 1790.

The only act of much consequence which the present Session has yet produced, is one for enumerating the Inhabitants as the basis of a reapportionment of the Representation. The House of Reps. has been cheifly employed of late on the Report of the Secy. of the Treasury. As it has been printed in all the Newspapers I take for granted that it must have fallen under your eye. The plan which it proposes is in general well digested, and illustrated &c supported by very able reasoning. It has not however met with universal concurrence in every heart. I have myself been of the number who could not suppress objections. I have not been able to persuade myself that the transactions between the U. S. and those whose services were most instrumental in saving their country, did in fact extinguish the claims of the latter on the justice of the former; or that there must not be something radically wrong in suffering those who rendered a bona fide consideration to lose 7/8 of their dues, and those who have no particular merit towards their Country, to gain 7 or 8 times as much as they advanced. In pursuance of this view of the subject, a proposition was made for redressing in some degree the inequality. After much discussion, a large majority was in the negative. The subject at present before a Committee of the whole, is the proposed assumption of the State debts. On this, opinions seem to be pretty equally divided. Virga. is endeavoring to incorporate with the measure some effectual provision for a final settlement and payment of balances among the States. Even with this ingredient, the project will neither be just nor palatable, if the assumption be referred to the present epoch, and by that means deprives the States who have done most, of the benefit of their exertions. We have accordingly made an effort but without success to refer the assumption to the State of the

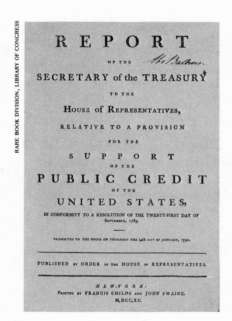

REPORT
OF THE
SECRETARY of the TREASURY
TO THE
HOUSE of REPRESENTATIVES,
RELATIVE TO A PROVISION
FOR THE
SUPPORT
OF THE
PUBLIC CREDIT
OF THE
UNITED STATES,
IN CONFORMITY TO A RESOLUTION OF THE TWENTY-FIRST DAY OF
SEPTEMBER, 1789.

PRESENTED TO THE HOUSE ON THURSDAY THE 14th DAY OF JANUARY, 1790.

PUBLISHED BY ORDER OF THE HOUSE OF REPRESENTATIVES.

NEW-YORK;
PRINTED BY FRANCIS CHILDS AND JOHN SWAINE.
M,DCC,XC.

Title page of Alexander Hamilton's Report on the Public Credit, *1790*

Edmund Pendleton

debts at the close of the war. This would probably add 1/3 more to the amount of the Debts, but would more than compensate for this by rendering the measure more just & satisfactory. A simple unequalified assumption of the existing debts would bear peculiarly hard on Virginia. She has paid I believe a greater part of her quotas since the peace than Massts. She suffered far more during the war. It is agreed that she will not be less a Creditor on the final settlement, yet if such an assumption were to take place she would pay towards the discharge of the debts, in the proportion of 1/5 and receive back to her Creditor Citizens 1/7 or 1/8, whilst Massts. would pay not more than 1/7 or 1/8, and receive back not less than 1/5. The case of S. Carola. is a still stronger contrast. In answer to this inequality we are referred to the final liquidation for which provision may be made. But this may *possibly* never take place. It will *probably* be at some distance. The payment of the balances among the States will be a fresh source of delay & difficulties. The merits of the plan independently of the question of equity, are also controvertible, tho' on the other side there are advantages which have considerable weight.

The House balked at assumption and sent the funding bill, *sans* assumption, to the Senate in June. But the advocates of assumption promised "no assumption, no funding." In short they would block any plan for establishing the national credit, thus jeopardizing the Union in its infancy, unless the state debts were included. As it happened, however, the Senate was at this time also entangled on the old nettle of a permanent seat of government. Madison and the Virginians, with most southerners, favored the location of the capital on the Potomac, while the rival claims of New York and Philadelphia divided the northerners. Thus the stage was set for the first sectional compromise under the Constitution. It would be a mistake to say that everything was settled between the principals, Madison and Hamilton, around Thomas Jefferson's dinner table. That famous dinner, arranged by the newly appointed Secretary of State, may have had more symbolic than actual importance. The result, at any rate, was a modified plan of assumption, which was quite acceptable to Madison, and the location of the capital on the Potomac after a temporary residence of ten years in Philadelphia. Votes were pledged and the two measures squeaked through Congress in July. Three hurried dispatches from Madison to Monroe chart the tortuous course of compromise.

New York, June 1, 1790.
The assumption has been revived, and is still depending. I do not believe it will take place, but the event may possibly be governed by circumstances not at present fully in view. The funding bill for the proper debt of the United States is engrossed for the last reading. It conforms in substance to the plan of the Secretary of the Treas. You will have seen by late papers that an experiment for navigation and commercial purposes has been introduced. It has powerful friends, and from the present aspect of the House of Representatives will succeed there by a great majority. In the Senate its success is not improbable, if I am rightly informed. You will see by the inclosed paper that a removal from this place has been voted by a large majority of our House. The other is pretty nearly balanced. The Senators of the 3 Southern States are disposed to couple the permanent with the temporary question. If they do, I think it will end in either an abortion of both, or in a decision of the former in favour of the Delaware. I have good reason to believe that there is no serious purpose in the Northern States to prefer the Potowmac, and that, if supplied with a pretext for a very hasty

This cartoon of the "Constitution" going to the devil with Congress on board and Robert Morris at the helm indicated public dissatisfaction with the assumption-residence compromise. Dissenters are being towed along by the majority on the way to Philadelphia.

decision, they will indulge their secret wishes for a permanent establishment on the Delaware. As Rhode Island is again in the Union, and will probably be in the Senate in a day or two, the Potowmac has the less to hope and the more to fear from this quarter.

New York, July 4, 1790

You will find by one of the Gazettes herewith sent, that the bill fixing the permanent seat of Government on the Potowmac, and the temporary at Philadelphia, has got through the Senate. It passed by a single voice only, Izzard and Few having both voted against it. Its passage through the House of Representatives is probable, but attended with great difficulties. If the Potowmac succeeds, even on these terms, it will have resulted from a fortuitous coincidence of circumstances which might never happen again.

The provision for the public debt has been suspended for some time in the Senate by the question relating to the seat of Government. It is now resumed in that House, and it is to be hoped will soon be brought to an issue. The assumption sleeps, but I am persuaded will be awakened on the first dawn of a favorable opportunity. It seems, indeed, as if the friends of the measure were determined to risk everything rather than suffer that finally to fail.

First page of an act concerning duties on distilled spirits in 1790

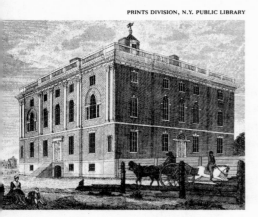

This house on Ninth Street in Philadelphia was intended for the President, but he never lived there.

New York, July 24, 1790.

After all the vicissitudes through which the assumption has passed, it seems at present in a fair way to succeed as part of the general plan for the public debt. The Senate have included it among their amendments to the funding bill, and a vote of yesterday in the House of Representatives indicates a small majority in favor of the measure. In its present form it will very little affect the interest of Virginia in either way. I have not been able to overcome my other objections, or even to forbear urging them. At the same time, I cannot deny that the crisis demands a spirit of accommodation to a certain extent. If the measure should be adopted, I shall wish it to be considered as an unavoidable evil, and *possibly* not the worst side of the dilemma.

In an end-of-session letter to his father, Madison described the final outcome of the vote on assumption.

N. Y. July 31. 1790.

The funding bill has at length passed the two Houses with a qualified assumption of the state debts.... The assumption was carried by a small majority in both Houses. Many who voted for it did so on a supposition that it was a lesser evil than to risk the effect of a rejection on the states which insisted on the measure. I could not bring myself to concur with them, but am sensible that there was serious danger of a very unfavorable issue to the Session from a contrary decision, and consider it as now incumbent on us all to make the best of what is done. The truth is that in a pecuniary light, the assumption is no longer of much consequence to Virginia, the sum allotted to her being about her proportion of the whole, & rather exceeding her present debt. She will consequently pay no more to the general Treasury than she now pays to the State Treasy. and perhaps in a mode which will be less disagreeable to the people, tho not more favorable to their true interests.

The Ways & means are now under consideration. The impost will be made equal to the federal debt. The provision for the State debts will be put off till the next session. It will be likely to consist chiefly of duties on rum distilled in the U.S. and on a few imported articles that will best bear a further augmentation.

We expect that an adjournment will take place in about a week. I shall set out for Virginia as soon thereafter as I can pack up my books papers &c. which will detain me here some days. Mr. Jefferson wishes me to wait for his setting out and as his company will be particularly grateful & also convenient I am not sure that I shall resist the invitation, if he finds that he can be ready for the Journey within a reasonable time. I shd. not hesitate, if I did not wish to be in Orange by the election, tho' as an attendance cannot be given at more than one of the 8 Counties, it does not seem worth while to sacrifice much to that consideration.

Madison and Jefferson often traveled to and from Virginia together now that Jefferson had been persuaded to become part of the government at home rather than Minister to France. Congress convened at the old stand, in Philadelphia, in the fall. Before long Hamilton submitted to the House his report on a national bank. The proposed bank, like the century-old Bank of England, would harness private interest and profit to public convenience. It would act as the financial arm of the government and also mount a large paper circulation in the form of bank notes, thereby multiplying the active capital of the country and stimulating enterprise. Of the capital of ten million dollars the government would furnish only one-fifth, the rest being subscribed by private investors, primarily in the form of public securities. In effect, the holders of the funded debt would be privileged to incorporate as a bank, empowered to engage in commercial business, and blessed with the largest account in the economy, that of the federal government. Leading the fight against the bill in the House, Madison dwelled less on the character of the bank as a financial institution or on its features of capitalist privilege than on its unconstitutionality. His principal speech was reported, in part, as follows.

Annals of Congress [February 2, 1791]

Is the power of establishing an incorporated Bank among the powers vested by the Constitution in the Legislature of the United States? This is the question to be examined.

After some general remarks on the limitations of all political power, he [Madison] took notice of the peculiar manner in which the Federal Government is limited. It is not a general grant, out of which particular powers are excepted; it is a grant of particular powers only, leaving the general mass in other hands. So it had been understood by its friends and its foes, and so it was to be interpreted....

Reviewing the Constitution...it was not possible to discover in it the power to incorporate a Bank. The only clauses under which such a power could be pretended are either:

1. The power to lay and collect taxes to pay the debts, and provide for the common defence and general welfare: or,

2. The power to borrow money on the credit of the United States: or,

3. The power to pass all laws necessary and proper to carry into execution those powers.

The bill did not come within the first power. It laid no tax to pay the debts, or provide for the general welfare. It laid no tax whatever. It was altogether foreign to the subject.

No argument could be drawn from the terms "common defence and general welfare." The power as to these general purposes was limited to acts laying taxes for them; and the general purposes themselves were limited and explained by the particular enumeration subjoined. To understand these terms in any sense, that would justify the power in question, would give to Congress an unlimited power; and would render nugatory the enumeration of particular powers; would supersede all the powers reserved to the State Governments. These terms are copied from the articles of Confederation; had it ever been pretended that they were to be understood otherwise than as here explained?

It has been said, that "general welfare" meant cases in which a general power might be exercised by Congress, without interfering with the powers of the States; and that the establishment of a National Bank was of this sort. There were, he said, several answers to this novel doctrine.

1. The proposed Bank would interfere, so as indirectly to defeat a State Bank at the same place.

2. It would directly interfere with the rights of the States to prohibit as well as to establish Banks, and the circulation of Bank notes. He mentioned a law in Virginia actually prohibiting the circulation of notes payable to bearer.

3. Interference with the power of the States was no

Madison led the fight in the House against Alexander Hamilton (above) and his report on a national bank.

constitutional criterion of the power of Congress. If the power was not given, Congress could not exercise it; if given, they might exercise it, although it should interfere with the laws, or even the Constitution of the States.

4. If Congress could incorporate a Bank merely because the act would leave the States free to establish Banks also, any other incorporations might be made by Congress. They could incorporate companies of manufacturers, or companies for cutting canals, or even religious societies, leaving similar incorporations by the States, like State Banks, to themselves. Congress might even establish religious teachers in every parish, and pay them out of the Treasury of the United States, leaving other teachers unmolested in their functions. These inadmissible consequences condemned the controverted principle.

The case of the Bank established by the former Congress had been cited as a precedent. This was known, he said, to have been the child of necessity. It never could be justified by the regular powers of the articles of Confederation....

The second clause to be examined is that which empowers Congress to borrow money.

Is this bill to borrow money? It does not borrow a shilling. Is there any fair construction by which the bill can be deemed an exercise of the power to borrow money? The obvious meaning of the power to borrow money, is that of accepting it from, and stipulating payment to those who are able and willing to lend.

To say that the power to borrow involves a power of creating the ability, where there may be the will, to lend, is not only establishing a dangerous principle, as will be immediately shown, but is as forced a construction as to say that it involves the power of compelling the will, where there may be the ability to lend.

The third clause is that which gives the power to pass all laws necessary and proper to execute the specified powers.

Whatever meaning this clause may have, none can be admitted, that would give an unlimited discretion to Congress.

Its meaning must, according to the natural and obvious force of the terms and the context, be limited to means

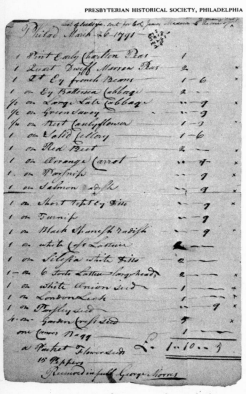

An invoice listing seeds, including beets, turnips, peas, and flowers, Madison purchased in March, 1791

When Hamilton's bank bill passed, plans were made to erect this building to house the Bank in Philadelphia, then the capital.

necessary to the end, and incident to the nature of the specified powers....

The essential characteristics of the Government, as composed of limited and enumerated powers, would be destroyed, if, instead of direct and incidental means, any means could be used, which, in the language of the preamble to the bill, "might be conceived to be conducive to the successful conducting of the finances, or might be conceived to tend to give facility to the obtaining of loans." He urged an attention to the diffuse and ductile terms which had been found requisite to cover the stretch of power contained in the bill. He compared them with the terms necessary and proper, used in the Constitution, and asked whether it was possible to view the two descriptions as synonymous, or the one as a fair and safe commentary on the other.

If, proceeded he, Congress, by virtue of the power to borrow, can create the means of lending, and, in pursuance of these means, can incorporate a Bank, they may do any thing whatever creative of like means....

With all this evidence of the sense in which the Constitution was understood and adopted, will it not be said, if the bill should pass, that its adoption was brought about by one set of arguments, and that it is now administered under the influence of another set? and this reproach will have the keener sting, because it is applicable to so many individuals concerned in both the adoption and administration.

In fine, if the power were in the Constitution, the immediate exercise of it cannot be essential; if not there, the exercise of it involves the guilt of usurpation, and establishes a precedent of interpretation levelling all the barriers which limit the powers of the General Government, and protect those of the State Governments. If the point be doubtful only, respect for ourselves, who ought to shun the appearance of precipitancy and ambition; respect for our successors, who ought not lightly to be deprived of the opportunity of exercising the rights of legislation; respect for our constitutents who have had no opportunity of making known their sentiments, and who are themselves to be bound down to the measure for so long a period; all these considerations require that the irrevocable decision should at least be suspended until another session.

Thomas Paine

It appeared on the whole, he concluded, that the power exercised by the bill was condemned by the silence of the Constitution; was condemned by the rule of interpretation arising out of the Constitution; was condemned by its tendency to destroy the main characteristic of the Constitution; was condemned by the expositions of the friends of the Constitution, whilst depending before the public; was condemned by the apparent intention of the parties which ratified the Constitution; was condemned by the explanatory amendments proposed by Congress themselves to the Constitution; and he hoped it would receive its final condemnation by the vote of this House.

But the bill passed and became law on February 25 after President Washington rejected the counsels of strict construction in favor of Hamilton's doctrine of implied powers. The split between Madison and Hamilton—between Jefferson and Hamilton, too—defined the fundamental constitutional issue in an emerging division of parties. Why Madison chose to take such a strict view of federal powers is not easily explained. Doubtless he was influenced by the remonstrance of the Virginia assembly against the assumption of state debts. Not only was that measure unconstitutional, it was, said the assembly, antirepublican and designed to prostrate agriculture at the feet of "a large monied interest." While he did not agree with this opinion of assumption, Madison recognized the widespread fears aroused by Hamilton's measures, especially to the southward, and he began to see these measures as forming a system of privilege that threatened the precarious balance of the republican experiment. The people in their conventions had adopted a strictly limited constitution, and it was to this constitution, not to the one he had advocated at Philadelphia or even in *The Federalist*, that Madison was bound. If its restraints were broken, there was no limit to which men like Hamilton, whose republican commitment was frail at best, might go. Madison once remarked that the Constitution had two enemies, "one that would stretch it to death, and one that would squeeze it to death." Death by stretching, he felt, was the danger in 1791.

Madison's hostility to Hamiltonian policy increased in the coming months. The speculative scramble for the Bank stocks implicated the government in the mean arts of jobbery and chicanery and helped to identify the "paper and stock" interest behind the Treasury program. Ideological affinity between this faction and the Burkian assault on the French Revolution was suggested by the controversy whipped up around the publication of Thomas Paine's *The Rights of Man*. The volume included an unintended preface by

Jefferson—actually a private letter printed without his permission—in which the Secretary of State recommended the book as a republican antidote to the "political heresies" lately abroad in the press—an unmistakable allusion to Vice President Adams's atrabilious "Discourses on Davila." British partisans loudly disapproved of Jefferson's remarks, fearing the Secretary's support of Paine would offend the British court. Madison feared that Adams's writings would be equally offensive to the French. Madison considered the French Revolution an emanation from the American—the awakening of the Old World to "the voice of liberty"—and felt that every true republican must wish for its success. In May, just as this affair was breaking, Madison and Jefferson set out on a leisurely excursion to Lake Champlain. On their return Madison lingered in New York and continued writing to Jefferson, who had gone on to Philadelphia, on the progress of speculation and ideological encounter.

N. York May 12, 1791.

I had seen Payne's pamphlet with the preface of the Philada. Editor. It immediately occurred that you were brought into the Frontispiece in the manner you explain[ed]. But I had not foreseen the particular use made of it by the British partizans. Mr. Adams can least of all complain; under a mock defence of the Republican Constitutions of his Country, he attacked them with all the force he possessed, and this in a book with his name to it whilst he was the Representative of his Country at a foreign Court [*A Defence of the Constitutions*, written while Adams was the first American Minister to Great Britain, 1785–88]. Since he has been the 2d. magistrate in the new Republic, his pen has constantly been at work in the same cause; and tho' his name has not been prefixed to his antirepublican discourses, the author has been as well known as if that formality had been observed. Surely if it be innocent & decent in one servant of the public thus to write attacks agst its Government, it can not be very criminal or indecent in another to patronize a written defense of the principles on which that govt. is founded. The sensibility of H. & B. [George Hammond and Phineas Bond, British Minister and Consul, respectively, to the United States] to the indignity to the Brit: Court is truly ridiculous. If offence cd. be justly taken in that quarter, what would France have a right to say to Burke's pamphlet [*Reflections on the French Revolution*] and the Countenance given to it & its author, particularly by the King himself? What in fact might not the U.S. say, whose revolution & demo-

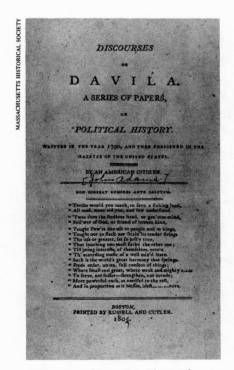

DISCOURSES
ON
D A V I L A.
A SERIES OF PAPERS,
ON
POLITICAL HISTORY.
WRITTEN IN THE YEAR 1790, AND THEN PUBLISHED IN THE
GAZETTE OF THE UNITED STATES.

BY AN AMERICAN CITIZEN.

John Adams

NON IGNARAT RUMORIS ANTE SALUTEM.

BOSTON,
PRINTED BY RUSSELL AND CUTLER.
1805.

Title page of Vice President John Adams's Discourses on Davila

cratic governments come in for a large share of the scurrility lavished on those of France.

N. York July 10. 1791

The Bank-Shares have risen as much in the Market here as at Philadelphia. It seems admitted on all hands now that the plan of the institution gives a moral certainty of gain to the subscribers with scarce a physical possibility of loss. The subscriptions are consequently a mere scramble for so much public plunder which will be engrossed by those already loaded with the spoils of indi-[vi]duals. The event shews what would have been the operation of the plan, if, *as originally proposed*, subscriptions had been limited to the 1st. of April and to the favorite species of stock which the Bank-Jobbers had monopolized. It pretty clearly appears also in what proportions the public debt lies in the Country—what sort of hands hold it; and by whom the people of the U.S. are to be governed. Of all the shameful circumstances of this business, it is among the greatest to see the members of the Legislature who were most active in pushing this Job, openly grasping its emoluments. [Philip] Schuyler [Senator from New York and Hamilton's father-in-law] is to be put at the Head of the Directors, if the weight of the N. Y. subscribers can effect it. Nothing new is talked of here. In fact stock-jobbing drowns every other subject. The Coffee House is in an eternal buzz with the gamblers.

New York, July 13, 1791.

Beckely [John Beckley, Clerk of the House of Representatives] has just got back from his Eastern trip. He says that the partizans of Mr. Adams's heresies in that quarter are perfectly insignificant in point of number; that particularly in Boston he is become distinguished for his unpopularity; that Publicola [author of a series of anti-Paine, pro-Adams letters] is probably the manufacture of his son [John Quincy] out of materials furnished by himself, and that the publication is generally as obnoxious in New England as it appears to be in Pennsylvania. If young Adams be capable of giving the dress in which Publicola presents himself, it is very probable he may have been made Editor of his father's doctrines.

...I mentioned to you some time ago an extract from a piece in the Poughkeepsie paper as a sensible comment on Mr. Adams's doctrines. The whole has since been republished here, and is evidently from a better pen than any of the Anti-Publicolas I have seen.

N. York Aug:8. 1791.

I take the liberty of putting the inclosed into your hands....You will find an allusion to some mysterious cause for a phoenomenon in the Stocks. It is surmized that the deferred [state] debt is to be taken up at the next session, and some anticipated provision made for it. This may either be an invention of those who wish to sell: or it may be a reality imparted in confidence to the purchasers or smelt out by their sagacity. I have had a hint that something is intended and had dropt from —— —— which has led to this speculation. I am unwilling to credit the fact, untill I have further evidence, which I am in a train of getting if it exists. It is said that packet boats & expresses are again sent from this place to the Southern States, to buy up the paper of all sorts which has risen in the market here. These & other abuses make it a problem whether the system of the old paper under a bad Government, or of the new under a good one, be chargeable with the greater substantial injustice. The true difference seems to be that by the former the few were the victims to the many; by the latter the many to the few. It seems agreed on all hands now that the bank is a certain & gratuitous augmentation of the capitals sub[s]cribed, on a proportion of not less than 40 or 50 PerCt. and if the deferred debt should be immediately provided for in favor of the purchasers of it in the deferred shape, & since the unanimous vote that no change shd. be made in the funding system, my imagination will not attempt to set bounds to the daring depravity of the times. The stockjobbers will become the pretorian band of the Government—at once its tool & its tyrant; bribed by its largesses, & overaweing it, by clamours & combinations.

John Quincy Adams by Copley

One of Madison's errands in New York was to persuade his old college friend Philip Freneau to go to Philadelphia and edit a national newspaper devoted to the republican cause. Such a vehicle of intelligence was necessary to combat the Federalist newspaper, John Fenno's *Gazette of the United States,* "a paper of pure Toryism" in Jefferson's opinion. Freneau finally consented and the *National Gazette* began publication in the fall. Madison was soon writing for it. His little essays on a variety of subjects in political economy and statecraft, several of which are excerpted here, became increasingly partisan as the political temperature soared in Philadelphia. Taken together, they form a kind of primer of the emerging Republican party.

Madison's college friend Philip Freneau (above) started publishing a newspaper (below) to which Madison contributed short political essays.

National Gazette.
By *PHILIP FRENEAU.*

"Consolidation" [December 3, 1791]
Much has been said, and not without reason, against a consolidation of the States into one government. Omitting lesser objections, two consequences would probably flow from such a change in our political system, which justify the cautions used against it. First, it would be impossible to avoid the dilemma, of either relinquishing the present energy and responsibility of a *single* executive magistrate, for some *plural* substitute, which by dividing so great a trust might lessen the danger of it; or suffering so great an accumulation of powers in the hands of that officer, as might by degrees transform him into a monarch. The incompetency of one Legislature to regulate all the various objects belonging to the local governments, would evidently force a transfer of many of them to the executive department; whilst the encreasing splendour and number of its prerogatives supplied by this source, might prove excitements to ambition too powerful for a sober execution of the elective plan, and consequently strengthen the pretexts for an hereditary designation of the Magistrate. Second, were the State governments abolished, the same space of country that would produce an undue growth of the executive power, would prevent that controul on the Legislative body, which is essential to a faithful discharge of its trust....

But if a consolidation of the States into one government be an event so justly to be avoided, it is not less to be desired, on the other hand, that a consolidation should prevail in their interests and affections; and this too, as it fortunately happens, for the very reasons, among others, which lie against a governmental consolidation. For, in the first place, in proportion as uniformity is found to prevail in the interests and sentiments of the different states, will be the practicability of accommodating *Legislative* regulations to them, and thereby of withholding new and dangerous prerogatives from the executive.

Again, the greater the mutual confidence and affection of all parts of the Union, the more likely they will be to concur amicably, or to differ with moderation, in the elective designation of the Chief Magistrate; and by such examples, to guard and adorn the vital principle of our republican constitution. Lastly, the less the supposed difference of interests, and the greater the concord and confidence throughout the great body of the people, the more readily must they sympathize with each other, the more seasonably can they interpose a common manifestation of their sentiments, the more certainly will they take the alarm at usurpation or oppression, and the more certainly will they *consolidate* their defence of the public liberty.

In December, 1791, Judge George Turner of the Northwest Territory gave this report of the Indians on the Ohio to Madison and Congress.

"Public opinion" [December 19, 1791]

Public opinion sets bounds to every government, and is the real sovereign in every free one.

As there are cases where the public opinion must be obeyed by the government; so there are cases, where not being fixed, it may be influenced by the government. This distinction, if kept in view, would prevent or decide many debates on the respect due from the government to the sentiments of the people.

In proportion as government is influenced by opinion, it must be so, by whatever influences opinion. This decides the question concerning a *Constitutional Declaration of Rights*, which requires an influence on government, by becoming a part of the public opinion.

The larger a country, the less easy for its real opinion to be ascertained, and the less difficult to be counterfeited; when ascertained or presumed, the more respectable it is in the eyes of individuals. This is favorable to the authority of government. For the same reason, the more extensive a country, the more insignificant is each individual in his own eyes. This may be unfavorable to liberty.

Whatever facilitates a general intercourse of sentiments, as good roads, domestic commerce, a free press, and particularly *a circulation of newspapers through the entire body of the people*, and *Representatives going from, and returning among every part of them,* is equivalent to a contraction of territorial limits, and is favorable to liberty, where these may be too extensive.

"Spirit of Governments" [February 20, 1792]
No Government is perhaps reducible to a sole principle
of operation. Where the theory approaches nearest to
this character, different and often heterogeneous principles mingle their influence in the administration. It is
useful nevertheless to analyse the several kinds of government, and to characterize them by the spirit which
predominates in each.

Montesquieu has resolved the great operative principles of government into fear, honor, and virtue, applying the first to pure despotisms, the second to regular
monarchies, and the third to republics. The portion of
truth blended with the ingenuity of this system, sufficiently justifies the admiration bestowed on its author.
Its accuracy however can never be defended against the
criticisms which it has encountered. Montesquieu was
in politics not a Newton or a Locke, who established immortal systems, the one in matter, the other in mind. He
was in his particular science what Bacon was in universal
science: He lifted the veil from the venerable errors
which enslaved opinion, and pointed the way to those
luminous truths of which he had but a glimpse himself.

May not governments be properly divided, according
to their predominant spirit and principles into three
species of which the following are examples?

First. A government operating by a permanent military
force, which at once maintains the government, and is
maintained by it; which is at once the cause of burdens
on the people, and of submission in the people to their
burdens. Such have been the governments under which
human nature has groaned through every age. Such are
the governments which still oppress it in almost every
country of Europe, the quarter of the globe which calls
itself the pattern of civilization, and the pride of humanity.

Secondly. A government operating by corrupt influence; substituting the motive of private interest in place
of public duty; converting its pecuniary dispensations
into bounties to favorites, or bribes to opponents; accommodating its measures to the avidity of a part of the nation instead of the benefit of the whole: in a word,
enlisting an army of interested partizans, whose tongues,
whose pens, whose intrigues, and whose active combinations, by supplying the terror of the sword, may support
a real domination of the few, under an apparent liberty

*Washington (standing at right) and
his first Cabinet: Henry Knox,
seated; Thomas Jefferson, Edmund
Randolph (back to artist), and
Alexander Hamilton, standing*

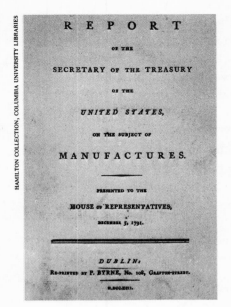

REPORT

OF THE

SECRETARY OF THE TREASURY

OF THE

UNITED STATES,

ON THE SUBJECT OF

MANUFACTURES.

PRESENTED TO THE

HOUSE OF REPRESENTATIVES,

DECEMBER 5, 1791.

DUBLIN:

Re-printed by P. BYRNE, No. 108, Grafton-street.

M.DCC.XCII.

Madison and Jefferson both opposed Hamilton's Report on Manufactures.

of the many. Such a government, wherever to be found, is an imposter. It is happy for the new world that it is not on the west side of the Atlantic. It will be both happy and honorable for the United States, if they never descend to mimic the costly pageantry of its form, nor betray themselves into the venal spirit of its administration.

Thirdly. A government, deriving its energy from the will of the society, and operating by the reason of its measures, on the understanding and interest of the society. Such is the government for which philosophy has been searching, and humanity been sighing, from the most remote ages. Such are the republican governments which it is the glory of America to have invented, and her unrivalled happiness to possess. May her glory be compleated by every improvement on the theory which experience may teach; and her happiness be perpetuated by a system of administration corresponding with the purity of the theory.

Political alignments took definite form in 1792. Congressmen spoke of "Mr. Madison's party." Leading Federalists said he had become "a desperate party leader." If this seemed a strange role for one who disliked parties, it was because he now realized that the natural countervailing action of competing interests, on which he had relied, was not working and that it was necessary to build a broad republican consensus to overcome the powerful combination—speculative, mercantile, manufacturing, Anglican—that Treasury influence had formed around the administration. Hamilton's *Report on Manufactures*, proposing a centralized system of economic development for the sprawling young agricultural country, not only bid defiance of the Constitution but disclosed the whole consolidating tendency of the administration. In Madison's view the choice was between two alternatives: consolidate power and divide the people or divide power and consolidate the people. The latter offered the only sure foundation of republican union.

The growing division in Congress was duplicated in Washington's Cabinet. Hamilton and Jefferson were increasingly at odds on issues of foreign policy, the former soft on Britain and hard on France, the latter just the reverse. By May, 1792, Hamilton was claiming that the two Virginians spearheaded a faction seeking to subvert the government. About Madison he was frankly puzzled. Whether his apostasy was the result of Jefferson's wily influence or the seductions of Virginia politics, he did not know; but it was Jefferson, more than Madison, whom he feared. In July, Hamilton himself took up the attack in Fenno's *Gazette*, charging Jefferson—and, to a lesser extent,

Madison—with hostility to the Constitution, to funding and credit, and to the administration he pretended to serve. He accused Jefferson of employing Freneau, a part-time clerk in his own department, in vicious newspaper warfare on the administration. Shocked by this development, Madison rode over to Monticello from Orange to talk strategy with Jefferson. In the public mind at least, Hamilton had built Jefferson into *the* Republican leader. While Jefferson held aloof from the turmoil, Madison and Monroe put their pens to work in his defense. Of Hamilton's charge regarding the *National Gazette,* Madison wrote to Attorney General Edmund Randolph.

Orange [Virginia,] Sepr. 13—1792

Your favor of the 12 Ult. having arrived during an excurtion into Albemarle [County], I did not receive it till my return on yesterday. I lose not a moment in thanking you for it; particularly for the very friendly paragraph in the publication in Fenno's paper. As I do not get his paper here, it was by accident I first saw this extraordinary maneuvre of Calumny; the quarter, the motive, and the object of which speak for themselves. As it respects Mr. Jefferson, I have no doubt that it will be of service both to him & to the public, if it should lead to such an investigation of his political opinions and character as may be expected. With respect to myself the consequence in a public view is of little account. In any view, there could not have been a charge founded on a grosser perversion of facts, & consequently against which I could feel myself more invulnerable.

That I wished & recomme[n]ded Mr. Freneau to be appd to his present Clerkship is certain. But the Department of State was not the only, nor as I recollect the first one to which I mentioned his name & character. I was governed in these recommendations by an acquaintance of long standing, by a respect for his talents, & by a knowledge of his merit & sufferings in the course of the revolution. Had I been less abstemious in my practice from Solicitations in behalf of my friends, I should probably have been more early in thinking of Mr. F. The truth is, that my application when made did not originate with myself. It was suggested by another Gentleman [Henry Lee] who could feel no motive but a disposition to patronize merit, & who wish'd me to cooperate with him. That with others of Mr. Freneau's particular acquaintances I wish'd & advis'd him to establish a press at Philada. instead of one meditated by him in N Jersey, is also certain. I advised the change because I thought his interest would

For the NATIONAL GAZETTE.

A candid State of PARTIES.

AS it is the bufinefs of the contemplative ftatefman to trace the hiftory of parties in a free country, fo it is the duty of the citizen at all times to underftand the actual ftate of them. Whenever this duty is omitted, an opportunity is given to defigning men, by the ufe of artificial or nominal diftinctions, to oppofe and balance against each other thofe who never differed as to the end to be purfued, and may no longer differ as to the means of attaining it. The moft interefting ftate of parties in the United States may be referred to three periods: Thofe who efpoufed the caufe of independence and thofe who adhered to the Britifh claims, formed the parties of the firft period; if, indeed, the difaffected clafs were confiderable enough to deferve the name of a party. This ftate of things was fuperfeded by the treaty of peace in 1783. From 1783 to 1787 there were parties in abundance, but being rather local than general, they are not within the prefent review.

The Federal Conftitution, propofed in the latter year, gave birth to a fecond and moft interefting divifion of the people. Every one remembers it, becaufe every one was involved in it.

Among thofe who embraced the conftitution, the great body were unqueftionably friends to republican liberty; tho' there were, no doubt, fome who were openly or fecretly attached to monarchy and ariftocracy; and hoped to make the conftitution a cradle for thefe hereditary eftablifhments.

Among thofe who oppofed the conftitu-

Madison's essay "A candid State of Parties" as it appeared in the National Gazette *September 26, 1792*

be advanced by it, & because as a friend I was desirous that his interest should be advanced. This was my primary & governing motive. That as a consequential one, I entertain'd hopes that a *free* paper meant for general circulation and edited by a man of genius, of republican principles, & a friend to the Constitution, would be some antidote to the doctrines & discourses circulated in favour of Monarchy and Aristocracy, & would be an acceptable vehicle of public information in many places not sufficiently supplied with it; this also is a certain truth; but it is a truth which I never could be tempted to conceal, or to wish to be concealed. If there be a temptation in the case it would be to make a merit of it.

But that the establishment of Mr. Fs. press was wished in order to sap the Constitution, and that I forwarded the measure; or that my agency negociated it, by an illicit or improper connection between the functions of a translating Clerk in a public office, & those of an Editor of a Gazette, these are charges which ought to be as impotent as they are malicious. The first is surely incredible, if any charge could be so: & the second is I hope at least improbable, & not to be credited, until unequivocal proof shall be subtituted for anonymous & virulent assertion.

The political temperature in Philadelphia soared with the approach of the fall elections. Washington—the only man capable of holding the government together—happily consented to another term at the urging of all concerned; but party spirit ran high in congressional contests. Seeking to advance the Republican cause, Madison contributed "A candid State of Parties" to the *National Gazette*.

[September 26, 1792]

The most interesting state of parties in the United States may be referred to three periods: Those who espoused the cause of independence and those who adhered to the British claims, formed the parties of the first period; if, indeed, the disaffected class were considerable enough to deserve the name of a party. This state of things was superseded by the treaty of peace in 1783. From 1783 to 1787 there were parties in abundance, but being rather local than general, they are not within the present review.

The Federal Constitution, proposed in the latter year,

MEMBERS OF CONGRESS.

SENATORS.

New-Hampshire.
John Langdon, No. 222, Market fl.
Paine Wingate, No. 155, n. Second fl.

Massachusetts.
George Cabot, No. 86, Union fl.
Caleb Strong, No. 58, n. Third fl.

Rhode-Island.
Theodore Foster, No. 29, Callow Hill fl.
Joseph Stanton, 125, f. Second fl.

Connecticut.
Oliver Ellsworth, No. 121, f. Third fl.
Roger Sherman, No. 155, n. Second fl.

Vermont.
Stephen R. Bradley, No. 159, Market fl.
Moses Robinson, No. 20, n. Third fl.

New-York.
Aaron Burr, No. 147, s. Second fl.
Rufus King, No. 104, Spruce fl.

New-Jersey.
Philemon Dickinson, Chesnut fl. upper end.
John Rutherford, No. 58, n. Fourth fl.

Pennsylvania.
Robert Morris, corner of Market and Sixth fl.

Delaware.
Richard Bassett.
George Read, No. 35, Dock fl.

Maryland.
Charles Carroll.
John Henry, No. 170, Market fl.

Virginia.
James Monroe, No. 128, Arch fl.
John Taylor.

Kentucky.
John Brown, corner of Third and Vine fl.
John Edwards, No. 48, Arch fl.

North-Carolina.
Benjamin Hawkins, No. 170, Market fl.
Samuel Johnston, No. 169, f. Third fl.

South-Carolina.
Pierce Butler, Market between Seventh and Eighth fl.
Ralph Izard, No. 165, Chesnut fl.

Georgia.
William Few, 14, Cherry Alley.
James Gunn.

REPRESENTATIVES.

New-Hampshire.
Nicholas Gilman, No. 9, n. Fourth fl.
Samuel Livermore, No. 235, Market fl.
Jeremiah Smith, No. 9, n. Fourth fl.

Massachusetts.
Fisher Ames, No. 231, Market fl.
Shearjashub Bourne, No. 58, Walnut fl.
Elbridge Gerry, No. 105, n. Front fl.
Benjamin Goodhue, No. 72, n. Third fl.
George Leonard, No. 65, Walnut fl.
Theodore Sedgwick, No. 104, Spruce fl.
George Thatcher, No. 235, Market fl.
Artemas Ward, No. 155, n. Second fl.

Rhode-Island.
Benjamin Bourne, No. 235, Market fl.

Connecticut.
James Hillhouse, No. 72, n. Third fl.
Amasa Learned, No. 67, Pine fl.
Jonathan Sturges, No. 72, n. Third fl.
Jonathan Trumbull, (Speaker) No. 67, Pine fl.
Jeremiah Wadsworth.

Vermont.
Nathaniel Niles, No. 155, n. Second fl.
Israel Smith, No. 20, n. Third fl.

New-York.
Egbert Benson, No. 104, Spruce fl.
James Gordon, No. 184, f. Front fl.
John Laurance, No. 159, Chesnut fl.
Cornelius C. Schoonmaker, No. 38, n. Third fl.
Peter Silvester, No. 118, Spruce fl.
Thomas Tredwell, No. 38, n. Third fl.

New-Jersey.
Elias Boudinot, N. 229, Market fl.
Abraham Clark, No. 68, Market fl.
Jonathan Dayton, No. 17, n. Third fl.
Aaron Kitchell, No. 68, Market fl.

Pennsylvania.
William Findley, No. 67, Vine fl.
Thomas Fitzsimons, corner of Spruce & 4th fl.
Andrew Gregg.
Thomas Hartley, No. 105, n. Front fl.
Daniel Heister, No. 67, Vine fl.
Israel Jacobs, 42, f. Second fl.
John Wilkes Kittera, 32, Market fl.
Frederick Augustus Muhlenberg, 62, n. Second fl.

Delaware.
John Vining.

Maryland.
Philip Key, 214, Market fl.
John Francis Mercer, City Tavern.
William Vans Murray, 81, f. Third fl.
Joshua Seney.
Upton Sheridine.
Samuel Sterret.

Virginia.
William B. Giles, 170, Market fl.
Samuel Griffin, 43, Spruce fl.
Richard Bland Lee, 53, Race fl.
James Madison, 170, Market fl.
Andrew Moore, 184, f. Front fl.
John Page, 214, Market fl.
Josiah Parker, 9, n. Fourth fl.
Abraham Venable, 170, Market fl.
Alexander White, 18 Chesnut fl.

Kentucky.
Christopher Greenup, 58, Arch fl.
Alexander D. Orr, Corner Vine and Third fl.

North-Carolina.
John Baptist Ashe, 131, Vine fl.
William Barry Grove, Corner Vine & Third fl.
Nathaniel Macon, do. do.
John Steele, 96, n. Third fl.
Hugh Williamson, Corner Vine and Third fl.

South-Carolina.
Robert Barnwell, 104, Spruce fl.
Daniel Huger, 9, n. Fourth fl.
William Smith, 162, Chesnut fl.
Thomas Sumpter, 110, n. Second fl.
Thomas Tudor Tucker, 9, n. Fourth fl.

Georgia.
Abraham Baldwin, 67, Vine fl.
John Milledge, do.
Francis Willis, 69, n. Sixth fl.

☞ The gentlemen to whose names no place of abode is annexed, have not arrived.

List of members of Congress in 1792 and their addresses in Philadelphia; Madison lived at Mrs. House's, 170 Market Street, as did a number of other senators and congressmen.

gave birth to a second and most interesting division of the people. Every one remembers it, because every one was involved in it.

Among those who embraced the constitution, the great body were unquestionably friends to republican liberty; tho' there were, no doubt, some who were openly or secretly attached to monarchy and aristocracy; and hoped to make the constitution a cradle for these hereditary establishments.

Among those who opposed the constitution, the great body were certainly well affected to the union and to good government, tho' there might be a few who had a leaning unfavourable to both. This state of parties was terminated by the regular and effectual establishment of the federal government in 1788; out of the administration of which, however, has arisen a third division, which being natural to most political societies, is likely to be of some duration in ours.

One of the divisions consists of those who from particular interest, from natural temper, or from the habits of life, are more partial to the opulent than to the other classes of society; and having debauched themselves into a persuasion that mankind are incapable of governing themselves, it follows with them, of course, that government can be carried on only by the pageantry of rank, the influence of money and emoluments, and the terror of military force. Men of those sentiments must naturally wish to point the measures of government less to the interest of the many than of a few, and less to the reason of the many than to their weaknesses; hoping perhaps in proportion to the ardor of their zeal, that by giving such a turn to the administration, the government itself may by degrees be narrowed into fewer hands, and approximated to an hereditary form.

The other division consists of those who believing in the doctrine that mankind are capable of governing themselves, and hating hereditary power as an insult to the reason and an outrage to the rights of man, are naturally offended at every public measure that does not appeal to the understanding and to the general interest of the community, or that is not strictly conformable to the principles, and conducive to the preservation of republican government.

This being the real state of parties among us, an experienced and dispassionate observer will be at no loss to decide on the probable conduct of each.

The antirepublican party, as it may be called, being the weaker in point of numbers, will be induced by the most obvious motives to strengthen themselves with the men of influence, particularly of moneyed, which is the most active and insinuating influence. It will be equally their true policy to weaken their opponents by reviving exploded parties, and taking advantage of all prejudices, local, political, and occupational, that may prevent or disturb a general coalition of sentiments.

The Republican party, as it may be termed, conscious that the mass of people in every part of the union, in every state, and of every occupation must at bottom be with them, both in interest and sentiment, will naturally find their account in burying all antecedent questions, in banishing every other distinction than that between enemies and friends to republican government, and in promoting a general harmony among the latter, wherever residing, or however employed.

Whether the republican, or the rival party will ultimately establish its ascendance, is a problem which may be contemplated now; but which time alone can solve. On one hand experience shows that in politics as in war, stratagem is often an overmatch for numbers: and among more happy characteristics of our political situation, it is now well understood that there are peculiarities, some temporary, others more durable, which may favour that side in the contest. On the republican side, again, the superiority of numbers is so great, their sentiments are so decided, and the practice of making a common cause, where there is a common sentiment and common interest, in spight of circumstancial and artificial distinctions, is so well understood, that no temperate observer of human affairs will be surprised if the issue in the present instance should be reversed, and the government be administered in the spirit and form approved by the great body of the people.

The Republicans scored impressive gains in the 1792 elections. Then, early in the new year, events abroad gave a fresh turn to American affairs. Against the invading armies of the "conspiracy of kings" (Great Britain, Spain, and Holland), France, now a republic, waged war to preserve and extend her revolution. Enthusiasm for France ran high in the United States. Republicans coupled her cause with the American and worried lest the failure of liberty abroad tip the political scales disastrously at home. Madison's opinion was unequivocal, as he made clear in a letter to George Nicholas, a political ally and the Attorney General of Kentucky.

Edmond Charles Genêt

Philada. Mar: 15 1793.
Our accounts from abroad are not of very late date nor of a very decisive cast. It is still a problem whether war will take place between England & France. The war in which the latter is at present engaged seems likely to be pushed by her enemies during the ensuing campaign. As yet her conduct has been great both as free and as martial nation. We hope it will continue so, and finally baffle all her enemies, who are in fact the enemies of human nature. We have every motive in America to pray for her success, not only from a general attachment to the liberties of mankind, but from a peculiar regard to our own. The symtoms of disaffection to Republi-[can gov]ernment have risen, & subsided among us in such visible [cor]respondence with the prosperous and adverse accounts from the French Revolution, that a miscarriage of it would threaten us with the most serious dangers to our present forms & principles of our governments.

War between Britain and France had, in fact, already begun. Not only was the United States an ally of France, pledged to defend her West Indian possessions, but the war inevitably threatened American peace on the high seas. Moreover, contrary dispositions toward these two great powers were woven into the texture of American politics. Federalists despised the infection of Jacobinical democracy, which they detected in their opponents, and wished trade and friendship with Britain. The Republican commitment to France involved matters of principle, of gratitude, and of hostility to Britain, as well as the shrewd political calculation that popular frenzy for France could be converted into party capital.

Madison was at home when the new French minister, Edmond Charles Genêt, arrived to a tumultuous welcome in the spring. Except for Jefferson, however, the administration received him coldly. (Hamilton had been opposed to receiving him at all.) On April 22, 1793, the President issued the Proclamation of Neutrality. It put the belligerents on the same level and enjoined "conduct friendly and impartial" toward both. Jefferson, although he disliked the proclamation, acquiesced in it and called upon his friends to do the same. Madison was at first puzzled and then revolted by the proclamation. The subsequent administration of the policy, he felt, gave an appallingly "anglified complexion" to the government. He expressed his views in three letters to Jefferson.

Orange [Virginia,] May 8th. 1793.
I anxiously wish that the reception of Genet may testify what I believe to be the real affections of the people. It is the more desireable as a seasonable plum after the bitter pills which it seems must be administered. Having neither the Treaty nor Law of Nations at hand I form no opinion as to the stipulations of the former or the precise neutrality defined by the latter. I had always supposed that the terms of the Treaty made some sort of difference, at least as far as would consist with the Law of Nations, between France & Nations not in Treaty, particularly G. Britain. I should still doubt whether the term *impartial* in the Proclamation is not stronger than was necessary, if not than was proper. Peace is no doubt to be preserved at any price that honor and good faith will permit. But it is no less to be considered that the least departure from these will not only be most likely to end in the loss of peace, but is pregnant with every other evil that could happen to us. In explaining our engagements under the Treaty with France, it would be honorable as well as just to adhere to the sense that would at the time have been put on them. The attempt [by

A view of the harbor of New York with the frigate Ambuscade, *which had brought Genêt to America*

195

Hamilton] to shuffle off the Treaty altogether by quibbling on Vattel [the author of *Law of Nations*] is equally contemptible for the meanness & folly of it. If a change of Govt. is an absolution from public engagements, why not from those of a domestic as well as of a foreign nature; and what then becomes of public debts &c &c. In fact, the doctrine would perpetuate every existing Despotism, by involving in a reform of the Govt. a destruction of the social pact, an annihilation of property, and a compleat establishment of the State of Nature. What most surprises me is that such a proposition shd. have been discussed.

Orange [Virginia,] June 13. 93.
I observe that the Newspapers continue to criticize the President's proclamations; and I find that some of the criticisms excite the attention of dispassionate & judicious individuals here. I have heard it remarked by such with some surprise that the P. should have declared the U.S. to be neutral in the unqualified terms used, when we were so notoriously & unequivally under *eventual engagements* to defend the American possessions of F. I have heard it remarked also that the impartiality enjoined on the people was as little reconciliable with their moral obligations, as the unconditional neutrality proclaimed by the Government with the express articles of the Treaty. It has been asked also whether the authority of the Executive extended by any part of the Constitution to a declaration of the *Disposition* of the U.S. on the subject of war & peace? I have been mortified that on these points I could offer no bona fide explanations that ought to be satisfactory. On the last point I must own my surprise that such a prerogative should have been exercised. Perhaps I may have not attended to some part of the Constitution with sufficient care, or may have misapprehended its meaning: But, as I have always supposed & still conceive, a proclamation on the subject could not properly go beyond a declaration of the fact that the U.S. were at war or peace and an injunction of a suitable conduct on the Citizen [Genêt]. The right to decide the question whether the duty & interest of the U.S. require war or peace under any given circumstances, and whether their disposition be towards the one or the other seems to be

One of the areas of friction between France and Great Britain was the West Indies. This print shows the capture of the disputed island of Tobago by the British in April, 1793.

essentially & exclusively involved in the right vested in the Legislature, of declaring war in time of peace; and in the P. & S. [Senate] of making peace in time of war. Did no such view of the subject present itself in the discussions of the Cabinet? I am extremely afraid that the P. may not be sufficiently aware of the snares that may be laid for his good intentions by men whose politics at bottom are very different from his own. An assumption of prerogatives not clearly found in the Constitution & having the appearance of being copied from a Monarchical model, will beget animadversion equally mortifying to him, & disadvantageous to the Government.

Orange [Virginia,] June 19, 1793. Every Gazette I see (except that of the U.S.) [Fenno's] exhibits spirit of criticism on the anglified complexion charged in the Executive politics. I regret extremely the position into which the P. has been thrown. The unpopular cause of Anglomany is openly laying claim to him. His enemies masking themselves, under the popular cause of France, are playing off the most tremendous batteries on him. The proclamation was in truth a most unfortunate error. It wounds the National honor, by seeming to disregard the stipulated duties to France. It wounds the popular feelings by a seeming indifference to the cause of liberty. And it seems to violate the forms & spirit of the Constitution, by making the executive Magistrate the organ of the disposition the duty & the interest of the Nation in relation to war & peace, subjects appropriated to other departments of the Government. It is mortifying to the real friends of the P. that his fame & his influence should have been unnecessarily made to depend in any degree on political events in a foreign quarter of the Globe: and particularly so that he should have any thing to apprehend from the success of liberty in another country, since he owes his pre-eminence to the success of it in his own. If France triumphs the ill-fated proclamation will be a millstone which would sink any other character, and will force a struggle even on his.

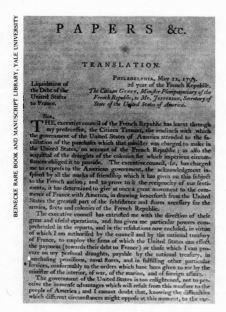

A paper on the liquidation of the American debt to France from Citizen Genêt to Jefferson, printed in a collection of 1793

Madison's confidence in the President was shaken, but he continued to defend him as a man misled and misused by the Federalists, with Hamilton the chief culprit. In June, as "Pacificus," Hamilton commenced a series of articles in Fenno's *Gazette* on the Proclamation of Neutrality. He upheld its constitutionality, declared the French alliance in abeyance, and denounced her revolution. "For God's sake, my dear sir," Jefferson implored Madison, "take up your pen, select the most striking heresies and cut him to pieces in the face of the public." Madison, as "Helvidius," complied, but found it the "most grating" task he had ever undertaken and broke off after scoring the narrow constitutional point earlier stated to Jefferson. "Citizen" Genêt, meanwhile, hoping to capitalize on popular support for the French cause, commissioned American privateers to attack British shipping, armed French prizes in American ports, and enlisted American adventurers in grandiose expeditions against Spanish and British territories in North America. By his intemperate—and illegal—actions, however, Genêt jeopardized his own cause and turned even Jefferson against him. No more calamitous appointment was ever made, Jefferson told Madison, and unless the Republicans abandoned Genêt they would sink with him. Still at Montpelier, Madison had some difficultly understanding the sudden metamorphosis of Genêt from hero into villain. But he toned down resolutions intended for Republican assemblages in the counties to counteract the anti-French blast of the Federalists. He explained the change of tactics to his coadjutor, Monroe.

[Orange, Virginia,] Sepr. 15. 93.

Since I parted from you I have had several letters from Mr. J. in which all the *facts* involving Genet are detailed. His conduct has been that of a mad man. He is abandoned even by his votaries in Philada. Hutcheson [Dr. James Hutchinson, Republican leader] declares that he has ruined the Republican interest in that place. I wish I could forward the details I have recd. but they are too confidential to be hazarded by the casual conveyance to which this is destined. They ought however to have no other effect on the steps to be pursued, than to caution agst. founding any of them on the presumed inculpability of Genet. As he has put himself on such unjustifiable ground, perhaps it is fortunate that he has done it in so flagrant a manner. It will be the more easily believed now that he has acted agst. the sense of his Constituents, and the latter will be the less likely to support him in his errors. I find that the Anglicans & Monocrats from Boston to Philada. are betrayed by the occasion into the most palpable discovery of their real views. They already lose sight of the Agent; and direct their hostilities *immediately agst. France*. This will do good, if proper use be made of it. You will see by the

L E T T E R S

OF

HELVIDIUS:

WRITTEN IN REPLY TO

PACIFICUS,

ON THE

PRESIDENT's PROCLAMATION OF NEUTRALITY.

Published originally in the Year 1793.

PHILADELPHIA:
PRINTED BY SAMUEL H. SMITH, No. 118, CHESNUT STREET.
M.DCC.XCVI.

Title page of Madison's Letters of Helvidius, *written in reply to those of Hamilton as "Pacificus" supporting the Proclamation of Neutrality*

late papers that G. B. has made war on our commerce, by interrupting uncontraband articles bound to unblockaded ports, and taking them to herself at her own price. This must bring on a crisis with us, unless the order be revoked on our demand, of which there is not the least probability.

What Madison described as the British "war on our commerce" helped to save Republicans from Genêt's ineptitude and enabled Jefferson, before he went into retirement at the year's end, to divert attention from French to British violations of American neutrality. In one of his last acts Jefferson dropped a bombshell into Congress: his *Report on Commerce* calling for retaliation against British restrictions on American trade and navigation. On January 3, 1794, Madison presented a series of resolutions in the House to implement this policy. France lurked behind the Republican plan, Federalists charged. On the contrary, Madison retorted, the policy was as old as the American Revolution and only looked to the national system of commerce that had been a paramount aim of the Constitution. The majority rallied to Madison's resolutions. He reported to Jefferson on the prospects in March.

Philada. March 2d. 1794.

I was in hopes every week to be able to furnish you with the proceedings on the subject grounded on your Commercial Report; and particularly with such of them as related to yourself. It has so happened that I never could find leisure to make out for the press, the share I had in them till very lately. The earlier part of my observations were sent to the Printer several weeks ago, but never made their appearance till Thursday evening last. The latter part is following, as you will find, as fast I can write it out, which from the extreme length of it, the brevity of my notes, and the time that has run since the observations were delivered, is a task equally tedious & laborious. The sequel will be forwarded to you as soon as it gets into print. As you are so little supplied with the current information it may be necessary to apprize you that after the general discussions on the measure proposed by me, had been closed, and the first general resolution agreed to by a majority of 5 or 6, several of the Eastern members friendly to the object insisted on a postponement till the first monday in March. It was necessary to gratify them, and the postponement was carried by a small majority against the

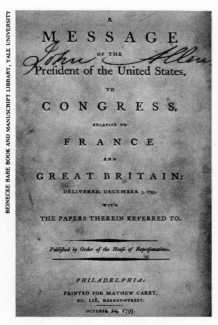

Title page of a volume of state papers concerning the relations of the United States with France and Great Britain at the end of 1793

The SECRETARY *of* STATE, *to whom was referred by the House of* REPRESENTATIVES, *the* REPORT *of a Committee on the written* MESSAGE *of the* PRESIDENT *of the* UNITED STATES, *of the 14th of February, 1791, with instruction to report to Congress the nature and extent of the* PRIVILEGES *and* RESTRICTIONS *of the* COMMERCIAL INTERCOURSE *of the United States with Foreign Nations, and the measures which he should think proper to be adopted, for the improvement of the Commerce and Navigation of the same, has had the same under consideration, and thereupon makes the following*

R E P O R T:

THE countries with which the UNITED STATES have their chief commercial intercourse, are, SPAIN, PORTUGAL, FRANCE, GREAT-BRITAIN, the UNITED NETHERLANDS, DENMARK, and SWEDEN, and their American possessions: and the articles of export which constitute the basis of that commerce, with their respective amounts, are—

	Dollars.
Bread-stuff, that is to say, bread-grains, meals, and bread, to the annual amount of	7,649,887
Tobacco	4,349,567
Rice	1,753,796
Wood	1,263,534
Salted fish	941,696
Pot and pearl-ash	839,093
Salted meats	599,130
Indigo	537,379
Horses and mules	339,753
Whale oil	252,591
Flax-seed	236,072
Tar, pitch and turpentine	217,177
Live provisions	137,743
Ships	
Foreign goods	620,274

Page from Jefferson's Report on Commerce, *which lists articles of export and their respective amounts*

"House flies plenty" appears to the right on a May 23, 1794, entry in a weather log kept by Madison family.

effects of the adverse party, who counted on the votes of the timid members if forced before they could learn the sense of their constituents. The Interval has produced vast exertions by the British party to mislead the people of the Eastern States. No means have been spared. The most artful & wicked calumnies have been propagated with all the zeal which malice and interest could invent. The blackest of these calumnies, as you may imagine have fallen to the lot of the mover of the Resolutions. The last Boston Paper contains a string of charges framed for the purpose of making the Eastern people believe that he has been the counsellor & abettor of Genet in all his extravagances, and a corrupt tool of France.... It appears however that in spite of all these diabolical manoeuvres, the town of Boston has been so far awakened as to have a Meeting in the town house, & a pretty unanimous vote for a committee to consider the subject & report proper instructions for their members in Congress.... I see by a paper of last evening that even in N. York a meeting of the people has taken place at the instance of the Republican party, and that a committee is appointed for the like purpose. As far as I know the names, the majority is on the right side. One motive for postponing the question so long was the chance of hearing from England, and the probability that the intelligence would strengthen the arguments for retaliation. Letters from Pinkney [Thomas Pinckney, Minister to Great Britain] have accordingly arrived. As yet they are under the seal of confidence but it is in

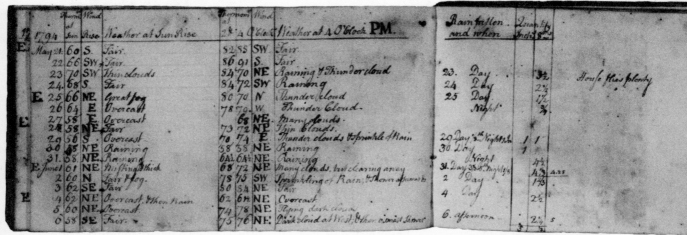

universal conversation that they mark precisely and *more strongly* than ever the unjust & unfriendly features which have characterized the British policy towards the U. States.

[Philadelphia,] Mar: 12. 1794.

The Merchants, particularly of N. England have had a terrible slam in the W. Indies. About a hundred vessels have been seized by the British for condemnation, on the pretext of enforcing the laws of the Monarchy with regard to the Colony trade. The partizans of England, considering a war as now probable are endeavoring to take the lead in defensive preparations, and to acquire merit with the people by anticipating their wishes. This new symtom of insolence & enmity in Britain, shews rather that she meditates a formal war as so[o]n as she shall have crippled our marine resources, or that she calculates on the pusilanimity of this country & the influence of her party, in a degree that will lead her into aggressions which our love of peace can no longer bear. The commercial propositions are in this state of things, not the precise remedy to be pressed as first in order; but they are in every view & in any event proper to make part of our standing laws till the principle of reciprocity be established by mutual arrangements.

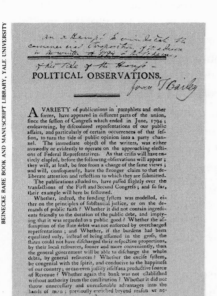

Some Political Observations, *which Jefferson ascribed to Madison, justifying the commercial resolutions Madison introduced in 1794*

Suddenly "more active medicine"—embargo or nonintercourse—seemed called for, and Madison's resolutions were set aside. The upshot in April, 1794, was the desperate mission of John Jay to negotiate a settlement with Britain. Madison expected no justice from Britain, unless forced by France, and both the Anglicanism of the envoy and Hamilton's ascendancy in the administration added to his misgivings.

While Madison awaited the outcome of Jay's mission, his thoughts turned to more personal matters. An unwilling bachelor at forty-three, his eye had fallen upon the attractive and vivacious Dolley Payne Todd, the twenty-six-year-old widow of a young Quaker lawyer who had died the year before, leaving her with a small son. The Todds had been known in Philadelphia's social and official circles for some time. Now, in the spring following her husband's death, Madison arranged for a formal introduction to the young widow, who wrote excitedly to a friend: "Thou must come to me. Aaron Burr says that the great little Madison has asked to be brought to see me this evening." The meeting was a success and Madison and Dolley were soon embarked on a whirlwind courtship. That summer, while she was recovering from a severe illness near her old home in Hanover County, Virginia, Dolley accepted his proposal of marriage and he replied to her affectionately.

> Orange [Virginia,] Aug: 18. 94:
> I recd some days ago your precious favor from Fredg. I cannot express, but hope you will conceive the joy it gave me. The delay in hearing of your leaving Hanover which I regarded as the only satisfactory proof of your recovery, had filled me with extreme...inquietude, and the consummation of that welcome event was endeared to me by the *stile* in which it was conveyed. I hope you will never have another *deliberation* on that subject. If the sentiments of my heart can guarantee those of yours, they assure me there can never be cause for it.

Madison and Mrs. Todd were married on September 15, 1794, at Harewood, the home of her sister Lucy, near Charles Town in what is now West Virginia. Madison notified his father of the marriage three weeks later, as soon as he could spare his father's servant, Sam.

> Harewood [Virginia,] October 5, 1794
> Dear & Hond Sir
> I have detained Sam by whom I send this so much longer than I intended & you expected that many apologies are due for the liberty. I hope it will be a sufficient one that I found him indispensable for a variety of little services, which I did not particularly take into view before I left Orange. These he can himself explain and I therefore leave the task to him; proceeding to the history of what relates to myself. On my arrival here I was able to urge so many conveniences in hastening the event which I solicited that it took place on the 15th ult: on the friday following we set out accompanied by Miss A. Payne, [Dolley's sister] and Miss Harriot Washington, on a visit to my sister Hite, when we arrived the next day, having stopped a night at Winchester with Mr. Bailmain. We had been a day or two only at Mr. Hites, before a slight indisposition which my wife had felt for several days, ended in a regular ague & fever. The fits tho' succeeded by compleat intermissions were so severe that I thought it prudent to call in a Physician from Winchester. Docr Mackay not being in the way Docr Baldwin attended, and by a decisive administration of the Bark soon expelled the complaint.

Dolley Madison as a young woman

Revolutionary Reminiscences of the Old Dominion... BY ALEXANDER BOTELER, 1860

Harewood House, home of Dolley's sister, where Madisons were wed

She has since recovered very fast & I hope notwithstanding a slight indisposition this morning which may be the effect of fatigue & change of weather, that no return is in the least to be apprehended. We left Mr. Hites the day before yesterday. Our time was passed there with great pleasure on our side, and I hope with not less on the other.... In 8 or 10 days we expect to set out for Philada—your daughter in law begs you and my mother to accept her best and most respectful affections, which she means to express herself by an early opportunity. She wishes Fanny [Madison's twenty-year-old sister] also be sensible of the pleasure with which a correspondence with her would be carried on....

I remain your affecte son

JS. MADISON JR

When the Madisons returned to Philadelphia for the next meeting of Congress, they moved into the home of James Monroe who had recently been appointed Minister to France. In November, 1794, Jay's Treaty was signed. It exceeded Madison's worst fears. Britain's pledge to evacuate the Northwest posts was the principal point gained, though this obligation descended from the peace of 1783. The treaty assumed American acquiescence in British maritime rule and practice, which had produced the crisis in the first place. Most damaging, in Madison's opinion, was the grant of "most favored nation" status to Britain. Not only was this unreciprocated on her side, but she must now profit freely from any commercial bargain the United States might make with friendly nations. The terms were made public in March, 1795; the Senate consented in June; and a whirlwind of indignation rolled across the land during the summer as the treaty awaited Washington's signature. Madison circulated his views among Republican leaders, including Robert R. Livingston of New York.

[Orange, Virginia,] Augst. 10. 1795.

Your favor of July 6, having been addressed to Williamsburg instead of *Orange Court House,* did not come to hand till two days ago. Your gloomy picture of the Treaty does not exceed my ideas of it. After yielding terms which would have been scorned by this country in the moment of its greatest embarrassments, & of G. Britains full enjoyment of peace & confidence, it adds to the ruinous bargain with this nation, a disqualification to make a good one with any other. In all our other Treaties it has been carefully stipulated that the nation to be treated as the most favored nations, & to come in for all new privileges that may be granted by the U. States, must pay for them the same or an equivalent price with the grantee. The proposed Treaty with G.B. disregarding this obvious rule of justice & equality, roundly agrees that no duty restriction or prohibition with respect to ships or merchandize shall be applied to G.B. which do not operate on all other nations (see Art. XV). Should any other nation therefore be disposed to give us the most precious & peculiar advantages in their trade, in exchange for the slightest preferences in ours, This article gives G.B. a negative on the transaction; unless it be so modified as to let her in for the favor without paying the price of it. But what nation wd. be willing to buy favors for another; especially when the inducement to buy & the value of the purchase, might depend on the peculiarity of the favor. It must be seen at once that this extraordinary feature would monopolize us to G.B. by precluding any material improvement of our existing Treaties, or the hope of any new ones that would be of much advantage to us. That so insidious an article should have occurred to Lord Grenville's jealousy of the U.S. & his policy of barring their connection with other Countries, and particularly with the French Republic, can surprise no one. The concurrence of the American Envoy in this & several other articles may not be so easily explained; but it seems impossible to screen him from the most illiberal suspicions without referring his conduct to the

Robert R. Livingston

blindest partiality to the British Nation & Govt. and to the most vindictive sensations towards the French Republic. Indeed the Treaty from one end to the other must be regarded as a demonstration that the Party to which the Envoy belongs & of which he has been more the organ than of the U.S. is a British party, systematically aiming at an exclusive connection with the British Governt. & ready to sacrifice to that object as well the dearest interests of our Commerce, as the most sacred dictates of national honor. This is the true key to this unparalleled proceeding; and can alone explain it to the impartial and discerning part of the public. The leaders of this party stand self-condemned in their efforts to palliate the Treaty by magnifying the necessity of the British commerce to the U.S. and the insufficiency of the U.S. to influence the regulation of it. . . . It is with much pleasure I can assure you that the sentiment & voice of the people in this state in relation to the attempt to prostrate us to a foreign & unfriendly Nation, are as decided & as loud as could be wished. Many even of those who have hitherto rallied to the most exceptionable party measures, join in the general indignation agst. the Treaty. The few who hold out will soon be under the dilemna of following the example, or of falling under imputations which must disarm them of all injurious influence. You will see by the Newspapers that the City of Richmd. has trodden in the steps of the other Cities by an unanimous address to the President. . . . With respect to the P. his situation must be a most delicate one for himself, as well as for his Country: and there never was, as you observe, a crisis where the friends of both ought to feel more solicitude, or less reserve. At the same time, I have reasons, which I think good, for doubting the propriety, & of course the utility, of uninvited communications from myself. He cannot, I am persuaded, be a stranger to my opinion on the merits of the Treaty; and I am equally persuaded that the State of the public opinion within my sphere, of information will sufficiently force itself on his attention.

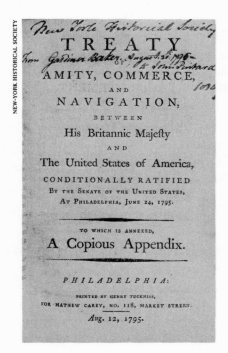

Jay's Treaty

Although the President shed his doubts and approved the treaty, its future still depended on appropriations by the House. The Republican majority set out to stifle the embryo monster, only to be frustrated for three months by Washington's refusal to communicate it. "The situation is truly perplexing," Madison wrote Jefferson. "It is clear that a majority if brought to the merits of the Treaty are agst. it. But as the Treaty is not regularly before the House, & an application to the President brings him personally into the question . . . there is some danger that eno' will fly off to leave the opponents . . . in a minority." Finally, on March 1, 1796, Washington sent the treaty to the House, and after several weeks of maneuver and debate, during which the antitreaty majority slowly wilted, the Republicans suffered mortifying defeat. Madison described the vexatious business to Jefferson.

Philada. May 1. 1796.

The Treaty question was brought to a vote on friday in Come. of whole. Owing to the absence (*certainly* casual & momentary) of one member, & the illness of another, the Committee were divided 49 & 49. The Chairman (Muhlenberg) decided in the affirmative, saying that in the House it would be subject to modification which he wished. In the House yesterday, an Enemy of the Treaty moved a preamble, reciting that altho' the Treaty was highly objectionable, yet considering all circumstances, particularly the duration for two years &c, & confiding in "the efficacy of measures that might be taken for stopping the spoliations & impressments &c," For this ingredient, which you will perceive the scope of, all who meant to persevere agst. the Treaty, with those who only yielded for the reasons expressed in it, ought to have united in voting, as making the pill a bitter one to the Treaty party, as well as less poisonous to the public interest. A few wrongheads however thought fit to separate, whereby the motion was lost by one vote. The main question was then carried in favr. of the Treaty by 51 agst. 48. This revolution was foreseen, and might have been mitigated tho' not prevented, if sooner provided for. But some who were the first to give way to the crisis under its actual pressure, were most averse to prepare for it. The progress of this business throughout has to me been the most worrying & vexatious that I ever encountered; and the more so as the causes lay in the unsteadiness, the follies, the perverseness, & the defections among our friends, more than in the strength or dexterity, or malice of our opponents. It is impossible for me to detail these causes to you now. My consolation under them is in the effect they have in riveting my future purposes. Had the preamble condemning the Treaty on its merits, exercising the discretionary power of the House, and requiring from the Ex. a stoppage of the spoliations &c, been agreed to, I have reason to believe, the Treaty party would have felt it a compleat defeat. You will be informed by the newspapers of the means practised for stirring up petitions &c, in favr. of the Treaty. The plan was laid in this City & circulated by a correspondence thro' the Towns every where. In the mean time the Banks, the British merchts. the insurance Comps. were at work in inflaming individuals, beating down the prices of produce, & sounding the tocksin of foreign war, & domestic convulsions. The success has been such as you would suppose. In several neighbouring districts the people have been so deluded as to constrain their Representatives to renounce their opposition to the Treaty. An appeal to the people on any pending measure, can never be more than an appeal to those in the neighbourhood of the Govt. & to the Banks, the merchts. & the dependents & expectants of the Govt. at a distance.

Philada. May 22. 1796

Congress are hurrying through the remnant of business before them, and will probably adjourn about saturday next. Petitions in favor of the Treaty still come in from distant places. The name of the President & the alarm of war, have had a greater effect, than were apprehended on our side, or expected on the other. A crisis which ought to have been so managed as to fortify the Republican cause, has left it in a very crippled condition; from which its recovery will be the more difficult as the elections in N.Y. Massachusetts & other states, where the prospects were favorable, have taken a wrong turn under the impressions of the moment. Nothing but auspicious contingences abroad or at home can repair the lost ground. Peace in Europe would have a most salutary influence, and accts. just recd. from France revive in some degree the hope of it with the Emperor, which will hasten of course a peace with England. On the other hand, a scene rather gloomy is presented by a letter I have just recd. from Col. M[onroe]. It is dated Feby. 27. The following extracts form the substance of it.

"About a fortnight past I was informed by the minister of foreign affairs that the governmt had at length resolved how to act with us in respect to our treaty with England;

Section of Madison's notes for speaking on Jay's Treaty in 1796

that they considered it as having violated or rather annulled our treaty of alliance with them and taken part with the coalised powers; that they had rather have a open enemy than a perfidious friend; that it was resolved to send an envoy extraordinary to the U.S. to discuss this business with us and whose powers would expire with the execution of the trust. I was astonished with the communication and alarmed with it's probable consequences. I told him it might probably lead to war and thereby separate us which was what our enemies wished and it hasarded much and without a probable gain, that from the moment a person of that character arrived their friends would seem to act under his banner and which circumstance would injure their character and lessen their efforts. In truth I did every thing in my power to prevent this measure and in which I am now told by the minister that I have succeeded. The Directors having resolvd to continue the ordinary course of representation only. But thro' this I hear strong sentiments will be conveyed — the whole of this is made known to the executive by me."

The Jay Treaty was the capstone of the British-centered Federalist system and an astounding defeat for the system of Jefferson and Madison, which was pegged to peace and friendship with France. France, now under the Directory, felt betrayed; and the United States had fled crisis with one power to run into crisis with the other. "It is probable," Madison opined to Jefferson, "that categorical steps on the part of F[rance] toward us are anticipated as a consequence of what has been effected by the British party here, and that such artifice will be practiced by it to charge them in some unpopular form, on its Republican opponents." He was right on both counts: the retaliation of France and the political use the Federalists would make of it.

Chapter 6

To the Revolution of 1800

The contest over the Jay Treaty was the opening gun in the presidential campaign of 1796. It shattered whatever illusions of concord remained in the nation's councils, made political passion a virtue, and split the parties into warring camps. Caught up in the conflict, Madison was nevertheless appalled by it. As long as Washington was President, such was the veneration accorded him that partisanship was not likely to run to violence; but he would soon retire and with him would go the last force for unity. John Adams was the Federalist heir apparent, though Hamilton contested the succession with his favorite, Thomas Pinckney. The Republican candidacy was thrust upon Jefferson by Madison and his friends. Jefferson had wanted Madison himself—"the greatest man in the world"—to run, but Madison would not think of it. Jefferson was older, more popular, and less scarred by the political wars. Besides, Madison intended to retire to Montpelier with his charming bride. The campaign was heated, not between the candidates but between their followers, and the outcome was still uncertain when Madison returned to Congress. As the votes came in, he reported the probable result to Jefferson.

Phila. Decr. 19. 1796

The returns from N. Hampshire Vermont, S.C. & Georga. are still to come in, & leave the event of the Election in some remaining uncertainty. It is but barely possible that Adams may fail of the highest number. It is highly probable, tho' not absolutely certain, that Pinkney will be third only on the list. You must prepare yourself therefore to be summoned to the place Mr. Adams now fills. I am aware of the objections arising from the inadequateness of the importance of the place to the sacrifices you would be willing to make to a greater prospect of fulfilling the patriotic wishes of your friends; and from the

*Draft of Washington's Farewell
Address incorporating Madison's
suggestions and corrections*

irksomeness of being at the head of a body whose sentiments are at present so little in unison with your own.
But it is expected that as you had made up your mind to
obey the call of your country, you will let it decide on the
particular place where your services are to be rendered.
It may even be said, that as you submitted to the election
knowing the contingency involved in it, you are bound
to abide by the event whatever it may. On the whole it
seems *essential* that you should not refuse the station
which is likely to be your lot. There is reason to believe
also that your neighbourhood to Adams may have a
valuable effect on his councils particularly in relation
to our external system. You know that his feelings will
not enslave him to the example of his predecessor. It is
certain that his censures of our paper system & the intrigues at New York for setting P [Pinckney] above him
have fixed an enmity with the British faction. Nor should
it pass for nothing, that the true interest of New England
particularly requires reconciliation with France as the
road to her commerce. Add to the whole that he is said
to speak of you now in friendly terms and will no doubt
be soothed by your acceptance of a place subordinate to
him. It must be confessed however that all these calculations, are qualified by his political principles and prejudices. But they add weight to the obligation from which
you must not withdraw yourself.

Madison's plea was quite unnecessary. If he must serve,
Jefferson would prefer the Vice Presidency. "The second office . . . is honorable and easy, the first is but splendid misery." On December 17 he had
written to Madison of his long friendship with Adams and said that in the
case of a tie vote the choice should go to the New Englander. Moderate
Federalists were soothed by the letter, which Madison quietly circulated in
Philadelphia, while High Federalists angrily charged Jefferson with hypocrisy and deception. Meanwhile, Jefferson wrote a warm congratulatory
letter to Adams, then worried over it lest his expressions of magnanimity
and cordiality be disbelieved or convey more than he intended. He finally
sent it under cover of his answer to Madison, instructing him to forward
or intercept the epistle as he thought best. "If Mr. Adams can be induced
to administer the government on its true principles, and to relinquish his
bias to an English constitution," Jefferson said, "it is to be considered
whether it would not be on the whole for the public good to come to a good
understanding with him as to future elections. He is perhaps the only sure

barrier against Hamilton's getting in." Madison, always cool to Adams, took alarm at the suggestion of a coalition between moderate Federalists and Republicans and shrewdly suppressed Jefferson's overture.

Philada. Jany. 15. 1797.

The last mail brought me your favor of Jany. 1. inclosing an unsealed one for Mr. A. & submitting to my discretion the eligibility of delivering it. In exercising this delicate trust I have felt no small anxiety, arising by no means however from an apprehension that a free exercise of it could be in collision with your real purpose but from a want of confidence in myself, & the importance of a wrong judgment in the case. After the best consideration I have been able to bestow, I have been led to suspend the delivery of the letter, till you should have an opportunity of deciding on the sufficiency or insufficiency of the following reasons. 1. It is certain that Mr. Adams, on his coming to this place, expressed to different persons a respectful cordiality towards you, & manifested a sensibility to the candid manner in which your friends had in general conducted the opposition to him. And it is equally known that your sentiments towards him personally have found their way to him in the most conciliating form. This being the state of things between you, it deserves to be considered whether the idea of bettering it is not outweighed by the possibility of changing it for the worse. 2. There is perhaps a general air on the letter which betrays the difficulty of your situation in writing it, and it is uncertain what the impression might be resulting from this appearance. 3. It is certain that Mr. A. is fully apprized of the trick aimed at by his pseudo-friends of N.Y. and there may be danger of his suspecting in memento's on that subject, a wish to make this resentment an instrument for avenging that of others.... 4. May not what is said of "the sublime delights of riding in the storm &c." be misconstrued into a reflexion on those who have no distaste to the helm at the present crisis? You know the temper of Mr. A. better than I do: but I have always conceived it to be rather a ticklish one. 5. The tenderness due to the zealous & active promoters of your election, makes it doubtful whether their anxieties & exertions ought to be depreciated by any thing implying the unreasonableness of them. I know that some individuals who have deeply committed them-

selves, & probably incurred the political enmity at least
of the P. elect, are already sore on this head. 6. Considering the probability that Mr. A.s course of administration may force an opposition to it from the Republican
quarter, & the general uncertainty of the posture which
our affairs may take, there may be real embarrassments
from giving written possession to him, of the degree of
compliment & confidence which your personal delicacy
& friendship have suggested.

I have ventured to make these observations, because
I am sure you will equally appreciate the motive & the
matter of them; and because I do not view them as inconsistent with the duty & policy of cultivating Mr.
Adam's favorable dispositions, and giving a fair start to
his Executive career.

The sequel may be briefly told. War with France
threatened the Adams administration at its start. The French were now
attacking American commerce; Monroe had been angrily recalled by
Washington; and diplomatic relations between the two countries were near

collapse. At the time of his inauguration Adams broached to Jefferson the plan of a bipartisan commission to France. Madison was the key to the plan. Would he go to France? Jefferson asked him, and he declined. Doubtless his own personal plans were too well settled to be laid aside for an arduous mission abroad. Even if this were not so, political considerations touching the independence of the Republican party would have led him to the same decision. And had this decision been different, the Hamiltonians in Adams's Cabinet would have vetoed Madison. Thus the spirit of conciliation quickly vanished. Madison's thoughts had turned to home and farm. He wrote to his father as he was about to leave Philadelphia.

Philada. March 12. 1797

I wrote you by the last mail, and add this by Mr. Jefferson. Lest my last should by any possibility have miscarried, I repeat my request that my name may not be suffered to get on the Poll for the County election. If Mr. Jefferson should call & say any thing to counteract my determination, I hope it will be regarded as merely expressive of his own wishes on the subject, & that it will not be allowed to have the least effect. In declining to go into the Assembly, should there really be a disposition to send me there I am sincere & inflexible. I hope I shall hear from you by the next mail, on the subject of Mordecai & the horses; being extremely anxious now to be on the journey, especially as we are to make visits to Berkeley & Fredk on the way home. At present the roads are made bad by a snow succeeded by rain which has nearly carried it off: but the winds of March will soon put them in order. If the same weather should have happened with you, it will have been a fair opportunity for sowing the Clover seed I sent, & which I hope got to hand in time for the purpose. The greater part of what I sent was purchased for a vessel intended to sail last fall, & cost me 15 dollrs. which with freight &c will exceed the Richmond price. I really think it was an error to be deterred by that price, considering the immense importance of the article, especially in laying a foundation for a meliorating plan of husbandry. The proper remedy for such a disappointment, I am told by a very experienced & intelligent farmer of this neighbourhood, is to sow in the fall on the stubble of the wheat or rye. He says this is his practice whenever he cannot get seed for spring sowing the fields, or when the seed does not take effect, & that the protection & putrefaction of the stuble, ensures a full crop the following year, so that there is no other loss,

The thirty-six gun Philadelphia (left) was constructed for the quasi war with France during the administration of John Adams (above in an engraving by H. Houston).

213

Page from the Madison family Bible
recording death of brother Ambrose

than the first fall pasture. I consider this as a valuable hint, to beginners, as it doubles the chance of getting Clover into a rotation.

You will see by the inclosed paper that the last accts. from Paris respecting the negociations for peace & the temper of France towards this Country, are not favorable. This resentment is the fruit of the British Treaty, which many of its zealous advocates begin now to acknowledge was an unwise & unfortunate measure. The accounts are not authentic, & probably not accurate; but coming through so many different channels they are thought to be true in substance.

So long engaged in public life, Madison had little practical knowledge of farming; but with other enlightened men of his time he had become a student of scientific agriculture, the principles of which he would apply to his own lands with considerable success. After the death of his younger brother Ambrose in 1793, the responsibility for management of the family estate fell increasingly to Madison. It was a large estate of some ten thousand acres (half of that being the Montpelier property), which together with approximately one hundred slaves would descend outright to Madison at his father's death. Grain had replaced tobacco as the main cash crop in the Piedmont; so long as armies marched in Europe and American carriers sailed the Atlantic, farming was profitable.

Madison put some of the profits into remodeling Montpelier. A portico of Jefferson's design was added and the entire house was elegantly finished. Dolley Madison presided over the hospitality of the mansion. A British diplomat, Sir Augustus Foster, visited Montpelier in 1807 when Madison was Secretary of State and described her as "a very handsome woman and tho' an uncultivated mind and fond of gossiping, was so perfectly good-tempered and good-humored that she rendered her husband's house as far as depended on her agreeable to all parties." Recalling the visit years later, Foster left this description (not always accurate) of the plantation.

"Notes on the U.S.A." [1833–35]

His house stands upon the Southwest Mountains, as they are called—a range of hills parallel to the Blue Ridge, and about twenty miles removed from it. The house has a fine view of the Ridge and of a well wooded plain that lies in front of it from whence the ascent is so gradual that the house scarcely appears to be upon an elevation. There is a portico to it of the plainest and most massive order of architecture, but which Palladio gives as a specimen of the Tuscan. Mr. Madison himself superintended the building which he had executed by the hands of common workmen to whom he prescribed the proportions to be observed. It is of brick which requires and is intended to be plastered. It occupies about a third part of the length of the house, being forty-seven feet wide, and together with its pediments it is as high as the house, viz., forty feet. There are four columns to this portico, of common bricks diminishing from a third, and having bases as well as plinths....

Mr. Madison has about ten or twelve hundred acres of land at this place which is called Montpellier, and as, from his situation in the republic, he was obliged to be often absent from home, he was under the necessity of trusting to his overseer a great deal. The latter had £60 Virginia currency of £48 sterling per annum, and was furnished with lodging and everything he or his family could want. Mr. Madison assured me that after providing for this overseer, clothing his Negroes, and deducting the expences for repairs, the profits which he derived from the estate did not exceed the overseer's pay.... The expence of a Negro he estimated at twenty-five or thirty dollars a year according to the situation, and you can only calculate, on an average, upon half the number of slaves being fit for service at any given time.

Great depredations are committed, and continue to be committed, unknown to the owners, in the vast extent of their forests, when they remain for a long while absent from their houses in the country. Tan yards being established in the smallest villages the owners of which employ people to go about barking the trees where they are least likely to be detected, and Mr. Madison assured me that for several years an overseer on a neighbouring property had been in the habit of breaking off the branches and tops of his pine trees in order to make lampblack (the smoke of burnt pines collected on canvas being the process employed) which he sold at a considerable profit.

There were wild turkeys in great numbers in the woods about Mr. Madison's place and I very much regretted not having brought my fowling piece as the Secretary of State had none to lend me. Mr. [Thomas] Macon, his brother-in-law [his younger sister Sarah's husband], lived but three miles off on an estate very prettily situated, and there were several other families scattered about in the neighbourhood. The Negro habitations are separate

Virginia, HOWE

Nineteenth-century engravings of a Blue Ridge vista (above) and the Madison family homestead

from the dwelling house both here and all over Virginia, and they form a kind of village as each Negro family would like, if they were allowed it, to live in a house by themselves. When at a distance from any town it is necessary they should be able to do all kind of handiwork; and, accordingly, at Montpellier I found a forge, a turner's shop, a carpenter, and wheelwright. All articles too that were wanted for farming or the use of the house were made on the spot, and I saw a very well constructed waggon that had just been completed. The slaves, however, are unwilling to make their own clothes, and during the Revolutionary War, it was very difficult to get them to spin or to card wool. Yet the cloth they did make was superior to the coarser English cloth because they threw the wool of best quality into the stuff in which the English use the worst. The Negro women too preferred by a great deal working in the fields to spinning and sewing. They appeared to me to be a happy thoughtless race of people when under a kind master as was the Secretary of State.

There are some very fine woods about Montpellier, but no pleasure grounds, though Mr. Madison talks of some day laying out space for an English park, which he might render very beautiful from the easy graceful descent of his hills into the plains below. The ladies, however, whom I have known in Virginia, like those of Italy generally speaking, scarcely even venture out of their houses to walk or to enjoy beautiful scenery. A high situation from whence they can have an extensive prospect is their delight and in fact the heat is too great in these latitudes to allow of such English tastes to exist in the same degree at least as in the mother country. A pleasure ground, too, to be kept in order, would in fact be very expensive, and all hands are absolutely wanted for the plantation. Great estates, and consequently great wealth were, it is true, in former days by no means uncommon in Virginia, and I have heard of a Mr. Carter who possessed eighty thousand acres, but the abolition of entails has nearly ruined them all. Many hard cases occurred after the act...was passed for the purpose in 1776, among which I was told by Mr. [John] Randolph of one that was in fact a great act in injustice on the part of Colonel Van, who, having received an estate entailed in 1775, took advantage of the act of the following year,

Guests at Montpelier commented upon the life of the slaves and noted the abundance of wild turkeys.

The Peaks of Otter, two mountains in the Blue Ridge to the south and west of Montpelier, typified the Virginia countryside Madison loved.

and left it away from his sisters to his widow who married again and left the rightful heiresses penniless. At the present day estates are very much subdivided and I believe that even so late as the commencement of the century nobody could be pointed out as possessed of twenty-five thousand acres.

On descending from Mr. Madison's I measured a chestnut tree that was eighteen feet in circumference and I saw several most beautiful umbrella magnolias of which the fruit makes an agreeable bitter that mixed in wine is considered a wholesome draft in hot weather.

It is a very delightful ride of twenty-eight miles from Montpellier to . . . Mr. Jefferson's seat at Monticello, the road lying at the foot of the Southwest Ridge.

For nearly a year following Adams's inauguration in 1797, Madison succeeded in placing himself *hors de combat.* The political scene became irresistible by 1798, however. In Madison's opinion, the Adams administration from its beginning had put the nation on a collision course with France. Foreign Minister Talleyrand and the Directory were not blameless; they had decided to follow the British example toward America's neutral commerce and had petulantly rebuffed Monroe's successor as Minister to the French court, Charles C. Pinckney. But Adams was the principal aggressor. Where he might have soothed, he provoked the French; where he might have checked the anglophile Federalists, he entered into their schemes and fastened an insane "war system" on the nation. Madison traced this criminal folly to Adams's apostasy from the principles of 1776, his adulation of the English constitution, and his contempt for the French Revolution. Not only was Adams to blame, but that blame was fundamentally a matter of antirepublican or "monarchical" principle. Madison voiced his opinion to Monroe after the President's saber-rattling speech to Congress in November, 1797.

[Montpelier,] Decr. 17. 97

I have not recd. a line from Philada. on the subject of the Speech, or indeed on any other. To me no explanation of the phenomenon is necessary, having been on the ground for observing the progressive apostasy from the principles of our Revolution & Governments, which marked the period of your absence. If events should not be unpropitious to the Monarchical party, you may prepare yourself for still more wonderful indications of its spirit & views. Those who tolerate at present the fashionable sentiments, will soon be ready to embrace & avow them. The active characters who promoted Mr. A. to his station, knowing him to be what he is, can not at bottom have been much averse to his political tenets, and will find in the spirit of party & in personal attachments & animosities, sufficient motives to go all lengths with him. Let us hope however that the tide of evil is nearly at its flood, and that it will ebb back to the true mark of which it has overpassed.

A few months later, in a letter to Jefferson, Madison made an interesting comparison between Adams and George Washington.

[Montpelier, February 18 or 19, 1798]

I am glad to find the public opinion to be taking the turn you describe on the subject of arming. For the public opinion alone can now save us from the rash measures of our hot-heated Executives; it being evident from some late votes of the House of Reps. . . . that a majority there as well as in the Senate are ready to go as far as the controul of their Constituents will permit. There never was perhaps a greater contrast between two characters, than between those of the present President & of his predecessor, altho' it is the boast & prop of the present, that he treads in the steps of his predecessor. The one cool considerate & cautious, the other headlong and kindled into flame by every spark that lights on his passions: the one ever scrutinizing into the public opinion, and ready to follow where he could not lead it: the other insulting it by the most adverse sentiments & pursuits: W. a hero in the field, yet overweighing every danger in the Cabinet. A. without a single pretension to the character of Soldier, a perfect Quixotte as a Statesman: the former cheif Magistrate pursuing peace every where with

French Foreign Minister Talleyrand

sincerity, tho' mistaking the means; the latter taking as much pains to get into war, as the former took to keep out of it. The contrast might be pursued into a variety of other particulars—the policy of the one in shunning connections with the arrangements of Europe, of the other in holding out the U.S. as a makeweight in its Balances of power: the avowed exultation of W. in the progress of liberty every where, & his eulogy on the Revolution & people of France posterior even to the bloody reign & fate of Robespierre—the open denunciations by Adams of the smallest disturbance of the antient discipline order & tranquility of Despotism, &c &c &c.

In the spring of 1798, the XYZ Affair exploded on the country. The three-man commission Adams had sent to France reported that Talleyrand, through his agents (identified only as X, Y, and Z in the dispatches), had demanded a loan and a bribe as the price of treating. Adams laid this nasty business before Congress in March, indignantly announced the end of negotiation, and called for enactment of bold new defense measures. Publication of the dispatches followed. Madison was shocked less by the venality of Talleyrand and his crew, which was not unexampled, than by their stupidity. He was also dismayed by the Federalists' calculated use of this pretext to annihilate the Republicans at home and to ally the country with Britain in war on France. That this was the plan became clearer as Congress laid new taxes, raised a provisional army (with Hamilton second-in-command to Washington), spread delusory fears of French subversion and invasion, enacted the repressive Alien and Sedition Acts, annulled the 1778 treaties of commerce and alliance with France, and embarked upon an undeclared naval war with that power. Several letters to Jefferson that spring charted Madison's reaction to events in Philadelphia.

[Montpelier,] Apl. 22 1798

My last was on the 15th. and acknowledged your preceding letters. I have since recd. that of the 12. under the same cover with the Gazettes; and the instructions & despatches, under a separate cover. The interruptions of company added to the calls of business have not left me time as yet to read over the whole of those papers. A glance at them, with the abstracts given of their intents, fully account for the state of astonishment produced in the public mind. And yet the circumstance that ought to astonish most perhaps, is the publication of them by the Ex. [executive] & Senate. Whatever probability there may be of individual corruption within the pale of the

French Govt. the evidence is certainly very insufficient to support such an attack on its reputation in the face of the world, even if we could separate the measure from its inevitable effect in blasting every chance of accomodation, if it should reach France before terms shall be finally settled. After this stroke in the politics of those two Branches of our Govt. no one who has not surrendered his reason, can believe them sincere in wishing to avoid extremities with the French Republic; to say nothing of the internal views to which they mean also to turn this extraordinary manoeuvre. There has not been time for any impressions on the public sentiment in this quarter, which the Despatches are calculated to make. The first will no doubt pretty much correspond with those made elsewhere; But the final impressions will depend on the further & more authentic developments which cannot be far behind, & wch. may by this time be arrived where you are. I find that in several places the people have turned out with their protests agst. the war measures urged by the Ex. Whether the proceeding will be general is what I cannot pretend to decide. In this County a Petition is to be handed about, which will I presume be pretty fully signed, if sufficiently circulated; unless the disaffected few among us, should be imbolded by the present crisis to circulate along with it, the impressions emanating from the Despatches wch. may stop the hands of wavering or cautious people. Altho' the thermo[me]ter on the mornings of the 15 & 16 inst: was at 31 & 32°. the fruit was not materially injured except in low situations, but having sunk during the night following to 24°. vegitation of every kind seemed to feel the blow. The Peaches & Cherries appear to [be] totally destroyed, and most of the apples. Even the young hickory leaves are in considerable proportion compleatly killed. The weather has since been more natural to the season.

A letter Madison wrote a neighbor, trying to track down a pocket-money weighing scale he had lent

[Montpelier,] May 13, 1798
The successful use of the Despatches in kindling a flame among the people, and of the flame in extending taxes armies & prerogative, are solemn lessons which I hope will have their proper effect when the infatuation of the moment is over. The management of foreign relations appears to be the most susceptible of abuse, of all the trusts committed to a Government, because they can be

concealed or disclosed, or disclosed in such parts & at such times as will best suit particular views; and because the body of the people are less capable of judging & are more under the influence of prejudices, on that branch of their affairs, than of any other. Perhaps it is a universal truth that the loss of liberty at home is to be charged to provisions agst. danger real or pretended from abroad. . . . If he [Adams] finds it thus easy to play on the prepossessions of the people for their own Govt. agst. a foreign, we ought not to be disappointed if the same game should have equal success in the hands of the Directory. We have had little or no rain for a month, and the evil has been increased by much windy & cold weather. The Thermr. yesterday morning was at 38° and the frost such as to kill the leaves of tender trees in low situations. I hope now you will soon be released from the thorny seat in which you are placed, and that I shall not be disappointed of the pleasure of seeing you on your way. You must so arrange your time as to be able to ride a mile while with me to see a Threshing machine I have lately built on Martins place. It is worked & attended by five or six hands at most, and I think promises more for general use than all the other modifications. I shall not describe it, because your own inspection will so soon give you a more perfect idea of it.

The Alien and Sedition Acts, enacted at the height of the war hysteria, seemed to Madison, as to most Republicans, to be aimed at the destruction of the opposition party. The Sedition Act outlawed "any false, scandalous and malicious writing" against the government, Congress, or the President. Every Republican newspaper was threatened. The Alien Act gave the President power to expel all foreigners deemed "dangerous to the peace and safety of the United States." This was meant for Frenchmen and Irishmen, who were almost invariably allied with the Republican cause. A companion measure, the Naturalization Act, raised the period of residency for American citizenship from five to fourteen years. The alien bill was before the Senate when Madison vented his wrath to Jefferson.

[Montpelier,] May 20. 1798

The Alien bill proposed in the Senate is a monster that must for ever disgrace its parents. I should not have supposed it possible that such an one could have been engendered in either House, & still persuade myself, that it can not possibly be fathered by both. It is truly to be

An act passed by the Fifth Congress "respecting alien enemies" in 1798

deplored that a standing army should be let in upon us by the absence of a few sound votes. It may however all be for the best. These addresses to the feelings of the people from their enemies, may have more effect in opening their eyes, than all the arguments addressed to their understandings by their friends. The President also seems to be co-operating for the same purpose. Every answer he gives to his addressers, unmasks more & more his principles & views. His language to the young men of Ph[il]a. is the most abominable & degrading that could fall from the lips of the first magistrate of an independent people, & particularly from a Revolutionary patriot. It throws some light on his meaning when he remarked to me, "that there was not a single principle the same in the American & French Revolutions".... The abolition of Royalty was it seems not one of his Revolutionary principles. Whether he always made this profession is best known to those who knew him in the year 1776. The turn of the elections in N.Y. is a proof that the late

occurrences have increased the noise only & not the number of the Tory party.... I forgot to acknowledge the
pamphlet containing the last despach from the Envoys
.... It is evidently more in the forensic than Diplomatic
stile and more likely in some of its reasonings to satisfy
an American Jury, than the French Government.

When Jefferson stopped at Montpelier on his return
from Philadelphia early in July, he was full of gloom yet somehow confident
that the evils of war and taxes and oppressive legislation would draw forth
the republican spirit of the people and produce their own remedy. But
during the summer months he decided a more radical cure was needed.
Because of the war party's hold on the federal government, this could only
originate in the states. Apparently without consulting Madison, he drafted
what became the Kentucky Resolutions of 1798. The resolutions introduced
by Madison's old friend George Nicholas and adopted by the Kentucky
legislature set forth the compact theory of the Union, declared the Alien
and Sedition Acts unconstitutional, and, without going to the length of
"nullification" as Jefferson had proposed, urged concerted state action for
their repeal. Madison saw Jefferson's draft at Monticello in October and
agreed to prepare similar resolutions for introduction in the Virginia
assembly. A man of cooler judgment and a more cautious politician, Madison adhered to Jefferson's reasoning but steered clear of his bold conclusion:
that in the case of federal usurpation of powers a nullification by the state
authorities is "the rightful remedy." The Virginia Resolutions of 1798
simply declared the right and duty of the legislature to interpose its authority when in its opinion certain federal laws were unconstitutional and to call
upon the sister states to join in securing their repeal. The resolutions were
followed by an address, also of Madison's authorship, defending the action.

"Address to the People"
[January 23, 1799]

Fellow-Citizens,— Unwilling to shrink from our representative responsibility, conscious of the purity of our
motives, but acknowledging your right to supervise our
conduct, we invite your serious attention to the emergency which dictated the subjoined resolutions....

It would be perfidious in those entrusted with the
guardianship of the State sovereignty, and acting under
the solemn obligation of the following oath, "I do swear
that I will support the Constitution of the United States,"
not to warn you of encroachments which, though clothed
with the pretext of necessity, or disguised by arguments
of expediency, may yet establish precedents which may

ultimately devote a generous and unsuspicious people to all the consequences of usurped power.

Encroachments springing from a government whose organization can not be maintained without the co-operation of the States, furnish the strongest excitements upon the State Legislatures to watchfulness, and impose upon them the strongest obligation to preserve unimpaired the line of partition. . . .

Exhortations to disregard domestic usurpation, until foreign danger shall have passed, is an artifice which may be forever used, because the possessors of power, who are the advocates for its extension, can ever create national embarrassments, to be successively employed to soothe the people into sleep, whilst that power is swelling, silently, secretly, and fatally. Of the same character are insinuations of a foreign influence, which seize upon a laudable enthusiasm against danger from abroad, and distort it by an unnatural application, so as to blind your eyes against danger at home.

The sedition act presents a scene which was never expected by the early friends of the Constitution. It was then admitted that the State sovereignties were only diminished by powers specifically enumerated, or necessary to carry the specified powers into effect. Now, Federal authority is deduced from implication; and from the existence of State law, it is inferred that Congress possess a similar power of legislation; whence Congress will be endowed with a power of legislation in all cases whatsoever, and the States will be stripped of every right reserved, by the concurrent claims of a paramount Legislature.

The sedition act is the offspring of these tremendous pretensions, which inflict a deathwound on the sovereignty of the States. . . .

It is vicious in the extreme to calumniate meritorious public servants; but it is both artful and vicious to arouse the public indignation against calumny in order to conceal usurpation. Calumny is forbidden by the laws, usurpation by the Constitution. Calumny injures individuals, usurpation, States. Calumny may be redressed by the common judicatures; usurpation can only be controlled by the act of society. Ought usurpation, which is most mischievous, to be rendered less hateful by calumny, which, though injurious, is in a degree less pernicious?

RESOLUTIONS

OF

VIRGINIA AND KENTUCKY,

PENNED BY

MADISON AND JEFFERSON,

IN RELATION TO THE

ALIEN AND SEDITION LAWS:

AND

DEBATES

IN THE

HOUSE OF DELEGATES OF VIRGINIA,

IN DECEMBER, 1798,

ON THE SAME.

RICHMOND:
PUBLISHED BY ROBERT I. SMITH.
Samuel Shepherd & Co. Printers.
1832.

Title page to a later publication of the Virginia and Kentucky Resolutions in opposition to the Alien and Sedition Acts of 1798

But the laws for the correction of calumny were not defective. Every libellous writing or expression might receive its punishment in the State courts, from juries summoned by an officer, who does not receive his appointment from the President, and is under no influence to court the pleasure of Government, whether it injured public officers or private citizens. Nor is there any distinction in the Constitution empowering Congress exclusively to punish calumny directed against an officer of the General Government; so that a construction assuming the power of protecting the reputation of a citizen officer will extend to the case of any other citizen, and open to Congress a right of legislation in every conceivable case which can arise between individuals....

...Remember that precedents once established are so much positive power; and that the nation which reposes on the pillow of political confidence, will sooner or later end its political existence in a deadly lethargy. Remember, also, that it is to the press mankind are indebted for having dispelled the clouds which long encompassed religion, for disclosing her geniune lustre, and disseminating her salutary doctrines.

The sophistry of a distinction between the liberty and the licentiousness of the press is so forcibly exposed in a late memorial from our late envoys to the Minister of the French Republic, that we here present it to you in their own words:

"The genius of the Constitution, and the opinion of the people of the United States, cannot be overruled by those who administer the Government. Among those principles deemed sacred in America, among those sacred rights considered as forming the bulwark of their liberty, which the Government contemplates with awful reverence and would approach only with the most cautious circumspection, there is no one of which the importance is more deeply impressed on the public mind than the liberty of the press. That this *liberty* is often carried to excess; that it has sometimes degenerated into *licentiousness,* is seen and lamented, *but the remedy has not yet been discovered. Perhaps it is an evil inseperable from the good with which it is allied; perhaps it is a shoot which cannot be stripped from the stalk without wounding vitally the plant from which it is torn. However desirable those measures might be which might correct without enslaving the press, they have never yet been devised in America.* No regulations exist which enable the Government to suppress whatever calumnies or invectives any individual may choose to offer to the public eye, or to punish such calumnies and invectives otherwise than by a legal prosecution in courts which are alike open to all who consider themselves as injured."

As if we were bound to look for security from the personal probity of Congress amidst the frailties of man, and not from the barriers of the Constitution, it has been urged that the accused under the sedition act is allowed to prove the truth of the charge. This argument will not for a moment disguise the unconstitutionality of the act, if it be recollected that opinions as well as facts are made punishable, and that the truth of an opinion is not susceptible of proof. By subjecting the truth of opinion to the regulation, fine, and imprisonment, to be inflicted by those who are of a different opinion, the free range of the human mind is injuriously restrained....

All the preceding arguments, arising from a deficiency of constitutional power in Congress, apply to the alien act; and this act is liable to other objections peculiar to itself. If a suspicion that aliens are dangerous constitute the justification of that power exercised over them by Congress, then a similar suspicion will justify the exercise of a similar power over natives; because there is nothing in the Constitution distinguishing between the power of a State to permit the residence of natives and of aliens. It is, therefore, a right originally possessed, and never surrendered, by the respective States, and which is rendered dear and valuable to Virginia...because her peculiar situation renders the easy admission of artisans and laborers an interest of vast importance.

But this bill contains other features, still more alarming and dangerous. It dispenses with the trial by jury; it violates the judicial system; it confounds legislative, executive, and judicial powers; it punishes without trial; and it bestows upon the President despotic power over a numerous class of men. Are such measures consistent with our constitutional principles? And will an accumulation of power so extensive in the hands of the Executive, over aliens, secure to natives the blessings of republican liberty?

If measures can mould governments, and if an uncon-

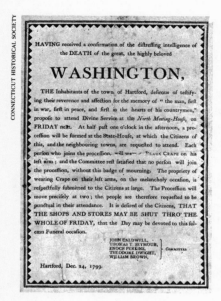

Broadside issued in Hartford, Connecticut, on death of George Washington on December 14, 1799

trolled power of construction is surrendered to those who administer them, their progress may be easily foreseen, and their end easily foretold. A lover of monarchy, who opens the treasures of corruption by distributing emolument among devoted partisans, may at the same time be approaching his object and deluding the people with professions of republicanism. He may confound monarchy and republicanism, by the art of definition. He may varnish over the dexterity which ambition never fails to display, with the pliancy of language, the seduction of expediency, or the prejudices of the times; and he may come at length to avow that so extensive a territory as that of the United States can only be governed by the energies of monarchy; that it cannot be defended, except by standing armies; and that it cannot be united except by consolidation.

Measures have already been adopted which may lead to these consequences. They consist—

In fiscal systems and arrangements, which keep a host of commercial and wealthy individuals imbodied, and obedient to the mandates of the treasury.

In armies and navies, which will, on the one hand, enlist the tendency of man to pay homage to his fellow-creature who can feed or honor him; and on the other, employ the principle of fear, by punishing imaginary insurrections, under the pretext of preventive justice.

In the extensive establishment of a volunteer militia, rallied together by a political creed, armed and officered

War on the high seas actually broke out between France and the United States in 1798. The American Constellation *captured the French frigate* L'Insurgente *in February, 1799, causing great excitement.*

227

by executive power, so as to deprive the States of their constitutional right to appoint militia officers, and to place the great bulk of the people in a defenceless situation.

In swarms of officers, civil and military, who can inculcate political tenets tending to consolidation and monarchy both by indulgencies and severities; and can act as spies over the free exercise of human reason.

In destroying, by the sedition act, the responsibility of public servants and public measures to the people, thus retrograding towards the exploded doctrine "that the administrators of the Government are the masters, and not the servants, of the people," and exposing America, which acquired the honour of taking the lead among nations towards perfecting political principles, to the disgrace of returning first to ancient ignorance and barbarism....

In transferring to the Executive important legislative powers; particularly the power of raising armies, and borrowing money without limitation of interest.

In restraining the freedom of the press, and investing the Executive with legislative, executive, and judicial powers, over a numerous body of men.

And, that we may shorten the catalogue, in establishing, by successive precedents, such a mode of construing the Constitution as will rapidly remove every restraint upon Federal power.

Let history be consulted; let the man of experience reflect; nay, let the artificers of monarchy be asked what further materials they can need for building up their favorite system.

These are solemn but painful truths; and yet we recommend it to you not to forget the possibility of danger from without, although danger threatens us from within. Usurpation is indeed dreadful; but against foreign invasion, if that should happen, let us rise with hearts and hands united, and repel the attack with the zeal of freemen who will strengthen their title to examine and correct domestic measures, by having defended their country against foreign aggression.

Pledged as we are, fellow-citizens, to these sacred engagements, we yet humbly and fervently implore the Almighty Disposer of events to avert from our land war and usurpation, the scourges of mankind; to permit our

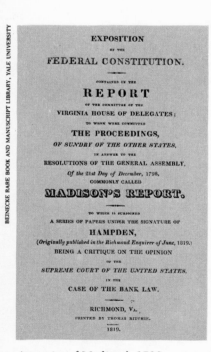

A reprint of Madison's 1799 report justifying the Virginia Resolutions

fields to be cultivated in peace; to instil into nations the love of friendly intercourse; to suffer our youth to be educated in virtue, and to preserve our morality from the pollution invariably incident to habits of war; to prevent the laborer and husbandman from being harassed by taxes and imposts; to remove from ambition the means of disturbing the commonwealth; to annihilate all pretexts for power afforded by war; to maintain the Constitution; and to bless our nation with tranquillity, under whose benign influence we may reach the summit of happiness and glory, to which we are destined by *nature* and *nature's God.*

In thus rushing to the defense of civil liberties, the Republican leaders ran the risk of provoking a crisis of union. This was not their intention. Their appeal to states' rights was only a tactic in the larger strategy of liberty; and they were pursuing, as Jefferson said, "a political resistance for political effect." The effect was slow in coming. The Sedition Act terrorized public opinion. Vigorously enforced by the administration with the aid of compliant judges and juries, it decimated the Republican press and clogged political avenues of change. Petitions for its repeal poured into Congress, with no other effect than to stiffen Federalist resolution. And several state legislatures, also Federalist dominated, vindicated the Alien and Sedition Acts in rebuff of the Virginia and Kentucky Resolutions. Jefferson concluded that the two states should renew their protests. Writing to Madison in midsummer, he even suggested that the states announce their intention, should the usurpations persist, of seceding from the Union.

This was too much for Madison. On a sultry Sunday afternoon he rode to Monticello and with little difficulty calmed his friend's feelings. Jefferson receded from the threat of secession, "not only in deference to his [Madison's] judgment, but because we should never think of separation but for repeated and enormous violations, so these, when they occur, will be cause enough of themselves." Kentucky, in 1799, briefly repeated its earlier protest. The Virginia assembly, where Madison was once again a delegate, adopted a lengthy report from his pen expounding the theory of federal union and vindicating human rights. Meanwhile, the initial cause of the controversy, the crisis with France, was on its way to a peaceful settlement, John Adams having broken with the High Federalists and dispatched a new trio of envoys to France. Jefferson was back in Philadelphia when Madison wrote to him from Richmond.

Richmond Decr. 29. 1799

My promise to write to you before your leaving Albemarle was defeated by a dysenteric attack which laid me

William Branch Giles

up for about a week, and which left me in a state of debility not yet thoroughly removed. My recovery has been much retarded by the job of preparing a vindication of the Resolutions of last Session agst. the replies of the other States, and the sophistries from other quarters. The Committee made their report a few days ago, which is now in the press and stands the order of the day for thursday next. A sett of Resolutions proposed by Mr. [William B.] Giles, instructing the Senators to urge the repeal of the unconstl. acts, the disbanding of the army, and the proper arrangement of the Militia, are also in the press and stand the order of the same day for the same Committee. It is supposed that both these papers, the latter perhaps with some modifications, will go through the H. of Delegates. The Senate, owing to inattention & casualties, is so composed as to render the event there not a little uncertain.... There is a report here that the Legislature of N. Carolina now in Session, have voted the Resolutions of Virginia under their table. The report is highly improbable, and I do not believe it. But it is impossible to calculate the progress of delusion, especially in a State where it is said to be under systematic management, and where there is so little either of system or exertion opposed to it. We had a narrow escape yesterday from an increase of pay to the members, which would have been particularly unseasonable & injurious both within & without the State. It was rejected on the third reading by a small majority; and was so much a favorite, with the distant members particularly, that I fear it has left them in rather an ill humour.

The late course of foreign events has probably made the same impression every where. If it should not render France less anxious to meet our advances, its good effects will be felt every way. If our Executive & their Envoys be sincere in their pacific objects, it will perhaps supply by their increased anxiety what may be lost on the other side. But there can be little confidence after what has been seen, that the negociation would be influenced by this temper of the Envoys, instead of that which perverted it in the hands of their predecessors. This possibility of failure in the diplomatic experiment, will present the most specious obstacle to an immediate discharge of the army. It would be useful for the Assembly to know how this matter is viewed where you are.

A Federalist cartoon of 1800 shows a watchful eye and American eagle preventing Jefferson from making a burnt offering of the Constitution on an "Altar of Gallic Despotism."

Richmond Jany. 4. 1800.

My last covered a copy of the Report on the Resolutions of last year. I now inclose a copy of certain resolutions moved by Mr. Giles, to which he means to add an instruction on the subject of the intercource law which has been so injurious to the price of our Tobo [tobacco]. It is not improbable that the Resolutions when taken up, may undergo some mollifications in the spirit & air of them. The Report has been under debate for two days. The attacks on it have turned chiefly on an alledged inconsistency between the comment now made, and the arguments of the last Session, and on the right of the Legislature to interfere in any manner with denunciations of the measures of the Genl. Govt. The first attack has been parried by an amendment admitting that different constructions may have been entertained of the term "States" as "parties" &c but that the sense relied on in the report must be concurred in by all. It is in fact concurred in by both parties. On examination of the debates of the last Session, it appears that both were equally inaccurate & inconsistent in the grounds formerly taken by them. The attack on the right of the Legislature to interfere by declarations of opinion will form a material point in the discussion. It is not yet known how far the opposition to the Report will be carried into detail.

Although the Sixth Congress, elected at the peak of the war frenzy, was overwhelmingly Federalist, all the signs in 1800 pointed to that "revolution of opinion" Jefferson and Madison had been awaiting for two years. In both Philadelphia and Richmond politicians were jockeying for position in the coming presidential contest. Republicans again united behind Jefferson, while Adams, in his bid for reelection, faced insurgency within the ranks. All the accumulated passion and fury of a decade of party conflict poured into the campaign; no one doubted that the outcome would determine the fate of republican government on the continent for a long time to come. Except within the Virginia Republican organization, Madison took little part in the campaign. He was in ill health and seems not to have stirred from Montpelier, having returned from Richmond early in the year.

Republicanism triumphed. By early December the electoral vote could be confidently predicted: 73 for Jefferson, 65 for Adams. Jefferson dashed off a letter to his running mate, Aaron Burr of New York, congratulating him on his election as Vice President. Unfortunately, as he soon discovered, Burr also received 73 electoral votes, which threw the choice into the House

231

of Representatives where the Federalists were in control. (Prior to the Twelfth Amendment in 1804—the direct result of the electoral tie in 1800 —ballots were cast only for President, the Vice Presidency going to the runner-up.) The Republicans had been on guard against just such a possibility, however remote. A Republican elector in some state would discard his vote for Burr, thereby preventing a tie with Jefferson. The result might have been secured in the Virginia "college of electors." But Burr had charged the Virginia Republicans with bad faith for failing to support him when he was second on the Republican ticket four years earlier. Madison, therefore, demanded a unanimous vote for the New Yorker in Virginia, being assured by Burr's friends that votes would be thrown away from him in New York or elsewhere. Burr failed to deliver on this promise to place Jefferson's election beyond hazard, and Republican electors north and south played Alphonse and Gaston to each other.

From the new capital on the Potomac, Jefferson informed Madison that "an absolute parity" between the Republican candidates seemed certain. "This has produced great dismay and gloom on the Republican gentlemen here, and equal exultation on the Federalists." Madison, in reply, shared his anxiety.

[Montpelier,] Jany. 10, 1801.

I find that the vote of Kentucky establishes the tie between the Repub: characters, and consequently throws the result into the hands of the H. of R. Desperate as some of the adverse party there may be, I can scarcely allow myself to believe that enough will not be found to frustrate the attempt to strangle the election of the people, and smuggle into the Chief Magistracy the choice creature of a faction. It would seem that every individual member, who has any standing or stake in society, or any portion of virtue or sober understanding must revolt at the tendency of such a manouvre. Is it possible that Mr. A[dams] shd. give his sanction to it if that should be made a necessary ingredient? Or that he would not hold it his duty or his policy, in case the present House should obstinately refuse to give effect to the Constn., to appoint, which he certainly may do before his office expires as early a day as possible, after that event, for the succeeding House to meet, and supply the omission. Should he disappt. a just expectation in either instance, it will be an omen, I think, forbidding the steps towards which you seem to be meditating. I would not wish to discourage any attentions which friendship, prudence, or benevolence may suggest in his behalf, but I think it not improper to remark, that I find him infinitely sunk in

Aaron Burr, the Republican vice-presidential candidate in 1800, received the same number of electoral votes as did Jefferson.

By Yesterday's Mails.

Highly Important and Interesting.

PENNSYLVANIA.   PHILAD. FEB. 14.

BY EXPRESS.

WASHINGTON, Feb. 11, half past 3, afternoon.

"ACCORDING to the rule of proceedings established by the House, they proceeded to the Senate Chamber, where (by Mr. *Nicholas* and Mr. *Rutledge,* the tellers on the part of the House, and Mr. *Wells* on the part of the Senate) the votes were counted and the result declared by the Vice-President, as follow:—

For THOMAS JEFFERSON,	73
AARON BURR,	73
JOHN ADAMS,	65
C. C. PINCKNEY,	64
JOHN JAY,	1

The tellers declared there was some informality in the votes of *Georgia,* but believing them to be the true votes, reported them as such.

The Vice-President then, in pursuance of the duty enjoined upon him, declared, that *Thomas Jefferson* and *Aaron Burr* being equal in the number of Votes, it remained for the House of Representatives to determine the choice.

The two Houses then separated, and the House of Representatives returned to their chamber, where seats had been previously prepared for the members of the Senate. A call of the members of the House, arranged according to States, was then made; upon which it appeared, that every member was present except Gen. *Sumpter,* who is unwell, and unable to attend. Mr. *Nicholson* of *Maryland,* was also unwell but attended and had a bed prepared for him in one of the committee rooms, to which place the ballot box was carried to him, by the tellers appointed on the part of the State.

The Columbian Centinel *of Boston reported the electoral deadlock.*

the estimation of all parties. The follies of his administration, the oblique stroke at his Predecessor in the letter to [Tench] Coxe...are working powerfully agst. him, added to these causes is the pamphlet of H[amilton, an open *Letter Concerning the Public Conduct and Character of John Adams*] which, tho' its recoil has perhaps more deeply wounded the author, than the object it was discharged at, has contributed not a little to overthrow the latter staggering as he before was in the public esteem.

On the supposition of either event, whether of an interregnum in the Executive, or of a surreptitious intrusion into it, it becomes a question of the first order, what is the course demanded by the crisis. Will it be best to acquiesce in a suspension or usurpation of the Executive authority till the meeting of Congs. in Decr. next, or for Congs. to be summoned by a joint proclamation or recommendation of the two characters havg a majority of votes for President. My present judgment favors the latter expedient. The prerogative of convening the legislature must reside in one or other of them; and if both concur, must substantially include the requisite will. The intentions of the people would undoubtedly be pursued. And if, in reference to the Constn: the proceeding be not strictly regular, the irregularity will be less in form than any other adequate to the emergency; and will be in form only rather than substance; whereas the other remedies proposed are substantial violations of the will of the people, of the scope of the Constitution, and of the public order & interest. It is to be hoped however that all such questions will be precluded by a proper decision of nine States in the H. of R.

The Federalist scheme to force an interregnum or to elect Burr was at length defeated. On the thirty-sixth ballot in the House of Representatives, Jefferson was elected. Madison had agreed to become Secretary of State in any government Jefferson might head. He had no intention of changing his mind, though his own feeble health and the declining state of his seventy-seven-year-old father combined to give him pause. Near the end of February his father died, which delayed Madison's departure. He sent Jefferson his apologies, along with his opinion of Adams's wholesale appointment of Federalist judges in the final hours of his administration.

Inventory of the estate of Madison's father, who died in February, 1801

[Montpelier, February 28, 1801]

Your favor of the 1st. instant was to have been acknowledged a week ago, but the irregularity of the post occasioned by high waters has delayed it to the present opportunity. I have now to acknowledge your two subsequent ones of the 12th. & 19th. In compliance with the last, I had proposed to leave home in a few days, so as to be with you shortly after the 4th. of March. A melancholy occurrence has arrested this intention. My father's health for several weeks latterly seemed to revive, and we had hopes that the approach of milder seasons would still further contribute to keep him with us. A few days past however he became sensibly worse, and yesterday morning rather suddenly, tho' very qui[e]tly the flame of life went out. It is impossible for me now to speak of my movements with precision. Altho' the exact degree of agency devolving on me remains to be known, a crowd of indispensible attentions must necessarily be due from me. In this posture of things I can only say that I shall wait the return of this post after this reaches, by which I hope to learn whether your intended continuance at Washington will admit, and the state of things will require, my being there before you leave it. By this information I shall be governed, unless imperiously controuled by the circumstances here.

The conduct of Mr. A. is not such as was to have been wished or perhaps expected. Instead of smoothing the path for his successor, he plays into the hands of those who are endeavoring to strew it with as many difficulties as possible; and with this view does not manifest a very squeamish regard to the Constn. Will not his appts. to offices, not vacant actually at the time, even if afterwards vacated by acceptances of the translations, be null?

The result of the contest in the H. of R. was generally looked for in this quarter. It was thought not probable that the phalanx would hold out agst. the general revolt of its partizans out of doors & without any military force to abet usurpation. How fortunate that the latter has been witheld; and what a lesson to America & the world, is given by the efficacy of the public will when there is no army to be turned agst. it!

Chapter 7

Secretary of State

The city of Washington was but a decade young in 1801. Sprawled along the Potomac between Georgetown and Alexandria, the embryo capital of three thousand people boasted few of the amenities of civilization. Men scoffed at its pretensions and groaned under its discomforts. Two "shining objects" relieved the dreary scene: the President's House, gleaming under its coat of whitewash, and a mile and a half away, the boxlike torso of the unfinished Capitol, its north wing alone awkwardly dominating the summit of Capitol Hill. Settlements clustered around these cardinal points, which were connected by a treacherous roadway through forest and marsh, Pennsylvania Avenue. Good houses were scarce. The Madisons, arriving on May 1, first stayed with the President, and not until the succeeding fall were they permanently installed in a large new brick house two blocks to the east.

The entire staff of the State Department, which was located in the same executive quarter of the city, consisted of one chief clerk, seven clerks, and a messenger. The department had certain "home office" responsibilities —registration of patents, supervision of the census, custody of public documents, printing of the laws, and so on. But Madison quickly found, as had his predecessors, that foreign affairs were all-consuming. He had never set foot outside the United States—he never would—and he had no diplomatic experience; still, he was uniquely qualified for the post of Secretary of State. He had a clear conception of the national interest and understood the intricate relationship of policy objectives to the balance of forces both in the Atlantic world and at home. He possessed a good head for business and those personal qualities of quiet dignity, tactful reserve, and dogged perseverance that were wanted in diplomacy. Above all, he knew the mind of the President. In law and in practice the Chief Executive had full responsibility for the conduct of foreign affairs. Jefferson, even more than his predecessors, would be his own Secretary of State. In every previous case— that of Jefferson himself, of Edmund Randolph, and of Timothy Pickering—

this subordination of the office had produced conflict with the President. But in the case of Jefferson and Madison it would work beautifully because of the perfect friendship, harmony, and trust between them.

Coming into executive employment for the first time since he had served on the governor's council in Virginia more than twenty years before, Madison had little time for anything outside the line of official duty. Of course he entered into the social life of the village capital, over which Dolley Madison presided as the surrogate First Lady of the widower President; but he sharply curtailed his private correspondence and curbed the partisan feelings that had impelled him for so long in opposition. Jefferson, in his inaugural address, had appealed for an end to political fanaticism and a restoration of harmony and affection. "We are all republicans: we are all federalists." He had made it equally evident, however, that the Republicans came into power dedicated to reform. In the administration's attempt to strike a balance between reconciliation and reform, Madison's weight was generally thrown into the former scale. More than any other American statesman, he could claim to be both "federalist" and "republican," and with these credentials he became the leading voice of moderation in the President's Cabinet.

The first test of administration policy came on the matter of patronage. Republicans looking to reform called for wholesale removal of Federalist officeholders, while the reconcilers urged a moderate course. Madison, significantly, removed none of the Federalist clerks in his department, persuaded Jefferson to retain Rufus King as Minister to Great Britain, and gave little satisfaction to Republicans craving the spoils of office. His stance is suggested in a letter to the Virginia party leader, Wilson Cary Nicholas.

Washington July 10. 1801

I can not at so late a day acknowledge your two favors . . . without an explanation which I am sure your goodness will accept as an apology. Having brought with me to this place a very feeble state of health, and finding the mass of business in the Department, at all times considerable, swelled to an unusual size by sundry temporary causes; it became absolutely necessary to devote the whole of my time & pen to any public duties, and, consequently to suspend my private correspondence altogether, notwithstanding the arrears daily accumulating. To this resolution I have thus far adhered. I must now endeavor to make some atonement for the delay and your case is among the first that is suggested both by obligation & inclination.

That one of your letters which is confidential has been imparted to no person whatever. The P. O. Genl. continues in the hands of Col. H. [Joseph Habersham] who though not perhaps sufficiently in the views of the

An 1808 print by William Birch shows the Capitol under construction, its two wings bridged by an eagle.

*An early engraving of Washington,
looking down Pennsylvania Avenue*

Administration, is much respected personally, & is warmly espoused politically also by some of the purest and most weighty of our friends. It will be difficult to make a satisfactory arrangement for this Dept. that will not involve translations &c. which will prevent a real vacancy. Besides this I am inclined to believe that the P. would be afraid to draw on Virga. agst. competitions which wd. abound from other States. The Indivi[du]al spoken of by you would, as you must be well assured, be perfectly desired as an associate in the public business, on every consideration, unless it be that of robbing another important station of his services.

Little has occurred which you have not found in the Newspapers. The task of removing, and appointing officers, continues to embarrass the Ex. and agitate particular parts of the Union. The degree, the mode & the times of performing it, are often rendered the more perplexing by the discord of information & counsel received from different persons whose principles & views are the same. In Connecticut the fever & murmur of discontent at the exercise of this power is the greatest. The removal of [Elizur] Goodrich [the customs collector at New Haven] & appt. of a respectable Repubn. have produced a Remonstrance to the President in the strongest terms that decorum would tolerate. The spirit in that State is so perverse that it must be rectified by a peculiar mixture of energy and delicacy. The Secyship. of the Navy is still unfilled.

The prospect in foreign affairs was brighter than it had been for years. An uneasy *detente* prevailed with Britain, while a new treaty with France, known as the Convention of 1800, removed the immediate source of difficulty with that power. Writing to Jefferson as early as January, Madison had been optimistic.

Toussaint L'Ouverture, leader of the rebel blacks in Santo Domingo

[Montpelier,] Jany 10, 1801.

France has sufficiently manifested her friendly disposition, and what is more, seems to be duly impressed with the interest she has in being at peace with us. G.B., however intoxicated with her maritime ascendancy, is more dependent every day on our commerce for her resources, must for a considerable length of time look in a great degree to this Country, for bread for herself, and absolutely for all the necessaries for her islands. The prospect of a Northern Confederacy of neutrals cannot fail, in several ways, to inspire caution & management toward the U.S. especially as, in the event of war or interruption of commerce with the Baltic, the essential article of naval Stores can be sought here only. Besides these cogent motives to peace and moderation, her subjects will not fail to remind her of the great pecuniary pledge they have in this Country, and which under any interruption of peace of commerce with it, must fall under great embarrassments, if nothing worse.

After eight years of war, peace was in the offing in Europe. The preliminary articles of the Peace of Amiens would be signed in October. Hopes for smooth sailing were jarred, however, by rumors of Spain's retrocession of Louisiana to France. So long as that vast province—with the port of New Orleans and the Floridas to the east—remained in the hands of Spain, the United States was content. For these Spanish dominions must fall, like ripe fruit from the tree, whenever the Americans were ready for them. Moreover, under the terms of Thomas Pinckney's 1795 treaty with Spain, the Americans enjoyed free navigation of the Mississippi and the privileges of the port. But French possession of Louisiana, and possibly the Floridas too, was another matter, signaling the rebirth under Napoleonic auspices of French empire in the New World. Napoleon had already embarked on the reconquest of Santo Domingo, the richest of the French colonies, then in control of rebel blacks led by Toussaint L'Ouverture; and Louisiana was part of his grand design in North America. At first Jefferson and Madison refused to take alarm. If the bargain had in fact been made, Napoleon's plans were involved in so many difficulties that they might never materialize. The reconquest of Santo Domingo would not be easy work. Whether or not the Floridas were included in the cession was unknown, but without them Louisiana would be of doubtful value to France. And

France dared not risk confrontation with the United States on the Mississippi lest she find herself again at war in Europe. Considerations such as these lay behind the surprisingly mild instructions Madison gave to Robert R. Livingston, newly appointed Minister to France, in the fall. Although Livingston was to urge reasons against the cession, he should do nothing that would "unnecessarily irritate our future neighbors, or check the liberality which they may be disposed to exercise in relation to the trade and navigation through the mouth of the Mississippi."

In the negotiations that led to the Louisiana Purchase nearly twenty months later, Jefferson called the tune and Madison played it. How much he may have influenced Jefferson's moves is uncertain; but on the record his part was to press the American case on Louis Pichon, the French chargé d'affaires, who in turn transmitted every perturbation to Talleyrand in Paris. He was also to carry out Jefferson's policy in instructions to American ministers abroad. Jefferson struck a bold new course in April, 1802. In a letter addressed to Livingston but left open for the benefit of its courier, Pierre Dupont de Nemours, through whom its sentiments would be conveyed to the First Consul himself, Jefferson gave stern warning to France. "There is on the globe one single spot, the possessor of which is our natural and habitual enemy. It is New Orleans, through which must pass the produce of three-eights of our territory, and from its fertility it will ere long yield more than half our whole produce and contain more than half our inhabitants. . . . The day France takes possession of New Orleans fixes the sentence which is to restrain her forever within her low water mark. It seals the union of two nations who in conjunction can maintain exclusive possession of the ocean. From that moment we must marry ourselves to the British fleet and nation." While Jefferson flourished this thunderbolt, Madison wrote more officially to Livingston in Paris, mentioning for the first time the possibility of a purchase.

Louisiana planter's house near the sought-after port of New Orleans

Washington, May 1st. 1802

The Cession of Louisiana to France becomes daily more and more a source of painful apprehensions. Notwithstanding the Treaty of March 1801 [which confirmed the retrocession], and notwithstanding the general belief in France on the subject, and the accounts from St Domingo that part of the armament sent to that island were eventually destined for Louisiana, a hope was still drawn from your early conversations with Mr Talleyrand that the French Government did not mean to pursue the object. Since the receipt of your last communications, no hope remains but from the accumulating difficulties of going thro' with the undertaking, and from the conviction you may be able to impress, that it must have an instant and powerful effect in changing the relations between France and the United States. The change is obvious, and the more it can be developed in candid and friendly appeals to the reflections of the French Government, the more it will urge it to revise and abandon the project. A mere neighbourhood could not be friendly to the harmony which both countries have so much an interest in cherishing: but if a possession of the mouth of the Mississippi is to be added to other causes of discord, the worst events are to be apprehended. You will consequently spare no efforts that will consist with prudence and dignity, to lead the Councils of France to proper views of this subject, and to an abandonment of her present purpose. You will also pursue by prudent means the enquiry into the extent of the Cession, particularly whether it includes the Floridas as well as New Orleans; and endeavor to ascertain the price at which these, if included in the Cession, would be yielded to the United States. I cannot in the present state of things be more particular on this head, than to observe that in every view it would be a most precious acquisition, and that as far as the terms could be satisfied by charging on the acquisition itself, the restitutions, and other debts to American Citizens, great liberality would doubtless be indulged by this Government. The President wishes you to devote every attention to this object, and to be frequent and particular in your communications relating to it.

Robert R. Livingston, a New York Republican, was Minister to France.

Some days later Madison wrote to Charles Pinckney, the Minister to Spain, to cover himself on that flank.

[Washington,] May 11th. 1802

We are still without a line from you since your arrival at Madrid, and feel an increasing solicitude to hear from you on the subject of Louisiana. The latest information from Paris has confirmed the fact that it was ceded by a Treaty prior to that of March 1801; and notwithstanding the virtual denial of the Cession in the early conversations between Mr Livingston and the [French] Minister of Foreign Relations, a refusal of any explanations at present, seems to admit that the Cession has taken place. Still there are chances of obtaining a reversal of the transaction. The repugnance of the United States to it is and will be pressed in a manner that cannot be without some effect. It is known that most of the French statesmen best informed on the subject, disapprove of it. The pecuniary difficulties of the French Government must also be felt as a check; whilst the prospect of a protracted and expensive war in St. Domingo must form a very powerful obstacle to the execution of the project. The Counsels of England appear to have been torpid on this occasion. Whether it proceed from an unwillingness to risk a fresh altercation with France, or from a hope that such neighbourhood between France and United States would lead to collisions which might be turned to her advantage, is more than I can decide. The latter consideration might justly have great weight with her, but as her eyes may be more readily turned to the immediate and certain purposes to be answered to her rival, it is to be presumed that the policy of England will contribute to thwart the acquisition. What the intentions of Spain may be, we wait to learn from you. Verbal information from inofficial sources has led us to infer that she disowns the instrument of Cession, and will vigorously oppose it. Should the Cession actually fail from this or any other cause, and Spain retain New Orleans and the Floridas, I repeat to you the wish of the President that every effort and address be employed to obtain the arrangement by which the Territory on the East Side of the Mississippi including New Orleans may be ceded to the United States, and the Mississippi made a common boundary, with a common use of its navigation, for them and Spain. The inducements to be held out to Spain, were intimated in your original instructions on this point. I am charged by the President now to add, that you may not only receive and transmit a proposition of guaranty of her territory beyond the Mississippi, as a condition of her ceding to the United States the Territory including New Orleans on this side, but in the case it be necessary may make the proposition yourself, in the forms required by our Constitution. You will infer from this enlargement of your authority, how much importance is attached to the object in question, as securing a precious acquisition to the United States, as well as a natural and quiet boundary with Spain. . . .

Charles Pinckney of South Carolina was the American Minister to Spain.

As the months passed and Jefferson and Madison summered in Virginia and returned to Washington in the fall, the problem of the Mississippi seemed no closer to resolution. The administration ardently wished a pacific settlement, whether with gold or boundary guarantees or both. Peace, said Jefferson, "is the most important of all things to us." Of next importance was time, which in this affair as in all things was believed to be on the American side. Napoleon had yet to make good his policy; no French expedition sailed for New Orleans; and war clouds again gathered in Europe. The clock was turned ahead dramatically in October, however. Madison's dispatch to Pinckney explained the situation.

[Washington,] November 27th. 1802

A letter from a confidential citizen at New Orleans, of which a copy is inclosed, has just informed us, that the Intendant at that place, by a proclamation from which an extract is also inclosed, had prohibited the deposit of American effects, stipulated by the Treaty of 1795; and as the letter is interpretted that the river was also shut against the external commerce of the U. States from that port. Whether it be the fact or not, that this latter prohibition has also taken place, it is evident that the useful navigation of the Mississippi essentially depends on a suitable depository for the articles of commerce that a privation of the latter is equivalent to a privation of both.

This proceeding is so direct and palpable a violation of the Treaty of 1795, that in candor it is to be imputed rather to the Intendant solely, than to instructions of his Government. The Spanish Minister takes pains to impress this belief and it is favoured by private accounts from New Orleans mentioning that the Governor did not concur with the Intendant. But from whatever source the measure may have proceeded the President expects that the Spanish Government will neither lose a moment in countermanding it, nor hesitate to repair every damage which may result from it. You are aware of the sensibility of our Western citizens to such an occurrence. This sensibility is justified by the interest they have at stake. The Mississippi is to them every thing. It is the Hudson, the Delaware the Potomac and all the navigable rivers of the Atlantic States formed into one stream. The produce exported thro' that channel last year amounted to $1,622,672 from the Districts of Kentucky and Mississippi only, and will probably be fifty [per] Cent more this year (from the whole Western Country, Kentucky alone has exported for the 1st half of this year $591,432 in value) a great part of which is now or shortly will be afloat for New Orleans and consequently exposed

Napoleon Bonaparte by Lefèvre

An 1803 permit of passage, signed by Madison and Jefferson, according neutral status to the ship O'Cain

to the effects of this extraordinary exercise of power. Whilst you presume therefore in your representations to the Spanish Government, that the conduct of its officer, is no less contrary to its intentions, than it is to its good faith, you will take care to express the strongest confidence, that the breach of the Treaty will be repaired in every way which justice and a regard for a friendly neighbourhood may require.

I have communicated the information received from New Orleans to the Chevalier D'Yrujo [Minister of Spain to the United States], with a view to obtain his immediate interposition, as you will find by the inclosed copy of a letter to him. He readily undertakes to use it with all the effect he can give it by writing immediately on the subject to the local authority at New Orleans.... It is to be hoped that the Intendant will be led to see the error which he has committed, and to correct it, before a very great share of its mischief will have happened. Should he prove as obstinate as he has been ignorant or wicked, nothing can temper the irritation and indignation of the Western Country but a persuasion that the energy of their own Government will obtain from the justice of that of Spain, the most ample redress.

The immediate crisis of closure was quietly resolved through the intercession of the Spanish envoy, Yrujo. Meanwhile, in order to still the clamor at home and exploit the crisis for maximum effect abroad, Jefferson appointed James Monroe minister extraordinary to join Livingston in negotiations for the purchase of New Orleans and the Floridas, supposing the Floridas were France's to sell. On March 2, 1803, Madison sketched the articles of the plan and authorized a purchase price of upward of ten million dollars. The time chosen for the experiment, he pointed out to the envoys, was one in which the grave danger of collision on the Mississippi had been strikingly brought into view. "The sensibility and unanimity in our nation which have appeared on this occasion, must convince France that friendship and peace with us must be precarious until the Mississippi shall be made the boundary between the United States and Louisiana; and consequently render the present moment favorable to the object with which you are charged." A later letter to Monroe and Livingston covered the last resort: the overture to Britain that Jefferson had earlier threatened.

[Washington,] April 18, 1803

The reasonable and friendly views with which you have been instructed by the President to enter into negocia-

Signatures of Livingston, Monroe, and François de Barbé-Marbois, French Finance Minister, on purchase treaty

tions with the French Government, justify him in expecting from them an issue favorable to the tranquillity and to the useful relations between the two Countries. It is not forgotten, however, that these views, instead of being reciprocal, may find, on the part of France, a temper adverse to harmony, and schemes of ambition, requiring, on the part of the United States, as well as of others, the arrangements suggested by a provident regard to events. Among these arrangements, the President conceives that a common interest may recommend a candid understanding and closer connection with Great Britain; and he presumes that the occasion may present itself to the British Government in the same light. He accordingly authorises you . . . to open a confidential communication with Ministers of the British Government, and to confer freely and fully on the precautions and provisions best adapted to the Crisis, and in which that Government may be disposed to concur; transmitting to your own, without delay, the result of these consultations.

The threat of this overture, combined with more compelling circumstances, made its execution unnecessary. Napoleon's dream of New World empire faded fast in the early months of 1803. Santo Domingo was lost. Spain would not yield the Floridas. War was again imminent in Europe and Napoleon turned his imperious gaze eastward toward Egypt, the Levant, and India. He could not defend Louisiana while marching to the east or risk American hostility in this new venture. "Irresolution and deliberation are no longer in season," he declared on April 11. "I renounce Louisiana." Monroe arrived in Paris the next day and the purchase treaty was quickly arranged. It was not the bargain the Americans had sought. It included the whole of Louisiana—the immense uncharted country between the Mississippi and the Rocky Mountains or beyond—together with New Orleans, but not the Floridas, for the price of approximately fifteen million dollars. Fortunately, Livingston and Monroe were guided by the spirit rather than the letter of their instructions. Madison warmly congratulated them not long after the treaty reached Washington.

[Washington,] July 29th. 1803

In concurring with the disposition of the French Government to treat for the whole of Louisiana, altho' the western part of it was not embraced by your powers, you were justified by the solid reasons which you give for it, and I am charged by the President to express to you his entire approbation of your so doing.

This approbation is in no respect precluded by the silence of your Commission and instructions. When these were made out, the object of the most sanguine was limited to the establishment of the Mississippi as our boundary. It was not presumed that more could be sought by the United States either with a chance of success, or perhaps without being suspected of a greedy ambition, than the Island of New Orleans and the two Floridas, it being little doubted that the latter was or would be comprehended in the Cession from Spain to France. To the acquisition of New Orleans and the Floridas the provision was therefore accommodated....

...In truth the communications in general between Mr Livingston and the French Government, both of prior and subsequent date, manifested a repugnance to our views of purchase which left no expectation of any arrangement with France by which an extensive acquisition was to be made, unless in a favorable crisis, of which advantage should be taken. Such was thought to be the crisis which gave birth to the extraordinary commission in which you are joined. It consisted of the state of things produced by the breach of our deposit at New Orleans, the situation of the French Islands, particularly the important Island of St Domingo; the distress of the French finances, the unsettled posture of Europe, the increasing jealousy between G Britain and France, and the known aversion of the former to see the mouth of the Mississippi in the hands of the latter. These considerations it was hoped might so far open the eyes of France to her real interest and her ears to the monitory truths which were conveyed to her thro' different channels, as to reconcile her to the establishment of the Mississippi as a natural boundary to the United States; or at least to some concessions which would justify our patiently waiting for a fuller accomplishment of our wishes under auspicious events. The crisis relied on has derived peculiar force from the rapidity with which the complaints and questions between France and Great Britain ripened towards a rupture and it is just ground for mutual and general felicitation that it has issued under your zealous exertions, in the extensive acquisition beyond the Mississippi.

With respect to the terms on which the acquisition is made, there can be no doubt that the bargain will be regarded as on the whole highly advantageous.

Artist's later rendition of the American flag raising in New Orleans

A fresco by Brumidi in the United States Capitol shows Livingston and Monroe negotiating the purchase of Louisiana with Barbé-Marbois.

The Louisiana Purchase gave Madison tremendous satisfaction. It planted the Americans on both banks of the Mississippi, all but eliminated European colonialism from the continent, buttressed the nation's power and independence, fixed its destiny westward, and secured room to grow in freedom for generations to come. Unlike Jefferson, he was little troubled by constitutional objections to this revolution in the American Union. From the acquisition of Louisiana, which he had not expected, he returned his attention to the more immediate objective, the Floridas. The boundaries of Louisiana were obscure. He asked Livingston and Monroe what "pretensions" the United States had to claim West Florida to the Perdido River, the present-day boundary between Alabama and Florida. Jefferson soon made that claim, determined to finesse West Florida from Spain. East Florida was also wanted, though the United States would pay two million dollars for it and throw half of Texas into the bargain. Monroe was expected to proceed to Madrid after finishing his business in Paris. Madison thought the crisis peculiarly favorable, as he wrote to Monroe.

[Washington,] July. 29 1803

You will be at no loss for the arguments most likely to have weight in prevailing on Spain to yield to our wishes. These Colonies, separated from her other territories on this Continent, by New Orleans, the Mississippi, and the whole of Western Louisiana are now of less value to her than ever; whilst to the United States, they retain the peculiar importance derived from their position, and their relations to us thro' the navigable rivers running from the U States into the Gulph of Mexico. In the hands of Spain they must ever be a dead expence in time of peace, indefensible in time of War, and at all times a source of irritation and ill blood with the United States. The Spanish Government must understand in fact that the United States can never consider the amicable relations between Spain and them definitively and permanently secured, without an arrangement on this subject, which will substitute the manifest indications of nature, for the artificial and inconvenient state of things now existing.

The advantage to be derived to your negotiations from the war which has just commenced, will certainly not escape you. Powerful, and it might be presumed, effectual use may be made of the fact, that Great Britain meant to seize New Orleans with a view to the anxiety of the United States to obtain it; and of the inference from that fact, that the same policy will be pursued with respect to the Floridas. Should Spain be engaged in the war it cannot be doubted that they will be quickly occupied by a British force, and held out on some condition or other, to the United States. Should Spain be still at peace, and wish not to lose her neutrality, she should reflect that the facility and policy of seizing the Floridas must strengthen the temptations of G. Britain to force her into the war. In every view, it will be better for Spain, that the Floridas should be in the hands of the United States, than of Great Britain; and equally so, that they should be ceded on beneficial terms by herself, than that they should find their way to us thro' the hands of Great Britain.

The Spanish Government may be assured of the sincere and continued desire of the United States to live in harmony with Spain; that this motive enters deeply into the solicitude of their Government for a removal of the danger to it, which is inseparable from such a neighbourhood as that of the Floridas; and that having, by a late Convention with G. Britain, adjusted every territorial question and interest with that Nation, and the Treaty with France concerning Louisiana having just done the same with her, it only remains that the example be copied into an arrangement with Spain, who is evidently not less interested in it than we are.

Cartoon of a hornet, Napoleon, stinging prairie dog Jefferson into coughing up two million dollars for East and West Florida

The opportunity passed, however, as more urgent business—the impressment of American seamen—called Monroe to London to replace Rufus King, who was retiring. Relations with Spain rapidly deteriorated. The Floridas negotiation was resumed in 1805, when Monroe finally joined Pinckney in Madrid; but it came to nothing then and dragged on for years. Spain would neither bite Madison's carrot nor jump at his stick.

The war in Europe slowly brought affairs with Britain into the foreground. The first British minister accredited to Jefferson's Republican administration, Anthony Merry, arrived in November, 1803. Merry and his imperious lady were appalled by Washington—drearier and more barbaric, they thought, than the worst parts of Spain. Madison took him in full regalia to be presented to the President, who was found, on Merry's account, "not merely in undress, but *actually standing in slippers down at the heels*, and both pantaloons, coat, and under-clothes indicative of utter slovenliness and indifference to appearances, and in a state of negligence actually studied." A day or two later Jefferson entertained the Merrys at dinner. The Madisons were present together with most of the tiny Washington diplomatic corps. When dinner was announced, Jefferson offered his arm to Dolley Madison, heedless of her demurring whispers, "Take Mrs. Merry," and escorted her to the place at his right. Mrs. Merry was seated well down the table, while her poor husband scurried to find what seat he could. "This will be cause of war," the Marchioness Yrujo muttered. Four days later the Merrys were similarly affronted as guests of the Secretary of State. And so it went. The Merrys were humiliated by Jefferson's introduction of the democratic custom of the country, pell-mell, into official society. The minister poured his heart out to his government, thereby threatening to turn a social spat into an international incident. It did not come to that, but Madison was obviously concerned and kept Monroe informed in London. In the private letter that follows he relates the next act in this diplomatic comic opera.

Washington Feby 16. 1804

In a private letter by Mr. Baring I gave you a detail of what had passed here on the subject of Etiquette. I had hoped that no farther jars would have ensued as I still hope that the good senses of the British government respecting the right of the government here to fix its rules of intercourse and the sentiments and manners of the country to which they ought to be adapted will give the proper instructions for preventing like incidents in future. In the mean time a fresh circumstance had taken place which calls for explanations.

The President desirous of keeping open for cordial civilities whatever channels the scruples of Mr. M[err]y might not have closed asked me what these were understood to be and particularly whether he would come and take friendly and familiar dinners with him. I undertook to feel his pulse thro' some hand that would do it the least impropriety. From the information obtained I inferred that an invitation would be readily accepted and with the less doubt as he had dined with me (his lady declining) after the offence originally taken. The invitation was accordingly sent and terminated in the note

Our Country BY BENSON J. LOSSING, 1877

Nineteenth-century engraving shows Jefferson's mode of dress that so shocked the British minister.

248

from him to me & my answer herewith inclosed. I need not comment on this display of diplomatic superstition, truly extraordinary in this age and country. We are willing to refer it to the personal character of a man accustomed to see importance in such trifles and over cautious against displeasing his government by surrendering the minutest of his or its pretentions. What we apprehend is that with these causes may be mingled a jealousy of our disposition toward England and that the mortifications which he has inflicted on himself are to be set down to that account. In fact it is known that this jealousy particularly since the final adjustment with France exists or is affected in a high degree and will doubtless give its colour to the correspondence of the legation with its government. To apply an antidote to this poison will require your vigilant and prudent attention. It can scarcely be believed that the British Govt. will not at once see the folly committed by its representative especially in the last scene of the farce and that it will set him to right in that respect. But it may listen with a different ear to suggestions that the U.S. having now less need of the friendship of Britain may be yielding to a latent enmity toward her. The best of all proofs to the contrary would be the confidential communications you possess, if it were not an improper condescension to disclose them for such a purpose. Next to that is the tenor of our measures, and the dictates of our obvious policy; on our appeal to both of which you may found the strongest assurances that the Govt. of the U.S. is sincerely and anxiously disposed to cultivate harmony between the two nations. The President wishes you to lose no opportunity and to spare no pains that may be necessary to satisfy the British Administration on this head and to prevent or efface any different impressions which may be transmitted from hence.

I collect that the cavil at the *pêle mêle* here established turns much on the alledged degradation of Ministers & Envoys to a level with chargés d'affaires. The truth is, & I have so told Mr. Merry that this is not the idea; That the President did not mean to decide any thing as to their comparative grades or importance; that these would be estimated as heretofore; that among themselves they might fix their own ceremonies, and that even at the Presidents table they might seat themselves in any subordination they pleased. All he meant was that no seats were to be designated for them, nor the order in which they might happen to sit to be any criterion of the respect paid to their respective commissions or Countries. On public occasions, such as Inaugural Speech &c. the Heads of Depts. with foreign ministers, and others invited on the part of the Govt. would be in the same *pêle mêle* within the space assigned them. It may not be amiss to recollect that under the old Congress, as I understand, and even in the ceremonies attending the introduction of the Govt. the foreign ministers were placed according to the order in which their Govts. acknowledged by Treaties the Independence of the U. States. In this point of view the *pêle mêle* is favorable both to G.B. and to Spain.

Madison approved of the new etiquette, even if he lacked Jefferson's zeal for it. The secretary of the British legation, Augustus Foster, said that a dinner at the Madisons was "more like a harvest-home supper, than the entertainment of the Secretary of State." In a capital so lacking in other diversions, a heavy burden of entertainment fell on the President and the Secretaries. The dry and stiff personality Madison exposed to the public seemed to mellow in the social circle. Men found him affable, good-humored, and full of anecdote. A vivid description of Madison as he appeared at this time is contained in a recollection by Edward Coles, who would later become his private secretary.

[December 23, 1854]

In his dress, he was not at all eccentric, or given to dandyism, but always appeared neat & genteel & in the costume of a well-bred & tasty old school gentleman. I have heard in early life he sometimes wore light-colored clothes. But from the time I first knew him, wh. was when he visited at my Fathers when I was a child, I never knew him to wear any other color than black; his coat being cut in what is termed dress fashion; his breeches short, with buckles at the knees, black silk stockings, and shoes with strings or long fair boot tops when out in cold weather, or when he road on horseback of which he was fond. His hat was of the shape and fashion usually worn by gentlemen of his age. He wore powder on his hair, which was dressed full over the ears, tied behind, and brought to a point above the forehead, to cover in some degree his baldness. . . . In height he was about five feet six inches, of small and delicate form, of

Dolley's sister Anna Payne Cutts

rather a tawny complexion, bespeaking a sedentary and studious man; his hair was originally of a dark brown color; his eyes were bluish, but not of a bright blue; his form, features, and manner were not commanding, but his conversation exceedingly so and few men possessed so rich a flow of language, or so great a fund of amusing anecdotes, which were made the more interesting from their being well-timed and well-told. His ordinary manner was simple, modest, bland, and unostentatious, retiring from the throng and cautiously refraining from doing or saying anything to make himself conspicuous.

In the summer of 1805 the Madisons traveled from Washington to Philadelphia, where the aptly named Dr. Philip Physick promised to cure Dolley of an ulcerated tumor near her knee, an ailment that had kept her almost completely immobilized since May. On the morning of their arrival in Philadelphia, Dolley wrote to her sister Anna.

[Philadelphia, July 29, 1805]
I feel as if my heart is bursting—no Mother, no Sister— but fool that I am, here is my beloved Husband sitting anxiously by me and who is my unremitting nurse. But you know how delicate he is—I tremble for him. On our way one night he [was] taken very ill with his old bilious complaint. I thought all was over with me. I could not fly to him and aid him as I used to do. But heaven in its mercy restored him next morning and he would not pause until he heard my fate from Doctr. P.

Madison in his customary black suit

[Philadelphia,] Wednesday 31st. July [1805]
My dear sister. We are at excellent lodgings in Lenson Street, & I feel quite like another being. My knee is better. Doct. P. has splintered it, that is fixed a bark nearly a yd. long & with a bandage has bound it so tight that I cannot even lift it from the bed—not a step can I take—but this process is to cure it without any thing, we hope, & the Doct. thinks. I'm in no pain but from the fixed position. I have had all the world to see me.... We have invitations to the House of one Dozen gentry but withstand all to be [at ease here]....

Under Dr. Physick's care Dolley's leg began to heal. But by the end of October she was still too ill to travel and Madison was forced to return to Washington alone. The separation occasioned a rare exchange of letters between the devoted couple, who were seldom apart.

[Philadelphia,] 23d: October 1805

A few hours only have passed since you left me my beloved, and I find nothing can releave the oppression of my mind but speaking to you in this *only* way.

The Doctor called before you had gone far and with an air of sympathy wished you could see how much better the knee appeared. I could only speak to assure him it felt better. Betsey Pemberton and Amy [Dolley's maid] are sitting beside me and seem to respect the grief they know I feel, at even a short separation from one who is all to me. I shall be better when Peter [the coachman] returns, not that any length of time could lessen my just regret, but an assurance that you are well and easy will contribute to make me So. I have sent the books and note to Mrs: Dallas. B. Pemberton puts on your hat to divert me, but I cannot look at her.

24th: of October. What a sad day! The watchman announced a cloudy morning at one o'clock, and from that moment I found myself unable to sleep from anxiety for thee my dearest husband—detention cold and accident seemed to menace thee! . . .

25th: This clear cold morning will favor your journey and enliven the feelings of my darling! I have nothing new to tell you. Betsey and myself sleep quietly together and the knee is mending. I eat very little and sit precisely as you left me. The doctor during his very short visits, talks of you, he says he regards you more than any man he ever knew and nothing could please him so much as passing his life near you—sentiments so congenial with one's own, and in *such cases*, like dew drops on flowers, exhilarate as they fall!

Adieu, my beloved, our hearts understand each other. In fond affection thine

DOLLY P. MADISON

Portion of letter Dolley wrote to her sister, Anna Cutts, August 19, 1805, beginning "My dearest Anna"

Philadelphia Novr: 1st: [1805]

I have great pleasure, my beloved in repeating to you what the Doctor has just now said, that the knee would be well in one day more and in two or three I might begin to ride—so that I may reasonably hope that a fortnight more will be the extent of my stay in Philadelphia. I am so impatient to be restored to you.

I wish you would indulge me with some information respecting the war with Spain and disagreement with England, as it is so generally expected here that I am at a loss what to surmise. You know I am not much of a politician but I am extremely anxious to hear (as far as you may think proper) what is going forward in the Cabinet—on this subject, I believe you would not desire your wife the active partizan, such as her neighbor Mrs: T, nor will there be the slightest danger whilst she is conscious of her want of talents, and her diffidence in expressing her opinions [on matters] always imperfectly understood by her sex....

Kiss my child for me and remember me to my friends. ... Adieu, my dear husband, Peter brings me no letters which really unfits me for writing more to any one,

Your ever affectionate

D.

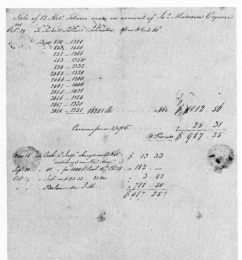

In November, 1805, Madison was asked to return some books he had borrowed from the Library of Congress (above); below, a bill of sale "made an account of Jas. Madison Esquire" for tobacco he had sold in Richmond.

[Washington, November 6, 1805]
Yours of the 1st. instant, my dearest gives me much happiness, but it can not be compleat till I have you again secure with me. Let me know the moment you can of the time you will set out that I may make arrangements for paying the Dr &c. My Tob[acc]o has been sold in Richd; but unfortunately the bills are not yet come on.... Your question as to our [situation] in regard to Spain & England is puzzling. As one gets into ill humor it is possible the other may change her circumstance.... Your friends are all well except Capt T [Thomas Tingey] who has been in extreme danger but is mending. Mrs T also has been unwell. I enclose a letter from Payne [Dolley's son, now fourteen years old]....

Your [own]
Affec

J.M.

The beginning of Jefferson's second administration in 1805 had coincided with William Pitt's return to power in Britain and the formation of the Third Coalition of European nations against Napoleon. All Europe was now engulfed in war; the United States was the last neutral of consequence. The Royal Navy, supreme on the seas, stepped up its harassment of American commerce; the impressment of American seamen soared to new heights; privateers infested American waters and plundered American trade. On July 23 a British admiralty court abruptly reversed the country's policy on the neutral carrying trade from enemy colonies. The decision in the case of the ship *Essex* marked a return to strict interpretation of the Rule of 1756, under which a trade closed in time of peace could not be opened in time of war. In 1793 Britain had enforced this rule with devastating effect against American carriers between French and Spanish colonies and the Continent. Since then the Americans had learned to evade the restriction by inserting an American port in the trade, landing the goods and paying the duties, then reexporting the "neutralized" cargoes to Europe. The admiralty courts came to accept the principle of the "broken voyage" as legitimizing the trade. In 1805 more than one-half of American exports were in fact reexports. The trade floated American prosperity. Now the *Essex* decision declared the trade fraudulent and made it subject to seizure and condemnation. Madison was still in Philadelphia attending his sick wife when he learned of this blow to American neutrality. He wrote to Monroe, who had just returned from defeat in Madrid to face a new crisis in London.

Philada. Sepr. 24, 1805

The decision in the Admiralty Courts of G.B. disallowing the sufficiency of landing, and paying duties on, Colonial produce of belligerent Colonies, re-exported from ports of the U.S., to protect the produce agst. the British Cruisers & Courts, has spread great alarm among merchants & has had a grevious effect on the rate of commerce. From the great amt. of property afloat subject to this new & shameful depredation, a dreadful sence of distress may ensue to our commerce. The subject was brought to attention by the case of the Aurora, which gives rise to the observations & instructions contained in my letter of 12 April last. I omitted in that letter to refer you to a case in Blackstone's reports, when Ld. Mansfield says, that it was a rule settled by the Lords of appeals that a transhipment off a central port, was equivalent to the landing, of goods from an enemy's colony, and that in the case of a landing there could be *no color* for seizure. As Mr. Kings correspondence may not be in London I think it not amiss to remind you of what passed with the British Govt. in 1801, in consequence of such seizures as are now sanctioned. A copy of the doctrine transmitted by the Govt. to the Vice admy. Courts as the law for their guidance is inclosed. If such a condemnation out of their own mouths has no effect, all meanings will be lost; and absolute submission, or some other resort in vindication of our neutral rights, will be the only alternative left.

IMPORTANT
AND
LUMINOUS COMMUNICATION
ON THE
SUBJECT OF THE
IMPRESSMENT OF AMERICAN AND FOREIGN
SEAMEN
AND OTHER PERSONS.

IT has become manifest to every attentive observer, that the early and continued aggressions of Great Britain on our persons, our property, and our rights, imperiously demand a firm stand—an effectual, though calm system of measures of arrestation. For this purpose, it is our duty to make ourselves completely masters of the great truths and arguments by which our rights have been elucidated, supported and maintained.

On the 17th of January, 1806, the President of the United States communicated to Congress an extract from a dispatch of James Madison Esq. our secretary of state, to James Monroe Esq. our minister in London, which contains many facts highly important, and observations and arguments perfectly satisfactory and conclusive against "*impressments* of seamen and passengers, whether Foreign or American, on board of our vessels." The republication of that document at this crisis will at once display some of the reasons on which the government has probably declined to sanction the recent draught of a treaty with Great Britain, and will elucidate the ground on which the question of *the impressment of persons*, both native and alien, has been rested by our administration.

Extract of a letter from the Secretary of State to James Monroe Esq. dated 5th January, 1804.

We consider a neutral flag, on the high seas, as a safeguard to those sailing under it. Great Britain, on the contrary, asserts a right to search for, and seize her own subjects ; and un-

Printed text of an 1804 letter from Madison to James Monroe in London on impressment of American seamen

I hope you will have recd. the instructions above referred to, and that your interposition will have had a good effect. I am engaged in a pretty thorough investigation of the original principle, to which so many shapes are given, namely, that "a trade not open in peace is not lawful in war," and shall furnish you with the result as soon as my remarks are digested. If I am not greatly deceived, it will appear that the principle is not only agst. the law of nations, but one which G.B. is precluded from assuming by the most conclusive facts & arguments derived from herself.

Madison's "pretty thorough investigation" resulted in a long diplomatic paper which marshaled all the authorities from Grotius through Vattel to show that the Rule of 1756 had no standing in international law. Close examination of treaties over a long period proved that Britain had often recognized the trade she now condemned. Indeed, her conduct had always been dictated by expediency. Force was the true foundation of the rule. "The question no longer is, whether the trade be right or wrong in itself, but on which side the superiority of force lies? The law of nations, the rights of neutrals, the freedom of the seas, the commerce of the world, are to depend, not on any fixed principle of justice, but on the comparative state of naval armaments." And why did Britain now return to strict enforcement of the old rule? Not to cut off supplies from her enemies, which might be justified militarily, but to force a dangerous rival, the United States, from the colonial trade and to monopolize it for herself even to the point of supplying her own enemies. Madison's argument was devastating. In law and learning and logic it showed him at his best; but it also disclosed the awful vulnerability of a statesman who could thus wrap himself in the heavy gray pedantry of the law. Britain was not interested in Madison's debater's points. Originally intended to be an official state paper, the report was withdrawn, and although published as a thick pamphlet and distributed to congressmen, it fell of its own weight. John Randolph, Madison's particular enemy in the House, contemptuously dismissed it as "a shilling pamphlet hurled against eight hundred ships of war."

The wave of captures following the *Essex* decision caused an uproar among the coastal merchants. Congress, in response, called for an extraordinary mission to Britain to seek a comprehensive settlement and backed this up with a Nonimportation Act triggered for nine months hence. Madison was cool to the plan. A settlement must take the form of a treaty, with concessions on both sides, and he wanted no successor to the Jay Treaty, the commercial articles of which had expired. Two years earlier he had committed to Monroe the project of a convention limited to neutral rights and impressment. Only military contraband and effectual blockade were to be admitted as exceptions to the freedom of neutral commerce. Impressment was to be virtually outlawed. This problem was peculiar to Anglo-American relations. In order to man her navy and recover her absconding subjects, Britain claimed the right to take seamen from American vessels on the high seas. In the process thousands of American citizens were cruelly pressed into His Majesty's service. Impressment assaulted the very existence of American nationality. Its abolition was made an ultimatum in any settlement with Britain. On Madison's recommendation Jefferson named William Pinkney of Maryland to join Monroe in the negotiations. Pinkney's Federalist background gave dissident Republicans, like Randolph, further opportunity to damn the administration's temporizing politics, which were charged to Madison. The instructions to Monroe and Pinkney ran to seven thousand words, including Madison's observations on the proposed treaty.

[Washington, May 17, 1806]

The 4th Article, besides the stipulation on the subject of contraband, relates to two other Subjects; 1. that of free Ships free goods, 2. that of a trade with enemies Colonies.

1. With respect to the first, the principle that a neutral flag covers the property of an enemy, is relinquished, in pursuance of the example of the Russian Treaty, on which the article is modelled.... The importance of that principle to the security of neutral Commerce, and to the freedom of the Seas, has at all times been felt by the United States; and although they have not asserted it as the established law of Nations, they have ever been anxious to see it made a part of that law. It was with reluctance of course that a contrary stipulation was authorized, and merely as a means of obtaining from Great Britain the recognition of a principle now become of more importance to neutral Nations possessing mercantile Capital, than the principle of "free Ships free goods." It is to be particularly kept in view therefore that such a contrary stipulation is to be avoided if possible; and, if unavoidable, that the stipulation be so modified as to interfere as little as possible with the spirit and policy of any provisions in favor of the principle which may be likely to be introduced into a treaty of peace among the present belligerent powers of Europe....

2. The vast importance of the Colonial Trade, with the circumstances and the excitement which have taken place since the date of the original instructions to Mr. Monroe, will require that the neutral right on this subject

John Randolph by Gilbert Stuart

While William Pinkney (above) and Monroe were negotiating neutral commercial rights, a bill of lading (below) for goods shipped to Madison from Marseilles in 1806 excepted liability for "Danger of the Seas."

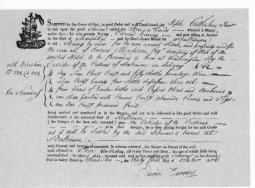

be provided for in an appropriate article, and in terms more explicit than are used in the article under review. As the right in this case, turns on the general principle, that neutrals may lawfully trade, with the exceptions of blockades and contraband, to and between all ports of an enemy, and in all articles, although the trade shall not have been open to them in time of peace, particular care is to be taken, that no part of the principle be expressly or virtually abandoned, as being no part of the law of Nations. On the contrary it is much to be desired that the general principle in its full extent, be laid down in the stipulation; but as this may not be attainable and as too much ought not to be risked by an inflexible pursuit of abstract right... you are left at liberty, if found necessary, to abridge the right in practice...; not omitting to provide that in case Great Britain should by her Treaties or instructions leave to any other nation the right in a greater extent than it is stipulated to the United States, they may claim the enjoyment of it in an equal extent.

The abuses which have been committed by Great Britain under the pretext that a neutral trade, from enemy Colonies, through neutral ports, was a direct trade, render it indispensable to guard against such a pretext by some express declaration on that point. The most that can be conceded on the part of the United States is, that *the landing of the goods, the securing the duties, and the change of the Ship,* or preferably, the landing of the goods alone, or with the securing the duties, shall be requiste to destroy the identity of the voyage and the directness of the trade; and that the ordinary documents of the Custom House Officers, shall be sufficient evidence of the facts or fact.

A satisfactory provision on this subject of trade with enemy Colonies, is deemed of so much consequence to the rights and interests of the United States... that as was enjoined with respect to the provision against impressment, no stipulation is to be entered into not consistent with a continuance of that act, unless the provision with respect to the Colonial trade be also obtained.

Napoleon's victories on the Continent and a new ministry in London suddenly raised Madison's hopes for the negotiations. By his calculation, certainly, the American commissioners held the winning hand.

He was, therefore, mortified by the treaty they signed on December 31, 1806. Jefferson angrily refused even to submit it to the Senate. Britain stood firm on impressment, offering only informal assurances of caution and forbearance in the practice. The warmth of Madison's feelings may be seen from his remarks to an American friend in England, George Joy.

> Washington May 22, 1807
>
> The Treaty signed with the British Commissrs. has not recd. the approbation of the President. Full justice is done to the talents & exertions of ours; but the terms admitted on the other side, do not satisfy the expectations on this. The case of impressments, particularly, having been brought to a formal issue, & having been the primary object of an Extry. Mission, a Treaty could not be closed which was silent on that subject; a subject which, whenever it shall no longer be seen thro' the mist with which practice enveloped rights, must excite wonder that the patience of the U.S. has remained so long unexhausted. That an officer from a foreign ship should pronounce any person he pleased, covered by the American flag on the high seas, to be not an Amn. Citizen, but a British subject, & carry this interested decision on the most important of all questions to a freeman, into execution on the spot, is so anomalous in principle, so grievous in practice, and so abominable in abuse, that the pretension must finally yield to sober discussion & friendly expostulation.

There were numerous other objections to the Monroe-Pinkney Treaty. Its commercial articles were unsatisfactory, despite British concessions on the reexport trade. In a note attached to the treaty Britain demanded, as a condition of compliance on her part, American retaliation against Napoleon's recent Berlin Decree, which declared lawful prize of all traffic with Britain. While Napoleon straddled the Continent and while the Florida purchase hung on his good offices with Spain, Jefferson and Madison would not be bullied into war against France.

So the treaty was returned for renegotiation. Madison penned new instructions. After detailed analysis of each article, he concluded with an essay on the natural advantages the United States possessed for the vindication of its cause against Britain. He believed now, as in 1794 and in 1789, that in any quarrel with the United States Britain must lose because her vital interests—in the West Indies, in the American market for her manufactures, in her dependence on American food and raw materials—could be mortally wounded, while those of the United States were invulnerable.

[Washington,] May 20th—1807

There are considerations moreover which cannot be without weight with a prudent Cabinet, however composed. They must know that, apart from the obstacles which may be opposed here to the use of British manufactures, the United States, by a mere reciprocation of the British navigation and Colonial laws, may give a very serious blow to a favorite system, a blow that would be felt perhaps as much too in its example, as in its immediate operation. Should this policy be adopted by the United States, as it respects the British West Indies, the value of those possessions would be either speedily lost, or be saved no otherwise than by a compliance with the fair reciprocity claimed by this Country. It can no longer be unknown to the most sanguine partisan of the Colonial Monopoly, that the necessaries of life and of cultivation, can be furnished to those Islands from no other source than the United States; that immediate ruin would ensue if this source was shut up; and that a gradual one would be the effect of even turning the supplies out of the present direct channel, into a circuitous one thro' neutral ports in the West Indies. . . .

It ought to occur moreover to the British Government that its marine may become as dependant as its Colonies on the supplies of the United States. As an auxiliary resource for naval stores, this Country must be at all times important to Great Britain. But it will be the sole and therefore an essential one in case that of the Baltic and even of the Black sea, should fail. And it may be justly remarked that a prohibition of this branch of our exports wd be a less sacrifice than that of any other important one; inasmuch as some of the articles of which it consists, being necessary to ourselves, and of an exhaustable nature, make it a problem whether the regulation would not in itself accord with our permanent interests.

Lastly it should not be forgotten that the United States are one of the Granaries which supply the annual deficit of the British harvests. The northern part of Europe, the usual concurrent resource is in a situation that must disable it, for some time, whatever the course of events may be, to spare any of its stock of food; nor can any substitute, other than the redundant harvests of the United States, be relied on to make up that deficiency. Add to this prospect, the possibility of an unfavorable

Nineteenth-century representation of the "British right of search"

season requiring enlarged importations of bread from the only source that can furnish it, and the risk of losing this would be an evil which no provident Counsels would neglect to guard against, by any measures equitable in themselves, or even by concessions neither dishonorable nor materially injurious.

On the other hand Great Britain having been led by her peculiar system to carry her commercial exclusions and restrictions to the utmost limit permitted by her immediate wants, would find no countervailing resources to be turned against the United States. She could not prohibit the importation of our productions. These are necessaries which feed her people, which supply her manufactories, which keep up her Navy, and which, by direct and indirect contributions to her revenue and credit strengthen all her faculties as a great power. As little could she prohibit the exportation of her manufactures to the United States. This is the last evil she would think of inflicting on herself. If it withheld from us the means of enjoyment, it would take from her own people the means of existence.

Would war be a better resort? That it would be a calamity to the United States is so well understood by them that peace has been cherished in the midst of provocations which scarcely permitted honor to listen to interest, to reason or to humanity. War they will continue to avert by every policy which can be reconciled with the essential duties which a nation owes to itself. But what will be the gain and the loss to Great Britain by a choice of this resort? The spoils of our defenceless commerce might enrich her greedy cruizers, and flatter the sentiment of national wealth. A temporary spasm might, at the same time, be produced in the affairs of the United States. But these effects weigh little against the considerations which belong to the opposite scale. To say nothing of the hostile use that might be made against Great Britain of 50,000 seamen, not less hardy or enterprizing than her own, nor of her vulnerable possessions in our neighbourhood, which tho' little desired by the United States, are highly prized by her, nor of the general tendency of adding the United States to the mass of nations already in arms against her; it is enough to observe, that a war with the United States involves a complete loss of the principal remaining market for her manufactures, and of the principal, perhaps the sole, remaining source of, supplies without which all her faculties must wither. Nor is it an unimportant circumstance, tho' it seems to have engaged little of her attention, that in the loss would be included, all the advantages which she now derives from the neutrality of our flag, and of our ports, and for which she could find no substitutes in distributing her manufactures, and even her fish to their necessary markets, and in obtaining the returns which she wants. The more these collateral advantages are enquired into, the more important will the interest appear which Great Britain has in preserving them.

These are views of the subject, which, tho' not to be presented to Great Britain with an air of menace or defiance, equally forbidden by respect to ourselves, and to her, may find a proper way to her attention. They merit hers as well as ours; and if they ought to promote on both sides, a spirit of accommodation, they show at the same time that Great Britain is not the party which has the least interest, in taking counsel from them.

Commodore James Barron

Whatever small chance remained for the treaty was blasted by the British attack on the U.S.S. *Chesapeake*. On June 22, 1807, just off Norfolk, the *Chesapeake* was hailed by the H.M.S. *Leopard* and ordered to submit to search for British seamen. When the American commander, Commodore James Barron, refused to submit, the *Leopard* poured broadsides into the defenseless frigate, killing three and wounding eighteen before its flag was struck. Four alleged deserters were then removed and the *Chesapeake* limped back to port. As the country rose in thunderous indignation, Madison sent Monroe his instructions.

[Washington,] July 6 1807
The documents herewith inclosed from No. 1 to No. 9 inclusive explain the hostile attack with the insulting pretext for it, lately committed near the Capes of Virga. by the British ship of war the Leopard on the American frigate the Chesapeake. No. 10 is a copy of the Proclamation issued by the President interdicting, in consequence of that outrage, the use of our waters and every other accomodation, to all British armed ships.

This enormity is not a subject for discussion. The immunity of a National ship of war from every species and purpose of search on the high seas, has never been contested by any nation. G.B. would be second to none in resenting such a violation of her rights, & such an insult to her flag. She may bring the case to the test of her own feelings, by supposing that instead of the customary demand of our mariners serving compulsively even on board her ships of war, opportunities had been seized for rescuing them in like manner, whenever the superiority of force or the chance of surprize might be possessed by our ships of war.

But the present case is marked by circumstances which give it a peculiar die. The seamen taken from the Chesapeake had been ascertained to be native Citizens of the U. States; and this fact was made known to the bearer of the demand, and doubtless, communicated by him to his commander [prior] to the commencement of the attack. It is a fact also, affirmed by two of the men with every appearance of truth that they had been impressed from American vessels into the British frigate from which they escaped, and by the third, that having been impressed from a British Merchant ship, he had accepted the recruiting bounty under that duress, and with a view to alleviate his situation, till he could escape to his own Country. Add that the attack was made during a period

After the Leopard *(at left in the picture below) poured broadsides into the* Chesapeake, *the British seized four alleged deserters (above).*

of negotiations, & in the midst of friendly assurances from the B. Government.

The printed papers herewith sent will enable you to judge of the spirit which has been roused by the occasion. It pervades the whole community, is abolishing the distinctions of party, and regarding only the indignity offered to the sovereignty & flag of the nation, and the blood of Citizens so wantonly and wickedly shed, demands in the loudest tone, an honorable reparation.

With this demand you are charged by the President. The tenor of his proclamation will be your guide in reminding the British Govt. of the uniform proofs given by the U.S. of their disposition to maintain faithfully every friendly relation; of the multiplied infractions of their rights by British naval Commanders on our Coasts & in our harbours; of the inefficacy of re-iterated appeals to the justice & friendship of that Govt., and of the moderation on the part of the U.S. which re-iterated disappointment had not extinguished; till at length no alternative is left but a voluntary satisfaction on the part of G.B. or a resort to means depending on the U.S. alone.

The nature & extent of the satisfaction ought to be suggested to the British Govt. not less by a sense of its own honor than by justice to that of the U. States. A formal disavowal of the deed, and restoration of the four seamen to the Ship from which they were taken, are things of course. Beyond these, the U States have a right to expect and require every solemnity of form & every other ingredient of retribution & respect, which, according to usage & the sentiments of mankind, are due in the strongest cases to the insulted rights & sovereignty of a nation. And it is the particular instruction of the President, that you do not allow it to be supposed, that any satisfaction of an inferior character, will be accepted by the U.S.

Should it be alledged as a ground for declining or diminishing the satisfaction in this case, that the U.S. have themselves taken it by the interdict contained in the Proclamation, the answer will be obvious. The interdict is a measure not of a reparation, but of precaution; and would besides be amply justified by occurrences prior to the extraordinary outrage in question.

The exclusion of all armed ships whatever from our

Broadside headlined "British Barbarity and Piracy!!" recounts a later naval incident described as "Leopard Outspotted."

This 1808 broadside was the work of Massachusetts Federalists who felt the French were the real enemies.

waters is in fact so much required by the vexations and dangers to our peace experienced from their visits, that the President makes it a special part of the charge to you, to avoid laying the U.S. under any species of restraint from adopting that remedy. Being extended to all Belligerent nations, none of them could of right complain; and with the less reason, as the policy of all nations has limited the admission of foreign ships of war into their ports, to such numbers as being inferior to the naval force of the Country, could be readily made to respect its authority & laws.

Jefferson, although he had only to nod to take the country to war, deliberately cooled the crisis and awaited British response to his demands. The Tenth Congress convened in the fall. Partly at Madison's instigation, the President adopted a high tone toward Britain and called for accelerated military preparations. Meanwhile the country's position became intolerable. Not only did Britain refuse to make amends for the *Chesapeake* affair; she also prepared new orders in council which would place the entire European continent under blockade. American commerce would be coerced into the monopolistic British system—again licensed, taxed, and "colonized" by George III. Napoleon, for his part, announced the extension of the Berlin Decree to the Americans, previously exempted. Between the emperor's tightening Continental System and the British orders American commerce was caught in the jaws of a vise, a maniacal war of blockades from which there seemed to be no appeal to reason and justice.

Thus it was that Jefferson recommended and Congress enacted on December 22 the Embargo Act shutting off American foreign commerce and navigation. Combined with the Nonimportation Act against Britain, only now put into effect, the embargo launched the system of "commercial coercion" Madison as well as Jefferson had long advocated. That the United States might, by withholding its trade, force justice on the marauding powers of Europe, especially Britain, was an idea as old as the nation itself. To no other idea had Madison clung so tenaciously during twenty years. The experiment would at last be made in a situation fraught with peril.

With the internal history of the embargo—the enforcement, the economic deprivations, the political opposition—Madison had little to do. These problems fell to Jefferson and Secretary of the Treasury Albert Gallatin. But the embargo was essentially an instrument of American diplomacy, which was Madison's province. Once its effects were felt abroad, Madison believed, either France would recede from her decree in order to force American conflict with Britain, or the stoppage of American trade would prove so ruinous to Britain as to bring her to justice. It was the same old neutral game, playing off one European empire against the other for America's benefit, but the stakes were higher than before. The diplomatic strategy took form in the spring of 1808. Pinkney in London, where he had succeeded Monroe, and John Armstrong, the minister in Paris, would each demand revocation of the obnoxious decrees, at the same time holding out the idea that compliance by one power would invite American hostilities against the other if it persisted in its edicts. The following is taken from Madison's instructions to Armstrong.

[Washington,] May 2d. 1808

The conditions on which the suspending authority is to be exercised will engage your particular attention. They appeal equally to the justice and the policy of the two great belligerent powers now emulating each other in violations of both. The President counts on your best endeavors to give to this appeal all the effect possible with the French Government. Mr Pinkney will be doing the same with that of Great Britain. The relation in which a recall of its retaliating decrees by either power, will place the United States to the other, is obvious; and ought to be a motive to the measure proportioned to the desire which has been manifested by each, to produce collisions between the U States and its adversary; and which must be equally felt by each to avoid one with itself.

Should wiser Councils or increasing distresses induce Great Britain to revoke her impolitic orders against neutral commerce, and thereby prepare the way for a removal of the Embargo as it applies to her, France could not persist in the illegal part of her decrees, if she does

Jefferson, prodded by Napoleon in the cartoon below right, informs dismayed citizens the ports must be closed to the British; below left, a turtle named "Ograbme" (embargo spelled backward) snaps at smuggler loading sugar on a British ship.

Cartoon of Jefferson and Madison dragging a ship into dry dock at Napoleon's instigation; Congress hotly debates the embargo at right.

not mean to force a contest with the United States. On the other hand should she set the example of revocation Great Britain would be obliged, either by following it, to restore to France the full benefit of neutral trade which she needs, or by perservering in her obnoxious orders after the pretext for them had ceased, to render collisions with the United States inevitable.

In every point of view therefore it is so clearly the sound policy of France to rescind so much at least of her decrees as trespass on neutral rights, and particularly to be the first in taking the retrograde step, that it cannot be unreasonable to expect that it will be immediately taken.

The repeal of her decrees is the more to be expected, above all if Great Britain should repeal or be likely to repeal hers, as the plan of the original decree at Berlin did not extend to a violation of the freedom of the seas, and was restricted to a municipal operation nearly an entire year notwithstanding the illegal British orders of Jany 1807, and as a return of France to that restricted scope of her plan, would so immaterially diminish its operation against the British commerce, that operation being so completely in the power of France on land, and so little in her power on the high seas.

But altho' we cannot of right demand from France more than a repeal of so much of her decrees as violate the freedom of the seas, and a great point will be gained by a repeal of that part of them, yet as it may not have the effect of inducing a repeal of the whole illegal system of the British Government which may seek pretexts, or plead a necessity for counteracting the unprecedented and formidable mode of warfare practiced against her, it will be desirable that as little room as possible should be left for this remaining danger to the tranquil enjoyment of our commercial rights.

These overtures failed. Napoleon, instead of snatching at the bait, made a mockery of the embargo. George Canning, the British Foreign Secretary, reacted with contempt. There was no accounting for Napoleon, but Madison blamed Canning's obstinacy on treacherous Federalist opposition to the embargo. Despite the mounting discontents of British merchants and manufacturers and workers, the government at Westminster adhered to its edicts in the delusory expectation planted by the madcap Federalists of producing a political revolution, perhaps even disunion, in the United States. Be that as it may, the discontents on American shores were no less real, and more compelling, than those in Britain. Madison's own reckoning of the "noble experiment" may be gleaned from his letters to Pinkney over several months.

Washington May 1. 1808

The colonizing & taxing features of the B. orders have so effectually re-inforced the other charges agst. them, that the public mind every where is rallying to the policy of the Embargo; and there can be no doubt that the efforts to render it unpopular are re-coiling on the authors of them. It has been somewhat eluded, but the last supplimental act will probably give it due effect. An indignation agst. the smugglers is moreover beginning to co-operate with those charged with its execution.

The B. Govt. may therefore calculate on the efficacy as well as the duration of the measure unless a repeal of its orders should obtain an exercise of the Power vested in the P. to open our ports in that event. To this prudent course it must be strongly impelled by the distresses of the W. Indies, the discontents at home, the alienation of our habits from her manufactures, and the vigorous means tak[en] to provide sub[s]titutes of our own; and by the apprehension that France may entitle herself to a removal of the Embargo as it applies to her, and thus expose G.B. to the dilemma of appearing to be forced into the measure by that example, or of encountering the consequences of adhering to her system after all pretext for it shall be at an end.

Washington July 21. 1808

Great efforts have been made to render the Embargo unpopular, and to promote evasions & violations of it. These efforts have not ceased & have not been without a certain degree of effect. With the means used by our own Citizens have been united great exertions from the Canadian & N. Scotia borderers. On the lakes combinations have been formed on both sides of the boundary, and it is believed, tho' not as yet proved, that a British party passed the boundary and carried away by force a quantity of Potash &c.... It is certain also that no inconsiderable quantities of provisions have been smuggled into the W. Indies. The Measure however cannot but have had a powerful effect in that quarter. The general price even of provisions shews it. And with respect to lumber so indispensible to their situation & pursuits, there is reason to believe that scarcely any supplies whatever have found their way. So that on the whole, connecting the Embargo with the Orders in Council, the W. India. interest has no reason to exult in the policy of the latter. Within ourselves, the body of the people have borne the privations with a firmness which leaves no doubt of their perserverence as long as they shall see the alternative with submission to the foreign Edicts. The sense of Natl. honor & independence seems to be entering deeper & deeper into the mass of the people, and the operation of the retaliating system on the onstanding navigation affords daily evidence of the good fortune of that which has been saved from the danger.

If the B. Orders continue much longer they will certainly have more than a temporary effect on B. manufactures. It is astonishing what a zeal for homespun has been excited, and I am persuaded that altho calculations may carry the extent and permanency of the substitutes in some cases too far, it will be found that the looms & wheels set up will be continued after the crisis is over in a degree beyond any idea entertained beyond the Atlantic....

George Canning

A storm of protest against the Embargo Act rolled over New England in the fall, providing Federalists with ammunition in their campaign against the act and against Madison who, with Jefferson's support, had emerged as the preeminent Republican candidate for President in the

1808 elections. Fearing that Federalist opposition would undermine the administration's position abroad, Madison wrote again to Pinkney as Congress convened.

Lord Erskine, British Minister to the United States, by Gilbert Stuart

Washington November 9th. 1808.

The conduct of the British cabinet in rejecting the fair offer made to it, and even sneering at the course pursued by the U.S., prove at once a very determined enmity to them, and a confidence that events were taking place here which would relieve it from the necessity of procuring a renewal of commercial intercourse by any relaxation on its part. Without this last supposition it is difficult to believe that, with the prospect at home and abroad in Europe, so great a folly would have been committed. As neither the public nor Congress have yet had time to disclose the feelings which result from the posture now given to our relations with Great Britain, I cannot speak positively on that subject. I shall be much disappointed, however, if a spirit of independence and indignation does not strongly reinforce the past measures with others which will give a severity to the contest of privations at least, for which the British government would seem to be very little prepared in any sense of the word. It was perhaps unfortunate, that all the intelligence from this country, previous to the close of your correspondence with Mr. Canning, was from a quarter and during a period most likely to produce miscalculations of the general & settled dispositions. You will see in the newspapers sufficient evidence of the narrow limits to which discontent was confined; and it may reasonably be expected that the counter-current will be greatly strengthened by the communications now going forth to the public.

Washington Decr. 5. 1808

Congs. seemed to be sufficiently determined, as you will observe, to resist the unjust and insulting Edicts of the Belligerents, and differ only as to the mode best suited to the case. The disposition to prefer war to the course hitherto pursued, is rather gaining than losing ground; and is even promoted by the efforts of those most opposed to war with G.B. who concur in deciding agst. submission, and at the same time contend that withdrawing from the Ocean is submission. It is very questionable however whether a preference of war, to be commenced within the present Session, is so general in Congs, or so much looked for by the nation, as to recommend the measure. Whether in case, the measure should be declined, any such substitute, providing for war, during the recess, as I have intimated in one of my last letters, will be acceptable, is more than I can undertake to say; nothing of the sort having been even brought into Conversation.

I find by conversation with Mr Erskine [the British minister] that he is himself favorably impressed by the documents laid before Congs. as to the fairness of our Conduct towards the two belligerents, and that he is willing I should believe that the impression will be the same [fo]r his Govt. As it may be conceived by him, however, to be politic to lull our feelings & suspicions, I am the less sure, that he calculates on any change in the Councils of his Govt. likely to do justice to those of this Govt.

As to the state of the public mind here, you will sufficiently collect it from the printed information now forwarded. I can not believe that there is so much depravity or stupidity in the Eastern States as to countenance the reports that they will separate from their brethren rather than submit no longer to the suspension of their commerce. That such a project may lurk within a Junto, ready to sacrifice the rights interests & honor of their Country, to their ambitious or vindictive views, is not to be doubted; but that the body of an intelligent people devoted to commerce & navigation with few productions of their own, and objects of unceasing jealousy to G.B. on acct. of their commerce & navigation, should be induced to abandon the Southern States for which they are the merchants & carriers, in order to enter into an Alliance with G.B. seems to be impossible.

Cartoon showing the death of the "terrapin policy," the embargo

By the end of November it was clear that Madison had won the election, despite opposition from left and right: from the Randolph faction of Republicans who believed he had betrayed the cause and who took up Monroe, alienated because of the rejected British treaty, as their candidate; and from eastern Federalists who accused him of selling out the nation to Napoleon. The vote of the electors in December was 122 for the Secretary of State and 47 for his Federalist opponent, Charles Cotesworth Pinckney. Although he lost four of five New England states and part of New York,

Madison's victory was still a vote of confidence in him and in the administration he had served. But the embargo issue remained, and the outgoing administration seemed incapable of leadership. In the early months of 1809 congressional opposition climaxed with a proposal to repeal the embargo and to enact in its place a milk-and-water nonintercourse law reopening trade with all the world except Britain and France. The President-elect kept William Pinkney informed of these late developments.

"Happy is the land, Who hails thee vested with the chief command" reads part of a poem by William Ray to Madison on March 22, 1809.

Washington Feby 11. 1809

My official letter by this conveyance leaves little of importance to be added to its contents. You will see with regret the difficulty experienced in collecting the mind of Congress to some proper focus. On no occasion were the ideas so unstable and so scattered. The most to be hoped for at present is that a respectable majority will finally concur in taking a course not essentially dishonoring the resolution not to submit to the foreign Edicts. The last vote taken, as stated in reports of their proceedings, 60 odd agst. 50 odd [for], implies that a non-intercourse with G.B. & F. including an Embargo on Exports to those two Nations, will be substituted for the general Embargo existing. And it is not improbable that 8 or 10 of the minority who prefer a simple adherence to the latter, will on finding it cannot be retained, join in the non-intercourse proposed. It is impossible however to foretell the precise issue of such complicated views.

If the non-intercourse as proposed, should be adopted, it will leave open a trade to all the Continent of Europe, except France....

The repeal of the Embargo has been the result of the opinion of many that the period prescribed by honor to that resort agst. the tyrannical Edicts agst. our trade, had arrived; but principally from the violence exerted agst. it in the Eastern quarter, which some wished to assuage by indulgence, and others to chastise into an American Spirit by the lash of British Spoliations. I think this effect begins to be anticipated by some who have been most clamorous for the repeal. As the Embargo is disappearing, the orders & decrees come into view, with the commercial & political consequences which they cannot fail to produce. The English market will at once be glutted; and the continental market particularly for the Sugar & Coffee in the Eastern Wharehouses will be sought at every risk. Hence Captures and clamors agst.

the authors of them. It can not I think be doubted that if the Embargo be repealed & the orders be enforced, that war is inevitable, and will perhaps be clamored for in the same quarter which now vents its disappointed love of gain agst. the Embargo.

There is reason to believe that the disorganizing spirit in the East, is giving way to the universal indignation of the parties elsewhere agst. it. It is explained in part also by the course of events abroad which lessens the prospect of British support, in case of a Civil war.

Finally on March 1, 1809, amidst much confusion, the embargo was repealed and the Nonintercourse Act was adopted, as Madison reported to Pinkney.

Washington Mar. 17. 1809
You will learn by the communications from the Dept. of State, that the discussions of Congs. on our foreign relations had an issue less operative than was at one time looked for. The aversions to war, the inconveniences produced by or charged on the embargo, the hope of favorable changes in Europe, the dread of civil convulsions in the East, and the policy of permitting the discontented to be reclaimed to their duty by losses at sea, had each a share in producing the Non-intercourse Act. Certain it is that no measure was ever adopted by so great a proportion of any public body which had the hearty concurrence of so small a one; and it seems to be as little satisfactory out of doors, as it was within.

Madison firmly believed, as did Jefferson and Pinkney, that the embargo would have succeeded had it been given a little more time. Repeal pulled the rug from under the British opposition to the orders in council just as it was aiming the knockout blow. Unfortunately, in this "contest of privations" time had run out at home. Madison's faith in the policy blinded him to the harsh realities of domestic discord and distress which could no longer be ignored except at grave peril to the nation itself. But defeat of "peaceable coercion" might have been tolerable for Madison had it been succeeded by a strategy of force, perhaps beginning with letters of marque or reprisal. The embargo had always been justified as the only alternative to submission or war. When its sequel was neither, but a halfway measure no one believed in, the credibility of American diplomacy was undermined and the future clouded in the extreme.

Chapter 8

Gathering Storm Clouds

Inauguration Day, March 4, 1809, "from its commencement to its close, was marked by the liveliest demonstrations of joy," according to the *National Intelligencer,* the administration newspaper in Washington. James Madison in his carriage, escorted by a troop of cavalry, arrived at the Capitol at noon and entered the splendid new chamber of the House of Representatives overflowing with people. Led to the front of the hall, he found Jefferson, feeling like "a prisoner released from his chains," seated to his right and Chief Justice John Marshall, who would administer the oath of office, to his left. Madison's brief address was commonplace—a piece of Republican homespun to match the suit of American cloth he wore in patriotic salute to the infant manufactures spawned by the embargo. After taking the oath, the new President left the hall to the roar of guns and proceeded to his home on F Street, which was thrown open to all and sundry. The day's festivities concluded with an inaugural ball at Long's Hotel. Margaret Bayard Smith, whose husband edited the *National Intelligencer,* wrote this breezy report in a personal letter.

> Saturday, March [4], 1809.
> To-day after the inaguration, we all went to Mrs. Madison's. The street was full of carriages and people, and we had to wait near half an hour, before we could get in,—the house was completely filled, parlours, entry, drawing room and bed room. Near the door of the drawing room Mr. and Mrs. Madison stood to receive their company. She looked extremely beautiful, was drest in a plain cambrick dress with a very long train, plain round the neck without any handkerchief, and beautiful bonnet of purple velvet, and white satin with white plumes. She was all dignity, grace and affability. Mr. Madison shook my hand with all the cordiality of old

Certificate of the tally of the electoral ballots, dated February 8, 1809, naming Madison the President and George Clinton Vice President

acquaintance....

...The crowd was immense both at the Capitol and here, thousands and thousands of people thronged the avenue. The Capitol presented a gay scene. Every inch of space was crowded and there being as many ladies as gentlemen, all in full dress, it gave it rather a gay than a solemn appearance,—there was an attempt made to appropriate particular seats for the ladies of public characters, but it was found impossible to carry it into effect, for the sovereign people would not resign their privileges and the high and low were promiscuously blended on the floor and in the galleries.

Mr. Madison was extremely pale and trembled excessively when he first began to speak, but soon gained confidence and spoke audibly. From the Capitol we went to Mrs. M's., and from there to Mr. Jefferson's....

Sunday morning. Well, my dear Susan, the chapter draws to a close. Last night concluded the important day, in which our country received a new magistrate.... The room was so terribly crowded that we had to stand on the benches; from this situation we had a view of the moving mass; for it was nothing else. It was scarcely possible to elbow your way from one side to another, and poor Mrs. Madison was almost pressed to death, for every one crowded round her, those behind pressing on those before, and peeping over their shoulders to have a peep of her, and those who were so fortunate as to get near enough to speak to her were happy indeed. As the upper sashes of the windows could not let down, the glass was broken, to ventilate the room, the air of which had become oppressive, but here I begin again at the end of the story. Well, to make up for it I will begin at

The President's House during the administration of James Madison

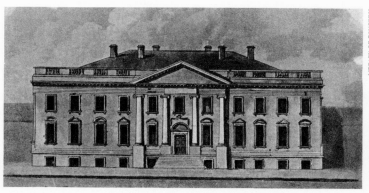

"Madison's March," which serenaded Madison and "his Lady" on March 4, 1809, his first Inauguration Day

the beginning. When we went there were not above 50 persons in the room, we were led to benches at the upper fire place. Not long afterwards, the musick struck up Jefferson's March, and he and Mr. [Isaac] Coles [Jefferson's private secretary] entered. He spoke to all whom he knew, and was quite the plain, unassuming citizen. Madison's March was then played and Mrs. Madison led in by one of the managers and Mrs. [Anna] Cutts [Dolley's sister] and Mr. Madison, she was led to the part of the room where we happened to be, so that I accidently was placed next her. She looked a queen. She had on a pale buff colored velvet, made plain, with a very long train, but not the least trimming, and beautiful pearl necklace, earrings and bracelets. Her head dress was a turban of the same coloured velvet and white satin (from Paris) with two superb plumes, the bird of paradise feathers. It would be *absolutely impossible* for any one to behave with more perfect propriety than she did. Unassuming dignity, sweetness, grace. It seems to me that such manners would disarm envy itself, and conciliate even enemies. The managers presented her with the first number,—"But what shall I do with it," said she, "I do not dance." "Give it to your neighbor," said Capt. Tingey. "Oh no," said she, "that would look like partiality." "Then I will," said the Capt. and he presented it to Mrs. Cutts. I really admired this in Mrs. M. Ah, why does she not in all things act with the same propriety? She would be too much beloved if she added all the virtues to all the graces. She was led to supper by the French Minister, Mrs. Cutts by the English Minister, she sat at the centre of the table, which was a cressent, the French and English ministers on each hand, Mrs. Cutts the next on the right hand, Mrs. [Robert] Smith [wife of the Secretary of State] the next on the left and Mr. Madison on the other side of the table opposite Mrs. M. . . . Mr. Jefferson did not stay above two hours; he seemed in high spirits and his countenance beamed with a benevolent joy. I do believe father never loved son more than he loves Mr. Madison, and I believe too that every demonstration of respect to Mr. M. gave Mr. J. more pleasure than if paid to himself. Oh he is a good man! And the day will come when all party spirit shall expire, that every citizen of the United States will join in saying "He is a good man." Mr. Madison, on the contrary, seemed spiritless and exhausted. While he was standing by me I said, "I wish with all my heart I had a little bit of seat to offer you." "I wish so too," said he, with a most woe begone face, and looking as if he could scarcely stand,—the managers came up to ask him to stay to supper, he assented, and turning to me, "but I would much rather be in bed" said he. Immediately after supper Mr. and Mrs. M. withdrew, the rest of the company danced until 12, the moment the clock struck that hour, the musick stopped, and we all came home tired and sick. "And such," said I as I threw myself on the bed, "such are the gaiety and pleasures of the world!"

The Madisons at once moved into the President's House and Dolley launched her remarkable career as First Lady. Large, bustling, vivacious, fashionable, "Queen Dolley" was everything her husband was not. Under her management the President's House, rudely furnished in Jefferson's time, acquired touches of elegance. So did the entertainment. The Wednesday afternoon "drawing rooms" recalled President Washington's celebrated levees (which Jefferson had abolished), though free of their stiffness and formality. In 1811 young Washington Irving stepped into "the blazing splendor" of this weekly salon. "Here I was most graciously received," he wrote, "found a crowded collection of great and little men, of ugly old women and beautiful young ones, and in ten minutes was hand in glove with half the people in the assemblage. Mrs. Madison is a fine, portly, buxom dame, who has a smile and pleasant word for everybody. Her sisters, Mrs. Cutts and Mrs. [Lucy Payne] Washington, are like the two merry wives of Windsor: but as to Jemmy Madison—ah poor Jemmy!—he is but a withered little apple-john." Dolley created an aura of glamour even around the Presidency of James Madison.

The unprecedented unity and harmony in the executive that Jefferson had maintained for eight years broke down at once under Madison. Contemplating no change of policy from the previous administration, he wanted as few changes of personnel as possible. Albert Gallatin was slated for the State Department; but when his enemies in Congress protested, Madison abandoned the plan, kept Gallatin in the Treasury, and gave the post to Robert Smith, formerly Secretary of the Navy, whose brother Samuel headed the troublesome faction in the Senate. The first of several bad decisions Madison made in the choice of his official family, it splintered the administration from the start. Smith's talent for intrigue exceeded his talent for diplomacy, so Madison continued to handle the important affairs of the State Department. More inept than Smith, though free of guile, were William Eustis and Paul Hamilton, appointed to the posts of War and Navy, respectively. Caesar Rodney stayed on as Attorney General. During eight years Jefferson had had three attorneys general but only one secretary in each of the four departments. During the same term Madison ran through as many attorneys general and fourteen secretaries. Weakness and discord in the Cabinet reflected, of course, Madison's own deficiencies of personality and leadership. Congress, too, escaped the President's control. Adhering rigidly to the constitutional separation of powers, Madison was reluctant to lead Congress. Jefferson, too, had bowed ceremoniously to the doctrine, but seeing that the alternative was chaos had controlled Congress through the unofficial apparatus of party leadership. Lacking Jefferson's political talents, Madison adopted a passive role toward Congress, which gained in power and prestige as the Presidency declined.

Foreign affairs virtually monopolized the President's agenda. He had no confidence in the Nonintercourse Act as an instrument of American neutrality. A trade legally open to all the world except Britain and France was, in fact, open to those nations as well, especially to a Britain that ruled the seas. France had every right to complain and did, while Britain was relieved of the pressure of the embargo and yet free to plunder American shipping as before. Madison was therefore pleasantly surprised in April by the offer of the British minister, David Erskine, to revoke the orders in council in exchange for normal trade between the two countries. Madison at once proclaimed the trade open and on the effective date, June 10, six hundred ships sailed confidently for Britain. Napoleon might be expected to reciprocate. Perhaps then the embargo had succeeded after all, for Erskine's instructions antedated the Nonintercourse Act. Madison sent Jefferson the good news.

Washington Apl. 24. 1809

You will see in the newspapers the result of the advances made by G.B. Attempts were made to give shapes to the arrangement implying inconsistency and blame on our part. They were however met in a proper manner & readily abandoned; leaving these charges in their full force, as they now bear on the other side. The B. Cabinet must have changed its course under a full conviction that an adjustment with this country, had become essential; & it is not improbable that this policy may direct the ensuing negociation; mingling with it, at the same time, the hope that it may embroil us with France. To this use it may be expected the Federalists will endeavor to turn what is already done, at the coming session of Congs. The steps deemed proper to give the proceeding a contrary turn will not be omitted. And if France be not bereft of common sense, or be not predetermined on war with us, she will certainly not play into the hand of

Pencil drawing of young Washington Irving in 1805 by John Vanderlyn

277

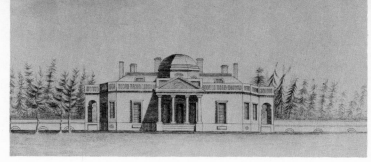

Monticello, Jefferson's home

her Enemy. Besides the general motive to follow the example of G.B. she cannot be insensible of the dangerous tendency of prolonging the commercial sufferings of her allies, particularly Russia, all of them already weary of such a state of things, after the pretext of enforcing it shall have ceased. She must be equally aware of the importance of our relations to Spanish America, which must now become the great object of Napoleons pride & ambition.

Jefferson hailed this "triumph of our forbearing and yet perservering system." Federalists, on the other hand, acclaimed the new President for boldly reversing Jefferson's course. Madison alluded to this mischievous and mistaken view of the matter in a subsequent letter to his friend at Monticello.

Washington May 30. 1809

The newfangled policy of the federal party, you will have noticed, has made a considerable figure in the newspapers. Some of the Editors are resuming the Old cant, and the others will doubtless soon follow the example. Nothing could exceed the folly of supposing that the principles & opinions manifested in our foreign discussion, were not, in the main at least, common to us; unless it be the folly of supposing that such shallow hypocrisy could deceive any one. The truth is, the sudden & unlooked for turn of the B. Cabinet, has thrown the party entirely off the Center. They have at present no settled plan. There is reason to believe that the leaders are soured towards England, and much less disposed than heretofore to render our interests subservient to hers. Expressions have been used by one at least of the Essex Cabinet [a group of New England Federalists], whether sincerely or insidiously may not be absolutely certain, from which it is inferred that a disposition exists in that quarter not even to continue the non-intercourse Act agst. France. Certain it is, that the desire of war with her is no longer manifested; and the deficiency of the English markets excites a keen appetite for a trade with the continent; and that a real uneasiness is felt lest the negociations with G.B. should end in sacrifices on our part, which they have been reproaching the Administration for not being ready to make. As one proof of their present feelings, the federal leaders shew a marked alienation from Erskine. The Elections in Massts. as well as in N.H. and N.Y. have issued unfavorably. But the smallness of the majority, and the overstrained exertions it has required, seem to depress rather than flatter the successful party. No confidence is felt in the permanency of the triumph.

Madison was at Montpelier near the end of July when he learned from Gallatin that Britain's Foreign Secretary Canning had repudiated the Erskine agreement. In his friendship for the United States the envoy had, in truth, violated his instructions. That something was amiss had been suggested by the new British order of April 26 which substituted the fiction of a far-flung blockade of the Continent—from Holland to Italy—for the harsh restrictions of the earlier system. Even if an improvement, the blockade contradicted the Erskine agreement and still interfered with neutral trade. Replying to Gallatin, Madison speculated on the reason for this latest act of British "fraud and folly."

Montpellier July 28. 1809

The conduct of the B. Govt. in protesting the arrangement of its Minister surprizes one in spite of all their examples of folly. If it be not their plan, now that they have filled their magazines with our supplies, and ascertained our want of firmness in witholding them, to adopt openly a system of monopoly & piracy, it may be hoped that they will not persist in the scandalous course in which they have set out. Supposing Erskine to have misunderstood or overstrained his instructions, can the difference between our trading directly & indirectly with Holland, account for the violent remedy applied to the case? Is it not more probable that they have yielded to the clamors of the London Smugglers in Sugar and Coffee, whose numbers & impudence are displayed in the scandalous & successful demand from their Govt. that it should strangle the lawful trade of a friendly nation lest it should interfere with their avowed purpose of

By the Virtue, Firmness and Patriotism of
JEFFERSON & MADISON,
Our Difficulties with England are settled—our Ships have been preserved, and our Seamen will, hereafter, be respected while sailing under our National Flag.

Heading of a proclamation issued by Madison in April, 1809, declaring prematurely that difficulties with England had been settled

Madison's stepson, John Payne Todd

carrying on a smuggling trade with their Enemies. Such an outrage on all decency, was never before heard of, even on the shores of Africa [by the Barbary pirates]. I have a private letter of late date from London, which says it was whispered that the Ministry were inclined to swallow the pill sent them; but that the King considered himself as insulted in what related to Berkley [Admiral George C. Berkeley, the responsible British officer in the *Chesapeake-Leopard* affair, whose punishment Madison had said was "due from His Britannic Majesty to his own honor"] and positively refused his consent. This is not impossible, and may assist in explaining the phenomenon. Still, I can not but hope...that things may take another turn, under the influence of the obvious & striking considerations which advise it. The sudden disavowal of Erskine by the Ministry took place in a moment of alarm...and the confusion is strongly marked on the expedient resorted to. Whilst they acknowledge the obligation to save the Amn. Merchts. from the snare, they not only leave it open for those not going directly from the U.S. but take no notice of the Mediterranean ports opened by the arrangement & shut by their decree. This is another presumption that the Holland market alone was in their thoughts, & that on acct. of the Smugglers who awed them.

In answer to a letter to Mr. [Robert] Smith, I have made a few observations on the several points for consideration; declining a return to Washington, as not necessary, but awaiting the result of your consultations on that as on other subjects. I venture to hope that my return will not be found necessary; the less so as you will be able to bring with you so full a view of the state of things, and the sentiments of your colleagues, that my decision as far as necessary, may be made as well here as at Washington.

The crisis was such, however, that Madison was forced to make the tiring journey to Washington in the August heat, staying just long enough to proclaim the restoration of nonintercourse with Britain. While at the capital, Madison wrote to his wife.

[Washington, August, 1809]
I hope you receid., my dearest, a letter written by the last mail. I write this in haste just to tell you that P[ayne]

& myself are well; & that I am making exertions to get thro' the necessary business, with a hope of setting out on my return tomorrow. It is very possible however that I may be detained till friday morning. I send you all the foreign news in the inclosed papers. That from France has a better complexion than preceding accts. of her temper towards the U.S. The tone of Cannings speech also is a little different from the arrogance of his instructions to Mr. Erskine. Payne writes. I must refer to his letter for what I am prevented from adding....

The bright promises of April shriveled in August. Anglo-American relations were in a worse state than before. The *Chesapeake* affair dragged on, impressment was still at issue, the orders in council still "colonialized" American trade, and the Erskine imbroglio frayed tempers on both sides. Back home in Virginia, Madison wrote to Jefferson.

Montpellier Aug. 16. 1809

I got home from my trip to Washington on Saturday last; having remained there three days only. You will have seen in the Procln. issued, the result of [our] consultation on the effect of what has passed on our relations with G.B. The enforcement of the non-intercourse act agst. her, will probably be cri[ticiz]ed by some friends and generally assailed by our adversaries, on the ground that the power given to the Ex. being special, was exhausted by the first exercise of it; and that the power having put out of force the laws to which it related, could under no possible construction restore their operation....

Erskine is in a ticklish situation with his Govt. I suspect he will not be able to defend himself agst. the charge of exceeding his instructions, notwithstanding the appeal he makes to sundry others not published. But he will make out a strong case agst. Canning, and be able to avail himself much of the absurdity and evident inadmissibility of the articles disregarded by him. He can plead, also that the difference between his arrangmt. & the spontaneous order of Apl. 26. is too slight to justify the disavowal of him....

We are looking out for Mr. & Mrs. Gallatin every day. Untill they arrive, and we learn also the periods of your being at & absent from Home, we do not venture to fix a time for our proposed visit to Monticello.

English mug honoring "Maddison"

281

Erskine was recalled, to be succeeded by Francis James Jackson, whose tone and temper were altogether different. Believing the United States the injured party in the Erskine matter, Madison expected an explanation from Jackson. Instead the minister accused Smith and Madison of conniving in Erskine's violation of instructions. Midway in this dialogue, Madison reported to William Pinkney in London.

Washington Ocr. 23. 1809

You will see in the communications from the Dept. of State what has passed with Mr. Jackson. No reply to Mr. S.s answer has yet been made. It appears that the B. Govt. continues to be equally ignorant of our character, & of what it owes to its own.... For it is impossible not to see that the avowed object is no longer to retaliate on an enemy, but to prevent our legitimate commerce from interfering with the London Smugglers of Sugar & Coffee. How can a nation expect to retain the respect of Mankind whose Govt. descends to so ignoble a career?

What will be the future course of Mr. Jackson, or that of his Govt. or of Congs. I do not undertake to anticipate, farther than that Congs. will in some form or other keep up a counteraction to the misconduct of both Belligerents. As to Mr. J. it can not be supposed that he has any effective authority to overcome the difficulties before him. Altho' we continue sincerely anxious to facilitate his doing so, yet no[t] a little indignation is felt, at the mean & insolent attempt to defraud the U.S. of the exculpatory explanation dictated by the respect due to them; and particularly at the insinuation in Jackson's answer that this Govt. colluded with Mr. E. in violating his instructions.

You will observe by the Gazettes that Mr. Onis, appointed by the Spanish Junta [controlled by Britain], is just arrived here as a Minister Plenipo: of Ferdinand; and that efforts are made to turn the question of his being received, to party purposes. The principle of neutrality on one hand, and on the other, the limited authority of the Executive...could never permit the reception of Mr. Onis in the actual state of things in Spain....

The public opinion or rather that of the discontented party has already undergone a considerable change in favor of the system pursued in our foreign relations, and the change is still going on. In Maryld. & Vermont, the fact is shewn by the late elections. And all accts. from the Eastward prognosticate that the next elections in Massts. N.H. & R. Island, will reverse those which took place during the fever which the Embargo was made to produce. Reflection alone would probably have brought about such a change. But it has been hastened by the disappointment of all parties, as to the Conduct of G.B. on the subject of Mr. Erskine's arrangement; and by the severe experience, that a trade limited to the B. dominions is but a mouthfull and not as the people were told it wd. be a bellyfull. The shipments to the W. Inds. have been ruinous. In the Mediterranean the losses, owing to captures, recaptures & markets glutted from Engd. will not be less than 25 or 30 per Ct. In the Baltic, & the N. of Europe, the speculations are still more entirely blasted. The lumber merchts. who struck at the great demand in England have been successful; and the others have been saved from loss, by the expected consequence of the Disavowal of Mr. Erskine.

The most remarkable feature in our internal prospects is the astonishing progress of manufactures, more especially in the Household way. Throughout the middle, S. & W. countries, they have taken a lasting root; it being found, that with the aid of the machineries accomodated to the family scale & of habit, cloathing & many other articles can be provided both cheaper & better than as heretofore. Passion is spur also to interest in the case. Nor is necessity without its influence; for in truth, the planters & farmers being deprived of the customary markets & prices for their produce, can no longer pay for their customary supplies from abroad.

New-York, Oct. 4.
SPANISH AFFAIRS.

Late last night the Spanish frigate Cornelia, capt. Don John Roderigues de Arias, arrived at the quarantine ground. She sailed from Cadiz on the 20th of August. This vessels has brought out his excellency Don Lewis de Onis, minister plenipotentiary and envoy extraordinary from his Catholic majesty Ferdinand the 7th to the United States of America. Also Don Bartholomew Rengenet, consul from his Catholic majesty for Philadelphia, their ladies, daughters and domestics, and Mr. Richard Bailey, of this city.

Article in the October 9, 1809, issue of the National Intelligencer *of Washington, D.C., announcing arrival of the Chevalier d'Onis from Cadiz*

Jackson's arrogance was not to be tolerated. After little more than a month, the talks were broken off, the minister dismissed and handed his passport. He struck out for a happier political clime, New England, where he was lionized by Anglomen, while back in Washington Congress condemned his "outrageous and insolent" conduct. The diplomatic rupture distressed Madison's old friend, George Logan, of Philadelphia. As good a Quaker as he was a Republican, Logan went to Washington to plead his cause and on his return home, apparently dissatisfied with the President's posture, wrote to him imploring peace. In his own mind Logan had already appointed himself the envoy of peace, intending to repeat in this crisis with Britain the intervention he had undertaken in 1798 with France—a mission that had produced the Logan Act making such personal diplomacy a crime. Madison, in reply to Logan, credited his good intentions but at the same time justified the administration's course toward Britain.

George Logan of Philadelphia

Washington Jany 19th 1810

I have received your favour of the 10th. Your anxiety that our country may be kept out of the vortex of war, is honourable to your judgement as a patriot, and to your feeling as a man. The same anxiety is, I sincerely believe, felt by the great body of the nation, & by its public councils; most assuredly by the Executive Branch of them. But the question may be decided for us, by actual hostilities against us, or by proceedings, leaving no choice but between absolute disgrace & resistance by force. May not also manifestations of patience under injuries & indignities, be carried as far, as to invite this very dilemma?

I devoutly wish that the same disposition to cultivate peace by means of justice which exists here, predominated elsewhere, particularly in G.B. But how can this be supposed, whilst she persists in proceedings, which comprise the essence of hostility; whilst . . . we see her converting the late reconciliation through one of her Ministers, into a source of fresh difficulties & animosities, thro' another. For in this light must be viewed, her disavowal of Mr. Erskine, and the impressions made thro' his successor. Had the disavowal been deemed essential to her interests, a worse plaister could not have been devised for the wound necessarily inflicted here. . . .

Notwithstanding all these grounds of discontent & discouragement, we are ready as the B. Govt. knows, to join in any new experiment, (& thro' either our diplomatic channel there, or hers here) for a cordial & comprehensive adjustment of matters between the two countries.

Let reparation be made for the acknowledged wrong commited in the case of the Chesapeak, a reparation so cheap to the wrongdoer, yet so material to the honour of the injured party; & let the orders in Council, already repealed as to the avowed object of retaliation, be repealed also as an expedient for substituting an illicit commerce, in place of that to which neutrals have, as such, an incontestible right. The way will then be opened for negotiation at large; and if the B. Govt. would bring into it the same temper as she would find in us; & the same disposition to insist on nothing inconsistent with the rule of doing as she would, or rather as she *will* be done by, the result could not fail to be happy for both.

Permit me to remark that you are under a mistake in supposing that the Treaty concluded by Messr. M[onroe] & P[inkney] was rejected because it did not provide that free ships should make free goods. It never was required nor expected that such a stipulation should be inserted.... Let me add that the acceptance of that Treaty would have very little changed the actual situation of things with G.B. The orders in council would not have been prevented but rather placed on stronger grou[n]d; the case of the Chesapeak, the same as it is; so also the case of impressments, of fa[c]titious blockades &c all as at present, pregnant sources of contention & ill humour.

From this view of the subject, I cannot but persuade myself, that you will concur in opinion, that if unfortunately, the calamity you so benevolently dread, should visit this hitherto favoured country, the fault will not lie where you would wish it not to lie.

Nathaniel Macon, Chairman of the House Committee on Foreign Affairs

Madison hoped to avoid war, but war was preferable to submission, and he mildly suggested that Congress look to the country's defenses. The Nonintercourse Act would expire with the current session. Although no one advocated its renewal, neither the administration nor Congress could agree on an alternative system to economic coercion. At Gallatin's initiative, Nathaniel Macon, Chairman of the House Committee on Foreign Affairs, introduced what became known as Macon's Bill. Essentially a navigation act, it would permit American ships to ply the seas at their own risk but close American ports to all British and French vessels. Madison thought well of the measure. After four months of wearisome debate, however, Macon's Bill died to be succeeded by Macon's Bill No. 2, enacted at the session's close. The last of a succession of experiments to vindicate American neutrality by commercial sanctions, the act reopened trade with both belligerents but provided that if either government revoked its edicts the President might prohibit intercourse with the other. According to one historian the act was "equivalent to alliance with England" inasmuch as it surrendered American commerce to the nation that controlled the Atlantic sea lanes. Doubtless Napoleon would see it in that light. Although Madison disliked the measure, he decided to make the best of it. Writing to Pinkney, who was pleased that Lord Wellesley had been named to replace Canning in the Foreign Ministry, Madison touched on the impasse over Jackson and then speculated at length on the fate of the new policy.

Washington May 23d 1810

You will learn from the Department of State, as you must have anticipated, our surprise that the answer of

Lord Wellesley, to your very just and able view of the case of Jackson, corresponded so little with the impressions of that Minister manifested in your first interviews with him. The date of the answer best explains the change; as it shows that time was taken for obtaining intelligence from this country, and adapting the policy of the answer to the position taken by the advocates of Jackson. And it must have happened that the intelligence prevailing at that date was of the sort most likely to mislead. The elections which have since taken place in the Eastern States, and which have been materially influenced by the affair of Jackson and the spirit of party connected with it, are the strongest of proofs, that the measure of the Executive coincided with the feelings of the Nation. In every point of view the answer is unworthy of the source from which it comes.

From the manner in which the vacancy left by Jackson is provided for, it is infered that a sacrifice is meant of the respect belonging to this Government, either to the pride of the British Government, or to the feelings of those who have taken side with it against their own. On either supposition, it is necessary to counteract the ignoble purpose. You will accordingly find that on ascertaining the substitution of a Chargé, to be an intentional degradation of the diplomatic intercourse on the part of Great Britain, it is deemed proper that no higher functionary should represent the United States at London.…

The Act of Congress transmitted from the Department of State, will inform you of the footing on which our relations to the Belligerent powers were finally placed. The experiment now to be made, of a commerce with both, unrestricted by our laws, has resulted from causes which you will collect from the debates, and from your own reflections. The new form of appeal to the policy of Great Britain and France on the subject of the Decrees and Orders, will most engage your attention. However feeble it may appear, it is possible that one or other of those powers may allow it more effect than was produced by the overtures heretofore tried.… Among the inducements to the experiment of an unrestricted commerce now made, were two which contributed essentially to the majority of votes in its favor; first a general hope, favored by daily accounts from England, that an adjustment of differences there, and thence in France, would

Lord Wellesley

Columbia teaches "Mounseer Beau" Napoleon and laggard John Bull a new lesson—to respect free trade and seamen's rights—in an 1813 cartoon.

render the measure safe & proper; second, a willingness in not a few, to teach the advocates for an open trade, under actual circumstances, the folly, as well as degradation of their policy. At the next meeting of Congress, it will be found, according to present appearances, that instead of an adjustment with either of the Belligerents, there is an increased obstinacy in both; and that the inconveniences of the Embargo, and non-intercourse, have been exchanged for the greater sacrifices as well as disgrace, resulting from a submission to the predatory systems in force. It will not be wonderful therefore, if the passive spirit which marked the late session of Congress, should at the next meeting be roused to the opposite point; more especially as the tone of the Nation has never been as low as that of its Representatives, and as it is rising already under the losses sustained by our Commerce in the Continental ports, and by the fall of prices in our produce at home, under a limitation of the market, to Great Britain. Cotton I perceive is down at 10 or 11 cents in Georgia. The great mass of Tobacco is in a similar situation. And the effect must soon be general, with the exception of a few articles which do not at present, glut the British demand. Whether considerations like these will make any favorable impression on the British Cabinet, you will be the first to know. Whatever confidence I may have in the justness of them, I must forget all that has past before I can indulge very favorable expectations. Every new occasion seems to countenance the belief, that there lurks in the British Cabinet, a hostile feeling towards this Country, which will never be eradicated during the present Reign; nor overruled, whilst it exists, but by some dreadful pressure from external or internal causes.

With respect to the French Govt. we are taught by experience to be equally distrustful. It will have however the same opportunity presented to it, with the British Govt., of comparing the actual state of things, with that which would be produced by a repeal of its Decrees; and it is not easy to find any plausible motive to continue the former as preferable to the latter. A worse state of things, than the actual one, could not exist for France, unless her preference be for a state of War. If she be sincere either in her propositions relative to a chronological revocation of illegal Edicts against Neutrals, or to a pledge from the United States not to submit to those of Great Britain, she ought at once to embrace the arrangement held out by Congress....

During the past year Napoleon had seized ten million dollars worth of American ships and cargoes in reprisal for the Nonintercourse Act. Considering the American trade as identical with the British, he made any Yankee vessel liable to seizure and sequestration in ports under French control. The practice was "legalized" by the Rambouillet Decree of March, 1810. Strictly in terms of maritime losses, France had become the greater enemy of American neutrality. Nevertheless, Madison continued to hold that "the original sin against neutrals lies with Great Britain" and that she remained the greater threat. France might pillage but she could not monopolize or colonize American trade. So Madison refused to shift the balance of American resistance from Britain to France.

Napoleon knew how to play the game for his benefit, and now, in August, he seized upon the invitation extended by Macon's Bill No. 2. On his order the Duke of Cadore, Foreign Minister, told John Armstrong, U.S. Minister to France, that the Berlin and Milan Decrees were revoked as of November 1, it being understood that Britain would lift her orders and sham blockades or that the United States would force her to reform. Madison learned of the Cadore letter by way of Pinkney and did not wait for confirmation. Historians disagree on whether he allowed himself to be duped by Napoleon or, rather, shrewdly adopted the fiction of French repeal in order to force the issue with Britain. At any rate, he took the letter at face value, interpreted the French repeal as unconditional, and on November 2 proclaimed nonintercourse with Britain subject to repeal of her orders within ninety days. At the same time, with Britain and France warring in Spain, he jumped at the chance to annex West Florida, which was already predominantly settled by Americans. Announcing possession of the area by the United States, Madison ordered Governor William Claiborne of the Orleans Territory to enter West Florida and to establish a civil government there. In writing to Armstrong, he discussed this latest chapter in the collapse of Spanish empire as well as the Cadore letter.

Washington Oct. 29th 1810

You will learn from the Department of State that altho' no direct authentication of the repeal of the French decrees has been received from you, a proclamation issues on the ground furnished by your correspondence with Mr. Pinkney. It is to be hoped that France will do what she is understood to be pledged for, and in a manner that will produce no jealousy or embarrassment here. We hope in particular that the sequestred property will have been restored.... The course which G.B. will take, is left by Wellesley's pledge, a matter of conjecture. It is not improbable that the orders in Council will be revoked and the sham blockades be so managed if possible, as to irritate France against our non-resistance without irritating this Country to the resisting point. It seems on the whole that we shall be at issue with G.B. on the ground of such blockades, and it is for us a strong ground.

You will see also the step that has been produced by the posture of things in W. Florida. If France is wise she will neither dislike it herself, nor promote resentment of it in any other quarter. She ought in fact, if guided by prudence and good information, to patronize at once, a general separation of S. America from old Spain. This event is already decided, and the sole question with France is whether it is to take place under her auspices, or those of Great Britain. The latter... is taking her measures with reference to that event; and in the mean time, is extorting commercial privileges [from West Florida residents] as the recompence of her interposition. In this particular her avarice is defeating her interest. For it not only invites France to outbid her; but throws in seeds of discord which will take effect the moment peace or safety is felt by the party of whom the advantage is taken.... It merits the consideration of France also, that in proportion as she discourages, in any way, a free intercourse of the U.S. with their revolutionary neighbours, she favors the exclusive commerce of her rival with them; as she has hitherto favored it with Europe,

Federalist handbill of 1811 warned that the French decrees had not been repealed and that American ships were still being detained.

by her decrees against our intercourse with it. As she seems to be recovering from the one folly, it may be hoped she will not fall into the other.

Britain yielded nothing, and Congress enacted into law the nonintercourse proclaimed by Madison. Napoleon, far from giving thought to reparations, continued his seizures, justified now on local customs regulations which, unlike the old decrees, were outside the scope of international law though their effect was the same. Britain insisted the French decrees were still in force. The United States insisted they were repealed. In this deadlock one country must yield or war must ensue. Whatever the truth of the matter, Madison stuck to the idea of repeal because it got him out of the scrape with France, rescued the nation from the disgraceful submission of the last two years, and restored peaceable coercion of Britain. Federalists, and some Republicans too, said the policy connived in Napoleonic fraud and deceit; they also denounced it as unconstitutional and destructive of commerce. Resolutions and addresses poured into the President from the eastern towns. To one of them, from New Haven, he sent his quiet answer.

Washington May 24. 1811.

I have recd. fellow Citizens, the petition which you have addressed to me representing the inconveniences experienced from the existing non-importation law, and soliciting that the National Legislature may be speedily convened.

It is known to all that the Commerce of the U.S. has, for a considerable period, been greatly abridged & annoyed by Edicts of the Belligerent powers; each professing retaliation only on the other; but both violating the clearest rights of the U.S. as a neutral nation. In this extraordinary state of things, the Legislature willing to avoid a resort to war, more especially during the concurrent aggressions of two great Powers, themselves at war, the one with the other, and determined on the other hand agst. an unqualified acquiescence, have endeavored by successive and varied regulations affecting the commerce of the parties, to make it their interest to be just.

In the Act of Congress out of which the existing non-importation has grown, the state of Commerce was no otherwise qualified than by a provision, that in case either of the Belligerents should revoke its unlawful Edicts, and the other should fail to do the same, our ports should be shut to the vessels & merchandize of the latter. This provision...was equally presented to

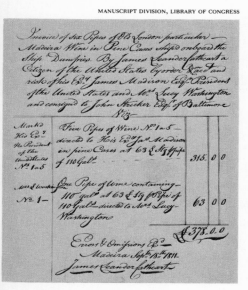

Invoice for pipes (casks) of wine ordered by Madison and Dolley's sister Lucy Washington in 1811

*An 1811 cartoon portrays the refusal
of Congress to renew the charter
of the Bank of the United States.*

the attention of both. In consequence of the communication the French Government declared that its Decrees were revoked. As the British Government had expressed reluctance in issuing its orders, and repeatedly signified a wish to find in the example of its adversary, an occasion for putting an end to them, the expectation was the more confident, that the occasion would be promptly embraced. This was not done; and the period allowed for the purpose having elapsed, our ports became shut to British Ships and merchandize. . . .

If appeals to the justice of the Belligerents, through their interests, involve privations on our part also, it ought to be recollected that this is an effect inseparable from every resort, by which one nation can right itself agst. the injustice of others.

If sacrifices made for the sake of the whole result more to some than to other districts or descriptions of Citizens, this also is an effect, which tho always to be regretted, can never be entirely avoided. Whether the appeal be to the sword, or to interruptions or modifications of customary intercourse, an equal operation on every part of the Community never happens. . . .

In estimating the particular measure which has been adopted by the national Councils, it may be reasonably expected therefore, from the candor of enlightened Citizens, that with the peculiarity of the public situation, they will be impressed also with the difficulty of selecting the course most satisfactory, and best suited to diminish its evils or shorten their duration: that they will keep in mind that a resort to war must involve necessary restrictions on commerce; and that were no measure whatever opposed to the Belligerent acts against our Commerce, it would not only remain under the severe restrictions now imposed by foreign hands, but new motives would be given for prolonging and invigorating them.

Feuding in Congress and in the Cabinet rocked the administration in 1811. The treasury faced declining revenues from the ban on British imports, yet additional funds were wanted for the country's defenses. Congress continued to starve the army and navy, however, and also defeated the bill to renew the charter of the Bank of the United States. Madison did not lift a finger to help Gallatin save the Bank, upon which the Secretary depended heavily and without which, in his opinion, the government could not finance a war. Old Republican feelings against the Bank, this last monument of Federalism, contributed to its demise, but much of the opposition was simply opposition to Gallatin. His enemies were not limited to "The Invisibles"—the followers of Senator Samuel Smith and his intriguing brother, the Secretary of State. But this faction was especially virulent, and it aimed to knock Gallatin out with the Bank. He did, in fact, threaten to resign. But Madison could not afford to lose him. His hand forced at last, he demanded Robert Smith's resignation. Smith chose to be fired, however, and then to smear the administration in the press. His publication (Madison called it "wicked") included the charge of executive collusion with France. The Cabinet crisis shook public confidence in the administration. To repair the public injury, and a painful personal one as well, Madison prevailed upon James Monroe to forget his old grudge (resulting from the rejection in 1807 of his treaty with Britain) and to become Secretary of State. Although Monroe entered the office half convinced Madison was the anglophobe his enemies portrayed, he soon fell in with the President's foreign policy.

During the summer the Virginia triumvirs—Jefferson, Madison, and Monroe—surveyed the diplomatic impasse, and the President returned to Washington in the fall all but finally committed to war. His message to the new Congress on November 5 was a call to arms. He reported the failure of the round of diplomacy commenced on the arrival of the latest British envoy, Sir Augustus Foster. Foster took the hard line: either the United States must make war on Napoleon's Continental System or submit its commerce to British orders. It was, Madison told Congress, "an indispensable condition of the repeal of the British orders, that commerce should be restored to a footing, that would admit the productions and manufactures of Great Britain...into markets shut against them by the Enemy; the United States being given to understand that, in the mean time, a continuance of their non-importation act, would lead to measures of retaliation." British privateers and cruisers hovered on American coasts and preyed on American carriers. Britain denied redress for old injuries and persisted in measures that amounted to commercial war on the United States. "With this evidence of hostile inflexibility in trampling on rights which no Independent Nation can relinquish, Congress will feel the duty of putting the United States into an armour, and an attitude demanded by the crisis, and corresponding with the national spirit and expectations."

The message appealed to the rising war fever. The West was especially volatile. News of the Battle of Tippecanoe reached the capital just as Congress commenced. This bloody encounter between frontier Americans and stubbornly resisting Indians in the Northwest was charged to British support of the Shawnee chief Tecumseh and his defensive confederacy. It sparked demands to take Canada, thereby ending the Indian menace, expelling the British, and satiating western land hunger. The Twelfth Congress soon gave

Battle of Tippecanoe, 1811

voice to these demands. Overwhelmingly Republican, it included a number of militant young patriots, primarily westerners—Henry Clay, Richard M. Johnson, Felix Grundy, John C. Calhoun, and others—who became known as War Hawks. Their influence was great but they did not drive Madison to war. Rather, they supplied the political nerve and muscle for the policy he had laid out, one which by measured steps led the nation to war on his own responsibility.

Unfortunately, the administration was deeply embarrassed by Napoleon, whose piratical acts against American commerce mocked the idea of repeal of his edicts. The country received nothing but outrages from France at the moment of arming for war on France's enemy. To clarify this anomalous situation, to obtain reparations and guarantees of respect in the future, Madison had sent Joel Barlow as Minister to France. Before the event of war with Britain, he desperately wished to be free of embarrassment with France, as was evident in his message to Barlow in November.

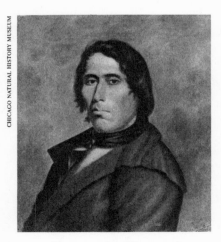

Shawnee chief Tecumseh

Washington Nov. 17. 1811

You will receive by this conveyance the proper communications from the Dept. of State. You will see in them, the ground now avowed for the B. Orders in Council. It must render them codurable with the war; for nothing but a termination of it will re-open the continental market to British products. Nor is it probable that peace will do it on its former extent. The Instruction which requires the U.S. as a neutral power to assert an obligation on one belligerent, to favor, by its internal reputations, the manufactures of another, is a fitter subject for ridicule than refutation. It accordingly has no countenance here even among the most devoted Champions of G.B. Whether some of them by arming themselves with simulated facts & sophisticated distinctions may not be embolded to turn out in her defence, will soon be seen. Nothing has yet passed in Congs. disclosing the sense of that Body, with respect to the moment &

*Madison's call to arms delivered
to Congress on November 5, 1811*

manner of meeting the conduct of G.B. in its present hostile shape. A disposition appears to enter at once on preparations, which will probably be put in force or not, as the effect of them on the British Councils, shall be ascertained in the course of the session. In the mean time it is not improbable that the merchant vessels may be permitted to arm for self-Defence. This can scarcely fail to bring on maritime reprisals and to end in the full extent of war, unless a change in the British system should arrest the career of events. All proceedings however relating to G. Britain will be much influenced by the conduct of France not only as it relates to a violation of our neutral rights; but of our national ones and that too not only in cases strictly French, but in those in Naples & elsewhere indirectly also, and to justice for the past as well as for the future. Altho' in our discussions with G.B. we have been justified in viewing the repeal of the French decrees as sufficiently substantiated to require a fulfillment of the pledge to repeal the order in Council; yet the manner in which the F. Govt. has managed the repeal of the Decrees, and evaded a correction of other outrages, has mingled with the conciliatory tendency of the repeal, as much of irritation and disgust as possible. And these sentiments are not a little strengthened by the sarcastic comments on that management with which we are constantly pelted in our discussions with the B. Govt. and for which the F. Govt. ought to be ashamed to furnish the occasion. In fact without a systematic change from an appearance of crafty contrivance, and insatiate cupidity, to an open manly & upright dealing with a nation whose example demands it, it is impossible that good will can exist; and that the ill will which her policy aims in directing against her enemy, should not, by her folly and iniquity be drawn off against herself. The late licenciousness of the F. privateers in the Baltic, the ruinous transmission of their cases to Paris, and the countenance said to be there given to such abuses, are kindling a fresh flame here: And if a remedy be not applied, & our merchantmen should arm, hostile collisions will as readily take place with one nation as the other. Were it not that our frigates would be in danger of rencounters with British Ships of superior force in that quarter, there could be no scruple at sending thither some of them, with orders to suppress by

Virginia, HOWE

In December, 1811, a number of the Madisons' friends were killed in a fire in the Richmond Theatre.

force the French and Danish depredations. I am aware that a pretext for these has been sought in the practice of our vessels in accepting British Convoy; but have they not in many instances at least been driven to this irregular step by the greater irregularities practised agst. them? We await the return of the [U.S.S.] Constitution not without a hope of finding the good effect of your remonstrances in a radical change of the French policy towards this Country.

Barlow got only a runaround in France. As late as April, 1812, Madison entertained the possibility of making war on both belligerents simultaneously. But Britain always loomed as the major enemy. During a tempestuous winter, when Washington was even visited by an earthquake, Madison fretted alternately over the glimmering hope of peace and the nation's laggard preparations for war. Of the army voted by Congress, he wrote sarcastically to Jefferson: "With a view to enable the Executive to step at once into Canada they have provided after two months delay, for a regular force requiring 12 to raise it; and after 3 months for a volunteer force, on terms not likely to raise it at all." Instead of new ships for the navy, Congress only reactivated old ones. Loans and higher tariffs were voted but not new taxes. The Republicans were a leaderless herd. Anti-Madisonian factions—Smith's Invisibles, Randolph's "Quids," the Clintonians of New York—blunted the best efforts of the administration party. It may have been some consolation to Madison that the government in London stood in worse straits. George III was insane, Ireland rebellious, and economic distress widespread. Angry opposition to the orders in council further jeopardized Spencer Perceval's government. Partly because of this situation, Madison delayed the decision for war. Even on April 1, when he asked Congress for an embargo preparatory to war, he clung to the hope that it might yet be an instrument of negotiating peace. He waited, too, to hear from France. Dispatches from both foreign capitals were expected on the return of the U.S.S. *Hornet*, which fixed the hour of decision. He wrote to Jefferson at this time.

Washington April 3. 1812
A late arrival from G.B. brings dates subsequent to the maturity of the Prince Regents Authority. It appears that Percival, &c. are to retain their places, and that they prefer war with us, to a repeal of their orders in Council. We have nothing left therefore, but to make ready for it. As a step to it an embargo for 60 days was recommended to Congs. on Wednesday and agreed to in the H. of Reps. by about 70 to 40. The Bill was before the Senate yes-

terday, who adjourned about 4 or 5 O Clock without a decision.... The temper of that body is known to be equivocal. Such a measure, even for a limited and short time, is always liable to adverse as well as favorable considerations; and its operation at this moment, will add fuel to party discontent, and interested clamor. But it is a rational & provident measure, and will be relished by a greater portion of the Nation, than an omission of it. If it could have been taken sooner and for a period of 3 or 4 months, it might have inlisted an alarm of the B. Cabinet.... Whether if adopted for 60 days, it may beget apprehensions of a protraction, & thence lead to admissible overtures, before the sword is stained with blood, cannot be foreknown with certainty. Such an effect is not to be counted upon. You will observe, that Liverpool was Secy. for the Foreign Dept. ad interim, & that Castlereah is the definitive successor of Wellesley [as Britain's Foreign Minister]. The resignation of this last, who has recd. no other appt is a little mysterious. There is some reason for believing that he is at variance with Percival; or that he distrusts the stability of the existing Cabinet, and courts an alliance with the Grenville party, as likely to overset it. If none of that party desert their colours, the calculation cannot be a very bad one; especially in case of war with the U.S: in addition to the distress of B. trade & manufactures, and the inflammation in Ireland: to say nothing of possible reverses in Spain & Portugal, which alone would cut up the Percival ascendency by the roots. From France we hear nothing. The delay of the Hornet is inexplicable, but on the reproachful supposition, that the F Govt. is waiting for the final turn of things at London, before it takes its course, which justice alone ought to prescribe, towards us. If this be found to be its game, it will impair the value of concessions if made, and give to her refusal of them, consequences it may little dream of.

Joel Barlow

The *Hornet* at last reached New York on May 19 and Madison read the fateful dispatches three days later. Castlereagh's letter to Foster confirmed what Madison thought he already knew: the British orders were "co-durable" with the war. He had, at least, hoped for some escape from the dilemma with France, but Napoleon, too, ran true to form. Madison relayed the sorry news to Jefferson.

Washington May 25. 1812

The inclosed letters came under cover to me, by the Hornet. France has done nothing towards adjusting our differences with her. It is understood that the B[erlin] & M[ilan] Decrees are not in force agst. the U.S. and no contravention of them can be established agst. her. On the contrary positive cases rebut the allegation. Still the manner of the F. Govt. betrays the design of leaving G.B. a pretext for enforcing her O[rders] in C[ouncil] And in all other respects the grounds of our complaints remain the same. The utmost address has been played off on Mr. Barlow's wishes & hopes; inasmuch that at the Departure of the Hornet which had been so long detained for a final answer, without its being obtained, he looked to the return of the Wasp which had just arrived, without despair of making her the Bearer of some satisfactory arrangement. Our calculations differ widely. In the mean time, the business is become more than ever puzzling. To go to war with Engd. and not with France arms the federalists with new matter, and divides the Republicans some of whom with the Quids make a display of impartiality. To go to war agst. both, presents a thousand difficulties; above all that of shutting all the ports of the Continent of Europe agst. our Cruisers who can do little without the use of them. It is pretty certain also, that it would not gain over the Federalists, who wd. turn all those difficulties agst. the Administration. The only consideration of weight in favor of this triangular war as it is called, is that it might hasten thro' a peace with G.B. or F: a termination, for a while at least, of the obstinate questions now depending with both. But even this advantage is not certain. For a prolongation of such a war might be viewed by both Belligts. as desireable with as little reason for the opinion, as has prevailed in the past conduct of both.

It only remained for the President to write his war message. He reviewed the long history of grievance with Britain, not omitting France from the tale, but as before excepting her from the wrath of American justice. Whatever the transgressions of France, they did not strike at the independence of the United States; besides, France could nowhere be attacked on the American continent, so the question of war with her was, in a sense, academic. The message went to Congress on the first day of June.

War Hawks included Richard M. Johnson (top) and Felix Grundy.

[June 1, 1812]

To the Senate and House of Representatives of the United States.

I communicate to Congress certain Documents, being a continuation of those heretofore laid before them, on the subject of our Affairs with Great Britain.

Without going back beyond the renewal in 1803, of the war in which Great Britain is engaged, and omitting unrepaired wrongs of inferior magnitude; the conduct of her Government presents a series of acts, hostile to the United States, as an Independent and neutral nation.

British cruisers have been in the continued practice of violating the American flag on the great high way of nations, and of seizing and carrying off persons sailing under it; not in the exercise of a Belligerent right founded on the Law of Nations against an Enemy; but of a municipal prerogative over British subjects. British jurisdiction is thus extended to neutral vessels in a situation where no laws can operate but the law of nations, and the laws of the Country to which the vessels belong; and a self-redress is assumed...which falls within the definition of War....

The practice, hence, is so far from affecting British subjects alone, that under the pretext of searching for these, thousands of American Citizens, under the safeguard of public law, and of their national flag, have been torn from their country, and from every thing dear to them, have been dragged on board ships of war of a foreign nation; and exposed, under the severities of their discipline, to be exiled to the most distant and deadly climes, to risk their lives in the battles of their oppressors, and to be the melancholy instruments of taking away those of their own brethren.

Against this crying enormity, which Great Britain would be so prompt to avenge if committed against herself, the United States have, in vain, exhausted remonstrances and expostulations. And that no proof might be wanting of their conciliatory dispositions, and no pretext left for a continuance of the practice, the British Government was formally assured of the readiness of the United States to enter into arrangements, such as could not be rejected, if the recovery of British subjects were the real and sole object. The communication passed without effect.

British cruisers have been in the practice also of violating the rights and the peace of our Coasts. They hover over and harass our entering and departing commerce. To the most insulting pretentions, they have added the most lawless proceedings in our very harbors; and have wantonly spilt American blood, within the sanctuary of our territorial jurisdiction. . . .

Under pretended blockades, without the presence of an adequate force, and sometimes without the practicability of applying one, our commerce has been plundered in every Sea; the great staples of our Country have been cut off, from their legitimate markets; and a destructive blow aimed at our agricultural and maritime interests. . . .

Not content with these occasional expedients for laying waste our neutral trade, the cabinet of Great Britain resorted, at length, to the sweeping system of Blockades, under the name of orders in Council; which has been moulded and managed, as might best suit its political views, its commercial jealouses, or the avidity of British cruisers.

To our remonstrances against the complicated and transcendent injustice of this innovation, the first reply was that the orders were reluctantly adopted by Great Britain, as a necessary retaliation on decrees of her Enemy proclaiming a general Blockade of the British Isles, at a time when the naval force of that Enemy dared not to issue from his own ports. She was reminded, without effect, that her own prior blockades, unsupported by an adequate naval force actually applied and continued, were a bar to this plea: that executed Edicts against millions of our property, could not be retaliation on Edicts, confessedly impossible to be executed: that retaliation to be just, should fall on the party setting the guilty example, not on an innocent party, which was not even chargeable with an acquiescence in it.

When deprived of this flimsy veil for a prohibition of our trade with her enemy, by the repeal of his prohibition of our trade with Great Britain; her Cabinet, instead of a corresponding repeal, or a practical discontinuance, of its orders, formally avowed a determination to persist in them against the United States, until the markets of her enemy should be laid open to British products: thus asserting an obligation on a neutral power to require one Belligerent to encourage, by its internal

John C. Calhoun (top) and Henry Clay were also militant patriots.

regulations, the trade of another Belligerent; contradicting her own practice towards all nations, in peace as well as in war. . . .

It has become indeed sufficiently certain, that the commerce of the United States is to be sacrificed, not as interfering with the Belligerent rights of Great Britain; not as supplying the wants of her enemies, which she herself supplies; but as interfering with the monopoly which she covets for her own commerce and navigation. She carries on a war against the lawful commerce of a friend, that she may the better carry on a commerce with an enemy; a commerce polluted by the forgeries and perjuries, which are, for the most part, the only passports by which it can succeed.

Anxious to make every experiment, short of the last resort of injured nations, the United States have witheld from Great Britain, under successive modifications, the benefits of a free intercourse with their market. . . . To these appeals her Government has been equally inflexible; as if willing to make sacrifices of every sort, rather than yield to the claims of justice, or renounce the errors of a false pride. . . .

In reviewing the conduct of Great Britain towards the United States, our attention is necessarily drawn to the warfare just renewed by the Savages, on one of our extensive frontiers; a warfare which is known to spare neither age nor sex, and to be distinguished by features peculiarly shocking to humanity. It is difficult to account for the activity, and combinations, which have for some time been developing themselves among tribes in constant intercourse with British traders and garrisons, without connecting their hostility with that influence; and without recollecting the authenticated examples of such interpositions, heretofore furnished by the officers and agents of that Government.

Such is the spectacle of injuries and indignities which have been heaped on our Country: and such the crisis which its unexampled forbearance and conciliatory efforts have not been able to avert. . . .

. . . We behold our Seafaring Citizens still daily victims of lawless violence committed on the great common and high way of nations, even within sight of the Country which owes them protection. We behold our vessels, freighted with the products of our soil and industry, or

Broadside printed in Philadelphia of the official declaration of war by Congress, approved by the President

Lord Castlereagh

returning with the honest proceeds of them, wrested from their lawful destinations, confiscated by prize Courts, no longer the organs of public law, but the instruments of arbitrary Edicts; and their unfortunate crews dispersed and lost, or forced, or inveigled in British ports, into British fleets: whilst arguments are employed, in support of these aggressions, which have no foundation but in a principle equally supporting a claim, to regulate our external commerce, in all cases whatsoever.

We behold, in fine, on the side of Great Britain a state of War against the United States; and on the side of the United States, a state of peace towards Great Britain.

Whether the United States shall continue passive under these progressive usurpations, and these accumulating wrongs; or, opposing force to force in defence of their national rights, shall commit a just cause into the hands of the almighty disposer of events; avoiding all connections which might entangle it in the contests or views of other powers, and preserving a constant readiness to concur in an honorable reestablishment of peace and friendship, is a solemn question, which the Constitution wisely confides to the Legislative Department of the Government. In recommending it to their early deliberations, I am happy in the assurance, that the decision will be worthy the enlightened and patriotic councils, of a virtuous, a free and a powerful Nation.

The House voted to declare war, 79 to 49, on June 4; the Senate followed, 19 to 13, on June 17. Ironically, on June 23 Britain suspended the orders in council. Fifteen years later, recalling the coming of the war in a letter to Henry Wheaton, Madison indicated that had the *Hornet* brought this news instead of Castlereagh's epistle to Foster, there would have been no war, the rest of the budget of causes in the war message presumably being negotiable.

Montpellier, Feb 26, 1827.

In none of the Comments on the Declaration of the last war has the more immediate impulse to it been sufficiently brought into view. This was the letter from Castlereah to Foster, which, according to the authority given, the latter put into the hands of the Secretary of State, to be read by him, and by the President also. In that letter it was distinctly and emphatically stated that the Orders in Council, to which we had declared we would not submit, would not be repealed, without a repeal of internal measures of France, which, not violating any neutral right of the U. States, they had no right to call on France to repeal, and which, of course, could give to G. Britain no imaginable right against the U.S. With this formal notice, no choice remained but between War and Degradation; a degradation inviting fresh provocations, and rendering war sooner or later inevitable.

It is worthy of particular remark that, notwithstanding the peremptory declaration of the British Cabinet in the letter of Castlereah, such was the distress of the British manufacturers produced by our prohibitory and restrictive laws, as pressed on the House of Commons by Mr. Brougham and others, that the Orders were soon after repealed, but not in time to prevent the effect of the declaration that they would not be repealed. The cause of the war lay, therefore, entirely on the British side. Had the repeal of the Orders been substituted for the declaration that they would not be repealed, or had they been repealed but a few weeks sooner, our declaration of war as proceeding from that cause would have been stayed, and negociations on the subject of impressments, the other great cause, would have been pursued with fresh vigor and hopes, under the auspices of success in the case of the orders in Council.

DECLARATION OF WAR,
BY EXPRESS!!!

A Messenger has just arrived in town from Boston, by express, bearing the important intelligence of a Declaration of War with England. Having been favored with a copy of the Letter from General Dearbon, we hasten to lay the following extract before the Public.
Argus Office, Portland, June 23, 1812,

Head-Quarters—Boston, June 22, 1812.
" Lieut Col Ripley
Sir,
Having received Official information of the Declaration of War, against Great-Britain, you will take every measure in your power for preparation for defence—I have sent an express with this, & wish you to forward this dispatch by an express that can be relied on, to Passamaquoddy—The express will proceed with all possible dispatch, and deliver this letter to the Commanding Officer of the U. S. troops at that place."

HENRY DEARBORN;

Broadside of a message from General Dearborn in Boston alerting Colonel Ripley in Maine to prepare for war

The decision for war resulted fundamentally from the Anglo-American conflict over neutral rights, and whatever may be said of Madison's wisdom in this matter, it is impossible to question his logic or his consistency. The other causes mentioned in the war message were not fundamental. But the conflict over neutral rights was in itself a symbol of much more. It involved the sovereignty and independence and commercial power of the United States against the pretensions of the mother country. It involved the honor of a new nation committed to the ways of peace in a world where force had always been the rule. It involved the ability of a free republican government—the only one on the face of the earth—to defend itself and survive. For Madison, who had been fighting the British lion all his life, the War of 1812 was morally justified as the Second War for American Independence.

A Picture Portfolio

Mr. Madison's War

A CALL TO ARMS

During the first three years of his Presidency, James Madison tried every means at his disposal to avoid the conflict that finally erupted and became known among his opponents as "Mr. Madison's War." But a series of British actions "hostile to the United States" led him in June, 1812, to present a war message to Congress (first and last pages below) citing, among other things, the continuing and intolerable impressment of American seamen, harassment of United States ships "in every Sea," and intrigues to arouse Indians along the western frontier to warfare. Madison knew that, despite the backing of a group of young western congressmen called the War Hawks, there was far from unanimity of opinion on such a war. The country was short of money and the American army was woefully inadequate. Madison at first put his faith in volunteer militiamen, such as the resplendent Philadelphia group shown at right assembling for a muster. But during the grim days in 1814 when the British marched into Washington itself, Madison had the opportunity to view the armies in combat at Bladensburg, Maryland. "I could never have believed," he admitted after seeing the British army make a shambles of his forces, "that so great a difference existed between regular troops and a militia force, if I had not witnessed the scenes of this day."

NATIONAL ARCHIVES

To the Senate and House of Representatives of the United States

I communicate to Congress certain Documents, being a continuation of those heretofore laid before them, on the subject of our affairs with Great Britain

Without going back beyond the renewal in 1803, of the war in which Great Britain is engaged, and omitting unrepaired wrongs of inferior magnitude, the conduct of her Government presents a series of acts, hostile to the United States as an Independent and neutral nation.

British cruisers have been in the continued practice of violating the American flag on the great high way of nations, and of seizing and carrying off persons sailing under it; not in the exercise of a Belligerent right, founded on the Law of Nations against an Enemy, but of a municipal prerogative over British subjects. British jurisdiction is thus extended to neutral vessels, in a situation where no laws can operate but the law of nations, and the laws of the Country to which the vessels

by its privateers and public ships; and that other outrages have been practiced on our vessels and our citizens. It will have been seen also, that no indemnity had been provided, or satisfactorily pledged for the extensive spoliations, committed under the violent and retrospective orders of the French Government against the property of our citizens, seized within the jurisdiction of France. I abstain at this time, from recommending to the consideration of Congress definitive measures with respect to that nation, in the expectation, that the result of unclosed discussions between our Minister Plenipotentiary at Paris and the French Government, will speedily enable Congress to decide, with greater advantage, on the course due to the rights, the interests, and the honor of our Country.

James Madison

Washington June 1st 1812

METROPOLITAN MUSEUM OF ART, ROGERS FUND

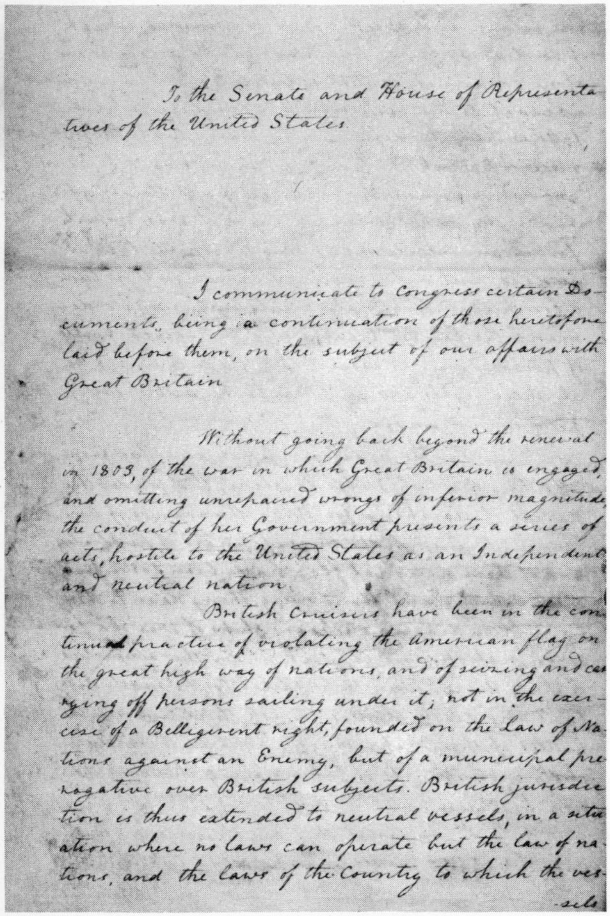

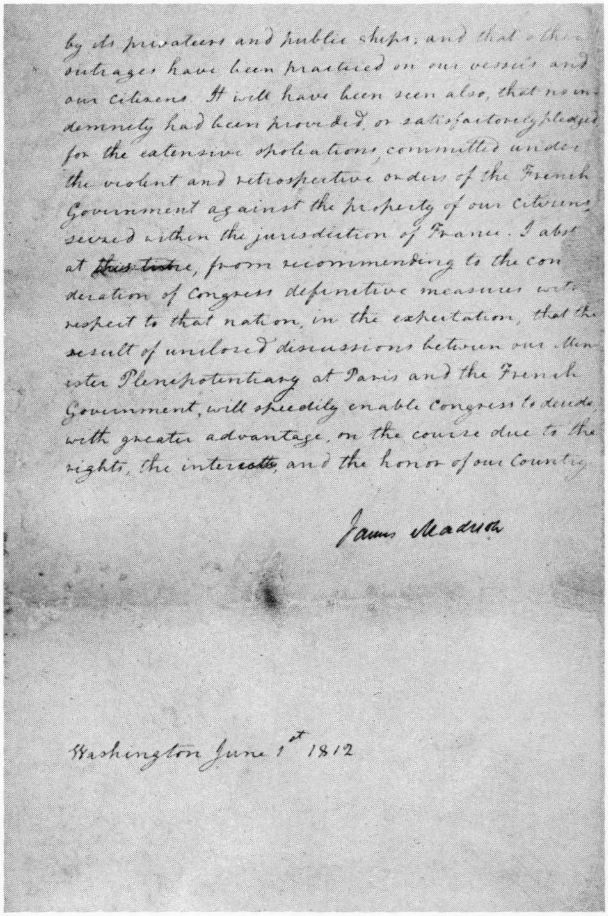

DESPAIR AND HOPE

Exactly three days after aging Brigadier General William Hull (above, left) plunged the country into despair by surrendering Detroit and losing twenty-five hundred American prisoners, his young nephew Isaac Hull (left) scored the war's first naval victory. On August 19, 1812, his frigate

Constitution, in a short and bloody battle, destroyed the *Guerrière* while the young American captain shouted in victory, "By Heaven, that ship is ours!" "Old Ironsides" is seen above firing broadsides after the mizzenmast of the *Guerrière* had snapped. Hull reported proudly: "From the smallest boy in the ship to the oldest seamen not a look of fear was seen."

DATES.	PLACE of ACTION.	VESSELS.	COMMANDERS.	RESULT & REMARKS.
August 19. 1812.	Lat.41 N. Long.55 W.	Constitution. Guerriere.	Isaac Hull. James R. Dacres.	Guerriere. captured after a close action of 10 minutes: completely dismasted, and was burnt.
August 13. 1812.	Banks of Newfoundland.	Essex. Alert.	David Porter. T.L.P. Laugharne.	Alert, captured after 8 minutes firing, and much cut to pieces: sent in and arived at New York.
Oct. 18. 1812.	Lat.37 N. Long.65 W.	Wasp. Frolick.	Jacob Jones. — Wingate.	Frolick captured after a close action of 42 minutes: Re-captured two hours after by the Poictiers of 74 guns.

DATES.	PLACE of ACTION.	VESSELS.	COMMANDERS.	RESULT & REMARKS
Oct. 25. 1812.	Lat.39 N. Long.29 W.	United States. Macedonian.	Stephen Decatur. John Carden.	Macedonian. captured after a spirited action of one hour & a half: sent in & arived at New York.
Decr. 29. 1812.	Lat.13 S. Long.38 W.	Constitution. Java.	Wm. Bainbridge. Henry Lambert.	Java. captured after a very warm engagement of one hour & a half: made a complete wreck & was blownup.

* Commodore Bainbridge commanded the Constitution in the action with the Java.

New Haven March 20th 1813 Published by A.Doolittle Engraver.

DRAMA ON THE HIGH SEAS

Following the success of the *Constitution*, more "Splendid Victories" over the British were won by the infant American navy in the first year of the war. The print above commemorates not only the *Constitution*, but the capture of the frigate *Macedonian* by the *United States* under the young and dashing Commodore Stephen Decatur (above, right) and the capture of the sloop of war *Frolic* by the *Wasp* with Captain Jacob Jones (above, far right) in command. The men of the weak and unprepared American navy, which had only seventeen ships when the war began, displayed nerve and seamanship in daring single-ship combat and stirred their countrymen's pride. Even the defeat of the *Chesapeake* by the *Shannon*, seen in the print opposite as the British swarmed aboard her, became a lasting inspiration when her mortally wounded captain, James Lawrence (right), commanded as he was carried below: "Don't give up the ship. Fight her till she sinks."

☞ Most Glorious News!

Sept. 21, 1813.

Copy of a letter from Com. PERRY to the Secretary of the Navy

U.S. Brig Niagara, off the Western Sister, Head of Lake Erie, Sept. 10, 1813, 4 P. M.

SIR—It has pleased the Almighty to give to the arms of the U. States a signal victory over their enemies on this Lake. The British squadron, consisting of two Ships, two Brigs, one Schooner and one Sloop, have this moment surrendered to the force under my command, after a sharp conflict.—I have the honor to be, sir, very respectfully, your obt servant,

O H PERRY.

Hon. Wm. Jones, Secretary of the Navy.

SOME PARTICULARS.

Chilicothe, September 14.

Last evening an express arrived in town from General Harrison's head quarters, bringing the highly gratifying intelligence of the capture of

the whole of the British fleet on Lake Erie by commodore Perry. The subjoined extracts of letters from two gentlemen at head quarters, contain the most essential particulars relative to that brilliant affair.

Camp Seneca, Sept. 12.

"An express has this moment arrived from Commodore Perry, dated the 10th inst. at 4 P. M. Head of Lake Erie, with the pleasing intelligence of the British fleet, consisting of two ships, two brigs and two schooners, being in our possession, with more prisoners on board than we had men to conquer them. A great many were killed on both sides."

Camp Seneca, Sept. 12.

"Victory perches on our Naval Standard! Commodore Perry has captured nearly if not all the enemy's fleet; two ships, two brigs, one sloop, and one schooner; and taken more prisoners than he had men on board."

War of 1812. LOSSING

SECURING THE NORTHWEST

The first fleet action of the War of 1812 was fought far from the ocean on Lake Erie, where in record time nine ships had been built to try to wrest control of that important lake from the British. Under the command of twenty-eight-year-old Commodore Oliver Hazard Perry—whose flagship was named the *Lawrence* and whose flag bore Lawrence's dying words—the small American fleet defeated an entire British squadron, even though Perry was forced to abandon the *Lawrence* and transfer to the *Niagara* in a rowboat in mid-battle (left). His report to the Secretary of the Navy was issued as a broadside on September 21, 1813, headlined "Most Glorious News!" (left, center). To General William Henry Harrison (left, bottom) he wrote: "We have met the enemy and they are ours," and he then transported Harrison's army to its rendezvous with British General Henry Proctor at Moraviantown on the Thames River in Ontario. Here the Americans won one of their few land victories over the British and their Indian allies (below).

Huzza for our Navy!

Another 15 minutes Job.

Being the 8th Naval Victory in which John Bull has been obliged to douce his flag, to the invincible skill of *American Tars.*

CHARLESTON, SUNDY MORNING, SEPT. 19th, 1813.

We have the satisfaction of announcing to the public that the United States sloop of war ARGUS is in the offing, with the British sloop of war BARBADOES her prize in company, taken after a desperate engagement of 15 minutes, carried by boarding.

Capt. Allen, of the Argus, has just come up, and we have conversed with a midshipman who states that she was taken off Halifax, but it was deemed expedient to proceed to this place for the purpose of escaping the British blockading squadrons. He also states that the captain, R. P. Davies, of the Barbadoes was killed, and the vessel was commanded the most part of the action by the 1st Lieut. Savage.

British loss, 97 killed and wounded. American loss, 12 killed and wounded. The Argus rates 16 and carries 20 guns, the Barbadoes rates 28 and carries 32 guns. She had previously captured, Aug. 22, the James Madison of 14 guns.

☞ This is the second Engagement in which Captain ALLEN has signalised himself, as he was 1st Lieut. of the U. States, was in the Engagement with the Macedonian, took Command of her and brought her into port.

Published 10 o'lc Sunday 26th September 1813.

A BOXING MATCH, or, Another Bloody Nose for JOHN BULL.

"HUZZA FOR OUR NAVY!"

Naval victories abounded. The cartoon at left of a boxing match between King George III and President Madison was a play on the name of the British brig *Boxer* which had been captured by the American *Enterprize* in September, 1813. In the same month a broadside (left, above) was issued to celebrate the "8th Naval Victory" for the "American Tars"—the *Argus* over the British *Barbadoes*. But it was not until a year later that one of the most decisive naval actions of the war was fought, once again on a lake and once again between an American and a British fleet. The British plan was to invade from Canada along Lake Champlain with a large and well-trained army of veterans supported by their entire Lake Champlain fleet. Their defeat on September 11, 1814, by the American fleet under the command of Commodore Thomas McDonough near Plattsburg (above), aided by land forces under General Alexander Macomb, ended the threat of a northern invasion once and for all.

313

WASHINGTON AFLAME

While the British were still preparing their invasion in the North, attention was diverted by the landing of British troops on the Maryland shore in August, 1814. After defeating the inept Americans at Bladensburg, General Robert Ross and "that undaunted seaman" Rear Admiral George Cockburn (left) marched into Washington. "You may thank old Madison for this," Cockburn said to some citizens en route; "it is he who has got you into this scrape." The British then set fire to every public building in the capital (below), except the Patent Office. Meanwhile, intrepid Dolley Madison, who had spent an anxious day "turning my spy glass in every direction," fled the White House, having first assured the safety of the Stuart portrait of George Washington (right).

"THE STAR-SPANGLED BANNER"

Flushed with their easy success in Washington, the British forces next eyed Baltimore, the third largest city in the United States. It was protected on the water side by Fort McHenry, whose commander Major George Armistead had ordered its huge flag (above, right) to be made "so large that the British will have no difficulty seeing it at a distance." The night assault beginning on September 13 lasted for twenty-five hours, as the Royal Navy poured bombs, shells, and rockets on the fort (above). Far out in the harbor on a flag-of-truce boat, a young American lawyer and occasional poet named Francis Scott Key stood on deck and watched. He anxiously awaited the dawn to see if Fort McHenry had withstood the withering attack. Greatly moved to see the flag still "gallantly streaming," Key wrote the words (right) that stirred the hearts of Americans overnight and later became the national anthem.

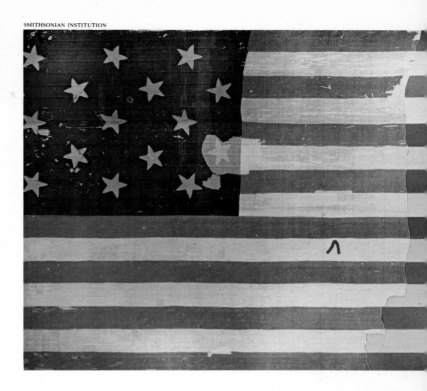

O say can you see, through by the dawn's early light,
What so proudly we hail'd at the twilight's last gleaming,
Whose broad stripes & bright stars, through the perilous fight,
O'er the ramparts we watch'd, were so gallantly streaming?
And the rocket's red glare, the bomb bursting in air,
Gave proof through the night that our flag was still there,
O say does that star spangled banner yet wave
O'er the land of the free & the home of the brave?

On the shore dimly seen through the mists of the deep,
Where the foe's haughty host in dread silence reposes,
What is that which the breeze, o'er the towering steep,
As it fitfully blows, half conceals, half discloses?
Now it catches the gleam of the morning's first beam,
In full glory reflected now shines in the stream,
'Tis the star-spangled banner — O long may it wave
O'er the land of the free & the home of the brave!

And where is that band who so vauntingly swore,
That the havoc of war & the battle's confusion
A home & a Country should leave us no more?
Their blood has wash'd out their foul footsteps' pollution.
No refuge could save the hireling & slave
From the terror of flight or the gloom of the grave,
And the star-spangled banner in triumph doth wave
O'er the land of the free & the home of the brave.

O thus be it ever when freemen shall stand
Between their lov'd home & the war's desolation;
Blest with vict'ry & peace may the heav'n rescued land
Praise the power that hath made & preserv'd us a nation!
Then conquer we must, when our cause it is just,
And this be our motto — "In God is our trust"
And the star-spangled banner in triumph shall wave
O'er the land of the free & the home of the brave. —

317

ONE-SIDED VICTORY

Unaware that a peace treaty had been signed on Christmas Eve, the British attacked the American forces under General Andrew Jackson at New Orleans on January 8, 1815. Entrenched behind a wall of earth, the Americans mowed down the arrogant redcoats (above), killing or wounding twenty-six hundred to their own loss of fifty-two—an incredible, one-sided victory.

DISSENSION AND PEACE

In November, 1814, Madison had written to Governor Wilson Cary Nicholas of Virginia that he was "not mistaken in viewing the conduct of the Eastern States as the source of our greatest difficulties in carrying on the war...." That December, a group of New England Federalists actually met in convention at Hartford, Connecticut, to draft proposals for amendments to the Constitution that would challenge what they termed Madison's military despotism and force him to resign. In the cartoon below, George III is shown trying to lure Massachusetts, Connecticut, and Rhode Island back into the British fold. But when the delegation from Hartford arrived in Washington, the Treaty of Ghent had already been signed and endorsed by Madison with the old seal of the United States (right) and news of Jackson's victory at New Orleans had reached the excited capital. "Their position," according to a French diplomat, "was awkward, embarrassing, and lent itself to cruel ridicule," and they quickly withdrew. Madison completed his term and retired in triumph to Montpelier in 1817. A government official going through the State Department papers at that time, so many of which had been drawn by Madison, remarked admiringly: "What history, what anecdote, what genius, what industry!"

To all and singular to whom these presents shall come, greeting:

Be it known, That I, James Madison, president of the United States of America, having seen and considered the within treaty, do, by and with the advice and consent of the Senate thereof, accept, ratify, and confirm, the same, and every clause and article thereof.

In testimony whereof I have caused the seal of the said United States to be hereunto affixed, and signed the same with my hand.

Done at the city of Washington, this seventeenth day of February, in the year of our Lord one thousand eight hundred and fifteen, and of the sovereignty and independence of the United States the thirty-ninth.

James Madison

Chapter 9

Second War for Independence

An accounting of American assets and liabilities as the War of 1812 began would include, on one side, command of the principal theater of operations, the enemy's preoccupation with the war in Europe, and superiority of available manpower and resources; on the other side was a feeble war machine, widespread public apathy and outright opposition in one quarter of the Union, and a government that possessed neither the organization nor the leadership to conduct war. The navy boasted seventeen oceangoing ships against a potential armada of seven hundred. The regular army, then well below its authorized peacetime strength of ten thousand, was to be raised to thirty-five thousand, but only five thousand had been recruited by June. Any additional muscle must come from volunteers and militia. To raise such an army, equip it, and officer it would take many months. Madison had asked Congress for a smaller elite force, one that could be brought into the field instantly to exploit the American advantage of choosing the time of hostilities. The army he got could not be mobilized for the first strike. The War Department consisted of the Secretary and eight clerks; commissary and quartermaster services scarcely existed; and officers to command the army were either tired Revolutionary War veterans or young men inexperienced in combat.

The American target was Canada. Taking it would be, said Jefferson in a flight of fancy, "a mere matter of marching." Some enthusiasts looked upon the acquisition of Upper Canada, from Lake Huron to the St. Lawrence, as the great aim of the war. But for the administration the attack on Canada was a means of waging war declared for maritime objectives, and it was to be a hostage for securing those objectives. The strategy of the first summer's campaign called for a three-pronged invasion of Canada. In the east, General Henry Dearborn was to advance along Lake Champlain for an assault on Montreal. In the center, General Stephen van Rensselaer was to attack across the Niagara River in western New York. And in the west, General William Hull at Detroit was to cut British lines to their Indian allies, capture Fort Malden and other posts across the Detroit River, and wrest control of Lake Erie from the enemy.

The campaign ended in crushing defeat. Poor generalship and the unreliability of state militia contributed to the collapse on all fronts. Dearborn, in particular, was hampered by hostility to the war in the eastern states. Both Massachusetts and Connecticut refused the President's orders to furnish militia for the Montreal campaign. Madison temporized with them rather than risk open rebellion. But the crucial defeat was the first one, in the west, in August. General Hull with a vastly superior force surrendered Detroit without firing a shot. Madison recalled the disaster at Detroit and spoke to the often repeated charge of the nation's unpreparedness for war in his 1827 letter to Henry Wheaton, a distinguished jurist.

General van Rensselaer established a toehold on Queenston Heights in Canada, but his army was dislodged by the British who crossed the Niagara River to retake the position.

Montpellier, Feby. 26, 1827.

But the war was commenced without due preparation: this is another charge. Preparations in all such cases are comparative. The question to be decided is, whether the adversary was better prepared than we were; whether delay on our side, after the approach of war would be foreseen on the other, would have made the comparative preparations better for us. As the main theatre of the war was to be in our neighbourhood, and the augmented preparations of the enemy were to be beyond the Atlantic, promptitude of attack was the evident policy of the U.S. It was in fact not the suddenness of the war as an Executive policy, but the tardiness of the Legislative provisions, which gave whatever colour existed for the charge in question. The recommendation of Military preparations went from the Executive on the fifth day of November, and so impressed was that Department of the Government with the advantage of despach in the measures to be adopted by Congress, that the recommendation was known to contemplate a force, of a kind & extent which it was presumed might be made ready within the requisite period. Unfortunately this consideration had not its desired effect on the proceedings in Congress. The Laws passed on the subject were delayed, that for filling up the peace establishment until the twenty-fourth of December, and that for the new Army to be raised, until the fourteenth of January: and such were the extent & conditions prescribed for the latter, that it could scarcely, under any circumstances, and by no possibility under those existing, be forthcoming within the critical season....

Yet, with all the disadvantages under which hostilities were commenced, their progress would have been very different, under a proper conduct of the initiative expedition into Upper Canada. The individual at the head of it [Hull] had been pointed out for the service by very obvious considerations. He had acquired during the Revolutionary War the reputation of a brave & valuable officer. He was of course an experienced one. He had been long the Chief Magistrate in the quarter contiguous to the theatre of his projected operations, with the best opportunities of being acquainted with the population & localities on the hostile as well as his own side of the dividing straight. He had also been the Superintendent of our Affairs with the Indian Tribes holding intercourse with that district of Country, a trust which afforded him all the ordinary means of understanding, conciliating, and managing their dispositions. With such qualifications and advantages which seemed to give him a claim above all others to the station assigned to him, he sunk before obstacles at which not an officer near him would have paused, and threw away an entire army, in the moment of entering a career which would have made the war as prosperous in its early stages, and as promising in its subsequent course, as it was rendered by that disaster, oppressive to our resources, and flattering to the hopes of the Enemy. By the surrender of Gen. Hull, the people of Canada, not indisposed to favour us, were turned against us; the Indians were thrown into the service of the Enemy; the expence & delay of a new armament

The bad news of Hull's defeat at Detroit is trumpeted to Madison in this British cartoon by Cruikshank.

Surrender by General William Hull

were incurred, the Western Militia & volunteers were witheld from offensive co-operation with the troops elsewhere, by the necessity of defending their own frontiers & families against incursions of the Savages; and a general damp spread over the face of our Affairs. What a contrast would the success so easy at the outset of the war have presented? A triumphant army would have seized on Upper Canada, and hastened to join the armies at the points below; the important command of Lake Erie would have fallen to us of course; the Indians would have been neutral or submissive to our will; the general spirit of the Country would have been kindled into enthusiasm; enlistments would have been accelerated, volunteers would have stepped forward with redoubled confidence & alacrity; the Militia would have felt a like animation; and what is not of small moment, the intrigues of the disaffected would have been smothered in their embryo State.

Writing to Jefferson before learning of General Hull's defeat at Detroit in August, 1812, Madison touched on the frustrations and difficulties of the early months of the war.

Washington Aug. 17. 1812

The seditious opposition in Mass. & Cont. with the intrigues elsewhere insidiously co-operating with it, have so clogged the wheels of the war, that I fear the campaign will not accomplish the object of it. With the most united efforts in stimulating volunteers, they would have probably fallen much short of the number required by the deficiency of regular enlistments. But under the discouragements substituted, and the little attraction contained in the volunteer act, the two classes together, leave us dependent, for every primary operation, on Militia, either as volunteers or draughts for six months. We are nevertheless doing as well as we can, in securing the maritime frontier, and in providing for an effective penetration into upper Canada. It would probably have been best if it had been practicable in time, to have concentrated a force which could have seized on Montreal & thus at one stroke, have secured the upper Province, and cut off the sap that nourished Indian hostilities. But this could not be attempted, without sacrificing the Western & N. W. Frontier, threated with an

A PROCLAMATION

BY THE

PRESIDENT OF THE UNITED STATES.

WHEREAS, information has been received that a number of individuals, who have deserted from the Army of the United States, have become sensible of their offence, and are desirous of returning to their duty....

A full pardon is hereby granted and proclaimed to each and all such individuals as shall, within four months from the date hereof, surrender themselves to the Commanding Officer of any Military Post within the United States, or the territories thereof.

IN TESTIMONY WHEREOF, I have caused the seal of the United States to be affixed to these presents, and signed the same with my hand.

DONE at the City of Washington, the 7th day of February, in the year of our Lord, one thousand eight hundred and twelve, and of the Independence of the United States, the thirty-sixth.

JAMES MADISON.

By the President,

JAMES MONROE,
Secretary of State.

Proclamation by President Madison granting pardon to deserters from army who surrendered themselves

War of 1812, LOSSING

Fort Mackinac (or Michilimachinac)

inundation of savages under the influence of the British establishment near Detroit. Another reason for the expedition of Hull was that the unanimity and ardor of Kentucky & Ohio, provided the requisite force at once for that service, whilst it was too distant from the other points to be assailed. We just learn, but from what cause remains to be known, that the important fort at Machilimackinac [on Mackinac Island in the straits joining lakes Huron, Michigan, and Superior] has fallen into the hands of the Enemy. If the re-enforcement of about 200 ordered from the Ohio, and on the way to Hull, should not enable him to take Malden, and awe the Savages emboldened by the British success, his situation will be very ineligible....

We have no information from England since the war was known there, or even, seriously suspected, by the public. I think it not improbable that the sudden change in relation to the Orders in Council, first in yielding to a qualified suspension, & then a repeal, was the effect of apprehensions in the Cabinet that the deliberations of Congs. would have that issue, and that the Ministry could not stand agst. the popular torrent agst. the Orders in Council, swelled as it would be by the addition of a war with the U.S. to the pressure of the non-importation Act. What course will be taken, when the declaration here, shall be known, is uncertain, both in reference to the American shipments instituted under the repeal of the Orders, and to the question between vindictive efforts for pushing the war agst. us, and early advances for terminating it. A very informal, & as it has turned out erronious communication of the intended change in the Orders, was hurried over, evidently with a view to prevent a declaration of war, if it should arrive in time. And the communication was accompanied by a proposal from the local authorities at Halifax sanctioned by Foster, to suspend hostilities both at sea & on land.... The insuperable objections to a concurrence of the Executive in the project are obvious.... As we do not apprehend invasion by land, and preparations on each side were to be unrestrained, nothing could be gained by us, whilst arrangements & re-enforcements adverse to Hull, might be decisive; and, on every supposition, the Indians wd. continue to be active agst. our frontiers, the more so in consequence of the fall of Machilimackinac. Nothing but triumphant operations on the Theatre which forms their connection with the Enemy, will controul their bloody inroads.

Indian chiefs had been beating a path to the national capital since Washington's time. Two delegations—forty chiefs in all—arrived opportunely in August, 1812. One of Sac, Fox, Osage, and other Missouri tribes had been sent by General William Clark; the other was of Sioux tribes from farther north. Both were dinner guests of the President, and of course they provided a colorful spectacle for the entire city. One enthralled spectator called their powwow at Greenleaf's Point "the most magnificent, imposing native human pagentry" ever seen outside the wilds. It was customary for the Great White Father to address visiting chiefs, and for this purpose a stylized rhetoric, naive and rich in metaphor, had long existed. Madison repeated the usual admonitions of peace, but also tried to explain the war to the Indians and wean them from the British.

Washington [August,] 1812

My red children,

You have come thro' a long path to see your father, but it is a straight and a clean path, kept open for my red children, who hate crooked walks. I thank the great spirit that he has brought you in health through the long journey; and that he gives us a clear sky & bright sun, for our meeting. I had heard from General Clarke of the good dispositions of several of the nations on & West of the Mississippi: and that they shut their ears to the bad birds hovering about them for sometime past. This made me wish to see the principal chiefs of those bands. I love to shake hands with hearts in them.

The red people who live on the same great Island with the White people of the 18 fires [the eighteen states], are made by the great spirit out of the same earth, from parts of it differing in colour only. My regard for all my red children, has made me desirous that the bloody tomahawk should be buried between the Osages, the Cherokees, & the Choctaws. I wish also that the hands of the Shawenee, & the Osage, should be joined in my presence, as a pledge to cherish & observe the peace made at St. Louis. This was a good peace for both. It is a chain that ought to hold them fast in friendship. Neither blood nor rust should ever be upon it....

A father ought to give good advice to his children, and it is the duty of his children to harken to it. The

Additional Instruction to the public and private armed vessels of the United States.

THE public and private armed vessels of the United States are not to interrupt any vessels belonging to citizens of the United States coming from British ports to the United States laden with British merchandize, in consequence of the alledged repeal of the British Orders in Council, but are on the contrary to give aid and assistance to the same; in order that such vessels and their cargoes may be dealt with on their arrival as may be decided by the competent authorities.

By command of the President of the United States of America,

Ja. Monroe   *Secretary of State.*

WASHINGTON CITY, AUGUST 28, 1812.

A broadside signed by James Monroe, Secretary of State, after repeal of the British orders in council

people composing the 18 fires, are a great people. You have travelled thro' their Country; you see they cover the land, as the stars fill the sky, and are thick as the Trees in your forests. Notwithstanding their great power, the British King has attacked them on the great water beyond which he lives. He robbed their ships, and carried away the people belonging to them. Some of them he murdered. He has an old grudge against the 18 fires, because when he tried to make them dig and plant for his people beyond the great water, not for themselves, they sent out warriors who beat his warriors, they drove off the bad chiefs he had sent among them, and set up good chiefs of their own. The 18 fires did this when they had not the strength they now have. Their blows will now be much heavier, and will soon make him do them justice. It happened when the 13 fires, now increased to 18, forced the British King, to treat them as an independent nation, one little fire [Canada] did not join them. This he has held ever since. It is there that his Agents and traders plot quarrels and wars between the 18 fires and their red brethren, and between one red tribe and another. Malden is the place where all the bad birds have their nests. There they are fed with false tales agst. the 18 fires, and sent out with bloody belts in their bills, to drop among the red people, who would otherwise remain at peace. It is for the good of all the red people, as well as the people of the 18 fires, that a stop should be put to this mischief. Their warriors can do it. They are gone & going to Canada for this purpose. They want no help from their red brethren. They are strong enough without it. The British, who are weak, are doing all they can by their bad birds, to decoy the red people into the war on their side. I warn all the red people to avoid the ruin this must bring upon them. And I say to you my children, your father does not ask you to join his warriors. Sit still on your seats: and be witnesses that they are able to beat their enemies and protect their red friends. This is the fatherly advice I give you.

I have a further advice for my red children. You see how the Country of the 18 fires is filled with people. They increase like the corn they put into the ground. They all have good houses to shelter them from all weathers, good clothes suitable' to all seasons: and as

FORT MALDEN NATIONAL HISTORIC PARK, ONTARIO

Fort Malden remained in British hands until October, 1813.

War of 1812, LOSSING

Victories such as that of the Wasp *over the* Frolic *(above) led to an expansion of the navy; its successes helped Madison win reelection.*

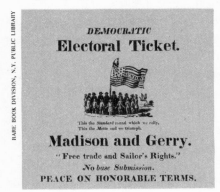

for food of all sorts, you see they have enough & to spare. No man woman or child of the 18 fires ever perished of hunger. Compare all this with the condition of the red people. They are scattered here & there in handfuls. Their lodges are cold, leaky, and smokey. They have hard fare, and often not eno' of it. Why this mighty difference? The reason, my red children, is plain. The white people breed cattle and sheep. They plow the earth and make it give them every thing they want. They spin and weave. Their heads and their hands make all the elements & the productions of nature useful to them. Above all; the people of the 18 fires live in constant peace & friendship. No Tomahawk has ever been raised by one agst. another. Not a drop of blood has ever touched the Chain that holds them together as one family. All their belts are white belts. It is in your power to be like them. The Ground that feeds one, by hunting, would feed a great band, by the plow and the hoe. The great spirit has given you, like your white brethren, good heads to contrive: strong arms, and active bodies. Use them like your white brethren; not all at once, which is difficult, but by little & little, which is easy. Especially live in peace with one another, like your white brethren of the 18 fires: and like them, your little sparks will grow into great fires.

Madison learned of Hull's ignominious surrender on the road to Montpelier. He turned around and, back in the capital, called an emergency meeting of the Cabinet. It was decided to retake Detroit, under a commander with blood in his veins, and also to build a naval force on Lake Erie. After all, 1812 was an election year. Victory somewhere would help revive flagging confidence in the administration and make the war popular. The West, where it was already popular, offered the best hope. But for the next several months Madison would hear of nothing but failure and defeat on land. The infant navy, on the other hand, scored impressive victories, beginning with the *Constitution*'s capture of the *Guerrière* in August. The President, who had shared the Republican prejudice against the navy, became its ardent champion.

The election of 1812 turned on the issue of war or peace. DeWitt Clinton was the candidate of the "peace party." In addition to being the leader of the New York Republicans, some of whom opposed the war and had long been at odds with the Republican leadership in Washington, Clinton was also taken up by the Federalists. An opposition broadside stated the issue.

Madison & War!
or,
Clinton and Peace.

Arise! ye Patriot Spirits! rise!
   The all-important hour's at hand
When, by your Votes, you must decide
   If War shall longer scourge our land! ...
Do you hate War — vote *not* for him
   Who's plung'd you *unprepar'd* in War, —
A War which was, no doubt, designed
   To lash you fast to Bona[parte]'s *Car!*
Think, think, upon those *blissful days*
   When Commerce spread her flowing sails,
And wafted to our *then* bless'd shore
   The choicest fruits of India's vales!
'Twas then the *"Golden Age"* of Peace, —
   The age when Patriots reign'd —
When Washington stood at the helm,
   And *Democratic power restrain'd!*

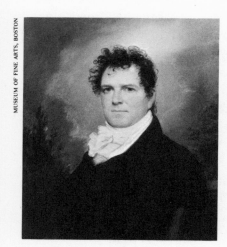

DeWitt Clinton by John W. Jarvis

The electoral vote, 128 to 89, gave Madison a clear-cut victory. But Clinton won three of the five New England states, plus New York, New Jersey, and Delaware; and the Federalists doubled their numbers in Congress. Persistent opposition to the war divided the country against itself and encouraged the enemy to exploit New England disaffection and thus draw that region into "common interest" with Old England. Trade was the bait. Early in the new year Britain threw a blockade around Delaware Bay and Chesapeake Bay. In May it was extended to the mouth of the Mississippi and some months later easterly to Long Island Sound. But New England ports were open until near the end of the war. Yankee merchants reaped handsome profits either in the disguise of neutrals or in trading with the enemy. To supply her colonies Britain issued special licenses for American imports, confined, however, to those from New England ports. Outraged by this "insidious discrimination," Madison sent a special message to Congress.

February 24th 1813
The policy [of Great Britain] now proclaimed to the world, introduces into her modes of warfare, a system equally distinguished by the deformity of its features, and the depravity of its character; having for its object to dissolve the ties of allegiance and the sentiments of loyalty in the adversary nation, and to seduce and

seperate its componant parts, the one from the other.

The general tendency of these demoralizing and disorganizing contrivances, will be reprobated by the civilized and Christian world; and the insulting attempt on the virtue, the honor, the patriotism, and the fidelity of our brethren of the Eastern States, will not fail to call forth all their indignation and resentment; and to attach more and more all the States, to that happy union and constitution, against which such insidious and malignant artifices are directed.

The better to guard, nevertheless, against the effect of individual cupidity and treachery, and to turn the corrupt projects of the Enemy against himself, I recommend to the consideration of Congress, the expediency of an effectual prohibition of any trade whatever, by Citizens or inhabitants of the United States, under special licences, whether relating to persons or ports; and in aid thereof a prohibition of all exportations from the United States in foreign bottoms; few of which are actually employed; whilst multiplying counterfeits of their flags and papers are covering and encouraging the navigation of the Enemy.

Brown's Indian Queen Hotel, site of Madison's second inaugural ball

A bill based on President Madison's recommendation passed the House but failed in the Senate. His call for a full-fledged embargo met the same fate in July. Finally, in December, Congress legislated the embargo and stiffened the nonimportation law. Whether in war or in peace Madison believed the British vulnerable to American commercial coercion. The embargo completed the alienation of affections in New England. But the President coolly let sedition run its course, fully confident that the good sense and republicanism of the mass of citizens would eventually assert itself. A letter to Federalist David Humphreys, the Connecticut manufacturer of Madison's suit of homespun, shows his forbearance.

Washington Mar. 23. 1813

Altho' it is neither usual, nor often eligible, to enter into political explanations on such an occasion, as the present, I am induced by the frank & friendly tenor of your remarks, to express (under the reserves which you will infer) my regret that you should be able to cite a prevailing opinion that "an alliance with France, and a systematic exclusion of Commerce" were within the views of the Administration.

To say nothing of the extreme improbability of such a

David Humphreys

policy on the first point, it is not easy to conceive a more formal disavowal, of it, than has been repeatedly made & published both by my predecessor & myself, particularly in the Messages relating to the war, which emphatically impugn political alliances or connections with any foreign power. In full conformity with these disavowals, is the letter from Mr. Barlow to Mr. Monroe lately published, from which it must be necessarily inferred that he was forbidden to enter into any arrangements with France beyond the subjects of indemnity & commerce. With such strong presumptions & decisive proofs before the public, it is impossible that a purpose in this Government of allying itself with that of France, can be seriously believed by any intelligent individual not in a temper to reject a Witness even from the dead. [Barlow had died.]

As to a systematic exclusion of commerce, a belief of it, is still more incomprehensible. Temporary abridgments or suspensions of it, must have for their object, its permanent freedom, as interruptions of peace, have for their object, a re-establishment of peace on improved foundations. In such a light only can the restrictive measures applied to our commerce be rationally viewed. The avowed object of them, in fact, was to liberate our commerce from restrictions equally obnoxious to all parties. Whether the means were well applied or not, may be made a question. The object itself never can.…

Viewing the topics which have so much agitated the public mind, in the light here presented, I have never allowed myself to believe that the Union was in danger, or that a dissolution of it could be desired, unless by a few individuals, if such there be, in desperate situations or of unbridled passions. In addition to the thousand affinities belonging to every part of the Nation, every part has an interest as deep as it is obvious, in maintaining the bond which keeps the whole together; and the Eastern part certainly not less than any other. Looking to the immediate & *commercial* effect of a dissolution, it is clear that the Eastern part would be the greatest loser, by such an event; and not likely therefore deliberately to rush into it; especially when it takes into view the groundlessness of the suspicions which alone could suggest so dreadful an alternative; and the turn which would probably grow out of it, to the relations with Europe. The great road of profitable intercourse for New England, even with Old England, lies through the Wheat, the Cotton & the Tobacco fields of her Southern & Western confederates. On what basis cd. N. E. & O. E. form commercial stipulations, on all the great articles, they would be in direct rivalship. The real source of our revolution was the commercial jealousy of G.B. towards that part of her then Colonies. If there be links of common interest between the two Countries, they wd. connect the S. & not the N. States, with that part of Europe.

The President's second inaugural address had underscored the administration's efforts to arrange a negotiated peace. "The sword was scarcely out of the scabbard," he had said, "before the enemy was apprized of the reasonable terms on which it would be resheathed." These terms included the abandonment of impressment, the protection of neutral commerce from illegal blockades and seizures, and indemnification for maritime losses. Britain spurned the overture. However, Emperor Alexander of Russia, hard pressed by Napoleon's armies, offered to mediate the Anglo-American war. Alexander's Armageddon was at hand, and he hoped to free Britain from the sideshow in America for the main event in Europe. By the time Madison learned of the emperor's offer, in March, 1813, the main event had occurred and Napoleon was in retreat from Russia. Madison promptly communicated the news to Jefferson.

Washington Mar. 10. 1813

CULVER PICTURES, INC.

Emperor Alexander I of Russia

If you do not receive the N.Y. Mercantile advertiser, the inclosed will give you the Russian acct. of the Catastrophe of the French Army. It is doubtless much exaggerated; but there is no doubt that the losses are beyond example. Whether they can be replaced so as to prevent the defection of allies, and to present another formidible countenance to the North, is uncertain. It does not appear that any thing like despondence is felt in Paris, and so many interests on the Continent have become associated with the ascendancy of Napoleon, that it will not be surprizing if with the terrors of his name, he should surmount his difficulties. In England the usual exultation is indulged, on the recent events: and united with the rage & jealousy produced by our little naval triumphs, account for the gigantic force she is bringing agst. us on the water. In the mean time Russia as you will observe is tendering her mediatory friendship; with the collateral view there is reason to believe, of deriving advantage from our neutral interference with British monopoly in the trade with her.

We shall endeavor to turn the good will of Russia to the proper acct. Whether England will accede to the mediation, or do so with evasive purposes remains to be seen.

Madison nominated two peace commissioners, Albert Gallatin and James A. Bayard, a Delaware Federalist, and dispatched them at once to St. Petersburg. They arrived there in July, just as Madison learned of Castlereagh's rebuff of Russian mediation. The Senate, meanwhile, turned down Gallatin because Madison declined to consider the Treasury office vacant. The obstructionism of the Senate had become chronic, but the rejection of Gallatin was more than an ordinary defeat. It stabbed at the President himself. He was, in fact, gravely ill at the time. Dolley wrote to Mrs. Gallatin via John Jacob Astor.

[Washington,] 29th. July [18]13

I cannot allow Mr Astor to leave us without his bearing a few lines, from me, to you, my beloved friend: You to whom my heart has often addressed itself, since our seperation and constantly sympathised with, on the subject of our dear Voyagers. You have heard no doubt, of the illness of my Husband but can have no idea of its extent, and the dispair, in which I attended his bed for nearly five weeks! Even now, I watch over him, as I would an infant, so precarious is his convalessence. Added to this, the disappointments & vexations, heaped upon him by party spirit. Nothing however has borne so hard, as the conduct of the Senate in regard to Mr Gallatin. Mr A will tell you many particulars, that *I aught not* to *write*, of the desertion of some whose support we had a right to expect; & of the *maneauvering* of others, allways hostile to superior merit. We console ourselves with the hope of its terminating both in the Public good, and Mr. Gallatins honorable triumph.

Just before setting out for Montpelier to recuperate from his illness, Madison reported to Gallatin on the Senate proceedings.

Washington, Aug 2, 1813

You will learn from the Secy. of State the painful manner in which the Senate have mutilated the Mission to St Petersburg. But the course & circumstances of the proceeding require more of explanation than may fall within his scope, and more indeed, than can well be conveyed on paper.

Albert Gallatin (above) and James A. Bayard (below) were sent to St. Petersburg as peace commissioners.

Previously to sending in the nomination of the Envoys, there was no indication, that, if the popularity of the object did not prevent opposition, it would extend beyond a portion of the Senate essentially short of a majority. And there is reason to believe that if a preliminary attempt to embarrass the subject had been decided on at the proper time, and before out-door means could be interposed, the desired & expected result would have been secured. Liberality however yielded to an adjournment of the question, and the opportunity afforded by it was industriously improved. The first step was, after formally ascertaining the arrangement under which you were included in the Mission, to obtain a vote declaring an incompatibility (without specifying whether Constitutional or otherwise) between the domestic & diplomatic appts. The tendency of this proposition to comprehend as many and to commit as much as possible, is obvious. It would seem notwithstanding that the vote of incompatibility was concurred in by some who regarded it not as an obstacle to an ultimate concurrence in the nomination, but rather as a protest throwing the whole responsibility upon the Executive. The next step was to communicate this opinion of the Senate to me, with a view either to extort a compliance, or to unite against the nomination all, or as many as possible, who had concurred in the vote of incompatibility. In this stage of the business it was the confident opinion of the supporters of the nomination that inflexibility on the part of the Ex would ensure a majority for it and their unanimous & urgent advice as well on general grounds, as on that particular calculation, not to yield to the irregular views of the adverse party. The event proved that the final purposes of certain individuals on whom the turning of the scale depended, had been miscounted. It is not easy to express the mixed feelings produced by the disappointment, or the painfulness of my own in particular. It was at first suggested from some friendly sources, as most advisable in such a posture of things to send in a renomination founded on a vacancy in the Secretaryship of the Treasury; and under certain points of view this expedient had its recommendations. They were met however by difficulties & considerations not to be got over. . . . It was apprehended by some of the best disposed & best informed of the Senate that a renomination would not secure the object. As it had become certain that the open & secret adversaries together amounted to a formidable number who would be doubly gratified by a double triumph, it was suspected that after succeeding in getting the Treasury vacated, it would be a prerequisite to a confirmation of the other appt. that the vacancy should be actually filled in order to prevent its being kept open for your return, which might be looked for within the term of six months; and that with this view a resolution might be obtained declaring the inconsistency of a protracted vacancy with the public service. . . . It is certain that some who had intimated an intended change of their votes, in case the Treasury Dept. should be vacated, had in view that the vacancy should be forthwith filled & even that a nomination to it should go in with the renomination. Whether a majority would have gone such lengths is uncertain; but strong symptoms existed of a temper in the Body capable of going very great lengths. And apart from all other considerations it would have been impossible even if it had been intended to make & fill a vacancy in the Treasy Dept that the consent of the Senate in the other case could be purchased by a pledge to that effect. Besides the degradation of the Ex., it would have introduced a species of barter of the most fatal tendency.

I have given you this summary that you may understand the true character of a proceeding which has given us so much concern. I will add to it two observations only, 1. that the Senate by resting their negative on the opin-

John Bull makes a new batch of ships (left) to send to the Great Lakes, and the Governor of Ohio invites more enlistments (above). Perry won on Lake Erie (right).

ion of official incompatibility tacitly acknowledge a personal fitness & so far defeat their own hostility: 2. that the whole proceeding according to every friendly opinion, will have the effect of giving you a stronger hold on the confidence & support of the Nation. Judging from the effect as already known this cannot fail to be the case.

I have just recovered strength eno', after a severe & tedious attack of bilious fever, to bear a journey to the Mountains whither I am about setting out. The Physicians prescribe it as essential to my thorough recovery, & security agst. a relapse at the present season.

The war went somewhat better for the Americans in 1813. In part this may be credited to long overdue changes in the War and Navy departments. The incompetence of Secretaries William Eustis and Paul Hamilton had made them public scandals. Executive duty finally overcame personal loyalty and Madison replaced them with John Armstrong and William Jones. In the case of Armstrong, the former Minister to France, Madison traded one problem for another. Ambitious, abrasive, and headstrong, the new Secretary of War created friction within the Cabinet and between himself and the commander in chief. On the wide Canadian front, a second campaign against Montreal failed; American forces made a strong bid to control Lake Ontario, raiding towns all along the northern shore, including York (Toronto), capital of Upper Canada; and Captain Oliver Perry's momentous victory on Lake Erie opened that region to American arms. General William Henry Harrison seized the opportunity, regained Detroit, drove the British back, and in the Battle of the Thames, where

This British cartoon dedicated to Madison shows Indians handing over a captured American general, daubed with paint, to a British officer.

Tecumseh was killed, virtually eliminated the Indian menace on the north-western frontier. On the southern frontier, a bloody Indian war pitted General Andrew Jackson and his volunteer army against the unruly Creeks, who finally capitulated the following summer.

Glory had sufficiently vanquished shame for Madison to offer a generally cheerful report on the state of the Union in December. He dwelled at length on British "barbarities" and "enormities," glossed over serious problems of finance and disaffection, and accented the redeeming features of the war.

Washington December 7th 1813

Battle of the Thames, October 5, 1813, in which Tecumseh was killed

It would be improper to close this communication without expressing a thankfulness, in which all ought to unite, for the numerous blessings with which our beloved Country, continues to be favored; for the abundance which overspreads our land, and the prevailing health of its inhabitants; for the preservation of our internal tranquility, and the stability of our free institutions; and above all for the light of divine truth, and the protection of every man's conscience in the enjoyment of it. And although among our blessings we cannot number an exemption from the evils of war; yet these will never be regarded as the greatest of evils by the friends of liberty and the rights of Nations. Our Country has before preferred them to the degraded condition which was the alternative, when the sword was drawn in the cause which gave birth to our national Independence; and none who contemplate the magnitude; and feel the value of that glorious event, will shrink from a struggle to maintain the high and happy ground, on which it placed the American people.

With all good Citizens, the justice and necessity of

resisting wrongs and usurpations no longer to be borne, will sufficiently outweigh the privations and sacrifices inseparable from a State of war. But it is a reflection, moreover, peculiarly consoling, that whilst wars are generally aggravated by their baneful effects on the internal improvements and permanent prosperity of the nations engaged in them, such is the favored situation of the United States, that the calamities of the contest into which they have been compelled to enter, are mitigated by improvements and advantages of which the contest itself is the source.

If the war has increased the interruptions of our Commerce, it has at the same time cherished and multiplied our manufactures; so as to make us independent of all other Countries for the more essential branches, for which we aught to be dependent on none; and is even rapidly giving them an extent which will create additional staples in our future intercourse with foreign markets.

If much treasure has been expended, no inconsiderable portion of it has been applied to objects durable in their value, and necessary to our permanent safety.

If the war has exposed us to increased spoliations on the Ocean, and to predatory incursions on the land, it has developed the national means of retaliating the former, and of providing protection against the latter; demonstrating to all that every blow aimed at our maritime independence, is an impulse accelerating the growth of our maritime power.

By diffusing through the mass of the nation the

Above: John Bull offers his terms of capitulation in detail from 1814 cartoon. Below: Cruikshank's satire of "British Valour and Yankee Boasting" after British Shannon *defeated the* Chesapeake

*America's naval heroes surround
scene of the Battle of Lake Erie.*

elements of military discipline and instruction, by augmenting and distributing warlike preparations applicable to future use; by evincing the zeal and valour with which they will be employed, and the cheerfulness with which every necessary burden will be borne; a greater respect for our rights, and a longer duration of our future peace, are promised than could be expected, without these proofs of the national character and resources.

The war has proved, moreover, that our free Government, like other free Governments, though slow in its early movements, acquires, in its progress, a force proportioned to its freedom; and that the Union of these States, the guardian of the freedom and safety of all and of each, is strengthened by every occasion that puts it to the test.

In fine, the war, with all its vicissitudes, is illustrating the capacity and the destiny of the United States to be a great, a flourishing, and a powerful nation; worthy of the friendship which it is disposed to cultivate with all others; and authorized, by its own example, to require from all, an observance of the laws of justice and reciprocity. Beyond these, their claims have never extended; and in contending for these, we behold a subject for our Congratulations, in the daily testimonies of increasing harmony throughout the nation, and may humbly repose our trust in the smiles of heaven, on so righteous a cause.

At the beginning of 1814, Madison accepted Castlereagh's sudden offer of direct negotiations. Congress approved a new commission consisting of Gallatin, who was released from the Treasury, Bayard, John Quincy Adams, then Minister to Russia, Henry Clay, and Jonathan Russell. Again Madison shuffled his Cabinet, always a painful political operation, and at the same time elevated a corps of vigorous young officers—Andrew Jackson, Winfield Scott, Jacob Brown, and several others—to command of armies in the field. Instant acceptance of the British overture stemmed less from confidence in the American position at the bargaining table than from realistic assessment of the French collapse and Allied ascendancy in Europe. Castlereagh was doubtless tired of the annoying little war in America, but he gave no sign of yielding on impressment and other matters, and if peace came to Europe, Britain could turn all her might to America. With the end of the Continental System, European ports were open to trade. Suddenly embargo and nonimportation were no longer in season. Madison recommended their repeal on March 31. A few days later, in Paris, Napoleon abdicated and retired to Elba. Britain at once reinforced her blockade and extended it from Maine to Louisiana. Admiral Sir Alexander Cochrane, in command, audaciously invited southern slaves to rebel. Madison's reaction to these fast-moving events may be gauged from letters to Jefferson and Monroe during a brief respite at Montpelier.

Montpelier May 10. 1814

We have recd. no information from our Envoys to the [neutral countries along the] Baltic for a very long time. From those last appointed there has not been time to hear after their arrival at Gothenburg. Neither have we any accts. from England, other than the newspaper paragraphs which you have seen. The B. Govt. can not do less than send negociators to meet ours; but whether in the spirit of ours is the important question. The turn of recent events in Europe, if truly represented, must strengthen the motives to get rid of the war with us; and their hopes by a continuance of it, to break down our Govt. must be more & more damped, by occurrences here as they become known there. The election in N. York alone crushed the project of the [Essex] Junto faction [to form a confederacy of northern states] so long fostered by and flattering the expectations of the B. cabinet. Still it is possible that new fallacies may suffice for a willingness to be deceived. Our difficulties in promising money without heavy taxes, and the supposed odium of these, will probably be made the most of by our internal enemies, to recommend the experiment of prolonged hostilities.

Montpelier May 21. 1814

The aggregate intelligence from Europe, with Cochrane's Procln. to the Blacks, warn us to be prepared for the worst measures of the Enemy and in their worst forms. They suggest the earliest attention to the wants of the Treasury, and the policy of securing them, with less scruple as to the terms. As it appears that Mr. Gallatin was in Holland, I hope he may have done something then, provisionally at least. We may count however on the influence of Engd. there as a collateral obstacle that may be fatal. It is not improbable that the intention of the Dutch Govt. to send a Minister here, is delayed, if not abandoned, in consequence of that interposition. . . .

But the strongest evidence of B. influence on the Continent, in opposition to our views, is seen in the unkind and even uncivil treatment of our Envoy in Russia. It is painful to see such a blot on the character of [Emperor] Alexander, as it is ominous to our expectations from his friendship & importance. Whilst the tide of B. ascendancy continues to direct the movements of that and probably the other sovereign having a common interest with us, we must be patient, in the hope that it will not be of long duration, and must endeavor to shorten it by all honorable means of conciliation.

Back in the capital in June, Madison met repeatedly with the Cabinet. Final plans were made for the summer campaign on the northern frontier—a campaign that tended to vindicate American arms but left the British in full possession of Canada. Convinced of an enemy buildup during the summer, and receiving nothing but discouragement from the commissioners in Europe, he proposed to the Cabinet a revision of peace terms. His own memoranda of these meetings explain the result.

submitted to Cabinet
June 23 & 24, 1814

1. Shall the surrender by G.B. of the practice of impressment, in a treaty, limited to a certain period be an ultimatum? Monroe, [the new Secretary of the Treasury George] Campbell, Armstrong, Jones—no. [Attorney General Richard] Rush inclining but not insisting otherwise.

2. Shall a treaty of peace, silent on the subject of Impressment be authorized? All no: but Armstrong & Jones, who were aye.

By the President of the United States of America.

A Proclamation

Whereas it is manifest that the Blockade, which has been proclaimed by the Enemy, of the whole Atlantic coast of the United States, nearly two thousand miles in extent, and abounding in ports harbours and navigable inlets, cannot be carried into effect, by any adequate force, actually stationed for the purpose; and it is rendered a matter of certainty and notoriety, by the multiplied and daily arrivals and departures of the public and private armed vessels of the United State; and of other vessels, that no such adequate force has been so stationed; And whereas a Blockade thus destitute of the character of a regular and legal blockade as defined and recognized by the established law of Nations, whatever other purposes it may be made to answer, forms no lawful prohibition

Proclamation issued by Madison on June 29, 1814, offering aid to all vessels running the enemy blockade

3.   Shall a treaty be authorized comprising an article, referring the subject of impressment along with that of Commerce to a seperate negotiation? Monroe, Campbell Armstrong & Jones aye — Rush for awaiting further information from Europe.

June 27. 1814.

in consequence of the letter from Messrs. Bayard & Gallatin of May 6 or 7. and of other accts from Europe, as to the ascendency & views of G. B. and the dispositions of the Great Contl. powers, the pending Question No. 2 was put to the Cabinet, and agreed to by Monroe, Campbell, Armstrong & Jones; Rush being absent: our Ministers to be instructed, besides trying the other conditions to make a previous trial, to insert or to annex some declaration or protest, agst. any inference from the silence of the Treaty on the subject of impressment, that the British claim was admitted or that of the U.S. abandoned.

The time had come to look to the defense of Washington. During the past year a British squadron had freely raided and pillaged in Chesapeake Bay, even into the Potomac. Rumors of invasion had often circulated in the capital. The First Lady heard tales of enemy plans to descend upon the city at night and set fire to the Capitol and President's House; and she confessed that, although she was a Quaker, "the old Tunesian Sabre" was always within her reach. Only after Napoleon's collapse, however, did the administration act on these fears. Madison perceived correctly that thousands of British troops in Europe would be transported to the bay with the capital a likely target. On July 1, over the dissent of the Secretary of War, Madison established a military district in the Potomac area, placed General William Winder in command, and directed him to carry out plans for its defense. Winder was hampered by Armstrong, who pooh-poohed danger to the capital and thought local militia sufficient for its defense. Armstrong had repeatedly presumed to act as commander in chief. Madison blew the whistle on him in early August, but by then it was too late. Panic descended on the city ahead of the invading army. Madison seemed unperturbed; not so his wife, who wrote to Mrs. Gallatin.

[Washington,] July 28. [18]14.

We have been in a state of purturbation here, for a long time. The depredations of the Enemy approaching within 20 miles of the City & the disaffected, makeing incessant difficulties for the Government. Such a place as this has

An ink and watercolor sketch of the Capitol made by Benjamin H. Latrobe, showing the building's appearance before a fire destroyed wooden corridor connecting wings

become I can not describe it. I wish (for my own part) *we were* at Phila. The people here do not deserve that *I* should prefer it & among other exclamations & threats they say if Mr. M. attempts to move from *this House*, in case of an attack, they will *stop him*, & that he shall *fall with it.* I am not the least alarmed at these things, but entirely disgusted, & determined to stay with him. Our preperations for defence by some means or other, is constantly retarded but the small force the British have on the Bay will never venture nearer than at the present 23 miles. I desired Mr. Astor to tell you the strange story they made, about your haveing recd. a letter from Mr. G. full of alarming information, such, as his having no prospect of making peace & urgeing you for your personal safety to quit N. York & reside in Phila. It had a distressing effect on our Loan & threw many in to consternation for a while but we were able to contradict & soften consequences. I was rejoiced at your last letter containing the acct. of my precious Payne's going to France from England.

A British fleet sailed up Chesapeake Bay in mid-August, dropped anchor at the mouth of the Patuxent River, discharged an army of four thousand veteran troops at Benedict on the west bank of the Maryland river, and this force at once advanced on the capital. There, as the populace fled, Armstrong calmly insisted the army's destination was Baltimore. The President, with Monroe and Winder, took charge of military operations while Armstrong sulked. On the twenty-second Madison rode a dozen miles or so east of the city to reconnoiter the enemy at Marlboro. Winder had assembled a motley force of seven thousand men, mostly raw militia, and taken his position at Old Fields halfway between Marlboro and Bladensburg, the gateway to the capital. Madison sent a confident report to Dolley the next day.

Mt. Williams about 6 or 7 miles from Washington. Tuesday Aug. 23.
We reached our quarters last evening at the Camp between 8 & 9 o'c. and made out very well. I have passed the forenoon among the troops, who are in high spirits & make a good appearance. The reports as to the enemy have varied every hour. The last & probably truest information is that they are not very strong, and are without cavilry and artillery, and of course that they are not in a condition to strike at Washington. It is be-

General William Winder

lieved also that they are not about to move from Marlbro unless it be from an apprehension of our gathering force, and on a retreat to their ships. It is possible, however they may have a greater force or expect one, than has been represented or that their timerity may be greater than their strength. I sent you a message last night by Col. M. and one today by messenger of Genl. Winder who set out at a moment when it was impossible to write. I have detained Shorter, that I might give you by him some final & certain information. We expect every hour to have something further from the camp concerning the Enemy.

That evening Madison returned to the capital and slept in the President's House for what was to be the last time. The next morning, August 24, as the British advanced on Bladensburg, he and most of the Cabinet officers rushed to the field to counsel with poor Winder. Soon they were fleeing in all directions. The Battle of Bladensburg passed quickly as the militia were routed. The Redcoats marched unopposed to Washington. Preceding them by several hours, Madison discovered that Dolley had fled the deserted city. Her last two days in the executive mansion are recorded in a breathless letter to her sister.

[Washington,] Tuesday Augt. 23d. 1814

Dear Sister

My husband left me yesterday morng. to join Gen. Winder. He enquired anxiously whether I had courage, or firmness to remain in the President's house until his return, on the morrow, or succeeding day, and on my assurance that I had no fear but for him and the success of our army, he left me, beseeching me to take care of myself, and of the cabinet papers, public and private. I have since recd. two dispatches from him, written with a pencil; the last is alarming, because he desires I should be ready at a moment's warning to enter my carriage and leave the city; that the enemy seemed stronger than had been reported and that it might happen that they would reach the city, with intention to destroy it.... I am accordingly ready; I have pressed as many cabinet papers into trunks as to fill one carriage; our private property must be sacrificed, as it is impossible to procure wagons for its transportation. I am determined not to go myself until I see Mr Madison safe, and he can accompany me, as I hear of much hostility towards him....

Countryside near Bladensburg

My friends and acquaintances are all gone; Even Col. C [Charles Carroll] with his hundred men, who were stationed as a guard in the enclosure. French John [Sioussat, the majordomo], with his usual activity and resolution, offers to spike the cannon at the gate, and to lay a train of powder which would blow up the British, should they enter the house. To the last proposition I positively object, without being able, however, to make him understand why all advantages in war may not be taken.

Wednesday morng., twelve o'clock. Since sunrise I have been turning my spyglass in every direction and watching with unwearied anxiety, hoping to discern the approach of my dear husband and his friends, but, alas, I can descry only groups of military wandering in all directions, as if there was a lack of arms, or of spirit to fight for their own firesides!

Three O'clock. Will you believe it, my sister? We have had a battle or skirmish near Bladensburg, and I am still here within sound of the cannon! Mr. Madison comes not; may God protect him! Two messengers covered with dust, come to bid me fly; but I wait for him.... At this late hour a wagon has been procured, I have had it filled with the plate and most valuable portable articles belonging to the house; whether it will reach its destination, the Bank of Maryland, or fall into the hands of British soldiery, events must determine.

Watercolors by George Heriot, 1815, portray the Capitol and White House after destruction by the British.

Our kind friend, Mr. Carroll, has come to hasten my departure, and is in a very bad humor with me because I insist on waiting until the large picture of Gen. Washington is secured, and it requires to be unscrewed from the wall. This process was found too tedious for these perilous moments; I have ordered the frame to be broken, and the canvass taken out it is done, and the precious portrait placed in the hands of two gentlemen of New York, for safe keeping. And now, dear sister, I must leave this house, or t[he] retreating army will make me a prisoner in it, by filling up the road I am direc[ted] to take. When I shall again write you, or where I shall be tomorrow, I cannot tell!!

Madison too beat a fast retreat, alone on horseback, first to Georgetown, then from place to place on both sides of the Potomac. The enemy entered Washington that night, fired the Capitol, burned the President's House, put a torch to every public building except the ramshackle Patent Office, and after twenty-four hours retired unscathed from destruction estimated at one and a half million dollars. From his last refuge Madison sent off a dispatch to Dolley who had found shelter with her sister Anna Cutts.

Brookville Aug. 27. 10 OC. [1814]

My dearest

Finding that our army had left Montgomery Court House we pushed on to this place, with a view to join it, or proceed to the City as further information might prescribe. I have just recd. a line from Col. Monroe, saying that the Enemy were out of Washington, & on the retreat to their Ships & advising our immediate return to Washington. We shall accordingly set out thither immediately. You will all of course take the same resolution. I know not where we are in the first instance to hide our heads; but shall look for a place on my arrival. Mr Rush offers his house in the six buildings, and the offer claims attention. Perhaps I may fall in with Mr. Cutts, and have the aid of his advice. I saw Mr. Bradley at Montgomery Ct. H. who told me that Mrs Cutts was well. *Jamey will give you some particulars wch. I have not time to write.

Truly yours

J. MADISON

*Since the above it is found necessary to detain Jamey, & send a Trooper

347

Madison, followed by his wife, returned to the ravaged city on the same day. The danger was not over. Enemy troops were still in the neighborhood. Madison gathered the Cabinet on the twenty-ninth to concert new defense measures. On September 1 he issued a proclamation denouncing Britain's act of "barbarism" against the capital and exhorting the people to unite to expel the invader. The humiliating disaster produced a torrent of accusation and recrimination. Madison did not escape blame, nor was he blameless. He had been indecisive, overly tolerant of weak or unreliable subordinates, courageous in his own person but timid in driving others, more intent on quieting than arousing the populace, and hopelessly naive about the fighting power of raw militia. Yet Monroe was probably right in later insisting that the capital could have been saved had the President's July orders been carried out. This put the onus on Armstrong. The city was enraged against him. He would have to go, though even in this extremity Madison was anxious to provide a dignified exit. He filed a memorandum of his last interview with Armstrong.

[after August 29, 1814]

In the evening of the 29th, of Augst. 1814 Being on Horseback I stopped at General Armstrong's lodgings for the purpose of communicating with him on the state of things in the District, then under apprehensions of an immediate visit from the force of the Enemy at Alexandria.

I observed to him that he could not be unaware of the great excitement in the District produced by the unfortunate event which had taken place in the City; that violent prejudices were known to exist against the Ad-

English woodcut (left) of burning of Washington illustrates massive destruction of public buildings; Octagon House (above) was saved because the French minister moved in, giving it diplomatic immunity, and the Madisons lived there while the gutted White House was restored.

The Octagon BY GLENN BROWN, 1917

ministration, as having failed in its duty to protect it, particularly agst. me & himself as head of the War Department; that threats of personal violence had, it was said, been thrown out agst us both, but more especially agst. him; that it had been sufficiently known for several days & before his return to the City (which was about one OClock P. M. of the 29th.) that the temper of the troops was such as made it expedient, if possible, that he should have nothing to do with them; that I had within a few hours recd. a message from the commanding General of the Militia informing me that every Officer would tear off his epaulets, if Genl. Armstrong was to have any thing to do with them; that before his arrival there was less difficulty, as Mr. Monroe who was very acceptable to them, had, as on preceding occasions of his absence, though very reluctantly on this, been the medium for the functions of Secretary of war, but that since his return & presence the expedient could not be continued, and the question was, what was best to be done. Any convulsion at so critical a moment could not but have the worst consequences.

He said he had been aware of the excitement agst. him; that it was altogether artificial, and that he knew the sources of it, and the intrigues by which it had been effected, which this was not the proper time for examining, that the excitement was founded on the most palpable falsehoods, and was limited to this spot; that it was evident he could not remain here..., he was ready to give up his appointment; or he could, with my permission, retire from the scene, by setting out immediately on a visit to his family in the State of N. York.

I observed that a resignation was an extent which had not been contemplated that if made under such circumstances, it might receive constructions which could not be desirable, either in a public or a personal view, that a temporary retirement, as he suggested, tho' also subject to be viewed in some lights not agreeable, was on the whole less objectionable, and would avoid the existing embarrassment, without precluding any future course which might be deemed most fit....

He returned to an exculpation of himself, and remarked that he had omitted no preparations or steps whatever for the safety of the place which had been enjoined on him.

Death of British General Robert Ross during the battle of Baltimore

I replied that as the conversation was a frank one, I could not admit this justification; that it was the duty of the Secretary of war not only to execute plans or orders committed to him, but to devise and propose such as would in his opinion be necessary & proper; that this was an obvious and essential part of his charge, and that in which related to military plans & proceedings elsewhere, he had never been scrupulous or backward in taking this course; that on the contrary he well knew from what on another occasion had passed between us, he had taken a latitude in this respect which I was not satisfied with; that it was due to truth & to myself, to say, that he had never appeared to enter into a just view either of the danger to the City wch. was to be apprehended; or of the consequences of its falling into the hands of the Enemy; that he had never himself proposed or suggested a single precaution or arrangement for its safety, every thing done on that subject having been brought forward by myself, and that the apparent difference of his views on that subject from mine had naturally induced a reduction of my arrangements to the minimum, in order to obtrude the less on a reluctant execution. I reminded him also that he had fallen short of the preparations even decided on in the Cabinet, in some respects, particularly in not having arms & equipments brought to convenient depots from distant ones, some of the Militia whom called on for the defence of the City, being obliged to get arms first at Harper's ferry.

I remarked that it was not agreeable thus to speak, nor on an occasion less urgent would it be done; that I had selected him for the office he filled from a respect to his talents, and a confidence that he would exert them for the public good, that I had always treated him with friendliness & confidence, and that as there was but a short distance before me to the end of my public career, my great wish, next to leaving my Country in a state of peace & prosperity, was to have preserved harmony and avoid changes, and that I had accordingly as he well knew acquiesed in many things, to which no other consideration would have reconciled me.... We parted as usual in a friendly manner; on the next morning he sent word by Mr. Parker that he should proceed immediately to visit his family; and on his arrival at Baltimore, transmitted his resignation....

The government, though inconvenienced by the devastation, was little hampered in its functions. Madison had already called Congress into session September 19, two months earlier than usual, in order to deal with urgent fiscal and military needs. Fortunately, at this moment, the humiliation of the capital was offset by news of American victory in the Battle of Lake Champlain and of the gallant defense of Fort McHenry which, besides inspiring "The Star-Spangled Banner," saved Baltimore and led to a British withdrawal from the Chesapeake. Congress, however, was no more cooperative with the administration than before. On the Treasury's recommendation, Congress approved the establishment of a national bank but because it omitted the provision most wanted, that of bank loans to the government, Madison vetoed the bill. The army was as depleted as the treasury, standing at about one-half the authorized strength of sixty-two thousand men. Monroe, Armstrong's successor in the War Department, proposed conscription to raise the army to one hundred thousand. The House rejected the measure with cries of tyranny.

Meanwhile, the Americans negotiated at Ghent. On the basis of Gallatin's pessimistic assessment in June, the administration threw away the remaining war aims and called for peace on the status quo antebellum. Almost at once, on October 8, new dispatches arrived detailing British demands to treat the United States as a conquered nation. Letters more than two months apart to two former presidents, Jefferson and John Adams, suggest Madison's response to this development.

Washington Oct. 10. 1814
We have just recd. despatches from Ghent which I shall lay before Congs. today. The British sine qua non. excluded us from fishing within the sovereignty attached to her shores, and from using these in curing fish—required a Cession of as much of Maine as wd. remove the obstruction to a direct communication between Quebec & Halifax, confirmed to her the Passamaquoddy Islands as always hers of right—included in the pacification the Indian Allies, with a boundary for them, (such as that of the Treaty of Greenville [with the Northwest Indians in 1795]) agst. the U.S. mutually guaranteed, and the Indians restrained from selling their lands to either party, but free to sell them to a *third* party—prohibited the U.S. from having an armed force on the Lakes or forts on their shores, the British prohibited as to neither—and substituted for the present N. W. limit of the U. S. a line running direct from the W. end of L. Superior to the Mississippi, with a right of G. B. to the navigation of this river. Our ministers were all present & in perfect harmony of opinion on the arrogance of such demands.

BOTH: *War of 1812,* LOSSING

Monument built to commemorate the Battle of Baltimore and the gallant defense of Fort McHenry

They wd. probably leave Ghent shortly after the sailing of the vessels just arrived. Nothing can prevent it, but a sudden change in the B. Cabinet not likely to happen, tho' it might be somewhat favored by indignant rupture of the negociation, as well as by the intelligence from this Country, and the fermentations taking place in Europe.

Washington Dcr. 17. 1814

The view of the discussions at Ghent presented by the private letters of all our Ministers there, as well as by their official dispatches leaves no doubt of the policy of the B. Cabinet.... Our Enemy knowing that he has peace in his own hands, speculates on the fortune of events. Should these be unfavorable he can at any moment, as he supposes, come to our terms. Should they correspond with his hopes, his demands may be insisted on, or even extended. The point to be decided by our Ministers is whether during the uncertainty of events, a categorical alternative of immediate peace or a rupture of the negociation would not be preferable to a longer acquiescence in the gambling procrastinations of the other party. It may be presumed that they will before this have pushed the negociations to this point.

It is very agreeable to find that the superior ability which distinguishes the notes of our Envoys extorts commendation from the most obdurate of their politi-

The Americans were victorious at the Battle of Plattsburgh (below) largely due to the naval triumph of Captain Macdonough's fleet on Lake Champlain, seen in background.

cal Enemies. And we have the satisfaction to learn that the cause they are pleading is beginning to overcome the prejudice which misrepresentations had spread over the Continent of Europe agst. it. The B. Govt. is neither inattentive to this approaching revolution in the public opinion there, nor blind to its tendency. If it does not find in it a motive to immediate peace, it will infer the necessity of shortening the war by bringing upon us [in] the ensuing Campain, what it will consider, as a force not to be resisted by us.

It were to be wished that this consideration had more effect in quickening the preparatory measures of Congress. I am unwilling to say how much distress in every branch of our affairs is the fruit of their tardiness....

View of the city of Ghent

His hopes for an early peace blasted, Madison prayed for more victories like Captain Thomas Macdonough's at Champlain to bring the British government to its senses. As an aid to this he prepared a propaganda paper on the causes and character of the war. With the return of peace to Europe, he argued, the original causes of the conflict, and hence the American demands, had been removed, but Britain kept up the fight with the view to "strangling the maritime power of the United States in its cradle and cutting off their commerce with other nations." Two extreme points on the compass, New Orleans and New England, drew Madison's fears. An attack on New Orleans had been expected since May, when General Jackson had been placed in command there. Subversion and disunion were the dangers in New England. But for the "traitors" in that quarter, Gallatin had said, a just peace would have already been signed. A young Virginian who called on the President in the fall described him as "miserably shattered and woe-begone" because of disunionism in the East. Madison did not disguise his anger on the subject in a letter to Wilson Cary Nicholas, Governor of Virginia.

Washington Novr. 26. 1814

You are not mistaken in viewing the conduct of the Eastern States as the source of our greatest difficulties in carrying on the war; as it certainly is the greatest, if not the sole inducement with the Enemy to persevere in it. The greater part of the people in that quarter have been brought by their leaders, aided by their priests, under a delusion scarcely exceeded by that recorded in the period of Witchcraft, and the leaders are becoming daily more desperate in the case they make of it. Their object is power. If they could obtain it by menaces,

Cartoon of Hartford Convention

their efforts would stop there. These failing, they are ready to go every length for which they can train their followers. Without foreign cooperation, revolts & separation will hardly be risked; and what the effect of so profligate an experiment may be first on deluded partizans, and next on those remaining faithful to the nation who are respectable for their consistency and even for their numbers, is for conjecture only. The best may be hoped, but the worst ought to be kept in view. In the meantime the Course to be taken by the Govt. is full of delicacy & perplexity; and the more so under the pinch which exists in our fiscal affairs, & the lamentable tardiness of the Legislature in applying some relief.

All the while, of course, Britain, her treasury empty and her attentions focused on the reconstruction of Europe, was backing away from the war in America. At the end of November her negotiators accepted the American formula and the treaty of peace was signed on Christmas Eve. As the good tidings crossed the Atlantic, the Battle of New Orleans was fought and won. Thus the American victory had no bearing on the outcome of the war, but that was not known at the time, and as the news spread across the country — it reached Washington on February 4 — there was great rejoicing at this vindication of American pride and power. The commissioners of the Hartford Convention, a group of New England Federalists who had long been restive under Jeffersonian Republicanism and had met to protest "Mr. Madison's War," arrived in the capital to present their demands in the midst of the rejoicing. They sheepishly retired. The Treaty of Ghent was in Madison's hands on February 14. Four days later he sent it to Congress with the following felicitations.

Washington February 18th 1815

The late war although reluctantly declared by congress, had become a necessary resort, to assert the rights and independence of the Nation. It has been waged with a success, which is the natural result of the wisdom of the Legislative Councils, of the patriotism of the people, of the public spirit of the Militia, and of the valor of the Military and Naval forces of the Country. Peace, at all times a blessing, is peculiarly welcome therefore, at a period, when the causes for the war have ceased to operate; when the Government had demonstrated the efficiency of its powers of defence; and when the Nation can review its conduct, without regret, and without reproach.

The Battle of New Orleans (above) was fought two weeks after Treaty of Ghent had been signed abroad. Madison later signed the treaty in this house at 21 Lafayette Square.

I recommend to your care and beneficences, the gallant men, whose achievements, in every department of the military service, on the land, and on the water, have so essentially contributed to the honor of the American name, and to the restoration of peace. The feelings of conscious patriotism and worth, will animate such men under every change of fortune and pursuit; but their Country performs a duty to itself, when it bestows those testimonials of approbation and applause which are, at once, the reward, and the incentive, to great actions.

The reduction of the public expenditures, to the demands of a peace establishment will doubtless engage the immediate attention of Congress. There are, however, important considerations, which forbid a sudden and general revocation of the measures, that have been produced by the war. Experience has taught us, that neither the pacific dispositions of the American people, nor the pacific character of their political institutions, can altogether exempt them from that strife, which appears, beyond the ordinary lot of Nations, to be incident to the actual period of the World; and the same faithful monitor demonstrates, that a certain degree of preparation for war, is not only indispensable to avert disasters in the onset; but affords also the best security, for the continuance of peace. The wisdom of Congress will, therefore, I am confident, provide for the maintenance of an adequate regular force; for the gradual advancement of the naval establishment; for improving all the means of harbour defence, for adding discipline, to the distinguished bravery of the Militia; and for cultivating the Military art, in its essential branches, under the liberal patronage of the Government.

The resources of our Country were, at all times, competent to the attainment of every national object; but they will now be enriched and invigorated by the activity, which peace will introduce, into all the scenes of domestic enterprize and labour. . . .

The termination of the Legislative Sessions will soon separate you, Fellow-Citizens, from each other, and restore you to your Constituents. I pray you to bear with you, the expressions of my sanguine hope, that the Peace, which has been just declared, will not only be the foundation of the most friendly intercourse between the United

355

States and Great Britain; but that it will, also be productive of happiness and harmony in every section of our beloved Country. The influence of your precepts and example, must be, every where, powerful: And while we accord in grateful acknowledgements, for the protection, which Providence has bestowed upon us, let us never cease to inculcate obedience to the laws, and fidelity to the Union, as constituting the palladium of the National independence and prosperity.

The American people, following their President, erased all the shame from the war and put upon it the face of glory. If the peace resolved none of the issues on which the war began, it nevertheless placed American independence on impregnable foundations and proved the strength of republican government and national character. The war, as Madison suggested, had been a great teacher—of patriotism, of union, of the firmness and energy that not even the most favored nation on God's footstool could ignore but at its peril. The war had ended gloriously precisely because it had been such an ordeal. To emerge stronger from trials of adversity, division, and disgrace was to emerge victoriously.

For the first time in six years the country was calm. Madison hastened to Montpelier in March and remained there except for one brief interlude in the capital until some weeks before Congress convened in December. His State of the Union message was a landmark in the history of the Republican party. In the opinion of doctrinaire Old Republicans, some of whom, like John Randolph, had never been convinced of Madison's political purity, the message "out-Federalized" Federalism. Politically, it seemed, Madison had traveled a circle back to the nationalism of his youth. And so he had. Yet this nationalism was different because it rested on the achievement of democracy and independence. It was nearly one hundred and eighty degrees to the left of Federalist nationalism, with its vitiating British connection, its narrow sectional views, and its distrust of democracy. In 1815, filled with the patriotic *élan* that followed the Peace of Ghent, Madison believed that the American political experiment had proved itself and that the Union could sustain a program of national improvement and consolidation. He therefore called upon Congress to establish a national bank and uniform currency, build a national defense, nurture manufactures, plan a system of roads and canals, and create a national university within the new "district of Columbia."

[December 5, 1815]

The arrangements of the finances, with a view to the receipts and expenditures of a permanent peace establishment, will necessarily enter into the deliberations of Congress, during the present Session. It is true that the improved condition of the public revenue will not only afford, the means of maintaining the faith of the Government with its Creditors, inviolate, and of prosecuting Successfully the measures of the Most liberal policy, but will also, justify an immediate alleviation of the burthens imposed by the necessities of the war. It is, however, essential, to every modification of the finances, that the benefits of an uniform national currency should be restored to the community.... If the operation of the State Banks cannot produce this result, the probable operation of a National Bank will merit consideration; and if neither of these expedients be deemed effectual, it may become necessary to ascertain the terms, upon which the notes of the Government (no longer required as an instrument of credit) shall be issued, upon motives of general policy, as a common medium of circulation.

Notwithstanding the security for future repose, which the United States ought to find in their love of peace, and their constant respect for the rights of other nations, the character of the times, particularly inculcates the lesson, that whether to prevent or repel danger, we ought not to be unprepared for it. This consideration will sufficiently recommend to Congress, a liberal provision for the immediate extension and gradual completion of the works of defence, both fixed and floating, on our maritime frontier; and an adequate provision for guarding our inland frontier, against dangers to which certain portions of it may continue to be exposed.

As an improvement in our military establishment, it will deserve the consideration of Congress, whether a corps of Invalids might not be so organized & employed.... I recommend also an enlargement of the military Academy already established, and the establishment of others in other sections of the Union. And I cannot press too much on the attention of Congress, such a classification and organization of the militia as will most effectually render it the safeguard of a free State....

The signal services which have been rendered by our navy, and the capacities it has developed for successful co-operation in the national defense, will give to that portion of the public force, its full value in the eyes of congress, at an epoch which calls for the constant vigilance of all Governments. To preserve the ships now in

Madison's message of December 4, 1815, communicating "successful termination of the war" to Congress

sound State; to compleat those already contemplated; to provide amply the imperishable materials for prompt augmentations; and to improve the existing arrangements, into more advantageous establishments, for the construction, the repairs, and the security, of vessels of war, is dictated by the soundest policy.

In adjusting the duties on imports, to the object of revenue, the influence of the Tariff on manufactures, will necessarily present itself for consideration. However wise the theory may be, which leaves to the Sagacity and interest of individuals, the application of their industry and resources, there are in this, as in other cases, exceptions to the general rule.... Under circumstances giving a powerful impulse to manufacturing industry, it has made among us a progress, and exhibited an efficiency, which justify the belief, that with a protection not more than is due to the enterprizing citizens whose interests are now at stake, it will become, at an early day, not only Safe against occasional competitions from abroad, but a source of Domestic Wealth, and even of external commerce.... It will be an additional recommendation of particular manufactures, where the materials for them are extensively drawn from our agriculture, and consequently impart and ensure to that great fund of national prosperity and independence, an encouragement which cannot fail to be rewarded.

Among the means of advancing the public interest, the occasion is a proper one for recalling the attention of Congress, to the great importance of establishing, throughout our Country, the roads and canals which can best be executed, under the National authority. No objects within the circle of political economy, so richly repay the expence bestowed on them; there are none, the utility of which is more universally ascertained and acknowledged; none that do more honor to the Governments, whose wise and & enlarged patriotism duly appreciates them. Nor is there any Country which presents a field, where nature invites more the art of man, to compleat her own work for his accomodation and benefit. These Considerations are strengthened moreover by the political effect of these facilities for intercommunication, in bringing and binding more closely together, the various parts of our extended confederacy....

The present is a favorable season also, for bringing

Certificate of membership in the Berkshire Agricultural Society of Massachusetts issued to Madison

*French army taking flight in the
Battle of Waterloo, June 18, 1815*

again into view, the establishment of a national seminary of learning within the district of Columbia, and with means drawn from the property therein subject to the authority of the General government. Such an institution claims the patronage of Congress, as a monument of their solicitude for the advancement of Knowledge, without which the blessings of liberty cannot be fully enjoyed, or long preserved; as a model instructive in the formation of other Seminaries; as a nursery of enlightened preceptors; and as a central resort of youth and genius from every part of their Country, diffusing, on their return, examples of those national feelings, those liberal sentiments, and those congenial manners, which contribute cement to our union, and strength to the great political fabric, of which that is the foundation.

Congress made a beginning on this program by chartering the Second Bank of the United States and adopting the first peacetime protective tariff. Meanwhile, events in Europe had given Madison some anxious moments in 1815. With the return of Napoleon, the peace looked more like an armistice, and if Europe again became a slaughterhouse America could not escape the carnage. Britain's hostility must again be felt—and indeed, actuated by zeal "to recover her lost reputation," more potently than before. Waterloo ended the immediate danger. Although Madison shed no tears for Napoleon, he could not help but regret the loss of France in the scales of power and the utter collapse of European liberty twenty-five years after its rise. An Anglo-American commercial treaty was signed in July, 1815. An important step forward, it nonetheless kept the Americans from the West Indies trade; and other serious matters—the Newfoundland fisheries and armament on the Great Lakes—remained in dispute between the two countries. Madison wrote of these problems to John Quincy Adams, now Minister to Great Britain, in the following year.

Washington May 10. 1816.
You will receive from the Secretary of State the communications relating to the topics in discussion with the B Govt. Being sincerely desirous of maintaining peace and friendship between the two Countries, we wish every fair experiment to be made for guarding against causes which may interrupt them. On questions such as impressments and blockades, on which we consider ourselves as standing on the ground of right and of public law, and consequently connect a defence of them with our honor & independence, collisions must be unavoidable in the

John Quincy Adams

event of wars in Europe, unless amicable adjustments precede them, or G B should be more yeilding than we are authorized to expect. It is much to be desired also that on questions not of right, but of prudence & reciprocity, as a discontinuance of armaments on the lakes, and the commerce with the West Indies, an understanding or stipulations satisfactory to both parties, should not be delayed. You will learn that with respect to the lakes Congs. declined to make appropriations for keeping pace with British armaments on them. But it is not to be inferred that if these should be actually carried on, they will not lead at another Session to a different policy. The effect of a display of British superiority on the upper lakes on the spirit of the Savages will be decisive. In this view only the question of naval superiority in that quarter is important to the U.S. whilst it is not so to Canada which has no apprehensions from Savage inroads. In any other view the extention of British armaments on the lakes would have nothing in them to be dreaded. In time of peace they are harmless and in the event of a future war, the object of the U. S. would be to take the lakes themselves, which the inducement would be strengthened by so rich a prize on them. This was the first object in the late war, and wd. have succeeded in any hands but those of Genl. Hulls. On future occasions, should they unfortunately not be precluded, the U. S. will have greater comparative means, with an application of them enlightened by experience. As to the commerce with the West Indies, there can be but one sentiment. What passed on that subject in Congs. is a proof that if intermediate negociation be not successful, it will be taken up at the next session, with a determination to put an end to the existing inequality. If G B will not admit American vessels into the W. India ports, American ports will be shut agst. B vessels coming from those ports. The consequence must be either that the intercourse will cease, which tho' disadvantageous to the U. S. will be not less so to G B: or that neutral ports will be interposed, which will furnish a greater proportion of the navigation employed, to the Amn than to the B tonnage. The present monopoly will be the less submitted to, as it is found to destroy the equality which was the object of the Commercial Convention in the branches of trade embraced by it.

The Rush-Bagot Convention of 1817 disarmed the Lakes and secured American rights to the fisheries. Free trade would take a little longer, but in time Britain would come to that policy as well. Meanwhile, Madison's term as President was coming to an end; in his last annual message he offered his own "farewell address" to the American people.

[December 3, 1816]

The period of my retiring from the public service being at little distance, I shall find no occasion more proper than the present, for expressing to my fellow Citizens, my deep sense of the continued confidence, and kind support which I have received from them. My grateful recollection of these distinguished marks of their favorable regard, can never cease; and with the consciousness, that if I have not served my Country with greater ability, I have served it with sincere devotion, will accompany me as a source of unfailing gratification.

Happily, I shall carry with me from the public Theatre, other sources, which those who love their country most, will best appreciate. I shall behold it blessed with tranquility and prosperity at home; and with peace and respect abroad. I can indulge the proud reflection, that the American people have reached in safety and success their fortieth year, as an independent nation; that for nearly an entire generation, they have had experience of their present constitution, the offspring of their undisturbed deliberations and of their free choice; that they have found it to bear the trials of adverse as well as prosperous circumstances; to contain in its combination of the federate and elective principles, a reconcilement of public strength with individual liberty, of national power for the defence of national rights, with a security against wars of injustice, of ambition or of vain glory, in the fundamental provision which subjects all questions of war to the will of the nation itself, which is to pay its costs, and feel its calamities. Nor is it less a peculiar felicity of this constitution, so dear to us all, that it is found to be capable, without losing its vital energies, of expanding itself over a spacious territory, with the increase and expansion of the community for whose benefit it was established.

And may I not be allowed to add to this gratifying spectacle, that I shall read in the character of the American people, in their devotion to true liberty, and to the constitution which is its palladium, sure presages, that

Above and at right, the first and last pages of Madison's "farewell address," given December 3, 1816

the destined career of my country will exhibit a Government, pursuing the public good as its sole object, and regulating its means by the great principles consecrated in its charter, & by those moral principles, to which they are so well allied: a Government, which watches over the purity of elections, the freedom of speech and of the press, the trial by Jury, and the equal interdict against encroachments and compacts, between religion and the State; which maintains inviolably the maxims of public faith, the security of persons and property, and encourages, in every authorised mode, that general diffusion of knowledge which guarantees to public liberty its permanency, and to those who possess the blessing, the true enjoyment of it: a Government, which avoids intrusions on the internal repose of other nations, and repels them from its own; which does justice to all nations with a readiness, equal to the firmness with which it requires justice from them; and which, whilst it refines its domestic code from every ingredient not congenial with the precepts of an enlightened age, and the sentiments of a virtuous people, seeks, by appeals to reason, and by its liberal examples, to infuse into the law which governs the civilised world, a Spirit which may diminish the frequency or circumscribe the calamities of war, and meliorate the social and beneficent relations of peace: a Government, in a word, whose conduct within and without, may bespeak the most noble of all ambitions, that of promoting peace on Earth, and good will to man.

These contemplations, sweetening the remnant of my days, will animate my prayers for the happiness of my beloved Country, and a perpetuity of the Institutions, under which it is enjoyed.

Having helped to set the government on the course of power and responsibility for the national welfare, Madison retreated to the safety of Republican dogma in the last act of his Presidency. His veto of the bonus bill, which created a permanent fund for internal improvements from the charter price and the dividends to be paid by the Bank, came as a jolt to national-minded Republicans who had been the mainstay of Madison's support in Congress since 1811. Although the President had not blinked at the Bank, he could not approve federally financed internal improvements without the sanction of a constitutional amendment, as he told Congress.

intrusions on the internal repose of other nations, and repels them from its own, which does justice to all nations with a readiness, equal to the firmness with which it requires justice from them; and which, whilst it refines its domestic code from every ingredient not congenial with the precepts of an enlightened age, and the sentiments of a virtuous people, seeks, by appeals to reason, and by its liberal examples, to infuse into the law which governs the civilized world, a spirit which may diminish the frequency or circumscribe the calamities of war, and meliorate the social and beneficent relations of peace: A Government, in a word, whose conduct, within and without, may bespeak the most noble of all ambitions, that of promoting peace on Earth and good will to man.

These contemplations, sweetening the remnant of my days, will animate my prayers for the happiness of my beloved Country, and a perpetuity of the institutions under which it is enjoyed.

James Madison
December 3d 1816.

March 3, 1817.

The legislative powers vested in Congress are specified and enumerated in the eighth section of the first article of the Constitution, and it does not appear that the power proposed to be exercised by the bill is among the enumerated powers, or that it falls by any just interpretation within the power to make laws necessary and proper for carrying into execution those or other powers vested by the Constitution in the Government of the United States.

"The power to regulate commerce among the several States" can not include a power to construct roads and canals, and to improve the navigation of water courses in order to facilitate, promote, and secure such a commerce without a latitude of construction departing from the ordinary import of the terms strengthened by the known inconveniences which doubtless led to the grant of this remedial power to Congress.

To refer the power in question to the clause "to provide for the common defense and general welfare" would be contrary to the established and consistent rules of interpretation, as rendering the special and careful enumeration of powers which follow the clause nugatory and improper. Such a view of the Constitution would have the effect of giving to Congress a general power of legislation instead of the defined and limited one hitherto understood to belong to them, the terms "common defense and general welfare" embracing every object and act within the purview of a legislative trust. It would have the effect of subjecting both the Constitution and laws of the several States in all cases not specifically exempted to be superseded by laws of Congress.... Such a view of the Constitution, finally, would have the effect of excluding the judicial authority of the United States from its participation in guarding the boundary between the legislative powers of the General and the State Governments....

A restriction of the power "to provide for the common defense and general welfare" to cases which are to be provided for by the expenditure of money would still leave within the legislative power of Congress all the great and most important measures of Government, money being the ordinary and necessary means of carrying them into execution.

If a general power to construct roads and canals, and to improve the navigation of water courses, with the train of powers incident thereto, be not possessed by Congress, the assent of the States in the mode provided in the bill cannot confer the power. The only cases in which the consent and cession of particular States can extend the power of Congress are those specified and provided for in the Constitution.

I am not unaware of the great importance of roads and canals and the improved navigation of water courses, and that a power in the National Legislature to provide for them might be exercised with signal advantage to the general prosperity. But seeing that such a power is not expressly given by the Constitution, and believing that it can not be deduced from any part of it without an inadmissible latitude of construction and a reliance on insufficient precedents; believing also that the permanent success of the Constitution depends on a definite partition of powers between the General and the State Governments, and that no adequate landmarks would be left by the constructive extension of the powers of Congress as proposed in the bill, I have no option but to withhold my signature from it, and to cherishing the hope that its beneficial objects may be attained by a resort for the necessary powers to the same wisdom and virtue in the nation which established the Constitution in its actual form and providently marked out in the instrument itself a safe and practicable mode of improving it as experience might suggest.

Festive election scene outside Independence Hall ushered in the Presidency of James Monroe.

Thus ended, on a somewhat ambiguous note, the Presidency of James Madison. No President since Washington retired from the office with greater public esteem. "Never was a country left in a more flourishing situation," Gallatin wrote in a personal tribute, or its people "more united at home and respected abroad." Madison was even fortunate in his successor, James Monroe, whose politics were virtually indistinguishable from his own. He lingered in Washington several days after the inauguration. "I am in the midst of preparations to get to my farm, where I shall make myself a fixture," he told Gallatin, "and where I anticipate many enjoyments, which if not fully realized, will be a welcome change from the labors and solicitudes of public life."

Chapter 10

Last of the Fathers

Sixty-six years of age when he retired to Montpelier, James Madison still had many years of happiness before him. He enjoyed good health, benign temperament, a fine estate, a loving family and many friends, the pleasures of his books and of farming, and the veneration of his countrymen. The mansion had been enlarged, with wings on either side, and the grounds much improved. Its central feature, a large drawing room, opened to the entire house and the luxuriant landscape beyond. "The drawing-room walls are covered with pictures," wrote one visitor, "some very fine, from the ancient masters, but most of them portraits of our most distinguished men, six or eight by Stewart [Gilbert Stuart]. The mantelpiece, tables in each corner and in fact wherever one could be fixed, were filled with busts, and groups of figures in plaster, so that the apartment had more the appearance of a museum of the arts than of a drawing-room." In the immediate household were Dolley and Madison's aged mother, who would live to the ripe age of ninety-eight. But the house was often filled with his wife's relatives and his own, as well as guests from far and near. Lacking children of his own, Madison doted on his nieces and nephews. Perhaps his favorite was young Richard Cutts, in his twelfth year when he received this patriarchal letter from "Uncle Madison."

> Montpellier. Jany. 4. 1829
>
> Your letter, my dear Richard, gave me much pleasure, as it shews that you love your studies, which you would not do if you did not profit by them. Go on, my good boy, as you have begun; and you will find that you have chosen the best road to a happy life, because a useful one; the more happy because it will add to the happiness of your parents, and of all who love you and are anxious to see you deserving to be loved.
>
> When I was at an age which will soon be yours, a book

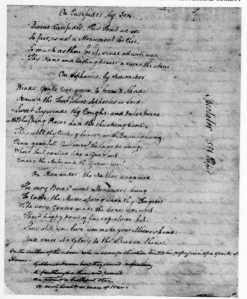

Excerpts from the Spectator, *which Madison recommended to his nephew Richard in 1829, appear on this page from his commonplace book, written when he was a young boy.*

fell into my hands which I read, as I believe, with particular advantage. I have always thought it the best that had been written, for cherishing in young minds a desire of improvement, a taste for Learning, and a lively sense of the duties, the virtues, and the proprieties of life. The work I speak of is the "Spectator" well known by that title. It had several Authors, at the head of them Mr. Addison, whose papers are marked at the bottom of each, by one of the letters in the name of the Muse, C.L.I.O. They will reward you for a second reading, after reading them along with the others.

Addison was of the first rank among the fine writers of the Age, and has given a definition of what he shewed himself to be an example. "Fine writing" he says "consists of sentiments that are natural, without being obvious"; to which adding the remark of Swift, another celebrated author of the same period, making a good style to "consist of proper words in their proper places," a definition is formed, which will merit your recollection, when you become qualified, as I hope you will one day be, to employ your pen for the benefit of others and for your own reputation.

I send you a copy of the "Spectator" that it may be at hand when the time arrives for making use of it; and as a token, also, of all the good wishes of your affectionate Uncle.

Montpelier, like Monticello only thirty miles away, was a republican mecca. Citizens great and ordinary and many distinguished foreign visitors beat a path to Madison's door. During the summer months the normal flow was swelled by the tide of tourists journeying to the Virginia springs. Under the arbor on the lawn, "Queen" Dolley spread dinner for as many as ninety guests at one time. The world came to Madison; and although he made the round of the plantations in the neighborhood,

only once in nineteen years did he venture more than a day's ride from home. A young Harvard professor, George Ticknor, accompanied by his wife and Daniel Webster, visited Montpelier in 1824. Ticknor wrote of the visit to a friend in Boston.

Album of Virginia BY ED. BEYER, 1858

On his return to America in 1824 (left), Lafayette visited Madison; George Ticknor (below) was also a guest at Montpelier. Others stopped en route to Warm Springs (above).

Monticello, December 16, 1824.

On Saturday morning we reached Mr. Madison's, at Montpellier, on the west side of what is called the Southwest Mountain; a very fine, commanding situation, with the magnificant range of the Blue Ridge stretching along the whole horizon in front, at the distance of from twenty to thirty miles. . . .

We were received with a good deal of dignity and much cordiality, by Mr. and Mrs. Madison, in the portico, and immediately placed at ease; for they were apprised of our coming an hour or two before we arrived, and were therefore all in order, to show a little of that ceremony in which Mrs. Madison still delights.

Mr. Madison is a younger-looking man—he is now seventy-four—than he was when I saw him ten years ago, with an unsuccessful war grinding him to the earth; and he is one of the most pleasant men I have met, both from the variety and vivacity of his conversation. He lives, apparently, with great regularity. We breakfasted at nine, dined about four, drank tea at seven, and went to bed at ten; that is, we went to our rooms, where we were furnished with everything we wanted, and where Mrs. Madison sent us a nice supper every night and a nice luncheon every forenoon. From ten o'clock in the morning till three we rode, walked, or remained in our rooms, Mr. and Mrs. Madison being then occupied. The table is very ample and elegant, and somewhat luxurious; it is evidently a serious item in the account of Mr. M.'s happiness, and it seems to be his habit to pass about an hour, after the cloth is removed, with a variety of wines of no mean quality.

On politics he is a little reserved, as he seems determined not to be again involved in them; but about everything else he talked with great freedom, and told an interminable series of capital stories, most of which have some historical value. His language, though not very rich or picturesque, was chosen with much skill, and combined into very elegant and finished sentences; and both Mr. Webster and myself were struck with a degree of good-sense in his conversation which we had

367

Robert Walsh

not anticipated from his school of politics and course of life. We passed our time, therefore, very pleasantly, and feel indebted to him for a hospitality which becomes one who has been at the head of the nation.

On Sunday forenoon we took a ride of a dozen miles across different plantations, to see the country and the people. Mr. Madison's farm—as he calls it—consists of about three thousand acres, with an hundred and eighty slaves, and is among the best managed in Virginia. We saw also one or two others that looked very well, but in general things had a very squalid appearance.

Madison maintained a lively interest in public affairs, but his principal business was farming. With little practical experience in this calling, he weathered the severe economic depression in Virginia agriculture after 1818 better and longer than most of his neighbors. Jefferson, who was broken by it, called Madison "the best farmer in the world." Within a year of his return, the prominent planters of the region named him president of the newly formed Agricultural Society of Albemarle. His address to the society in 1818 combined enlarged philosophical views of the place of agriculture in the advance of civilization with a detailed "catalogue of errors" in Virginia husbandry. Most of these errors were well known to scientific agriculturists, as were most of the correctives proposed—deep plowing, crop rotation, the use of manures, improvement of livestock, reforestation, contour plowing—but they were still novel in the common practice of American agriculture and would remain so for decades to come. The address was printed in the *American Farmer* and circulated widely in the United States and abroad.

After nearly forty years on the national scene, Madison was impressed by the changes in the manners and morals of his native state. In 1819 the Philadelphia journalist Robert Walsh solicited his aid in the defense of American character and institutions against the verbal onslaught of carping English critics after the war. In all areas—slavery, religion, property, education—Madison wrote, he saw striking progress since the Revolution.

Montpellier Mar 2. 1819

In reference to the actual condition of slaves in Virga. it may be confidently stated, as better beyond comparison, than it was before the Revolution. The improvement strikes every one who witnessed their former condition, and attends to their present. They are better fed, better clad, better lodged, and better treated in every respect; insomuch that what was formerly deemed a moderate treatment wd. now be a rigid one, and what

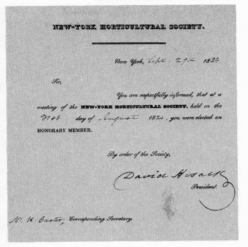

Certificate of membership that Madison received from the New-York Horticultural Society in 1824

View of Richmond in 1819

formerly a rigid one would now be denounced by the public feeling. With respect to the great article of food particularly it is a common remark among those who have visited Europe, that it includes a much greater proportion of the animal ingredient, than is attainable by the free labourers even in that quarter of the Globe. As the two great causes of the general melioration in the lot of the slaves since the establishment of our Independence, I should set down   1. the sensibility to human rights, and sympathy with human sufferings excited and cherished by the discussions preceding, & the spirit of the Institutions growing out of that event. 2. the decreasing proportions which the slaves bear to the individual holders of them: a consequence of the abolition of entails, & the rule of primogeniture, and of the equalizing tendency of parental affection unfettered from old prejudices, as well as from the restrictions of law.

With respect to the moral features of Virga. it may be observed, that the pictures which have been given of them are, to say the least, outrageous caracatures, even when taken from the state of Society previous to the Revolution; and that so far as there was any ground or colour for them, the same cannot be found for them now.

Omitting more minute or less obvious causes tainting the habits and manners of the people under the Colonial Govt. the following offer themselves.   1. the negro slavery chargeable in so great a degree on the very quarter which has furnished most of the libellers. It is well known that during the Colonial dependence of Virga. repeated attempts were made to stop the importations of slaves each of which attempts, was successively defeated by the foreign negative on the laws, and that one of the first offsprings of independent & republican legislation was an Act of perpetual prohibition   2. the too unequal distribution of property favored by laws derived from the British code, which generated examples in the opulent class, inauspicious to the habits of the other classes.   3. the indolence of most & the irregular lives of many of the established Clergy consisting, of in a very large proportion of foreigners, and these in no inconsiderable proportion, of men willing to leave their homes in the parent Country when their demerit was an obstacle to a provision for them, and whose

369

degeneracy here was promoted by their distance from the controuling eyes of their kindred & friends, by the want of Ecclesiastical superiors in the Colony, or efficient ones in G.B. who might maintain a salutary discipline among them, and finally by their independence both of their congregations and of the Civil authority for their stipends. 4. A source of contageous dissipation might be traced in the British Factors, chiefly from Scotland, who carried on the general trade external & internal of the Colony. These being interdicted by their principals from marrying in the Country, being little prone to apply their leisure to intellectual [pursuits] and living in knots scattered in small towns or detached spots affording few substitutes of social amusements easily fell into irregularities of different sorts, and of evil example....

With the exception of slavery these demoralizing causes have ceased or are wearing out; and even that as already noticed, has lost no small share of its former character. On the whole the moral aspect of the State may at present be fairly said to bear no unfavorable comparison with the average standard of the other States. It certainly gives the lie to the foreign Calumniators whom you propose to arraign.

That there has been an increase of religious instruction since the revolution can admit of no question. The English Church was originally the established religion: the character of the clergy that above described. Of other sects there were but few adherents, except the Presbyterians who predominated on the W. side of the Blue ridge Mountains. A little time previous to the Revolutionary struggle the Baptists sprang up, and made a very rapid progress. Among the early acts of the Republican Legislature were those abolishing the Religious establishment and putting all Sects at full liberty and on a perfect level. At present the population is divided, with small exceptions, among the Protest[ant]: Episcopalians, the Presbyterians the Baptists & the Methodists.... On a general comparison of the present & former times, the balance is certainly & vastly on the side of the present, as to the number of religious teachers the zeal which actuates them, the purity of their lives, and the attendance of the people on their instructions. It was the universal opinion of the Century preceding the last,

Drawing of a slave auction from the sketchbook of artist Lewis Miller

Although Madison felt the living conditions of slaves had improved, whippings such as the one portrayed in this illustration from a book published in 1817 still occurred.

that civil Govt. could not stand without the prop of a religious establishment, & that the Christian religion itself, would perish if not supported by a legal provision for its Clergy. The experience of Virginia conspicuously corroborates the disproof of both opinions. The Civil Govt. tho' bereft of everything like an anointed hierarchy possesses the requisite Stability and performs its functions with complete success: Whilst the number, the industry, and the morality of the priesthood & the devotion of the people have been manifestly increased by the total separation of the Church from the State.

On the subject of education I am not eno' informed to give a view of its increase.... Those who are best able to compare the present intelligence of the mass of the people, with that antecedent to the revolution, will all agree I believe on the great superiority of the present.

However much the condition of Virginia's blacks may have improved, Madison could not rest until slavery was abolished. Slavery was a moral crime, a curse to the society, and a menace to the Union. In his youth he had hoped to rid himself of dependence on slave labor and he had expected with most revolutionary Virginians that the system would fall before the advance of liberty and enlightenment. Instead, the monster had fastened its hold on Virginia and the states to the south. Simply to free the slaves was no solution, in Madison's opinion. The system must be eradicated and its benighted victims removed from society. To Madison, the coexistence of the two races in a state of freedom and equality was inconceivable. With the birth of the idea of colonization, he came to believe that the problem could be solved. He was one of the founders of the American Colonization Society in 1817, and until the end of his life he clung desperately to its program. In a letter to an acquaintance, Robert J. Evans, he sketched his own more ambitious version of that program.

Montpellier June 15. 1819

A general emancipation of slaves ought to be 1. gradual. 2. equitable & satisfactory to the individuals immediately concerned. 3. consistent with the existing & durable prejudices of the nation.

That it ought, like remedies for other deep rooted, and wide spread evils, be gradual, is so obvious that there seems to be no difference of opinion on that point.

To be equitable & satisfactory, the consent of both the Master & the slave should be obtained. That of the Master will require a provision in the plan for compensating a loss of what he has held as property guaranteed by the laws, and recognized by the constitution. That of the slave requires that his condition in a state of freedom, be preferable in his own estimation, to his actual one in a state of bondage.

To be consistent with existing and probably unalterable prejudices in the U.S. the freed blacks ought to be permanently removed beyond the region occupied by or allotted to a white population. The objections to a thorough incorporation of the two people, are with most of the Whites insuperable, and are admitted by all of them to be very powerful. If the blacks, strongly marked as they are by physical & lasting peculiarities, be retained amid the whites, under the degrading privation of equal rights political or social, they must be always dissatisfied with their condition as a change only from one to another species of oppression; always secretly confederated agst. the ruling & privileged class; and always uncontrolled by some of the most cogent motives to moral and respectable conduct. The character of the freed blacks, even where their legal condition is least affected by their colour, seems to put these truths beyond question. It is material also that the removal of the blacks be to a distance precluding the jealousies & hostilities to be apprehended from a neighboring people stimulated by the contempt known to be entertained for their peculiar features; to say nothing of their vindictive recollections, or the predatory propensities which their State of Society might foster. Nor is it fair, in estimating the danger of Collusions with the Whites, to charge it wholly on the side of the Blacks. There would be reciprocal antipathies doubling the danger.

The colonizing plan on foot, has as far as it extends a due regard to these requisites; with the additional object of bestowing new blessings civil & relegious on the quarter of the Globe most in need of them. The Society proposes to transport to the African Coast, all free & freed blacks who may be willing to remove thither; to provide by fair means, & it is understood with a prospect of success, a suitable territory for their reception; and to initiate them into such an establishment as may gradually, and indefinitely expand itself.

The experiment under this view of it, merits encouragement from all who regard slavery as an evil, who wish

Madison's letter of June 15, 1819, giving his views on colonization

to see it diminished and abolished by peaceable & just means; and who have themselves no better mode to propose. Those who have most doubted the success of the experiment must at least have wished to find themselves in an error.

But the views of the Society are limited to the case of blacks already free, or who may be *gratuitously* emancipated. To provide a commensurate remedy for the evil, the plan must be extended to the great mass of blacks, must embrace a fund sufficient to induce the Master as well as the slave to concur in it. Without the concurrence of the Master, the benefit will be very limited as it relates to the Negroes; and essentially defective, as it relates to the U. States; And the concurrence of Masters, must for the most part, be obtained by purchase. . . .

Happily . . . if slavery as a national evil is to be abolished, and it be just that it be done at the national expence, the amount of the expence is not a paramount consideration. It is the peculiar fortune, or rather a providential blessing of the U.S. to possess a resource commensurate to this great object, without taxes on the people, or even an increase of the Public debt.

I allude to the vacant territory the extent of which is so vast, and the vendible value of which is so well ascertained.

Supposing the number of slaves to be 1,500,000. and the price to average 400. d[ollar]rs the cost of the whole would be 600 millions of dollrs. . . .

This will require 200 Mils. of acres at 3 dolrs. per acre; or 300 Mills. at 2 dollrs. per acre a quantity, which tho' great in itself, is perhaps not a third part of the disposable territory belonging to the U.S. And to what object so good so great & so glorious, could that peculiar fund of wealth be appropriated? Whilst the sale of territory would on one hand be planting one desert with a free & civilized people, it would on the other, be giving freedom to another people, and filling with them another desert. And, if in any instances, wrong has been done by our forefathers to people of one colour in dispossessing them of their soil, what better atonement is now in our power than that of making what is rightfully acquired a source of justice & of blessings to a people of another colour? . . .

It is evident however that in effectuating a general

emancipation of slaves in the mode which has been hinted, difficulties of other sorts would be encountered. The provision for ascertaining the joint consent of the masters & slaves; for guarding agst. unreasonable valuations of the latter; and for the discrimination of those not proper to be conveyed to a foreign residence, or who ought to remain a charge on Masters in whose service they had been disabled or worn out and for the annual transportation of such numbers, would require the mature deliberations of the National Councils. The measure implies also the practicability of procuring in Africa, an enlargement of the district or districts, for receiving the exiles, sufficient for so great an augmentation of their numbers.

Perhaps the Legislative provision best adapted to the case would be an incorporation of the Colonizing Society or the establishment of a similar one, with proper powers under the appointment & superintendence of the national Executive....

One difficulty presents itself which will probably attend every plan which is to go into effect under the Legislative provisions of the National Govt. But whatever may be the defect of the existing powers of Congress, the Constitution has pointed out the way in which it can be supplied, And it can hardly be doubted that the requisite powers might readily be procured for attaining the great object in question, in any mode whatever approved by the nation.

If these thoughts can be of any aid in your search of a remedy for the great evil under which the nation labors, you are very welcome to them. You will allow me however to add that it will be most agreeable to me, not to be publickly referred to in any use you may make of them.

Principally because of slavery, Madison feared for the duration of the Union. The Missouri question raised a mighty storm in 1820. Madison disapproved of the Missouri Compromise's prohibition of slavery above the latitudinal line 36°30′ in the Louisiana Purchase lands. Whatever its motives, the effect of the restriction, Madison thought, was to cause a division of parties along a geographical line and hence to weaken, perhaps eventually to destroy, national political consensus. And whatever the value of restricting slavery above the Ohio in 1787 when the door to the African trade was open, Madison believed that gradual emancipation would be more readily accomplished now by diffusion of the slaves over a vast area, thereby lightening the burden in the South and bringing more shoulders under it. Finally, he felt that since slavery was a local institution, Congress could not control its destiny in any new or old state. Madison expressed these views of the Missouri Compromise and its sequel, the so-called Second Missouri Compromise, in letters to President Monroe and his old friend Lafayette.

Speaker of the House Henry Clay supported Missouri Compromise.

Montpellier Feby. 10. 1820

I find the idea is fast spreading that the zeal with which the extension, so called, of slavery is opposed, has with the coalesced *leaders,* an object very different from the welfare of slaves, or the check to their increase; and that the real object is, as you intimate, to form a new State of parties founded on local instead of political distinctions; thereby dividing the republicans of the North from those of the South, and making the former instrumental in giving the opponents of both an ascendancy over the whole. If this be the view of the subject at Washington, it furnishes an additional reason for a conciliatory proceeding in relation to Maine.

I have been truly astonished at some of the doctrines & declarations to which the Missouri question has led. . . .

I have observed as *yet,* in none of the views taken of the ordinance of 1787 interdicting slavery N.W. of the Ohio, an allusion to the circumstances, that when it passed, the Congs. had no authority to prohibit the importation of slaves from abroad; that all the States had, and some were in the full exercise of, the right to import them; and consequently, that there was no mode in which Congress could check the evil, but the indirect one of narrowing the space open for the reception of slaves. Had the federal authority then existed to prohibit directly & totally the importation from abroad, can it be doubted that it would have been exerted, and that a regulation having merely the effect of preventing an interior dispersion of slaves actually in the U.S. and creating a distinction among the States in the degrees of their sovereignty, would not have been adopted? or perhaps thought of?

Montpellier Novr. 25. 1820

Here, we are, on the whole, doing well, and giving an example of a free system, which I trust will be more of a pilot to a good port, than a Beacon, warning from a bad one. We have, it is true, occasional fevers; but they are of the transient kind, flying off through the surface, without preying on the vitals. A Government like ours has so many safety-valves, giving vent to overheated passions, that it carries within itself a relief against the infirmities from which the best of human Institutions can not be exempt. The subject which ruffles the surface of public affairs most at present, is furnished by the transition of the "Territory" of Missouri, from a state of nonage, to a maturity for self-Government, and for a membership in the Union. Among the questions involved in it, the one most immediately interesting to humanity, is the question whether a toleration or prohibition of slavery westward of the Mississippi, would most extend its evils. The humane part of the argument agst. the prohibition turns on the position, that whilst the importation of slaves from abroad is precluded, a diffusion of those in the Country, tends at once to meliorate their actual condition, and to facilitate their eventual emancipation. Unfortunately the subject which was settled at the last session of Congress by a mutual concession of the parties, is reproduced on the arena, by a clause in the Constitution of Missouri; distinguishing between free persons of colour, and white persons, and providing that the Legislature of the new State shall exclude from it the former. What will be the issue of the revived discussion is yet to be seen. The Case opens the wider field, as the Constitutions and laws of the different States are at variance in the civic character given to free people of colour; those of most of the States, not excepting such as have abolished slavery, imposing various disqualifications which degrade them from the rank & rights of white persons. All these perplexities develope more & more, the dreadful fruitfulness of the original sin of the African trade.

Nineteenth-century illustration of the capture of rebel Nat Turner

The best hope for slavery reform in Virginia came in the wake of the hideous Nat Turner insurrection of 1831 in Southampton County, Virginia, in which fifty-seven whites were slain before the rebels were hunted down and captured or killed. But the state legislature, meeting after the massacre, slammed the door once and for all on emancipation in any form. Only the most slender thread of hope remained, but Madison clung to it. While northern abolitionists discredited colonization as a cheat and a sham and Southerners united on the theory of African slavery as the norm of history, the injunction of the Bible, and the bulwark of southern civilization, Madison stared down despair. The English author and reformer, Harriet Martineau, visited him in 1835, only a year before his death. Crippled by rheumatism, deaf in one ear, losing his sight, "his little person wrapped in a black silk gown, a warm gray and white cap upon his head, which his lady took care should always sit becomingly," Madison had lost none of his talent for spirited conversation. He talked of many things, from the diminutive size of Roman farms to the absurdities of geology, but most of all he talked of slavery.

Madison as Harriet Martineau saw him: "his little person wrapped in a black silk gown, a warm gray and white cap upon his head...."

Retrospect of Western Travel [1838]

With regard to slavery he owned himself almost to be in despair. He had been quite so till the institution of the Colonization Society. How such a mind as his could derive any alleviation to its anxiety from that source is surprising. I think it must have been from his overflowing faith; for the facts were before him that in eighteen years the Colonization Society had removed only between two and three thousand persons, while the annual increase of the slave population in the United States was upward of sixty thousand.

He talked more on the subject of slavery than on any other, acknowledging, without limitation or hesitation, all the evils with which it has ever been charged. He told me that the black population in Virginia increases far faster than the white; and that the licentiousness only stops short of the destruction of the race; every slave girl being expected to be a mother by the time she is fifteen. He assumed from this, I could not make out why, that the negroes must go somewhere, and pointed out how the free states discourage the settlements of blacks; how Canada disagrees with them; how Hayti shuts them out; so that Africa is their only refuge. He did not assign any reason why they should not remain where they are when freed. He found, by the last returns from his estates, that one third of his own slaves were under five years of age. He had parted with some of his best land to feed the increasing numbers, and had yet been obliged to sell a dozen of his slaves the preceding week. He observed that the whole Bible is against negro slavery; but that the clergy do not preach this, and the people do not see it. He became animated in describing ... the eagerness of the clergy of the four denominations to catch converts among the slaves, and the effect of religious teaching of this kind upon those who, having no rights, can have no duties. He thought the condition of slaves much improved in his time, and, of course, their intellects. This remark was, I think, intended to apply to Virginia alone, for it is certainly not applicable to the southwestern states. He accounted for his selling his slaves by mentioning their horror of going to Liberia, a horror which he admitted to be prevalent among the blacks, and which appears to me decisive as to the unnaturalness of the scheme. The willing mind is the first requisite to the emigrant's success. Mr. Madison complained of the difficulty and risk of throwing an additional population into the colony, at the rate of two or three cargoes a year; complained of it because he believed it was the fault of the residents, who were bent upon trading with the interior for luxuries, instead of raising food for the new comers.... Mr. Madison admitted the great and various difficulties attending the scheme, and recurred to the expression that he was only "less in despair than formerly about slavery." He spoke with deep feeling of the sufferings of ladies under the system, declaring that he pitied them even more than their negroes, and that the saddest slavery of all was that of conscientious Southern women. They cannot trust their slaves in the smallest particulars, and have to superintend the execution of all their own orders; and they know that their estates are surrounded by vicious free blacks, who induce thievery among the negroes, and keep the minds of the owners in a state of perpetual suspicion, fear, and anger.

Mr. Madison spoke strongly of the helplessness of all countries cursed with a servile population in a conflict with a people wholly free; ridiculed the idea of the Southern States being able to maintain a rising against the North; and wondered that all thinkers were not agreed in a thing so plain. He believed that Congress has power to prohibit the internal slave trade. He mentioned the astonishment of some strangers, who had an idea that slaves were always whipped all day long, at seeing his negroes go to church one Sunday. They were gayly dressed, the women in bright-coloured calicoes; and, when a sprinkling of rain came, up went a dozen umbrellas. The astonished strangers veered round to the conclusion that slaves were very happy; but were told

Harriet Martineau

of the degradation of their minds; of their carelessness of each other in their nearest relations, and their cruelty to brutes.

If slavery headed Madison's agenda of unfinished business from the Revolution, the conquest of ignorance stood not far behind. In 1785 he had tried and failed to win legislative approval of Jefferson's comprehensive plan of public education. Jefferson, always the captain of this cause, revived his plan in 1814. This time the Virginia assembly eliminated the provisions for elementary and secondary schools but gave Jefferson his dream of a state university. Madison must have wondered, as Jefferson did, at the folly of the legislature in thus choosing to raise the apex without laying the foundations in the schools. Since knowledge will ever govern ignorance, Madison observed, a popular government without popular education "is but a prologue to a Farce or a Tragedy, or perhaps both." His essentially civic conception of education, as an ally of republican government, is developed in a letter to William T. Barry of Kentucky.

[Montpelier,] Aug. 4 1822

Learned Institutions ought to be favorite objects with every free people. They throw that light over the public mind which is the best security against crafty & dangerous encroachments on the public liberty. They are nurseries of skilful Teachers for the schools distributed throughout the Community. They are themselves Schools for the particular talents required for some of the public Trusts, on the able execution of which the welfare of the people depends. They multiply the educated individuals from among whom the people may elect a due portion of their public agents of every description more especially of those who are to frame the laws; by the perspicuity, the consistency, and the stability, as well as by the just & equal spirit of which the great social purposes are to be answered.

Without such Institutions, the more costly of which can scarcely be provided by individual means, none but the few whose wealth enables them to support their sons abroad, can give them the fullest education; and in proportion as this is done, the influence is monopolized which superior information everywhere possesses. At cheaper & nearer seats of Learning parents with slender incomes may place their sons in a course of Education putting them on a level with the sons of the richest. Whilst those who are without property, or with but little,

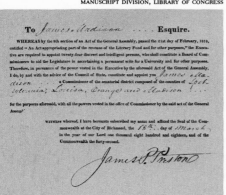

In 1818 Madison had been appointed a commissioner "to aid the Legislature in ascertaining a permanent scite for a University."

must be peculiarly interested in a System which unites with the more Learned Institutions, a provision for diffusing through the entire Society the education needed for the common purposes of life....

But why should it be necessary in this case, to distinguish the Society into classes according to their property? When it is considered that the establishment and endowment of Academies, Colleges, and Universities are a provision not merely for the existing generation, but for succeeding ones also; that in Governments like ours a constant rotation of property results from the free scope to industry, and from the laws of inheritance, and when it is considered moreover, how much of the exertions and privations of all are meant not for themselves, but for there posterity, there can be little ground for objections from any class, to plans of which when contributing to a permanent plan for the education of the poor, ought to reflect that he is providing for that of his own descendants; and the poor man who concurs in a provision for those who are not poor that at no distant day it may be enjoyed by descendants from himself. It does not require a long life to witness these vicisitudes of fortune.

It is among the happy peculiarities of our Union, that the States composing it derive from their relations to each other and to the whole, a salutary emulation, without the enmity involved in competitions among States alien to each other. This emulation, we may perceive, is not without its influence in several important respects; and in none ought it to be more felt than in the merit of diffusing the light and the advantages of public Instruction....

Throughout the Civilized World, nations are courting the praise of fostering Science and the useful arts, and are opening their eyes to the principles and the blessings of Representative Government. The American people owe it to themselves, and to the cause of free Government to prove by their establishments for the advancement and diffusion of Knowlege, that their political Institutions, which are attracting observation from every quarter, and are respected as Models, by the newborn States in our own Hemisphere, are as favorable to the intellectual and moral improvement of man, as they are conformable to his individual & social Rights. What spectacle can be more edifying or more seasonable, than that of Liberty & Learning, each leaning on the other for their mutual & surest support?

Madison was closely associated with Jefferson in founding the University of Virginia. It was to be, among other things, a secular institution in strict conformity to the principle of separation of Church and State. The idea of a "godless university" was novel, threatening to Virginia's evangelical leadership, and the university rose over its opposition. For Madison, freedom of religion was involved with freedom of mind and therefore with what would later be called academic freedom. It was the one principle upon which there could be no compromise. He stated his views in a letter to Edward Everett, then a professor and later president of Harvard—a university that still labored under the constraints of its Puritan founding.

Montpellier Mar. 19. 1823

Edward Everett of Harvard

I am not suprised at the dilemma produced at your University, by making Theological Professorships an integral part of the System. The anticipation of such an one, led to the omission in ours; the Visitors being merely authorized to open a public Hall for religious occasion, under *impartial* regulations; with the opportunity to different Sects to establish their Theological Schools, so near that the Students of the University may respectively attend the religious exercises in them. The Village of Charlottesville, where different Religious Worships will be held, is also so near that resort may be conveniently had to them.

A University with Sectarian professorships, becomes of course, a Sectarian Monopoly: with professorships of rival sects, it would be an arena of Theological Gladiators: without any such professorship, it must incur for a time at least, the imputation of irreligious tendencies if not designs. The last difficulty was thought more manageable, than either of the others.

On this view of the subject, there seems to be no alternative but between a public University without a Theological professorship, or Sectarian Seminaries without a University.

I recollect to have seen a great many years ago, a project of a paper by Govr [of New Jersey William] Livingston, father of the present Judge [Henry Brockholst Livingston on the Supreme Court], intended to comprehend & conciliate College Students of every denomination, by a Form composed wholly of texts & phrases of Scripture. If a trial of the expedient was ever made, it must have failed, notwithstanding its winning aspect, from the single cause that many sects reject all set forms of worship.

The difficulty of reconciling the Christian mind to the absence of religious Tuition from a University, established by Law & at the common expense, is probably less with us than with you. The settled opinion here is that religion is essentially distinct from Civil Govt. and exempt from its cognizance; that a connexion between them is injurious to both; that there are causes in the human breast which ensure the perpetuity of religion without the aid of the law; that rival sects with equal rights, exercise mutual censorships in favor of good morals; that if new sects arise with absurd opinions or overheated imaginations, the proper remedies lie in time, forbearance, and example: that a legal establishment of Religion without a toleration, could not be thought of, and with a toleration, is no security for public quiet & harmony, but rather a source itself of discord & animosity: and finally, that these opinions are supported by experience, which has shewn that every relaxation of the Alliance between Law & Religion, from the partial example of Holland, to its consumation in Pennsylvania, N. Jersey &c. has been found as safe in practice as it is sound in Theory.

Jefferson dedicated the university to "the illimitable freedom of the human mind." Still, his anxiety for the political purity of the School of Law and Government—one of the ten schools envisioned—led him to propose that the Board of Visitors prescribe correct texts. These ranged from Algernon Sydney's *Discourses* and Locke on civil government to Madison's Virginia Report on the Alien and Sedition Laws. If one reads between the lines of Madison's letter in response, it seems clear that he disliked the proposition—though in this, as in all things connected with the university, he had not the heart to quarrel with Jefferson. He confined himself to suggesting an amendment that softened the resolution.

Montpellier Feby. 8. 1825
I have looked with attention over your intended proposal of a textbook for the Law School. It is certainly very material that the true doctrines of Liberty, as exemplified in our Political System, should be inculcated on those who are to sustain and may administer it. It is at the same time, not easy to find Standard books that will be

Virginia, HOWE

The University of Virginia

both guides & guards for the purpose. Sydney & Locke are admirably calculated to impress on young minds the right of Nations to establish their own Governments, and to inspire a love of free ones, but afford no aid in guarding our Republican Charters against constructive violations. The Declaration of Independence tho' rich in fundamental principles, and saying everything that could be said in the same number of words, falls nearly under a like observation. The "Federalist" may fairly enough be regarded as the most authentic exposition of the text of the federal Constitution as understood by the Body which prepared & the Authorities which accepted it. Yet it did not foresee all the misconstructions which have occurred; nor prevent some that it did foresee. And what equally deserves remark, neither of the great rival parties have acquiesced in all its Comments. It may nevertheless be admissible as a Schoolbook, if any will be that goes so much into detail. It has been actually admitted into two Universities if not more, those of Harvard & Rh. Island; but probably at the choice of the Professors, without an injunction from the superior authority. With respect to the Virginia Document of 1799 there may be more room for hesitation.... In framing a political creed, a like difficulty occurs as in the case of religion tho the public right be very different in the two cases. If the Articles be in very general terms, they do not answer the purpose: if in very particular terms, they divide & exclude where meant to unite & fortify. The best that can be done in our case seems to be, to avoid the two extremes, by referring to selected Standards without requiring an unqualified conformity to them, which indeed might not in every instance be possible. The selection would give them authority with the Students, and might controul or counteract deviations of the Professor. I have for your consideration, sketched a modification of the operative passage in your draught, with a view to relax the absoluteness of its injunction, and added to your list of Documents, the Inaugural Speech and the Farewell Address of President Washington. They may help down what might be less readily swallowed, and contain nothing which is not good; unless it be the laudatory reference in the Address to the [Jay] Treaty of 1795 with G.B. which ought not to weigh against the sound sentiments characterizing it.

After all, the most effectual safeguard against heretical intrusions into the School of politics, will be an Able & Orthodox Professor, whose course of instruction will be an example to his Successors, and may carry with it a Sanction from the Visitors.

Madison saw Jefferson for the last time, at Monticello, in September, 1825. The collaboration of these two philosophical statesmen over half a century was one of the wonders of the world. The pilgrims who took in Montpelier as well as Monticello usually found Madison the more inviting figure. He seemed happier, friendlier, better informed on current affairs, and more resilient to change than the Sage of Monticello. "He appears less studied, brilliant, and frank, but more natural, candid and profound than Mr. Jefferson," one observer noted. "Mr. Jefferson has more imagination and passion, quicker and richer conceptions. Mr. Madison has a sound judgment, tranquil temper and logical mind." At eighty-two, as he labored to put the university into operation, Jefferson struggled against death and bankruptcy. In January, 1826, he appealed to the legislature for permission to dispose of the bulk of his property by lottery—a favor granted but to no avail. A month later, in his last letter to Madison, he explained his plight and closed with a moving farewell.

> Monticello. February 17, 1826
>
> The friendship which has subsisted between us, now half a century, and the harmony of our political principles and pursuits, have been sources of constant happiness to me through that long period. And if I remove beyond the reach of attentions to the University, or beyond the bourne of life itself, as I soon must, it is a comfort to leave that institution under your care, and an assurance that it will not be wanting. It has also been a great solace to me, to believe that you are engaged in vindicating to posterity the course we have pursued for preserving to them, in all their purity, the blessings of self-government, which we had assisted too in acquiring for them. If ever the earth has beheld a system of administration conducted with a single and steadfast eye to the general interest and happiness of those committed to it, one which, protected by truth, can never know reproach, it is that to which our lives have been devoted. To myself you have been a pillar of support through life. Take care of me when dead, and be assured that I shall leave with you my last affections.
>
> TH: JEFFERSON

M adison replied to his old friend a short time later.

Montpellier Feby. 24. 1826.

I had noticed the disclosures at Richmond with feelings which I am sure I need not express: any more than the alleviation of them by the sequel. I had not been without fears that the causes you enumerate were undermining your estate. But they did not reach the extent of the evil. Some of these causes were indeed forced on my attention by my own experience. Since my return to private life (and the case was worse during my absence in public) such have been the unkind seasons, & the ravages of insects, that I have made but one tolerable crop of Tobacco, and but one of Wheat; the proceeds of both of which were greatly curtailed by mishaps in the sale of them. And having no resources but in the earth I cultivate, I have been living very much throughout on borrowed means. As a necessary consequence, my debts have swelled to an amount, which if called for at the present conjuncture, would give to my situation a degree of analogy to yours. Fortunately I am not threatened with any rigid pressure, and have the chance of better crops & prices, with the prospect of a more leisurely disposal of the property which must be a final resort.

You do not overrate the interest I feel in the University as the Temple thro' which alone lies the road to that of Liberty. But you entirely do my aptitude to be your successor in watching over its prosperity. It would be the pretension of a mere worshipper "remplacer" the Tutelary Genius of the Sanctuary. The best hope is, in the continuance of your cares, till they can be replaced by the stability and self growth of the Institution. Little reliance can be put even on the fellowship of my services. The past year has given me sufficient intimation of the infirmities in wait for me. In calculating the probabilities of survivorship, the inferiority of my constitution forms an equation at least with the seniority of yours. . . .

You cannot look back to the long period of our private friendship & political harmony, with more affecting recollections than I do. If they are a source of pleasure to you, what ought they not be to me? We can not be deprived of the happy consciousness of the pure devotion to the public good, with which we discharged the trusts committed to us. And I indulge a confidence that sufficient evidence will find its way to another generation, to

Harper's New Monthly Magazine, JULY, 1863

Monticello, where Madison saw his friend Jefferson for the last time

ensure, after we are gone, whatever of justice may be witheld whilst we are here. The political horizon is already yielding in your case at least, the surest auguries of it. Wishing & hoping that you may yet live to increase the debt which our Country owes you, and to witness the increasing gratitude, which alone can pay it, I offer you the fullest return of affectionate assurances.

Jefferson died on July 4, 1826, the fiftieth anniversary of American independence. Nicholas P. Trist, one of the Monticello family, informed Madison, who replied at once.

Jefferson and John Adams both died on July 4, 1826, fifty years after the Declaration of Independence. A friend sent Madison this dirge.

Montpellier July 6. 1826

I have just recd. yours of the 4th. A few lines from Doctr Dunglison had prepared me for such a communication; and I never doubted that the last scene of our illustrious friend would be worthy of the life which it closed. Long as this has been spared to his country and to those who loved him, a few years more were to have been desired for the sake of both. But we are more than consoled for the loss, by the gain to him; and by the assurance that he lives and will live in the memory and gratitude of the wise and good, as a luminary of science, as a votary of liberty, as a model of patriotism, and as a benefactor of human kind. In these characters I have known him, and not less in the virtues and charms of social life for a period of fifty years, during which there was not an interruption or diminution of mutual confidence and cordial friendship for a single moment in a single instance. What I feel therefore now need not, I should say, can not be expressed. If there be any possible way in which I can *usefully* give evidence of it do not fail to afford me the opportunity.

As Jefferson had wished, Madison succeeded him as rector of the university, a position that combined the duties of a president with those of a chairman of the board. Most of the business was transacted through young Trist stationed at Monticello. In one of his many letters to him, Madison departed from the business at hand to write a little essay on the Utopian experiment of Robert Owen, who had called at Montpelier in 1825 while en route to the new paradise, New Harmony, Indiana. For all his faith in man's capacity for justice, improvement, and self-government, Madison could not indulge Owen's dream of an egalitarian socialist society.

The streak of Calvinism in his thought, crossed now with the Malthusian teachings of the classical economists, caused him to look skeptically on Owen's scheme, though he wished to see it tried for the good it might hold for mankind.

Robert Owen

Montpellier Apl. 1827

The Harmony Gazette has been regularly sent me; but in the crowd of printed things I receive, I had not attended to the Essays to which you refer me. The present situation of G. Britain which gave rise to them is full of instruction and Mr. Owen avails himself of it with address, in favour of his panacea. Such diseases are however too deeply rooted in human society to admit of more than great palliatives.

Every populous country is liable to contingenc[i]es that must distress a portion of its inhabitants. The chief of them are 1. unfruitful seasons, increasing the price of subsistence without increasing that of labour; and even reducing the price of labour, by abridging the demand of those whose income depends on the fruits of the Earth.

2. The sudden introduction of labour-saving machinery, taking employment from those whose labour is the only source of their subsistence.

3. The caprice of fashion, on which the many depend, who supply the wants of fancy. Take for a sufficient illustration a single fact. When the present King of England was Prince of Wales, he introduced the use of Shoe strings instead of Shoe buckles. The effect on the condition of the Bucklemakers was such that he received addresses from many thousands of them, praying him as the Arbiter of fashion, to save them from starving, by restoring the taste for buckles in preference to strings.

4. To the preceding occurrences to which an insulated community would be liable, must be added a loss of foreign markets to a manufacturing and commercial community from whatever of the various causes it may happen. Among these causes may be named even the changeableness of foreign fashion. The substitutions of shoe strings for shoe-buckles in the U.S., had a like effect with that in England, on her bucklemakers.

Mr. Owen's remedy for these vicissitudes, implies that labour will be relished without the ordinary impulses to it; that the love of equality will supercede the desire of distinction; and that the increasing leisure from the improvements of machinery will promote intellectual cultivation, moral enjoyment, and innocent amusements, without any of the vicious resorts for the ennui of idleness....

The state of things promising most exemption from the distress exhibited in G. Britain, would be a freedom of commerce among all nations, and especially with the addition of universal peace. The aggregate fruits of the Earth, which are little varied by the Seasons, would then be accessible to all: The improvements of machinery, not being adopted every where at once, would have a diminished effect where first introduced: and there being no interruptions to foreign Commerce, the vicissitudes of fashion, would be limited in their sudden offset in one country by the numerous markets abroad for the same or similar articles.

After all there is one indelible cause remaining, of pressure on the condition of the laboring part of mankind: and that is, the constant tendency to an increase of their numbers, after the increase of food has reached its term. The competition for employment then reduces wages to their minimum, and privation to its maximum: and whether the evil proceeding from this tendency be checked, as it must be by either physical or moral causes, the checks are themselves but so many evils. With this knowledge of the impossibility of banishing evil altogether from human society, we must console ourselves with the belief that it is overbalanced by the good mixed with it, and direct our efforts to an increase of the good proportion of the mixture.

A circular announcing the Western Volunteer, a newspaper in Frankfort, Kentucky; the publisher, Henry Banks, asked Madison to subscribe.

Republicanism for Madison was fundamentally a matter of balancing the will of the majority with the rights of minorities through a properly constituted government. The principal unfinished business in this regard was the Virginia Constitution of 1776, which he, though unhappily not Jefferson, would at last have an opportunity to reform. In 1829 the freeholders of Orange elected him a delegate to the convention to revise the constitution. The assemblage in Richmond was dazzling. Two former presidents, Madison and Monroe, Chief Justice John Marshall, Speaker of the House of Representatives Philip P. Barbour, vintage Jeffersonians John Randolph and William B. Giles, and even a President-to-be, John Tyler, were among its members. Representation was the great issue, and it divided Virginia geographically along the line of the Blue Ridge. The existing system took no account of population. New Virginia—the rapidly growing West—

was unfairly dominated by old Virginia. Western reformers, taking up the half-century-long Jeffersonian attack on the constitution, advocated a "one man, one vote" system on the basis of white population only. But the power and the wealth of Virginia, particularly the property in slaves who could not vote but were counted in apportioning the legislature, were concentrated in the East, and easterners demanded protection for these interests against the will of a hostile majority. Suffrage was a related issue. Somewhere between one-third and one-half of Virginia's adult white males were disfranchised under the freehold suffrage qualification, an intolerable vestige of the past in this new age of democracy. Both these matters were referred to a committee chaired by Madison, the lone survivor of the revolutionary convention. He cast the decisive vote in the committee for the white basis in the lower house of the assembly. This was unacceptable to the eastern majority in the convention, however, and Madison himself yielded his convictions to the eastern bloc. Early in December, the old gentleman, his small frame draped in a threadbare "snuff-colored" coat, his hair powdered, his voice low and weak, addressed the convention.

[December 2, 1829]

Having been for a very long period withdrawn from any participation in proceedings of deliberative bodies, and under other disqualifications now, of which I am deeply sensible, though, perhaps less sensible than others may perceive that I ought to be, I shall not attempt more than a few observations which may suggest the views I have

This painting by George Catlin shows Madison addressing the Virginia Convention at Richmond in 1829.

taken of the subject and which will consume but little of the time of the Committee, now become precious.

It is sufficiently obvious, that persons and property, are the objects on which Governments are to act: and that the rights of persons, and the rights of property are the objects for the protection of which Government was instituted. These rights cannot well be separated. The personal right to acquire property, which is a natural right, gives to property when acquired a right to protection as a social right. The essence of Government is power, and power lodged as it must be in human hands, will ever be liable to abuse. In Monarchies the interests and happiness of all may be sacrificed to the caprice and passion of a despot. In Aristocracies, the rights and welfare of the many may be sacrificed to the pride and cupidity of a few. In Republics, the great danger is that the majority may not sufficiently respect the rights of the minority. Some gentlemen, consulting the purity and generosity of their own minds, without adverting to the lessons of experience, would find a security against that danger in our social feelings; in a respect for character: in the dictates of the monitor within; in the interests of individuals: in the aggregate interests of the community.

But Man is known to be a selfish as well as a social being. Respect for character though often a salutary restraint, is but too often overruled by other motives. When numbers of men act in a body respect for character is often lost, just in proportion as it is necessary to control what is not right. We all know that conscience is not a sufficient safeguard, besides that conscience itself may be deluded; many being misled by an unconscious bias into acts which an enlightened conscience would forbid. As to the permanent interest of individuals in the aggregate interests of the community, & in the proverbial maxim that honesty is the best policy; present temptation is too often found to be an over match for those considerations. These favourable attributes of the human character are all valuable as auxiliaries, but they will not serve as a substitute for the coercive provisions belonging to government and law. They will always, in proportion as they prevail, be favourable to a mild administration of both; but they can never be relied on as a guaranty of the rights of the minority against a Majority disposed to take unjust advantage of its power. The only effectual

Among the impressive delegates to the convention was Philip P. Barbour, Speaker of the House.

safeguard to the rights of the minority must be laid in such a basis & structure of the Government itself as may afford, in a certain degree, directly or indirectly, a defensive authority in behalf of a minority having right on its side.

To come more nearly to the subject before the Committee, viz: that peculiar feature in our community which calls for a peculiar division in the basis of our Government, I mean the coloured part of our population. It is apprehended, if the power of the Commonwealth shall be in the hands of a majority, who have no interest in this species of property, that, from the facility with which it may be oppressed by excessive taxation, injustice may be done to its owners. It would seem therefore, if we can incorporate that interest into the basis of our system, it will be the most apposite and effectual security that can be devised. Such an arrangement is recommended to me by many very important considerations. It is due to justice: due to humanity: due to truth; to the sympathies of our nature: in fine, to our character as a people, both abroad and at home, that they should be considered, as much as possible, in the light of human beings; and not as mere property. As such they are acted upon by our laws; and have an interest in our laws. They may be considered as making a part, tho a degraded part of the families to which they belong. If they had the complexion of the Serfs in the north of Europe, or of the Villeins, formerly in England; in other terms, if they were of our own complexion, much of the difficulty would be removed. But the mere circumstance of complexion cannot deprive them of the character of men. The Federal number, as it is called [the three-fifths clause of the Constitution (Article I, Section 3) apportioning representation and direct taxes according to the number of free persons and three-fifths of the slaves of each state], is particularly recommended to attention in forming a basis of representation, by its simplicity, its certainty, its stability, and its permanency...

Should the federal number be made to enter into the basis in one branch of the Legislature and not into the other, such an arrangement might prove favourable to the slaves themselves. It may be, and I think it has been suggested, that those who have themselves no interest in this species of property, are apt to sympathize with

John Randolph of Roanoke was a long-time antagonist of Madison's.

the slaves more than may be the case with their masters; and would, therefore, be disposed, when they had the ascendency to protect them from laws of an oppressive character; whilst the masters, who have a common interest with the slaves, against undue taxation, which must be paid out of their labour, will be their protectors when they have the ascendency.

The Convention is now arrived at a point where we must agree on some common ground, all sides relaxing in their opinions, not changing, but mutually surrendering a part of them. In framing a Constitution, great difficulties are necessarily to be overcome; and nothing can ever overcome them but a spirit of compromise. Other nations are surprised at nothing so much as our having been able to form Constitutions in the manner which has been exemplified in this country. Even the Union of so many States is, in the eyes of the world, a wonder; the harmonious establishment of a common Government over them all, a miracle. I cannot but flatter myself, that, without a miracle, we shall be able to arrange all difficulties. I never have despaired, notwithstanding all the threatening appearances we have passed through. I have now more than a hope—a consoling confidence that we shall at last find that our labours have not been in vain.

Here was the last reprise of an old theme, and the dissonance of "interests" finally drowned the melody of democracy. What Madison was saying, though he seemed not to recognize it, was that slavery and democracy—even the democracy of the white community—were irreconcilable. Suffrage reform was finally compromised by the convention with Madison's support. He opposed going to universal white male suffrage but advocated admitting householders and taxpaying heads of families. Although he did not speak on this question, he developed his thoughts in a personal memorandum that focused his fears of the coming challenge to democracy from the massive growth of population on the Malthusian law.

[1829]

It is a law of nature, now well understood, that the earth under a civilized cultivation is capable of yielding subsistence for a large surplus of consumers, beyond those having an immediate interest in the soil; a surplus which must increase with the increasing improvements in agriculture, and the labor-saving arts applied to it. And it is a lot of humanity that of this surplus a large proportion is necessarily reduced by a competition for employment to wages which afford them the bare necessaries of life. That proportion being without property, or the hope of acquiring it, can not be expected to sympathize sufficiently with its rights, to be safe depositories of power over them.

What is to be done with this unfavored class of the community? If it be, on one hand, unsafe to admit them to a full share of political power, it must be recollected, on the other, that it cannot be expedient to rest a Republican Gov. on a portion of the society having a numerical & physical force excluded from, and liable to be turned against it; and which would lead to a standing military force, dangerous to all parties & to liberty itself.

This view of the subject makes it proper to embrace in the partnership of power, every description of citizens having a sufficient stake in the public order, and the stable administration of the laws; and particularly the House keepers & Heads of families; most of whom "having given hostages to fortune," will have given them to their Country also. . . .

It would be happy if a State of Society could be found or framed, in which an equal voice in making the laws might be allowed to every individual bound to obey them. But this is a Theory, which like most Theories, confessedly requires limitations & modifications, and the only question to be decided in this as in other cases, turns on the particular degree of departure, in practice, required by the essence & object of the Theory itself.

It must not be supposed that a crowded state of population, of which we have no example here, and which we know only by the image reflected from examples elsewhere, is too remote to claim attention.

The ratio of increase in the U.S. shows that the present

12 Millions will in	25 years be	24 Mils.
24 " " "	50 " "	48 "
48 " " "	75 " "	96 "
96 " " "	100 " "	192 "

There may be a gradual decrease of the rate of increase; but it will be small as long as agriculture shall yield its abundance. G. Britain has doubled her population in the last 50 years; notwithstanding its amount in proportion to its territory at the commencement of that period, and Ireland is a much stronger proof of the effect of an increasing product of food, in multiplying the consumers.

How far this view of the subject will be affected by the Republican laws of descent and distribution, in equalizing the property of the citizens and in reducing to the minimum mutual surplusses for mutual supplies, cannot be inferred from any direct and adequate experiment. One result would seem to be a deficiency of the capital for the expensive establishments which facilitate labour and cheapens its products on one hand, and, on the other, of the capacity to purchase the costly and ornamental articles consumed by the wealthy alone, who must cease to be idlers and become labourers. Another the increased mass of labourers added to the production of necessaries by the withdrawal for this object, of a part of those now employed in producing luxuries, and the addition to the labourers from the class of present consumers of luxuries. To the effect of these changes, intellectual, moral, and social, the institutions and laws of the Country must be adapted, and it will require for the task all the wisdom of the wisest patriots.

Supposing the estimate of the growing population of the U.S. to be nearly correct, and the extent of their territory to be 8 or 9 hundred Mil of acres, and one fourth of it to consist of inarable surfaces, there will in a century or a little more, be nearly as crowded a population in the U.S. as in G. Britain or France, and if the present Constitution (of Virginia) with all its flaws, lasted more than half a century, it is not an unreasonable hope that an amended one will last more than a century.

If these observations be just, every mind will be able to develop & apply them.

Lafayette by Charles Willson Peale

After the convention adjourned, Madison reflected on its work in a letter to Lafayette. The old hero, long a friend of the black man, had hoped Madison would take up the cause of emancipation in Richmond. He explained why he did not, and could not, and speculated on the chances of ratification of the revised constitution. (It was approved in April on a straight sectional vote, the East for, the West against.)

Montpellier Feby 1. 1830
The Convention which called forth your interesting remarks & generous solicitudes, was pregnant with dif-

ficulties of various sorts, and at times, of ominous aspects. Besides the ordinary conflicts of opinion concerning the structure of Government, the peculiarity of local interests real or supposed, and above all, the case of our coloured population which happens to be confined to a geographical half of the State, and to have been a disproportionate object of taxation, were sources of jealousies & collisions which infected the proceedings throughout, and were finally overcome by a small majority only. Every concession of private opinion, not morally inadmissable, became necessary in order to prevent an abortion.... On the whole, the probability is, that the Constitution as amended will be sanctioned by the popular votes, and that by a considerable majority. Should this prove to be the case, the *peculiar* difficulties which will have been overcome, ought to render the experiment a new evidence of the capacity of men for Self-Government, instead of an argument in the hands of those who deny & calumniate it. The Convention was composed of the Elite of the Community, and exhibited great talents in the discussions belonging to the subject. Mr. Monroe, and still more myself, were too mindful of the years over our heads, to take an active part in them. The same consideration was felt by Mr. Marshall. I may add that each of us was somewhat fettered by the known & in some important instances, by the expressed will of our *immediate* Constituents.

Your anticipations with regard to the slavery among us, were the natural offspring of your just principles & Laudable sympathies. But I am sorry to say that the occasion which led to them, proved to be little fitted for the slightest interposition on that subject. A sensibility, morbid in its degree, was never more awakened among those who have the largest stake in that interest, and are most violent against any Governmental movement in relation to it. The excitability at the moment, happened also to be augmented by party questions between the South & the North, and the efforts used to make the circumstance common to the former, a sympathetic bond of co-operation. I scarcely express myself too strongly in saying, that an allusion in the Convention to the subject you have so much at heart, would have been a spark to a mass of Gunpowder. It is certain nevertheless, that Time "the great Innovator" is not idle in its salutary preparations. The Colonization Societies are becoming more and more one of its agents. Outlets for the freed blacks are alone wanted for a rapid erasure of that blot from our Republican character.

I observe in the foreign Journals the continued struggle between the Good & Evil principles on your side of the atlantic.

The cause that lay heaviest on Madison's heart and mind in these declining years was the cause of the Union and the Constitution. As the last of the founders, whose career surveyed the entire history of the nation, Madison became an acknowledged authority, almost an oracle, to historians, statesmen, and patriots seeking to light America's troubled course with the torch of the past. He thus came into public possession of his chief title to fame, Father of the Constitution. Men often inquired of him about some detail presumably buried in his voluminous record of the debates of the Federal Convention. He consistently refused disclosure even after the veil of secrecy was lifted by the publication in 1821 of the fragmentary record kept by Robert Yates, the New York Antifederalist. At that time Thomas Ritchie, editor of the Richmond *Enquirer,* tried to negotiate the publication of Madison's notes. Madison declined, as he continued to do as long as he lived.

Montpelr. Sep 15 1821

It is true as the public has been led to understand, that I possess materials for a pretty ample view of what passed in that Assembly. It is true also that it has not been my intention that they should for ever remain under the veil of secrecy. Of the time when it might be not improper for them to see the light, I had formed no particular determination: In general it had appeared to me that it might be best to let the work be a posthumous one, or at least that its publication should be delayed till the Constitution should be well settled by practice, & till a knowlege of the controversial part of the proceedings of its framers could be turned to no improper account. Delicacy also seemed to require some respect to the rule by which the Convention prohibited a promulgation without leave of what was spoken in it, so long as the policy of that rule could be regarded as in any degree unexpired. As guide in expounding and applying the provisions of the Constitution the debates and incidental decisions of the Convention can have no authoritative character. However desirable it be that they should be preserved as a gratification to the laudable curiosity felt by every people to trace the origin and progress of their political institutions, & as a source perhaps of some lights on the Science of Govt. the legitimate meaning of the Instrument must be derived from the text itself; or if a key is to be sought elsewhere, it must be not in the opinions or intentions of the Body which planned & proposed the Constitution, but in the sense attached to it by the people in their respective State Conventions where it recd. all the authority which it possesses.

Such being the course of my reflections I have suffered a concurrence & continuance of particular inconveniences for the time past, to prevent me from giving to my notes the fair & full preparations due to the subject of them. Of late, being aware of the growing hazards of postponements, I have taken the incipient steps for executing the task; and the expediency of not risking an ultimate failure is suggested by the Albany publication from the notes of a N. York member of the Convention. I have not seen more of the volume than has been extracted into the newspapers. But it may be inferred from these samples, that it is not only a very mutilated but a very erroneous edition of the matter to which it relates. There must be an entire omission also of the proceedings of the latter period of the Session from which Mr. Yates & Mr. Lansing [also a New York delegate] withdrew in the temper manifested by their report to their Constituents: the period during which the variant & variable opinions, converged & centered in the modifications seen in the final act of the Body.

It is my purpose now to devote a portion of my time to an exact digest of the voluminous materials in my hands. How long a time it will require under the interruptions & avocations which are probable I can not easily conjecture.

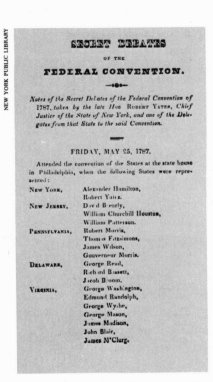

Published notes by Robert Yates of debates of 1787 Federal Convention

A jealous guardian of his reputation, especially as it touched the Constitution, Madison spent much paper and ink defending himself from charges of inconsistency. In the process he sometimes ran into new inconsistencies. Thus he repeatedly insisted that the Constitution should be construed in the sense given to it by the ratification conventions, since it was they who made the compact. Yet he held that *The Federalist,* a partisan work, was the most "authentic exposition" and that, in the instance of the national bank, a power deemed unconstitutional in 1791, or 1788, or 1798, might become valid through "the construction put on the Constitution, by the nation, which having made it had the supreme right to declare its meanings."

But Madison's most vexatious problem arose from the apparent discrepancy, if not contradiction, between the celebrated Resolutions of 1798 and the fervent unionism of his twilight years. During the 1820s the Virginia and Kentucky Resolutions were resurrected and mustered into the service of a revival of states' rights in Virginia politics. On the high authority of Jefferson and Madison, the movement assailed the tendency toward "consolidation" in the central government. Federal internal improvements and the protective tariff were the main targets, though the judicial nationalism of Chief Justice John Marshall was also condemned. Madison disapproved of Marshall's "latitudinarian" constructions of the Constitution; even more, however, he disapproved of the campaign mounted by Virginia's Old Republicans against the federal judiciary, which he believed essential to the preservation of the Union. Similarly, while he thought protectionism had gone far enough, he did not consider it responsible for Virginia's economic ills (slavery and the open door to the West were of first importance) nor an unconstitutional exercise of power by Congress.

By the end of the decade the states' rights doctrine employed by Jefferson and Madison to combat the Alien and Sedition Acts had been transformed under the hand of John C. Calhoun into the South Carolina doctrine of nullification. For the next several years Madison kept his pen working overtime to expose the heresy of that doctrine. From the celebrated Webster-Hayne debate of 1830 until the end of the great controversy in 1833, he found himself in the unenviable position of being quoted on both sides of the question and, even worse, on neither side correctly. Daniel Webster of Massachusetts associated him with the theory of unitary national sovereignty, while Robert Hayne of South Carolina associated him with the theory of state sovereignty. Both were in error, Madison said. The true theory was that of divided sovereignty. The Union originated in a compact of the people of the states, who divided the powers of government between two spheres, each government supreme in its sphere, and made the judiciary of the whole nation the final arbiter in cases requiring adjudication of the compact. The idea that a single state could nullify an act of the central government was an absurdity. To Hayne, who had sent him his famous Senate speech on the subject, Madison returned a four-thousand-word rebuttal, a copy of which went to a young admirer, Edward Everett of Massachusetts. When Everett expressed the wish to publish it, Madison recast the essay and it appeared in the *North American Review* in October, 1830.

Montpellier August 28th. 1830.

In order to understand the true character of the Consti-

Painting by G.P.A. Healy depicts
Daniel Webster replying to Hayne.

John Marshall

tution of the United States, the error, not uncommon, must be avoided, of viewing it through the medium, either of a Consolidated Government, or of a Confederated Government, whilst it is neither the one nor the other; but a mixture of both. And having in no model, the similitudes and analogies applicable to other systems of Government, it must more than any other, be its own interpreter according to its text and *the facts of the case.*

From these it will be seen, that the characteristic peculiarities of the Constitution are   1. the mode of its formation.   2. the division of the supreme powers of Government between the States in their united capacity, and the States in their Individual capacities.

1. It was formed not by the Governments of the component States, as the Federal Government for which it was substituted was formed: Nor was it formed by a majority of the people of the United States, as a single community, in the manner of a consolidated government.

It was formed by the States, that is by the people in each of the States, acting in their highest sovereign capacity; and formed consequently by the same authority which formed the State Constitutions.

Being thus derived from the same source as the Constitutions of the States, it has, within each State, the same authority as the Constitution of the State; and is as much a Constitution, in the strict sense of the term within its prescribed sphere, as the Constitutions of the States are, within their respective spheres: But with this obvious and essential difference, that being a compact among the States in their highest sovereign capacity, and constituting the people thereof one people

John C. Calhoun

for certain purposes, it cannot be altered or annulled at the will of the States individually, as the Constitution of a State may be at its individual will.

2. And that it divides the Supreme powers of Government, between the Government of the United States, and the Governments of the Individual States, is stamped on the face of the Instrument; the powers of war and of taxation, of commerce and of treaties, and other enumerated powers vested in the government of the United States....

Between these different Constitutional governments, the one operating in all the States, the others operating separately in each, with the aggregate powers of government divided between them, it could not escape attention, that controversies would arise concerning the boundaries of jurisdiction; and that some provision ought to be made for such occurrences. A political system that does not provide for a peaceable and authoritative termination of occurring controversies, would not be more than the shadow of a Government; the object and end of a real government being, the substitution of law and order, for uncertainty confusion and violence....

The Constitution ... for its safe and successful operation, has expressly declared, on one hand 1. "that the Constitution and the laws made in pursuance thereof and all treaties made under the authority of the United States, shall be the Supreme law of the land; 2. that the Judges of every State shall be bound thereby, anything in the Constitution and laws of any State, to the contrary notwithstanding; 3. that the Judicial power of the United States shall extend to all cases in law and equity arising under the Constitution, the laws of the United States, and treaties made under their authority &c."

On the other hand, as a security of the rights and powers of the States, in their individual capacities, against an undue preponderance of the powers granted to the Government over them in their united capacity, the Constitution has relied on 1. the responsibility of the Senators and Representatives in the Legislature of the United States to the Legislatures and people of the States 2. the responsibility of the President to the people of the United States; and 3. the liability of the Executive and judiciary functionaries of the United States to impeachment....

How far this structure of the Government of the United States be adequate and safe for its objects, time alone can absolutely determine. Experience seems to have shewn that whatever may grow out of future stages of our national career, there is, as yet a sufficient controul, in the popular will, over the Executive and Legislative Departments of the Government. When the alien and sedition laws were passed in contravention of the opinions and feelings of the community, the first elections that ensued, put an end to them. And whatever may have been the character of other acts, in the judgment of many of us, it is but true, that they have generally accorded with the views of a majority of the States and of the people. At the present day it seems well understood, that the laws which have created most dissatisfaction, have had a like sanction without doors; and that whether continued varied or repealed—a like proof will be given of the sympathy and responsibility of the Representative body, to the Constituent body. Indeed the great complaint now is, against the results of this sympathy and responsibility in the Legislative policy of the nation. . . .

Those who have denied or doubted the supremacy of the Judicial power of the United States and denounce at the same time a nullifying power in a State, seem not to have sufficiently adverted to the utter inefficiency of a supremacy in a law of the Land, without a supremacy in the exposition and execution of the law; nor to the destruction of all equipoise between the Federal Government and the State Governments if . . . no constitutional controul of any sort belonged to the United States over the States. Under such an organization, it is evident that it would be in the power of the States, individually, to pass unauthorised laws, and to carry them into compleat effect, anything in the Constitution and laws of the United States to the contrary notwithstanding. This would be a nullifying power in its plenary character; and . . . would be equally fatal to the constituted relation between the two Governments.

Should the provisions of the Constitution as here reviewed, be found not to secure the Government and rights of the States, against usurpations and abuses on the part of the United States, the final resort within the purview of the Constitution, lies in an amendment

401

*Portrait of the aged James Madison
painted by Asher B. Durand in 1833*

of the Constitution according to a process applicable
by the States.

And in the event of a failure of every Constitutional
resort, and an accumulation of usurpations and abuses,
rendering passive obedience and non-resistance a greater
evil, than resistance and revolution, there can remain
but one resort, the last of all; an appeal from the can-
celled obligations of the Constitutional compact, to
original rights and the law of self preservation. This is
the ultima ratio under all Governments, whether consolidated, confederated, or a compound of both; and it
cannot be doubted that a single member of the Union,
in the extremity supposed, but in that only, would have
a right, as an extra and ultra constitutional right, to
make the appeal.

This brings us to the expedient lately advanced,
which claims for a single State, a right to appeal against
an exercise of power by the Government of the United
States decided by the State to be unconstitutional,
to the parties to the Constitutional compact: the decision
of the State to have the effect of nullifying the act of the
Government of the United States, unless the decision
of the States be reversed by three fourths of the parties. . . .

Can more be necessary to demonstrate the inadmissibility of such a doctrine, than that it puts in the power of the smallest fraction over one fourth of the United States, that is, of seven states out of twenty four, to give the law, and even the Constitution to seventeen States; each of the seventeen having as parties to the Constitution, an equal right with each of the seven, to expound it, and to insist on the exposition. That the seven might, in particular instances be right, and the seventeen wrong, is more than possible. But to establish a positive and permanent rule giving such a power, to such a minority, over such a majority, would overturn the first principle of free government, and in practice necessarily overturn the government itself. . . .

In favor of the nullifying claim for the States, individually, it appears . . . that the proceedings of the Legislature of Virginia in 98 & 99 against the Alien and Sedition Acts, are much dwelt upon.

That the Legislature could not have intended to sanction such a doctrine, is to be inferred from the debates in the House of Delegates, and from the address of the two Houses, to their Constituents, on the subject of the Resolutions. The tenor of the debates, which were ably conducted and are understood to have been revised for the press by most if not all of the speakers, discloses no reference whatever to a constitutional right in an individual State, to arrest by force the operation of a law of the United States. Concert among the States for redress against the Alien and Sedition Laws, as acts of usurped power, was a leading sentiment; and the attainment of a concert, the immediate object of the course adopted by the Legislature, which was that of inviting the other States "to *concur,* in declaring the acts to be unconstitutional, and to *co-operate* by the necessary and proper measures; in maintaining unimpaired the authorities rights and liberties reserved to the States respectively and to the people." That by the necessary and proper measure to be *concurrently* and *co-operatively* taken, were meant measures known to the Constitution, particularly the ordinary controul of the people and Legislatures of the States, over the Government of the United States, cannot be doubted; and *the interposition* of this controul, as the event shewed, was equal to the occasion. It is worthy of remark, and explanatory of the intentions of the Legislature, that the words "not law, but utterly null, void, and of no force or effect" which had followed, in one of the Resolutions, the word "unconstitutional," were struck out by common consent. Tho the words were in fact but synonomous with "unconstitutional"; yet to guard against a misunderstanding of this phrase as more than declaratory of opinion, the word unconstitutional, alone was retained, as not liable to that danger.

The letter to Everett demolished nullification as a theory and may have contributed to its actual defeat in 1833. Although he approved the action, Madison also labeled "heretical" the strident nationalism of President Jackson's proclamation against South Carolina's attempt to nullify the tariff. The last act of the drama was Henry Clay's Compromise Tariff of 1833. Madison applauded it heartily as going some way toward meeting the just objections of the South without impairing the foundations of the Union.

All through this crisis Madison was a semi-invalid at Montpelier. Rheumatism crippled his wrists and hands until he was forced to dictate many of his letters. The disease let up in 1833 but the body slowly gave out. The next year he resigned as rector of the university. Those who saw him in these last years testify that his mind and spirits were as lively as ever. He could not shake his anxiety over the fate of the Union. And he worried over the deterioration of his estate. For several years he had been forced to sell land and slaves to keep afloat. The economic depression of Virginia

Last page of Madison's will, 1835

MANUSCRIPT DIVISION, LIBRARY OF CONGRESS

*Dolley Madison lived until 1849.
This mutilated daguerrotype was
made during her last decade.*

agriculture had finally caught up with him, though it had been helped
along by the constant drain of dollars—$40,000 during twenty years—to
pay the debts of his profligate stepson, Payne Todd. Madison had hoped
to emancipate and colonize the Montpelier slaves by his will. But with
bankruptcy staring him in the face, this became quite impossible.

He died quietly and serenely at Montpelier on June 28, 1836, at the age
of eighty-five. That morning breakfast had been brought to him in bed. His
niece, noticing that he could not swallow, asked him what was wrong, to
which the former President replied, "Nothing more than a change of *mind*,
my dear." Then, according to his servant, "His head instantly dropped, and
he ceased breathing as quietly as the snuff of a candle goes out." He was
buried the next day in the family burial ground half a mile south of his house.
Soon afterward, Dolley moved back to Washington where, although plagued
by debts, she reigned for another decade as the grande dame of the capital's
social life. She died in 1849, at the age of eighty-one.

Having served his country and his fellow man for sixty years, Madison
had to be forgiven nothing and nothing had to be mourned in his death.
He was not a religious man in the conventional sense. His life was given up
to a political religion, what Harriet Martineau called "his inexhaustible
faith that a well-founded commonwealth may...be immortal; not only
because the people, its constituency, never die, but because the principles

of justice in which such a commonwealth originates never die out of the people's heart and mind." Since his youth he had seldom speculated on religious questions. In 1825 an evangelical minister tried to press these questions upon him. Madison replied to the Reverend Frederick Beasley.

Montpr. Novr. 29, 1825

I have duly recd. the copy of your little tract on the proofs of the Being & Attributes of God. To do full justice to it, would require not only a more critical attention than I have been able to bestow on it, but a resort to the celebrated work of Dr. [Samuel] Clarke, which I read fifty years ago only, and to that of Dr. [Daniel] Waterland [who argued with Clarke about the Trinity in 1712] also which I never read.

The reasoning that could satisfy such a mind as that of Clarke ought certainly not to be slighted in the discussion. And the belief in a God All Powerful wise & good, is so essential to the moral order of the world & to the happiness of man, that arguments which enforce it cannot be drawn from too many sources nor adopted with too much solicitude to the different characters & capacities to be impressed with it.

But whatever effect may be produced on some minds by the more abstract train of ideas which you strongly support, it will probably always be found that the course of reasoning from the effect to the cause, "from nature to nature's God," will be of the more universal & more persuasive application.

The finiteness of the Human understanding betrays itself on all subjects, but more especially when it contemplates such as involve infinity. What may safely be said seems to be that the infinity of time & space forces itself on our conception, a limitation of either being unconceivable: that the mind prefers at once the idea of a self-existing cause to that of an infinite series of causes & effects which augments, instead of avoiding the difficulty: and that it finds more facility in assenting to the self-existence of an invisible cause possessing infinite power, wisdom & goodness, than to the self-existence of the universe visibly destitute of those attributes and which may be [the] effect of them. In this comparative facility of conception & belief, all philosophical reasoning on the subject must perhaps terminate. But that I may not get farther beyond my depth, and without the resources which bear you up in fathoming efforts, I hasten

Unsigned note announcing the death of James Madison on June 28, 1836

406

to thank you for the favour which has made me your debtor, and to assure you of my esteem & my respectful regards.

In the end, faith in the Union had become the core of Madison's political religion. The crisis of nullification had passed, but other dangers, above all slavery, threatened to destroy the Union and with it the world's best hope for liberty and self-government. In 1834, when eighty-three years old, Madison penned a solemn appeal to his countrymen to cherish the Union. It was the political testament of the last Founding Father.

"Advice To My Country" [Fall of 1834]

As this advice, if it ever see the light will not do it till I am no more, it may be considered as issuing from the tomb, where truth alone can be respected, and the happiness of man alone consulted. It will be entitled therefore to whatever weight can be derived from good intentions, and from the experience of one who has served his country in various stations through a period of forty years, who espoused in his youth and adhered through his life to the cause of its liberty, and who has borne a part in most of the great transactions which will constitute epochs of its destiny.

The advice nearest to my heart and deepest in my convictions is that the Union of the States be cherished and perpetuated. Let the open enemy to it be regarded as a Pandora with her box opened; and the disguised one, as the Serpent creeping with his deadly wiles into Paradise.

Following Madison's death, Congress resolved to shroud chairs of Speaker and Senate president in black and to wear crepe armbands for thirty days.

The President of the United States having communicated to the two Houses of Congress the melancholy intelligence of the death of their illustrious and beloved fellow Citizen, James Madison, of Virginia, late President of the United States; and the two Houses sharing in the general grief which this distressing event must produce —

Resolved, by the Senate and House of Representatives of the United States in Congress assembled, That the Chairs of the President of the Senate and of the Speaker of the House of Representatives be shrouded in black during the residue of the session, and that the President of the Senate, the Speaker of the House of Representatives, and the members and officers of both Houses, wear the usual badge of mourning for thirty days. —

Resolved, That it be recommended to the people of the United States to wear crape on the left arm, as mourning, for thirty days. —

Resolved, That the President of the United States be requested to transmit a Copy of these Resolutions to Mrs. Madison, and to assure her of the profound respect of the two Houses of Congress for her person and character, and of their sincere condolence on the late afflicting dispensation of Providence.

Selected Bibliography

Adams, Henry. *History of the United States During the Administrations of Jefferson and Madison.* 9 vols. New York: Charles Scribner's Sons, 1889–91.

Beirne, Francis F. *The War of 1812.* New York: E. P. Dutton, 1949.

Brant, Irving. *The Fourth President: A Life of James Madison.* Indianapolis: Bobbs-Merrill, 1970.

————. *James Madison.* 6 vols. Indianapolis: Bobbs-Merrill, 1941–61.

————. *James Madison and American Nationalism.* Princeton: Van Nostrand, 1968.

Burns, Edward McNall. *James Madison: A Philosopher of the Constitution.* rev. ed. New York: Octagon Books, 1968.

Clark, Allen Culling. *Life and Letters of Dolly Madison.* Washington: W.F. Roberts, 1914.

Cunningham, Noble E., Jr. *The Jeffersonian Republicans in Power: The Formation of Party Organization, 1789–1801.* Chapel Hill: University of North Carolina Press, 1957.

Dangerfield, George. *The Era of Good Feelings.* New York: Harcourt, Brace, 1952.

De Conde, Alexander. *Entangling Alliance: Politics and Diplomacy under George Washington.* Durham: Duke University Press, 1958.

Farrand, Max, ed. *The Records of the Federal Convention of 1787.* rev. ed. 4 vols. New Haven: Yale University Press, 1937.

Hunt, Gaillard. *The Life of James Madison.* New York: Doubleday, Page, 1902.

Ketcham, Ralph. *James Madison: A Biography.* New York: Macmillan, 1971.

Koch, Adrienne. *Jefferson and Madison: The Great Collaboration.* New York: Alfred A. Knopf, 1950.

————. *Madison's "Advice to My Country."* Princeton: Princeton University Press, 1966.

Lord, Walter. *The Dawn's Early Light.* New York: W.W. Norton, 1972.

Madison, James. *Letters and Other Writings of James Madison, Fourth President of the United States.* Edited by William C. Rives and Philip R. Fendall. 4 vols. Philadelphia: J.B. Lippincott, 1865.

————. *The Papers of James Madison.* Vols. 1–7, Edited by William T. Hutchinson and William M.E. Rachal et al. Vol. 8–, Edited by Robert A. Rutland and William M.E. Rachal et al. Chicago: University of Chicago Press, 1962–.

————. *The Papers of James Madison Purchased by Order of Congress...* Edited by Henry D. Gilpin. 3 vols. Washington: Langtree & O'Sullivan, 1840.

————. *The Writings of James Madison, Comprising His Public Papers and His Private Correspondence.* Edited by Gaillard Hunt. 9 vols. New York: G.P. Putnam's Sons, 1900–1910.

Padover, Saul, ed. *The Complete Madison: His Basic Writings.* New York: Harper, 1953. Republished as *The Forging of American Federalism: Selected Writings of James Madison.* New York: Harper & Row, 1965.

Perkins, Bradford. *The First Rapprochement: England and the United States, 1795–1805.* Philadelphia: University of Pennsylvania Press, 1955.

————. *Prologue to War: England and the United States, 1805–1812.* Berkeley: University of California Press, 1961.

Riemer, Neal. *James Madison.* New York: Washington Square Press, 1968.

Rives, William C. *History of the Life and Times of James Madison.* 3 vols. Boston: Little, Brown, 1859–68.

Rossiter, Clinton. *1787: The Grand Convention.* New York: Macmillan, 1966.

Smelser, Marshall. *The Democratic Republic, 1801–1815.* New York: Harper, 1954.

Smith, Margaret Bayard. *The First Forty Years of Washington Society.* Edited by Gaillard Hunt. New York: Charles Scribner's Sons, 1906.

White, Leonard D. *The Jeffersonians: A Study in Administrative History, 1801–1829.* New York: Macmillan, 1951.

Acknowledgments

Unless otherwise specifically credited below, all documents reproduced in this volume are from the James Madison Papers, Library of Congress, Washington, D.C., the greatest collection of Madison documents in existence. In addition the Editors would like to thank the following individuals and institutions for permission to reprint documents in their possession:

American Art Association, Anderson Galleries catalogue, 1936, page 344(bottom)–345
George B. Cutts, Brookline, Mass., pages 251(bottom), 252–53(top), 365–66
Mrs. Theodore P. Dixon, Jr., Darien, Conn., pages 267(bottom), 268, 271–72, 282–83
Greensboro, N.C., Historical Museum, page 253(center)
Historical Society of Pennsylvania, Philadelphia, pages 22–39, 202(bottom)–203, 250(bottom)–251(top), 280(bottom)–281(top)
Massachusetts Historical Society, Boston, pages 238, 352–53(top), 359(bottom)–360, 381(bottom)–382(top), 398(bottom)–404(top)
National Archives, Washington, D.C., pages 58(bottom)–61, 239–43(top), 244(bottom)–247, 254–57, 261(bottom)–267(top), 269–70, 330(bottom)–331(top), 338–40, 354(bottom)–359(top), 361–62
New-York Historical Society, New York, N.Y., pages 279(bottom)–280(top), 334(center), 343(bottom)–344(top)
Pierpont Morgan Library, New York, N.Y., pages 323–25(top), 394(bottom)–396(top)
Princeton University, Princeton, N.J., page 258
University of Virginia Library, Charlottesville, page 251(center)
Virginia State Library, Richmond, pages 91–94

The Editors also make grateful acknowledgment for the use of documents from the following works:

Davis, Richard Beale, ed. *Jeffersonian America, Notes on the United States of America Collected in the Years 1805–6–7 and 11–12 by Sir Augustus John Foster.* San Marino, Cal., 1954. Pages 214(bottom)–217
Gilpin, Henry D., ed. *The Papers of James Madison.* 3 vols. Washington, D.C., 1840. Pages 72(bottom)–73(top)
Hillard, George S., ed. *Life, Letters, and Journals of George Ticknor.* 2 vols. Boston, 1876. Pages 367–68(top)
Hunt, Gaillard, ed. *The First Forty Years of Washington Society.* New York, 1906. Pages 273–76(top)
———. *The Writings of James Madison.* 9 vols. New York, 1900–1910. Pages 223(bottom)–229(top), 363–64
Proceedings and Debates of the Virginia Convention . . . 1829–30. Winchester, Va., 1830. Pages 389–92(top)
Martineau, Harriet. *Retrospect of Western Travel.* 3 vols. London, 1838. Pages 377–79(top)
Richardson, James D., ed. *A Compilation of the Messages and Papers of the Presidents.* Washington, D.C., 1907. Pages 298–301(top)
Robertson, David, comp. *Debates and Other Proceedings of the Convention of Virginia . . . June, 1788 . . .* Richmond, 1805. Pages 157–61

The Editors also wish to express their appreciation to the many institutions and individuals who made available their pictorial materials for use in this volume. In particular the Editors are grateful to:

American Antiquarian Society, Worcester, Mass. —Georgia B. Bumgardner
Anne S. K. Brown Military Collection, Brown University, Providence, R.I.
Library of Congress, Manuscript Division, Washington, D.C. —Carolyn H. Sung
Maryland Historical Society, Baltimore
National Archives, Washington, D.C.
New-York Historical Society, New York, N.Y. —Wilson G. Duprey
New York Public Library, New York, N.Y.
The Papers of the Continental Congress, National Archives, Washington, D.C. —Kenneth E. Harris
The Papers of James Madison, University of Virginia, Charlottesville, Va.
Presbyterian Historical Society, Philadelphia, Pa.
Princeton University Archives, Princeton, N.J. —Nancy Graham
Virginia Historical Society, Richmond—Mary S. Southall
Yale University Art Gallery, New Haven, Conn.

Finally, the Editors would like to thank Russell Ash in London and John D. Knowlton in Washington, D.C., for advice and assistance in obtaining pictorial material, Thomas Froncek for editing, and Mary-Jo Kline for compiling the chronology and bibliography.

Index

Boldface indicates pages on which illustrations appear.

Abolitionists, 376
"Act for Establishing Religious Freedom" (Jefferson), **94**
Adams, John, 46, 65, 68–69, **132**, 166, 183–85, 351–52
  death of, 386
  election of 1796, 209–12
  election of 1800, 231–32
  as President, 212–13, 217–19, 222, 229, 233–34
  Cabinet, 218
Adams, John Quincy 184, **185**, 341, 359, **360**
"Address to the States," 76, 77, 78
"Advice to My Country," 407
Africa, 280, 372, 374
Agricultural Society of Albemarle, 368
Agriculture, 368, 392–94
Alexander I, Emperor, 333, 342
Alien and Sedition Acts, 219, 221–22, 229, 398, 403
Allen, Ethan, 37
Almanac of 1788, 155
American Colonization Society, 371–74, 377, 396
American Farmer, 368
American Revolution, 26, 37-38, 40, 75, 118, 222
  money for, 46, 50, 55
  peace treaty, 169
    instructions, **68**
    preliminary, 69
    cartoon of, **69**
  Proclamation of Peace, **68**
Anglican Church, 26, 28, 41, 90, 370
Annapolis, Md., 81
Annapolis Convention, 100–3, 107
Antifederalists, 156, 161, 166,

168, 396
Argus (ship), 313
Armistead, Major George, 316
Armstrong, John, 265, 288–89, 337, 342–44, 348–51
Army, 291, 295, 304. *See also* Continental Army, Militia
  provisional, 219
  standing army, danger of, 156
  in War of 1812, 322–23, 351
Arnold, Benedict, 64
Articles of Confederation, 45, 51, 69–70, 72, 137, 179–80
  revision of, 100
Astor, John Jacob, 334, 344
Atotarho, **86**

Baltimore, Md., 316, 344
  Battle of, monument commemorating, **351**
Bank notes, 179
Bank of the United States, **181**, 291–92, **291**, 356–57, 359, 398
  proposal for, 178
  Second Bank of the United States, 359
  shares in, 182, 184–85
  unconstitutionality, 178–82
  veto of, 351
Banks, Henry, 388
Baptists, 41, 91, 370
Barbadoes (ship), 313
Barbary pirates, 280
Barbour, Philip P., 388
Barlow, Joel, 293, 295, **296**, 297, 332
Barron, Commodore James, **261**
Barry, William T., 379
Bartram, William, 138
Bayard, James A., 334, **335**, 341, 343

Beasley, Reverend Frederick, 406
Beckley, John, 184
Bedford, Gunning, Jr., 22
Berkeley, Admiral George C., 280
Berkshire Agricultural Society membership certificate, **358**
Berlin Decree, 258, 266, 288, 297
Bill of Rights, **124**, 161–63, 165, 168
Billy (slave), 81
Birch, William, 236
Bladensburg, Md., 304, 315, 344, **345**, **346**
  Battle of, 345
Bland, Theodorick, **61**, 61–63, 71
Blue Ridge Mountains, 14–16, 113, 214, **215**
Bond, Phineas, 183
Bonus bill, veto of, 362
Boston, Mass., 27, 31, 37, 184, 200
  State House, **154**
Boston Tea Party, 31
Boudinot, Elias, 79
Boxer (ship), 313
Boyd, Julian P., 9
Boyle, Caleb, 63
Brackenridge, Hugh Harry, 21–22, 29
Bradford, William, 7, 22, **23**, 25
  Madison's letters to, 24–39, **24**
Bradford family bookstore and coffee house, **25**
Brant, Irving, 9
Brick Church, 15–16
Brown, General Jacob, 341
Brown, Mather, 132
Brown's Indian Queen Hotel, **331**

Buffon, Comte George Louis de, 82
Bunker Hill, Battle of, 37
Burr, Aaron, 22, 201, 231, **232**, 233

Cadore, Duke of, 288–89
Calhoun, John C., 293, **299**, 398, **400**
Campbell, George, 342–43
Canada, 61, 295, 313, 322, 324, 328, 337, 360
  Upper, 322, 324–25, 337
Canals, 356, 358, 363
"Candid State of Parties, A," **191**, 192–93
Canning, George, 267, **268**, 269, 279, 281, 285
Capitol, the, 235, **236**, 273, **344**, **346**
  burning of, 347
Carpenters' Hall, Philadelphia, **32**, 33
Carr family, 89
Carroll, Colonel Charles, 346–47
Castlereagh, Lord, 296, **301**, 302, 334, 341
Catlin, George, 389
Certificate of election (1809), **274**
Charleston, S.C., 45
Chesapeake (ship), 261–62, 264, 280–81, 284–85, **308**, 339
Chesapeake Bay, 343–44, 351
Christianity, 90, 93
Chronology, 10–11
Church and State, 94
  separation of, 90–91, 371, 381
  union of, 26–27, 30, 41
Claiborne, William, 289
Clark, General William, 327
Clay, Henry, 293, **299**, 341, **375**, 404
Clergy, the, 29, 35, 39, 90, 93, 95, 369–70
Clinton, DeWitt, 329, **330**
Clinton, George, **103**, 166, 274
Clinton, Sir Henry, 45
Clintonians, 295
Cliosophic Society, 20
Cochrane, Admiral Sir Alexander, 341–42
Cockburn, Rear Admiral George, **315**
Coercive Acts, 31
Coles, Edward, 250
Coles, Isaac, 275
College of New Jersey. *See* Princeton University
Commerce, regulation of, 96–100, 105, 169, 172, 199, 255–56, 264–71, 353
Compromise Tariff of 1833, 404
Concord, Mass., skirmish at, 37
Confederation, the, 69, 72, 78, 96, 103, 105, 130, 147, 155, 159
Congress. *See* U.S. Congress
Connecticut, 48, 54, 57, 99, 134, 139, 154, 237, 320, **320**, 323, 325
  liberty of, 29, 41
  rights of, 30, 91, 163
"Consolidation," 186–87

Constellation (ship), 227
Constitution (ship), 295, **307**, 329
Constitutional Convention. *See* Federal Convention of 1787
Continental Army, 45, 47, 72–74
Continental Association, 33–34
Continental Congress, 7, 32, 39, 43, 45–56, 58, 62–63
  money problems, 46–48
  peace commission of, 65
  Second, 36
Contraband, 256
Convention of 1800, 237–38
Conway, Nelly. *See* Madison, Nelly Conway
Copley, John Singleton, 185
Cornwallis, General Charles, 61, 64–65
Cotton, 333
Coxe, Tench, 233
Creek Indians, 338
Crown Point, N.Y., 37
Cutts, Anna Payne, **251**, 252, 275–76, 347
Cutts, Richard, 365

Deane, Silas, 46, 51
Dearborn, General Henry, 322–23
Decatur, Captain Stephen, **308**
Declaration of Independence, 383
Defense of the Constitutions of Government of the United States of America, A (Adams), 132, 183
Delaware, 56–57, 70, 107, 154, 330
Delaware River, 175–76
Democracy, 392
Depression, economic, 96
Despotism, 158, 164, 196
Detroit, 307, 323, 326, 329
  surrender of, **324**
Dickinson, John, 20, 137
"Discourses on Davila" (Adams), 183, **183**
District of Columbia, 356, 359
Dunmore, Lord, 31, 37–38, **38**, 40
  Palace, site of, **39**
Dupont de Nemours, Pierre, 239
Durand, Asher B., 402
Duties
  on distilled spirits, repeal of, **176**
  import, 13, 72, 168, 170

Eastern states. *See* New England
East Florida, 246, **247**. *See also* the Floridas
East India Company, 27
Education, 356, 379–84
  public schools, 90, 379
Elections, 140–42, 145, 152
  of 1788, 166–67
  of 1796, 209
  of 1800, 231–33
  of 1808, 268–71
  of 1812, 329–30
Emancipation, 394
Embargo Act, 264–68, 271, 283, 287

cartoons of, **265**, **266**
  repeal of, **270**, 271–72, 341
Enlightenment, 20
Enterprize (ship), 313
Episcopal Church, 91
Erskine, David, **269**, 277, 280–84
Erskine agreement, 279
Essex (ship), 254–55
Essex Cabinet, 278, 341
Europe, 188, 219, 237–38, 242, 244, 247, 253–54, 265, 271–72, 322, 332, 341–42, 353, 359–60. *See also* names of countries
  blockade of, 279, 285, 297
  trade with, 169–70
Eustis, William, 276, 337
Evans, Robert J., 371
Everett, Edward, **381**, 398, 404
Exports, 149, 170, 242, 254, 271
  embargo on, 70

Federal Convention of 1787, 7–8, 22, 123, 130, 158, 396–97
  debates in, 130–31, 136–43, 397
  Madison's notes on, 7–8, **122**, 130–32, 396–97
Federalism, 136, 292, 356
Federalist, The, **124**, 135, 139, 150, 182, 383, 397
  excerpt from Number 39, **153**, 150–54
  Number 10, **152**
Federalists, 150, 156, 186, 189, 194, 198–99, 208–11, 217, 219, 229, 231–33, 236, 267, 269–70, 277–78, 290, 297, 320, 329–30, 354
Fendall, Philip R., 9
Fenno, John, 186, 197–98
Ferguson, Adam, 20
Fisheries, 67–68, 101, 359, 361
Floridas, the, 58, 69, 238–47, **247**
Floyd, Kitty (Catherine), 78–79, 81, **121**
Fort McHenry, **316**, 351
Fort Mackinac, **326**, 326
Fort Malden, 323, 326, **328**
Fort Stanwix, 84–86
  plan of, **86**
  treaty at, **87**
Fort Ticonderoga, 37
Foster, Sir Augustus, 214, 292, 296, 301, 326
Founding Fathers, 6, 9, 13
France, 84, 101, 183–84, 283
  alliance with U.S., 46, 51, 65–69, 87, 104, 172, 198
  anti-Gallic sentiment in U.S., 65, **231**
  commercial relations with U.S., 61, 169–70, 210, 212, 217, 265–67, 271, 277, 279, 286, **287**, 288–91, 293, 295–97, 302, 341
  in Continental wars, 193, 196, 244
Floridas, control of, 238–47, **247**, 258
  foreign policy of U.S. toward,

189, 194–99, 208, 229–30, 237–38, 258, 265–67, 281, 288–91, 293, 295–97, 302, 331–32, 359
Louisiana, purchase of, from, 129, 238–41, 243–45, 247
Mississippi, control of, 58, 61, 69, 84–85, 238–39, 243–45
war with, 212, 219, **227**, 279
Francisco, Peter, **64**
Franklin, Benjamin, 45–46, 51, 68–69, 130, 142, **143**
Freedom of the seas, 256, 266
Free trade, 172, 361
French and Indian War, 15
French Revolution, 183, 194, 217, 219, 222
Freneau, Philip, 21–22, 24, 185, **186**, 190–91
Frolic (ship), 308, **329**
Funding controversy, 173, 175, 177
cartoon, **175**

Gallatin, Albert, 264, 276, 279, 281, 285, 291–92, 334, **335**, 341, 342, 351, 353, 364
Gallatin, Mrs. Albert, 334, 343
Galloway, Joseph, 20, 132
Gardoqui, Diego de, **100**, 100, 102
Gazette of the United States, 186
Genêt, Edmond Charles, **194**, 194–200
George III, King, 295, 313, in cartoons, **35**, **313**, **320**
Georgetown, D.C., 347
Georgia, 45, 57, 61–62, 104, 149, 287
Gerry, Elbridge, 142, **147**
Ghent, 351–52, **353**
Treaty of, **320**, 354, 356
Giles, William B., **230**, 230–31, 388
Gilpin, Henry, 9
Goodrich, Elizur, 237
Great Britain, 64, 84, 135, 387–88, 393. *See also* War of 1812
blockade of, 299
commercial relations with U.S., 61, 96–101, 168–70, 172, 199, 217, 254–72, 277–302, 330–33, 341, 359–60
cartoon of, **287**
embargo against, 295, 331
foreign policy of U.S. toward, 189, 219, 236–37, 241, 244–45, 247–50, 254–72, 277–302, 326, 341–42, 352–53
on frontier, 69
Jay's Treaty with, 203, **205**–9, 214
navy, 253, 260, 316
Parliament, 31, 33, 146
relations with Colonies, 13, 34
relations with Indians, 85, 326–28, 319
in Revolution, 45, 55, 62, 64, 65–69
cartoons of, **67**, **69**

peace treaty, 195–96
in War of 1812, 319, 343–45, 348
war with France, 193–96, 219, 253
Great Lakes, 359, 361. *See also* names of lakes
Grundy, Felix, 293, **298**
Guerrière (ship), 307, 329

Habersham, Joseph, 236
Hamilton, Alexander, 76, **124**, 142, 150–51, **51**, 162, 172, 174, 178, 182, **188**, 189, 194, 198, 201, 209, 211, 219
pamphlet of, 233
Hamilton, Paul, 276, 337
Hammond, George, 183
Hampden-Sydney College, 20
Hampton Roads, Va., 43
Hancock, John, 20
Harewood House, 202, **203**
Harrison, Benjamin, 90
Harrison, William Henry, **311**, 337
Hartford, Conn., 226
Hartford Convention, 320, 354
cartoon, **354**
Harvard University, 381
Hayne, Robert, 398, **399**
Healy, G. P. A., 399
"Helvetius," 198
Henry, John, 113
Henry, Patrick, 36, 40–41, 43, 89–90, 94, 132–33, 154–56, **157**, 158–59, 161, 166
home of, **159**
Heriot, George, 346
Holland, 101, 104, 169, 193, 342, 382
Hornet (ship), 295–97, 301
House, Mrs. Mary, 121, 130, 192
Hull, General William, **307**, 323–26, 360
surrender of, **325**, 329
Hull, Isaac, **307**
Hume, David, 47, 136
Humphreys, Charles, 32
Humphreys, David, 331, **332**
Hunt, Gaillard, 9
Hutcheson, Francis, 20
Hutchinson, James, 198

Impeachment, 145, 171, 400
Imports, 32, 149
duties on, 13, 71–73, 75–76, 168, 170
Impost. *See* Imports, duties on
Impressment, 247, 254, 256, 300–1, 304, 342–43
Indians, 15, 51, 85–86, 104, 292, 300, 304, 324–25, 327, 351
Turner's report of, **187**
in War of 1812, **311**, 323, 326–27, 338
Ingersoll, Jared, **145**
Invisibles, The, 292, 295
Ireland, 295–96
Iroquois Indians, 85
Irving, Washington, 276, **277**

Jackson, Andrew, 319–20, 338, 341, 353

Jackson, Francis James, 282–83, 286
Jay, John, 58, 60, 62–63, **63**, 66, 68–69, 100, 102, **124**, 150, **151**, 201
Jays Treaty, **205**, 205–9, 214, 255, 383
Jefferson, Thomas, 8, 40, **81**, 94, 102–3, 113, **129**, 172, 183, 201, 208, 211, 214, 231, 272, 398
character of, 44, 384
death of, 386
description of, 248
in election of 1800, 231–33
as Governor of Virginia, 43, 55
Hamilton and, 182, 189–90
letters to, 47–49, 53–55, 70–71, 79–81, **80**, 98–100, 143–50, 154–56, 166–67, 168–71, 195–97, 199–201, 206–8, 211–12, 218–21, 229–31, 238, 277–79, 281, 295–97, 325–27, 333–34, 341, 351–52, 382–84, 385
letter from, 384
Madison and, 43–44, 78, 82–90, 95, 178, 183, 236, 275, 381, 384–86
as Minister to France, 165
papers of, 6
as President, **129**, 235–36, 238–39, 241–43, 232–34, 248–50, **248**, 256, 258, 264, 276–77
in cartoons, **247**, **265**, **266**
Cabinet, 127, 236
foreign affairs, 236–37
public school system, plan for, 90
as Republican leader, 190, 198, 229
in retirement, 273–75, 278, 292, 295, 379, 382, 384
as Secretary of State, 174, **188**, 189–90, 194–95, 198–99
Report on Commerce, 200
as Vice President, 213, 223
in cartoon, **231**
Johnson, Richard M., 293, **298**
Johnson, Zachary, 155
Jones, Gabriel, 155
Jones, Captain Jacob, 308
Jones, Joseph, 49–50, **50**, 52, 55, 58, 62
Jones, William, 337, 342–43
Joy, George, 258

Kames, Lord, 20
Kentucky, 52, 229, 232, 242, 326
Kentucky Resolutions, 223, **225**, 229, 398. *See also* Virginia Resolutions
Key, Francis Scott, 316
King, Rufus, 236, 247
Kirkland, Samuel, 85
"Knights of the Golden Horseshoe," 14
Knox, Henry, **188**

Lafayette, Marquis de, 8, 84–85, 85, 86–87, **367**, **394**, 394
Lake Champlain, 183, 313, 322,

352, 352–53
Battle of, 351
Lake Erie, 311, 323, 325, 329, 337
Battle of, **340**
Lake Ontario, 337
Latrobe, Benjamin H., 344
Lawrence, Captain James, **308**
Lawrence (flagship), 311
League of Armed Neutrality, 61
Lee, Arthur, 46, 51, 65, 72–73, 85–87
Lee-Adams faction, 65, 72
Lee-Deane affair, 51
Lee, General Charles, 35
Lee, Henry (Lighthorse Harry), 22, 190
Lee, Richard H., 36, 40
Lee, William, 43
Leopard (ship), 261, **262**, 280
Letter Concerning the Public Conduct and Character of John Adams (Hamilton), 233
Letters of Helvetius, **198**
Lexington, Mass., 37
Liberia, 378
Library of Congress, 9, 253
L'Insurgente (frigate), **227**
Liverpool, Lord, 296
Livingston, Henry Brockholst, 381
Livingston, Robert R., **204**, 204, 239, **240**, 245, **246**
Livingston, William, 381
Locke, John, 41, 382–83
Logan, George, 283, **284**
Logan Act, 283
London Coffee House, **25**
Louisiana, 60, 237–40, 243–44, 246–47
planter's house in, **239**
Louisiana Purchase, 129, 238, 246, 374
Luckey, George, 29

McDonough, Commodore Thomas, **313**, 353
Macedonian (ship), 308
McGuire, James C., 8
Macomb, General Alexander, 313
Macon, Nathaniel, **285**
Macon's Bill, 285
No. 2, 285, 288
Maddison, John (ancestor), 14
Madison, Ambrose (grandfather), 14
Madison, Ambrose (brother), 82
death, 214
Madison, Dolley (wife), 7–8, 127, 201, **202**, 203, 214, 236, 251–53, 273–76, 315, 343, 345, 347, 365–67, **405**
death, 405
description of, 273, 275–76
letters of, 251–53, **252**, 334, 343–47
Madison's letters to, **127**, 202, 253, 344–45, 347
marriage, 127, 202–3
Madison, James
and American Revolution, 7, 13, 33, 45–68
manifesto drafted, **66**
ancestry, 14

autobiography, 13–14, 41–42
birth, 14
character of, 44, 235, 250, 277, 367, 384
chronology, 10–11
classmates of, 21–22
as conversationalist, 377
copybook of, **114**
correspondence, 6–9
on Council of State in Virginia, 7, 42
death, 8, 405
announcement of, **406**
congressional mourning of, **407**
delegate to Congress of the Confederation, 69, 71, 96, 102, 121
delegate to Continental Congress, 7, 43, 51, 58, 65, 121
committee report, **70**
credentials, **47**
notes on debate, 72
instructions to Jay, **60**
instructions to peace commissioners, **68**
delegate to Federal Convention, 123, 130–43
notes on debates, 7–8, **122**, 130–31, 396–97
and Virginia Plan, 133–35
delegate to Virginia Convention, 7, 40–41, **41**
to convention of 1829–30, 388–92
delegate to Virginia House of Delegates, 83
statutory reform, 89–90
description, 44, 161, 250–51, 276, 367, 377, 389
education, 13, 16–22, 114, 117
in political theory, 20
engagement to Kitty Floyd, 78
essays of, 46, 48, 186–89, 398–404
farewell address of, 361, **362**, 363–64
as farmer, 368
as Father of the Constitution, 123, 130–65, 396
The Federalist, 124, 150
Hamilton and, 182
health of, 22, 27, 29, 233, 334, 337, 377, 404
in House of Representatives, 166–208
intellect of, 7–8
Jefferson and, 43–44, 78, 82–90, 95, 178, 236, 275, 284–86
library of, 82–83, **83**, 87–88
marriage, 127, 202–3
as nationalist, 69, 71, 96, 136, 139, 356
papers of, 7, 14
pictures of, **27**, **37**, **121**, **127**, **251**, **377**, **389**, **402**
poem by, 21
and politics, 26, 44, 51, 118
Presidency
Cabinet, 276–77, 291, 329,

341–42, 348
election, 270
certificate of (1809), **274**
to second term, 330
foreign affairs, 272, 277
inauguration, 273
second inaugural address, 333
State of the Union messages
1813, 338–40
1815, 356, **357**, 358–59
in War of 1812. *See also* War of 1812
call to arms, **294**
cartoons, **312**, **324**
declaration of war, **300**
defense of Washington, D.C., 315, 343–45, 347–50
proclamation pardoning deserters, **326**
war message, 297–301, **304**
rector of University of Virginia, 386
retirement, 320, 365
Secretary of State, 127, 129, 233, 235–72
in cartoon, **266**
patronage, use of, 236
speeches of, 134–35, 137–41, 157–61, 178–82, 223–29, 368, 389–92
views on
academic freedom, 381
civil liberties, 30, 147–48, 229
education, 379–81
freedom of the press, 225–26
government, 137–39, 164, 220–21, 362, 390–91
division of power in, 146
enlarged sphere of, 106, 136
executive department of, 109, 139–40, 144–45, 166, 171, 400
federal vs. national, 151–53
foreign department of, 170
judiciary, 109, 140, 146–47, 400
legislative department of, 109–10, 137–39, 140, 145, 301
national, 151–53
national vs. local, 146
oppression in, 163
powers of, 109–10, 144, 151–52, 157, 163–64, 178–79, 181–82, 363–64, 400
removal from office, 171–72
republican form of, 106, 135, 139, 148
state, 160, 163, 179
treasury department of, 170
war department of, 170
manipulation of foreign affairs, 220–21
monarchy, 227

money, 46–47
national defense, 356–58, 363
national and state
  universities, 356, 359, 379
religion, 26–27, 405–7. *See also* Church and State and Religious freedom
rights of minority, 92, 158
slavery, 81, 389, 391–92, 395
the Union, 407
Utopianism, 386–88
will, **404**
Madison, James, Sr. (father), 14, 81–82, 114, 177, 202, 213
  account book of, **17**
  death of, 233
  inventory of estate, **234**
Madison, Reverend James (second cousin), 42–43, **43**, 118
Madison, Nelly Conway (mother), 14, 114, 365
Madison family, **114**, 200, 214
"Madison's March," **275**
Maine, 351, 375
Manufactures
  American, 170, 189, 283, 356, 358
  British, 170, 259–60, 296
  promotion of, 20–21
Marlboro, Md., 344–45
Marshall, John, 44, 155, 273, 388, 398, **399**
Martin, Luther, **147**
Martin, Reverend Thomas, 16–18, 114
Martineau, Harriet, 7, 377, **378**, 405
Maryland, 45, 51–57, 104, 154, 282, 315, 344
  Constitution, 74
Mason, George, 40–41, 55, 91, 142, **147**, 154–55
Massachusetts, 55, 57, 75, 99, 101–2, 104, 107, 154, 174, 207, 279, 282, 320, **320**, 323
Mayo Bridge, Richmond, Va., **118**
Mazzei, Philip, 64
"Memorial and Remonstrance against Religious Assessments," 91
Mercer, John Francis, 74–75, **75**
Merry, Anthony, 248–49
Merry, Mrs. Anthony, 248
Methodists, 91, 370
Middle States, 155–56
Milan Decree, 288, 297
Militia, 322–23, 325, 345, 350, 355
Miller, Lewis, 370
Minutemen, 38
Mississippi River, 51, 54, **59**, 68–69, 156, 245
  free navigation on, 58–62, 64, 68, 84–85, 100–1, 239–42, 351
Missouri, 375–76
Missouri Compromise, 374–75
"Money," 46–47
Monroe, James, 82, 96, 100, 167, 174, 190, 198, 203, 207, 212,

217, 243–44, **246**, 246–48, 254–55, 261, 265, 284, 332, 341–44, 347–49, 375, 388
  elected President, **364**
  as Secretary of State, 292
  as Secretary of War, 351
Monroe-Pinckney Treaty, 258, 261, 285
Montesquieu, Baron de, 89, 188
Monticello, 44, 55, 82, 384, **385**
Montpelier, 6–7, 16, 82, **113**, 118, 214, **215**, 365–68
  description of, 214–17
Montreal, 322–23, 337
Moraviantown, Ontario, 311
Morris, Gouverneur, 142, **144**
Morris, Robert, 51, 71–74, **74**, 141
  in cartoon, **175**
  home of, **140**
Morristown, N.J., 45
Mount Vernon, 168, **169**

Napoleon I, 238, **242**, 244, 247, 257–58, 267, 285, 288, 290, 292–93, 296, 333, 341, 359
  in cartoons, **265**, **266**, **287**
  Third Coalition against, 253
Nassau Hall, Princeton, 17–18, **18**, 20, **117**
National bank. *See* Bank of the United States
National Gazette, 186–89, 197–98
  Hamilton's attack on Jefferson, 189–91
  Madison's essays in, 186–89, 191–93
National Intelligencer, 273
National university, proposal for, 356, 359
Nationalism, 356, 398
Nationalists, 69, 71, 73, 78, 96, 136, 139
Naturalization Act, 221
Navy, 291
  duties of, 71
  in War of 1812, 307–8, 311, 313, 329
Neutrality, American, 253, 285, 290–91, 293, 299, 302, 330
Neuville, Baroness Hyde de, 113
New England (or "the eastern states"), 58, 75, 154, 156, 163, 184, 200, 201, 210, 268, 270–72, 282, 283, 286, 320, 323, 330–33, 353
Newfoundland, 68–69, 359
New Hampshire, 55–56, 154, 156, 161, 279, 282
New Harmony, Ind., 386
New Jersey, 56–57, 99, 154, 190, 330, 382
New Jersey Plan, 137, 139
New Orleans, 58, 60, **129**, 238–42, 247, 319–20, 353
  Battle of, **355**
New York City, 96, 99, 102, 174, 184–85, 200
  Federal Hall, **124**, 168
  harbor of, **195**
  Lower, view of, **98**
  Old City Hall, **96**

New York Horticultural Society
  membership certificate, **369**
New York State, 35, 54, 56–57, 84, 154, 156, 161, 207, 270, 279, 295, 322, 329–30, 341
  paper money issued by, **49**
Niagara (ship), 311
Niagara River, 322
Nicholas, George, 155, 194, 223
Nicholas, Wilson Cary, 236, 320, 353
Nonimportation movement, 13, 21
Nonimportation Act, 255, 326, 331
  repeal of, 341
Nonintercourse Act, 272, 277, 280, 287–88, 290
Northern states, 71, 108, 136, 141, 156, 174–75, 375–78, 395
North American Review, 398–404
North Carolina, 37, 57, 61, 230
Northwest, the, 292, 311
"Notes on Ancient and Modern Confederacies," 103
Notes on the State of Virginia (Jefferson), 89
Nullificaton, doctrine of, 398, 403–4

Octagon House, **349**
Ohio, 52–53, 326, 374–75
Ohio River, 51, 54, 60
Oneida Indians, 86
Onis, Chevalier d' 282, 283
Orange County, Va., 14–15, 33, 82–83, 119, 166–67, 388
Orange County Committee of Safety, 33
Orange County militia, 33
Owen, Robert, 386, **387**

"Pacificus," 198
Paine, Thomas, **182**, 182–83
Paper money, 46, **49**, 102, 104, 109, 132, 185
Paris, 65
  Treaty of, 58
Paterson, William, 137
Patuxent River, 344
Payne, Anna C., 9
Payne, John C., 8
Peace of Amiens, 238
Peaks of Otter, **217**
Peale, Charles Willson, 121, 137, 394
Pendleton, Edmund, 36, 40, 52, 55, 89, 102, 155, 173, **174**
Pennsylvania, 51, 55–57, 99, 154, 382
Pennsylvania Journal, 22
Pennsylvania State House, **121**, **123**
Perceval, Spencer, 295–96
Perry, Commodore Oliver Hazard, **311**, 337
Philadelphia, Pa., 6–7, 21–22, 27, 31–33, 40, 45, **50**, 78, 102–3, 121, 123, 127, 130, 174, 176, 178, 184–86, 190–91
  Congress Hall, **149**